W9-BSN-942

A READY REFERENCE TO PHILOSOPHY EAST AND WEST

Eugene F. Bales
Conception Seminary College
Conception, Missouri

UNIVERSITY
PRESS OF
AMERICA

Lanham • New York • London

Copyright © 1987 by

University Press of America,® Inc.

4720 Boston Way
Lanham, MD 20706

3 Henrietta Street
London WC2E 8LU England

Printed in the United States of America

British Cataloging in Publication Information Available

Library of Congress Cataloging-in-Publication Data

Bales, Eugene F., 1946-
A ready reference to philosophy East and West / Eugene F. Bales.
p.   cm.
Includes index.
ISBN 0-8191-6640-5 (alk. paper)
1. Philosophy—History.   I. Title.
B72.B34   1987
109—dc19   87-19842
                                                  CIP

All University Press of America books are produced on acid-free
paper which exceeds the minimum standards set by the National
Historical Publication and Records Commission.

TABLE OF CONTENTS

A QUICK ALPHABETICAL INDEX TO PHILOSOPHERS

Name	Page

A QUICK ALPHABETICAL INDEX TO PHILOSOPHICAL THEORIES AND MOVEMENTS

-A-

Anarchism, in Proudhon, 84
      in Kropotkin, 99
Aristotelianism, 11, 36
Atomism, in Empedocles, 4
      in Democritus, 5
      in Epicurus, 19
      in Leibniz, 59
      in Hobbes, 61
      in Alexander, 149
      in Whitehead, 167

-B-

Buddhism and Philosophy, 178, 251

-C-

Carvaka (Materialist) School, 210
Ch'an School of Chinese Buddhist Philosophy, 255
Christianity and Philosophy, 24
Confucianism, 228, 244
Confucianism, in Confucius, 228
      in Mencius, 230
      in Hsün Tzu, 232
      in Tung Chung-Shu, 244
      in Yang Hsiung, 246
      in Wang Ch'ung, 246

-D-

Deconstruction, in Derrida, 136

-E-

Emotivism, in Stevenson, 170
Empiricism, in Ockham, 42
      in Bacon, 48
      in Locke, 63
      in Berkeley, 65
      in Hume, 67
      in Russell, 145
Epicureanism, 19
Evolutionism, in Spencer, 93
      in Alexander, 149
      in Aurobindo, 221
      in K'ang Yu-wei, 274

PREFACE

This manual is written for everyone seeking a readily accessible account of the history of philosophy. Undergraduate students and those taking philosophy courses without necessarily majoring in the subject will find it to be a helpful study aide. The non-technical treatment of the subject matter makes it a useful reference for the general reader as well.

The overall structure of the book was designed to reflect the concerns of the intended readers. Chapters 1-8 are devoted to the history of Western philosophy; contemporary Western thinkers are the focus of Chapters 7 and 8. In order to include only those thinkers that students are likely to encounter in undergraduate courses, the first six chapters are intentionally summary and lacking in detail when compared with the chapters on contemporary thought. This reflects the emphasis of undergraduate courses, which typically include a substantial amount of contemporary readings.

Chapters 9 and 10 cover the history of Indian and Chinese philosophy respectively. The inclusion of Eastern thinkers, as well as the emphasis on a wide variety of contemporary Western thinkers, is intended to make this brief work even more useful to the general reader.

The primary limitation of this work is an obvious one. The breadth of discussion, which is the aim of this manual, has been purchased at the price of depth of treatment. Those who want more extensive discussion of the philosophers found in this volume should look elsewhere; the intention here is to provide only a very introductory account of each philosopher.

This short book has gone through several earlier revisions. The inspiration for doing it at all came from my students. The encouragement to persist in doing it I owe to my wife Deborah. The time to complete it I owe to a sabbatical granted me by Conception Seminary College. To all—my thanks.

The author welcomes any advice on how to make this book of greater utility for the general reader.

INTRODUCTION

Philosophy is by all accounts an unusual academic discipline. Defining what unites all the various thinkers discussed in this volume is not an attainable, let alone easy, task. Despite that, some provisional clarification of the nature of philosophy is in order here.

Traditionally, philosophy has been concerned with asking fundamental questions about the nature of reality, and how it is possible for us to have knowledge of it. The world as we perceive it seems to be constituted by a plurality of objects and events, organisms and persons, existing in space and time. One might ask about this plurality of things whether it is really as we see it, or whether there is some fundamental unity "behind the scenes", as it were. If there is some kind of unified reality beyond what we perceive--the essence of the belief called "monism"--then there are many possibilities as to the nature of that reality--God, creativity, matter, spirit, and so forth. Or we might admit that the world is radically disunified; or we might insist that, while there are many individual and independent realities, none of them is absolutely unrelated to the other. We might espouse, that is, either radical pluralism or moderate pluralism. The possibilities of interpretation are endless.

There is another question that appears on the horizon in much of philosophy, often in the same breath as the first question concerning the nature of reality. For if I say that I know something about the nature of reality, just how is it possible for the human mind to know this or anything else? Are there some things that could not be known because of the nature of the human mind, human knowledge, and human perception? Here the question is not what ultimately exists, but what do I know (given the nature of my mind), and how do I know it?

If the first question is called alternatively metaphysics or ontology because it is concerned with the nature of being itself (ontology), beyond the domain of the merely physical (metaphysics), the second is called epistemology, and is concerned with the nature and limits of knowledge. Whole eras or movements of philosophy have been marked by the dominance of one as opposed to the other of these concerns; but no era or movement has failed to be concerned with both issues.

There are many other issues that philosophers have been concerned with besides these two. Logic, ethics, politics, the foundations of aesthetics, the nature of religion, human oppression and suffering, and so forth--all of these and many more have come to be the subject of philosophical questioning.

Philosophizing does not tend to recognize conceptual borders, as though there were some area in life which was immune from its questions. Every imaginable experience has been the starting point of philosophical questioning and thinking. Starting points are as numerous in philosophy as the experience of human beings themselves. And each starting point raises new and often unexpected questions about the fundamental issues. Thus, to take an important contemporary issue: if we begin from the moral and perceptual experience of women, rather than men (and one must remember that most philosophers of note have historically been unmarried males), will the nature of reality appear in a different light? Is there a distinct epistemology or theory of knowledge that characterizes the standpoint of someone who is relatively disadvantaged in society, as opposed to one who is relatively advantaged? Will the ethical good appear in a different light than it has heretofore?

The point to be made is simply that philosophy has a radical open-endedness in terms of its starting-point that prevents anyone from ever successfully bringing it to a nice, neat finale, or organizing it into a whole whose borders are as clear as a row of flowers. If the starting-points are endless, it is not surprising that philosophy is forever casting new light on old questions, and often raising new questions as well. It is also not surprising that philosophy never seems to go anywhere. But those who expect it to have gone somewhere, and are accordingly either disappointed or satisifed, have confused it with a kind of religion. Philosophy has very strong relations with religion at various points in its history; but it has never been very slavish to any religion anywhere in the world. That is because philosophical thinking has its own task, quite apart from any ulterior uses others may give it. And that task is as limited and as unlimited as the human spirit itself.

CHAPTER 1

PHILOSOPHY IN THE GREEK CITY-STATE

A. EARLY PRE-SOCRATICS AND THE ORIGINS OF PHILOSOPHY

Western philosophy has its recorded origins in the 6th century B.C., principally within various Greek colonies. There were two Greek-speaking regions that were important at this time: the first consisted of a number of communities scattered along what is now the Western coast of Turkey: this was called Ionia. The second was in southern Italy and was called Magna Graecia or the Greek West.

1. The Ionian School flourished in the sixth century B.C. until the city of Miletus was destroyed in 494 B.C. Three philosophers are associated with this school: Thales, Anaximander, and Anaximenes. Little is known about them, since they left no written works. But it is possible to discern their significance through fragments preserved by later writers.

All three of these men asked a most unusual question: What is it that accounts for both the diversity and unity of things in the universe? It was this question that seems to have initiated the philosophical quest, though, as we shall see, that quest broadened out to include many other questions as well.

The answers that these men gave to this question seem terribly unsophisticated today; yet in their own time they must have seemed quite thoughtful and profound. Thales (fl. 585 B.C.), for example, speculated that the universe or kosmos is ultimately made up of drops of water. Why water? Water is the source of life, and life is associated with divinity. Thus for Thales, water accounted not only for the life of things in the kosmos, but also for the holiness or divinity of things that are alive. Water was not only an ultimate scientific and metaphysical explanation, it was also a theological explanation. For Thales, God, Water, and Life were one and the same.

Anaximander (fl. 550 B.C.), who was an acquaintance of Thales, took a different approach. He suggested that the kosmos was made up of opposites, namely the hot and the cold, the wet and the dry. Now these opposites came to be separated out from one another by a "whirling" movement within what Anaximander called the "Unbounded." This Unbounded was apparently material in nature, and Anaximander, like Thales, had no hesitation in identifying it with God. Anaximander's explanation of the nature of things focused not just on what everything had in common (the "unbounded"), but also on the differences that obviously existed.

These differences could all be reduced to two sets of opposites; and Anaximander wanted to point out that to explain the world one needed both an explanation of unity and diversity. It is for this reason that many have regarded Anaximander as a much more brilliant thinker than Thales, though of course with such thin evidence at hand caution is the order of the day in making such judgments.

Anaximenes (fl. 550 B.C.) attempted to explain the movement of all things in the kosmos in terms of two opposed processes: rarefaction, whereby things become lighter or aerier, and condensation, whereby things become heavier or more solid. Ultimately the kosmos is made up of air, however, which is both the Divine and the source of all life. Air, after all, was a sine qua non of living animals. Thus, Anaximenes' logic closely parallels Thales; yet his analysis of movement into rarefaction and condensation was clearly a step beyond Thales, insofar as it presupposes Anaximander's concern with the diversity of things. But Anaximenes was concerned about movement more than about the kinds of things in the world.

The significance of these philosophers lies not so much in their answers (obviously) as their questions. They were the first apparently to postulate a single unobserved substance as the foundation of the world in which we live. Their philosophizing was speculative, but their speculation clearly depended on the empirical qualities of things such as water and air. And two of these three thinkers sought to answer the question of why there are many things, and not just one.

2. The most significant philosopher in Magna Graecia at this time actually founded his own religious cult. His name was Pythagoras (c. 570-495 B.C.), and his followers were known as Pythagoreans. The Pythagoreans held that the human soul was immortal, and that it was subject to further reincarnations if it did not separate itself from the body in this life. The separation could be helped by abstinence: the Pythagoreans had very strict and unusual dietary rules. These beliefs about the soul were extraordinary for the average Greek; it is likely that they were borrowed from other cultures living at the far eastern edge of the Mediterranean area.

In any case, the soul, by abstaining from various foods, could reflect the harmony and beauty of the kosmos. Now the kosmos was rational in nature; specifically, all things were made up of "numbers", that is, of mathematical points or units. The entire kosmos or universe could thus be understood mathematically. The extraordinary importance of this idea did not really emerge until the advent of modern science, whose presupposition is precisely this: everything in the universe is mathematically measurable. The Pythagoreans were not scientists, however; they were a religious cult whose doctrine centered on a mystical appreciation of numbers.

Although both the Ionians and the Pythagoreans speculated about the nature of the kosmos, their influence was in different directions. The Ionians' philosophy became the starting-point for later scientific or empirical trends of thought, while the Pythagoreans' thinking became the basis for more rationalistic, mathematical, and religious trends of thought. One can see the final outcome of both these trends in the thought of Plato and Aristotle.

B. LATER PRE-SOCRATICS

1. <u>Heraclitus</u> (536-470 B.C.) and <u>Parmenides</u> (530-460 B.C.) were perhaps two of the very greatest Presocratic philosophers, and they were as different from one another as the Ionians and the Pythagoreans.

<u>Heraclitus'</u> philosophy is preserved in a number of sayings, some of which are quite short and often cryptic. He believed that all Reality is One. Yet this One is necessarily made up of many parts, all of which are in constant motion. This motion is in the nature of a perpetual internal conflict, which proceeds in a rational, orderly and law-like way. The law-like character of the perpetual conflict Heraclitus termed Logos; Logos was the nature of the movement of all things in the world.

Since the nature of all things was conflict, Heraclitus felt that of the four elements—earth, air, fire, and water—it was fire whose qualities best resembled the motion of the universe. Thus Fire is the nature of the One Reality; and this is God. Fire or God is the Logos which gives rise to a law-like movement of opposed things. This theory is still far removed from Christian theology; but it must never be forgotten that this meaning of Logos was part of the "sediment" of Greek culture that St. John took for granted in the opening lines of his Gospel.

<u>Parmenides</u> was also convinced that Reality was One. However, this led him to deny that it (Reality) had any parts or movement. He says that whatever is, is; whatever is not, is not, and cannot come to be. Being or Reality is eternal, unchangeable, uncreated, and imperishable. It cannot be divided into parts, and it therefore has no movement. Being and Thought are at one with each other; sense-perception must be invalid since it reveals a world of changing and multiple realities. These latter are unreal and deceptive.

3

One of Parmenides' disciples named Zeno (490 B.C.--?) strengthened this unusual philosophy by posing a series of curious word puzzles which have intrigued mathematicians and philosophers ever since. One example is sufficient: Suppose you are driving from New York to Los Angeles. To get to Los Angeles, you would necessarily have to get to a point midway between New York and Los Angeles, say St. Louis. To get from New York to St. Louis, one would have to get to a point midway between New York and St. Louis, say Cincinnati. This line of reasoning never comes to an end, since there are an infinite number of points between New York and Los Angeles, between New York and St. Louis, and between New York and Cincinnati. But to cross an infinite number of points would require an infinite number of moments in time, since travelling from point to point requires some amount of time. It follows that it is quite impossible to drive from New York to Los Angeles in less than an infinite period of time. If it appears in ordinary life that we do in fact travel from New York to Los Angeles in a finite period of time, such movement must be an illusion. Thus there is no such thing as movement, and all things are at rest and at one.

2. There emerged out of the Ionian and Parmenidean schools a tendency toward more complex theories of nature. Three philosophers are especially important: Empedocles (500-440? B.C.), Anaxagoras (500-428 B.C.) and Democritus (460-400 B.C.).

Empedocles accepted Parmenides' notion of Being as uncreated and indestructible. However, he held that motion was real. His explanation of motion is of some interest.

Being is made up of four chief kinds of atoms: earth, air, fire, and water. Each object in sense-perception is constituted of different arrangements or combinations of these four kinds of atoms. The movement of these atoms occurs because of the universal principles of Love and Hate, that is, of attraction and repulsion. Thus the atoms, like Parmenides' Being, are eternal and unchangeable by nature; but, like the Logos of Heraclitus, they do move according to principles which are forever in conflict.

Anaxagoras also accepted the reality of motion. But he apparently felt that Empedocles' theory of four different kinds of atoms was arbitrary. If four, why not ten? or twenty? or better, why not an infinite number of kinds of atoms, each of which could be divided endlessly. Thus anything can change into anything else, and similarly everything is in everything else. But while this is an effective criticism of Empedocles' arbitrary list of atoms, it does not explain the world of trees and animals in sense perception. For if everything is in everything else, then everything in sense perception would be a mixture of things, and nothing would have an identifiable shape or form. To explain how

4

things come to have such a shape or form, Anaxagoras suggested that the forms or shapes of things were due to a source external to the universe. For Anaxagoras this external source of order could only be a kind of cosmic mind. Nous (the Greek word for "mind") was infinite for Anaxagoras; it had complete knowledge of the world. The world in turn was related to this mind as its idea.

Democritus was perhaps the most famous atomist of all, and has been more closely linked with contemporary scientific atomism than any other Greek thinker. For Democritus, there are two kinds of realities: an infinite Void or space, and an infinite number of atoms (literally, in-divisibles). Each of these atoms is infinitely small and invisible, and all of them lack qualities such as color, shape, etc. These atoms, which move about in the infinite Void, are all perfectly alike, eternal, and indestructible. The entire world consists of combinations or aggregates of these atoms. Indeed even the human mind and its sense-perception can be reduced to atoms of some sort. Curiously, Democritus ended by denying the validity of sense-perception, since the latter did not reveal a world constituted of atoms. It was only the thinking mind that knew the world to be so constituted. Thus Democritus' atomism was rationalistic, rather than empiricistic; and in this respect Democritus was worlds away from the contemporary scientific approach which rests on empiricism for its evidence of atomism.

Empedocles, Anaxagoras, and Democritus obviously built on the theories of Heraclitus and Parmenides, as well as on the Ionians. But in one respect these three—especially Anaxagoras and Democritus—introduced and emphasized a new element in philosophical speculation: namely, the role of the mind. The next great movement in philosophy would come when philosophers turned from asking about the universe to asking about the nature of the human mind.

C. THE SOPHISTS

With the rise of Athens as a great city-state, there emerged a flowering of art, philosophy, and political thought. Certainly the achievement of Athens represents one of the finest of the human spirit. With this achievement, philosophy underwent some important changes. Those changes are associated with a group of travelling teachers who came to be known as "Sophists". The term merely means "those who are knowledgeable"; but because later generations came to dislike their teachings, the term "sophist" has acquired a thoroughly pejorative character. It now designates someone who only pretends to be knowledgeable, but in fact is not. This is not really a fair characterization of these philosophers.

Their most important contribution was to substitute humanity for nature as the object of philosophical interest. This was a truly momentous change and paved the way for Plato and Aristotle. The sophists were the first true humanists. Several examples should suffice.

Protagoras (480-410 B.C.) held as his basic point of view that "Man is the measure of all things". He applied this both to ethical truths and to religious beliefs, as well as to the objects of sense-perception. Now this sounds like a relativism which could only end in complete rejection of all traditional beliefs; and indeed Protagoras concluded that absolute truth was inaccessible to the mind. But ordinary life remained undisturbed by this skepticism, since, for Protagoras, knowledge was subordinate to practice. Thus outwardly Protagoras' philosophy and behavior were quite traditional; inwardly, however, he was skeptical of the validity of most traditional beliefs.

Gorgias (483-375) has often been considered the first nihilist in Western thought. Actually his arguments were probably concocted to prove the absurdity of Parmenides' philosophy. His argument is simple, although strange: (1) Nothing is real. For if anything existed it must have come into being from nothing. But from nothing comes nothing. Therefore nothing whatever exists. (2) If anything did exist, it could not be known. This is true because if anything were known, Nothingness could not be known. But Nothingness can be known. (3) If there were knowledge of being, this knowledge could never be spoken or communicated to another. This is true because language is distinct from thought; there is never a perfect correlation between the two. Thus, to recapitulate: (1) Nothing exists; (2) even if it did, it couldn't be known; and (3) even if it could be known, it could not be spoken. In the end Gorgias renounced the search for absolute truth and confined himself to the teaching of rhetoric or the art of persuasion.

Other sophists include Thrasymachus of Chalcedon who held an early version of the might-makes-right political theory, and Antiphon of Athens who held that all men are equal and denounced the institution of slavery.

Main works of all presocratics: All that remains of the writings of the presocratics are literary fragments. These are not always easy to interpret or understand, and it is best to consult a commentary on them. The usual reference in English for these fragments and for a well-regarded interpretation of them, is G. S. Kirk and J. E. Raven, The Presocratic Philosophers: A Critical History with a Selection of Texts (Cambridge University Press, 1957).

D. SOCRATES (470-399 B.C.)

Perhaps the greatest of all the Athenian philosophers was Socrates. Socrates' life and teachings were recorded by his disciple Plato in the famous Platonic dialogues which are among the masterpieces of world literature. Socrates himself left no writings whatever. This has created a rather sticky problem for scholars: how much that is spoken by Socrates in the Platonic dialogues is really Socrates and how much is really Plato? A similar problem arises with the New Testament and the sayings of Jesus. Indeed both problems were raised for the first time by 19th century German scholars. While there remain problems of interpretation, no one today seriously questions the historical reality of either Socrates or Jesus, and there is considerable agreement about the teachings of both.

Socrates was, like the other sophists, a traveling teacher. Unlike his fellows, however, he did not accept money for his teaching. He considered his teaching to be a kind of inspired vocation.

The typical structure of a Platonic dialogue has Socrates claiming that he does not know what X (justice, virtue, courage, are some examples) is. Someone else then offers a definition of X; and Socrates proceeds meekly to demolish the proposed definition. Almost none of the genuinely Socratic dialogues ends with a positive conclusion about anything. Yet one can gather the outlines of some of Socrates' beliefs.

Socrates began his studies with the later atomists, especially Anaxagoras. But he became frustrated with such cosmic speculation and turned to humanity as the center of his concern. He was also influenced by the concern of the Pythagoreans for the cultivation of the soul.

Socrates believed that the soul was a distinct entity from the body, that it had undergone many reincarnations previously; and that unless it purified itself in this life, it would continue to undergo more miserable reincarnations. But Socrates differed from the Pythagoreans by insisting that purification of the soul was to be achieved by the pursuit of knowledge, virtue, and happiness, which he held to be one and the same.

For Socrates the nature of the soul was thinking. Now the soul's primary desire was for happiness; and happiness could only come through the pursuit of virtue. But what was the relation between virtue and knowledge? Were they two different things altogether? Socrates did not think so. He held that all virtues were the same in nature, and that virtue in essence was a kind of knowledge. To be good was to know the good; by contrast, to be evil was to not know the good. It was inconceivable for Socrates that someone could know what was good, but not do it. Further, Socrates believed that a person only acts voluntarily when he or she does what is good. When one does what is evil, one is always acting involuntarily. Since doing evil was a matter of ignorance, not will, it followed that the solution to the problem of human wrong-doing was education.

Socrates believed that virtue could be taught, but he was not always clear as to how it could be taught. Generally, learning occurs when the student discovers something which has been apparently caused by the teacher, but which the student recognizes he or she has known all along. Thus knowledge is entirely a priori or independent of experience, although it may well have been incidentally "triggered" by experience. Our knowledge is imprinted on our soul in a previous life; and thus all acquisition of knowledge in this life is simply a form of remembering what the soul once knew but forgot at birth.

What is it, then, that is the object of knowledge? What does the soul know when it knows Virtue as such? It was in answer to this question that Socrates proposed a highly influential theory crucial to many later metaphysical theories. (That Socrates [as opposed to Plato] proposed the following theory has been debated extensively in the philosophical literature; there are many who question the interpretation that follows.)

Consider the case of an ordinary triangle. I perceive in front of me a triangular shaped object. I know what triangularity is. I might be tempted to say that the triangularity is right there in front of me—in the object. But this is not correct for Socrates. For every specific instance of triangularity is not quite perfect; what I know when I know "triangularity" is perfect triangularity. Socrates speaks of a Form of Triangularity or the Idea of Triangularity, meaning Perfect Triangularity. Now this triangular object participates in, or imitates, or resembles this Perfect Triangularity; and so do all the other instances of tri-angular-shaped objects I may come across in my experience. Thus, my experience of objects serves to remind me of the Forms or Ideas which I came to know in a previous life but forgot in the process of being born.

The same analogy can be used with regard to the knowledge of just things, of virtuous things, of good things, and so forth. Socrates himself did not extend the theory beyond knowledge of mathematical or moral realities, however; it was left to later philosophers to do this.

By re-achieving this knowledge of forms, the soul becomes good, virtuous, and ultimately happy. Although Socrates always

8

claimed to be ignorant, the extraordinary account of his execution in Plato's dialogue called the Phaedo leaves no doubt that Socrates was indeed "the wisest and the best of men." It is still a moving account today after 2500 years.

E. PLATO (429-348 B.C.)

Of all Socrates' pupils, Plato was by far the most gifted both as a philosopher and as a writer. Indeed on both counts Plato is among the great geniuses of the human race.

Plato's writings (with the exception of a number of letters whose authenticity is still debated) are all in the form of dialogues. Plato, like Socrates, never presented any systematic or formal philosophical treatise. Yet the dialogues are full of insights and ideas both profound and suggestive.

Plato's own thought is difficult to distinguish from that of his great teacher. At the start, he assumes the truth of Socrates' theory of the Forms, and then advances the theory well beyond this.

For Plato, as well as for Socrates, the fundamental datum of knowledge is the Form or Idea (eidos). These Forms exist beyond this material kosmos in a kind of intelligible kosmos. They are entirely spiritual or non-material in nature and thus immutable; and they are each distinct and simple.

Plato distinguishes three steps in the progression of the soul's knowledge from this world to the world of the Forms. First, there is mere sensation (aisthesis) of things. Second, there is the more general knowledge of sense objects which is essentially probable and tentative in nature. This Plato calls doxa, that is, opinion or belief. Third, there is knowledge (episteme) of the Forms of all things; this kind of knowledge is called wisdom (sophia).

Plato held the theory of knowledge as Recollection or Remembering (as did Socrates). This theory implied that the source of knowledge was the realm of Forms; and that sense experience was only the occasion, not the real cause, of knowledge.

Plato discussed in some detail this realm of Forms. Specifically, all forms participated in either the Form of Movement or the Form of Rest; all participated in either the Form of Sameness or that of Difference; and all participated in the Form of Being. Beyond these five highest kinds of Forms, however there is the Form of the Good. The Form of the Good is the source of the existence of all other forms.

What is the way in which this world of physical things comes into being, then? Plato distinguishes in each physical thing a determinate element and an indeterminate element. The determinate element is the reflection of some form. The indeterminate element is an infinite potentiality whose nature is simply the lack of all the qualities the Forms possess.

Plato's proof for the existence of God centers on the need for a soul-like existence to "combine" this indeterminate potentiality and the forms. This deity is called a Demiurge or creative God. But God for Plato does not create all things out of nothing. God's creativity is strictly conceived on the analogy of an artist who arranges previously existent items. God, however, does differ from the human soul in that God possesses perfect knowledge of the World of Forms. It is to be noted that this Demiurge is distinct from both the Form of the Good and the Form of Being; they are objects of God's thought, and not identical with the essence of God.

Plato's notion of the human soul (psyche) also went beyond Socrates' beliefs. He accepted with Socrates the pre-existence of the soul, the merely accidental union of soul and body in this life, and the future immortality of the soul. But he also suggested a theory of the Soul's ethical progress based upon the Soul's three faculties of knowledge, viz., sensation, opinion, and wisdom. Each of these three aspects of knowledge has its own corresponding virtue. The virtue of temperance (sophrosyne) corresponds to sensation; the virtue of fortitude (andreia) to opinion; and the virtue of wisdom (sophia) to knowledge itself. The last point underscores the fact that Plato accepts the identity of knowledge and virtue, just as Socrates did: thus wisdom is both the highest form of knowledge, and simultaneously the highest virtue.

Plato's theory of the State closely parallels that of the Soul. Indeed he suggested that the State is the Soul "writ large". If the Soul is characterized by three essential functions and/or virtues, so in fact is the State. Thus, the largest group of citizens in the state consists of laborers or artisans whose function is to provide for the material needs of all the members of the State. Their particular virtue as a social class is that of temperance. They thus correspond to the lowest level of the Soul.

The second group or social class is that of the soldiers whose function is to protect the state from any harm. As a group they have no wealth or property; their specific virtue as a class is fortitude or courage.

10

The third and highest social class is that of the leaders or archontes. These have complete power of legislation and administration. To do this effectively Plato requires them to have studied philosophy extensively; it is they and they alone who have sufficient knowledge to govern society wisely. Their specific virtue, needless to say, is wisdom.

When all three classes in this society are each practicing their specific virtue, the State exists in a harmony which is called justice (dikaiosyne). Justice is the proper functioning of each part of the Soul or State in its specific manner.

This theory of the State is certainly not democracy as we understand it, nor is it simply totalitarianism. Rather it represents an attempt to differentiate social classes on the basis of their knowledge or talents. Only an elite for Plato are knowledgeable enough to govern wisely. Thus government is by the wise for Plato, not by the strong. Plato clearly did not believe that wisdom resided with the masses. In this respect he apparently shared the sympathies of his teacher Socrates. Both philosophers were at odds with their own society which was democratic in sentiment.

Main works: Protagoras (concerned with the unity of virtue); Euthyphro (on the nature of piety or holiness); Apology (the account of Socrates' trial); Gorgias (written about 387 B.C.; concerned with the Sophists and their teaching); Meno (written after 387 B.C.; on the teachability of virtue); Cratylus (on the nature of language); Symposium (after 385 B.C.; on love); Phaedo (very close in time of composition to the Symposium; an account of Socrates' death); Republic (written over a period of perhaps 20 years, finished around 374 B.C.; Plato's longest work, concerned with justice in the individual and the state); Parmenides (after 370 B.C.; on the nature of the one or unity); Theaetetus (c. 368 B.C.; on the nature of knowledge); Phaedrus (after 374 B.C.; on love and a number of other topics); Sophist (continuation of Theaetetus); Politicus (continuation of the Sophist); Philebus (on the relation of pleasure and goodness); Timaeus (metaphysical account of the universe); Laws (probably Plato's last work, on government).

F. ARISTOTLE (384-322 B.C.)

Plato's most famous pupil was Aristotle. It is to be regretted that many of Aristotle's original works have perished. Most of what is known about Aristotle is contained in lecture notes either that he wrote for his classes or that students copied during his classes. His works therefore are often very difficult reading, and bear no comparison on literary grounds with Plato.

Aristotle's philosophical concern extended to virtually every subject under the heavens. His mind was enormously probing and wide-ranging: he studied natural objects with an almost scientific sense of detail; he systematized and organized the entire field of logic which remained virtually unmodified in essentials until only the last few centuries; he suggested theories of metaphysics, psychology, politics, ethics, and art that have continued to inspire thinkers till this day. It is futile to ask whether he or Plato was truly the greatest mind of ancient Greece; both were geniuses and both were unique.

The most important and crucial distinction in Aristotle's metaphysics is that between act (energeia) and potency (dynamis). Everything that exists in the ordinary world has a degree of both. For an object to be in act is for it to be a fully perfect thing, not lacking in anything. Strictly speaking, the only being fully in act for Aristotle is God. Conversely, for something to be in potency is for it to lack something proper to itself and thus be imperfect. That which lacks perfection altogether is called prime matter (prote hyle) or pure potentiality (potency). God and Prime Matter are the two extremes between which all other realities are situated. It must be kept in mind that for all beings other than God and Prime Matter, act and potentiality are not two kinds of objects like apples and oranges. Rather, they are inseparably one in reality, though distinct from one another, and distinguishable by the mind. The distinction between act and potency is not based on any empirical experience as such, but it is a valid analysis of the nature of real objects.

The universe in which we live was considered by Aristotle to be eternal. He thought this because the heavenly bodies all moved in a circular motion, and circular motion was considered by the Greeks to be metaphysically perfect and hence eternal. Aristotle also thought the heavens were made, not merely of earth, air, fire, and water, but of a fifth element called ether which had no admixture of prime matter with it. The earth was at the center of the universe and did not share in the movement of the heavenly sphere. One can readily see why scientists such as Galileo were so anti-Aristotelian. The reported reluctance of one person during Galileo's lifetime to look through a telescope and behold the rather earth-like features of the moon was based on the Aristotelian belief that the moon was made of ether, not earthly elements.

For Aristotle all objects in this world could be logically analyzed not only into act and potency, but also into substance (hypokeimenon) and accident (symbebekos), and into matter (hyle) and form (eidos). A substance is defined as something that exists in and by itself, without the need for some other substratum. An

12

accident is defined as something that has no existence except in a substance; as such, an accident "modifies" the substance. An example will clarify the relationship. Suppose I perceive a large gray rock. The rock has a large number of accidents such as "grayness", "largeness", "roughness", and so forth. These accidents do not exist all by themselves; rather we perceive them as <u>unified</u>, as inhering <u>in</u> <u>something</u>. This something is what Aristotle calls substance.

Aristotle's doctrine of the 10 Categories (that there are exactly 10 such categories is a medieval invention, not Aristotle's) was a doctrine of the categories of substances and accidents. The first category is simply that of substance; the other nine—action, passivity, quality, quantity, place, time, relation, posture, and habit—are types of accidents.

Besides the distinction between substance and accident, there is also that of matter and form. Every substance is composed of both matter and form. The matter is, of course, prime matter and is the cause of the thing's individuality; the form is some kind of actual reality. Matter and form are obviously parallel to the distinction between act and potency. Substance is form insofar as it is in act; it is matter insofar as it is in potency. It is the presence of potency that accounts for the possibility of one substance becoming another. In such change, the form may change, but the prime matter remains the same.

It should also be clear that while Aristotle's theory of matter is relatively close to that of Plato's, his theory of form is very much at odds with Plato's theory of Forms. Plato's Forms exist in a world apart from this world; Aristotle's forms are in some sort of unity with the objects in this world. Aristotle's metaphysics is in this respect much more "this-worldly" than Plato's. It will be essential to keep this distinction in mind later on when discussing the influx of Aristotelianism in the middle ages, and Christianity's initial reaction to such thinking.

So far we have been discussing the actual natures of everyday objects: substance and accident, matter and form. Given these distinctions within the nature of things, how do things change? Aristotle offers us an account of change in his theory of the four kinds of causes (<u>aitia</u>).

The <u>material</u> <u>cause</u> of an object, let us say a statue, is similar to the marble out of which the statue is made. In this sense, marble is like prime matter in being able to be made into many different things, only one of which is the statue itself.

The <u>formal</u> <u>cause</u> is that cause of an object whereby the marble acquires specific form or (in this case) shape.

13

The efficient cause is that agent which caused the statue with its matter and form to come to be. In this case, the efficient cause is the sculptor.

The final cause is that purpose or idea in the sculptor's mind which caused the agent to make the statue in such-and-such a way.

Aristotle claimed that each natural object was constituted by all four kinds of causes. But he especially emphasized the importance of final causes or purposes in natural objects. It is perhaps rather difficult for us today to understand how a rock, for example, could be said to have a purpose (telos), since the notion of final cause was strongly rejected by early scientists like Galileo.

Each particular kind of living object in the world had a specifically different kind of soul, for Aristotle. The plant, for example, had a vegetable soul whose function was simply to reproduce.

The animal had a soul with two functions: the first reproductive, the second perceptual. The animal could actually sense other objects: for example, a cat can see a ball rolling and chase it.

The human soul is more complex than either of these. Besides· reproduction and sensation, the human soul also has a third function: intellection. There are two phases of intellection, one passive, one active. First, a sense image or phantasm is "impressed" on that part of the soul known as the passive intellect (it is passive because it is only potentially in the process of knowing). The act of knowledge is a function of the active intellect. The function of the active intellect is to separate the spiritual from the material elements of the phantasm. The spiritual element—that is, the form, the act, the substance of a thing—is expressed in a concept, which is the way in which the active intellect knows the real objects in the world. Concepts are essentially simple: there is a concept of a "horse", of a "rock", of a "tree". Concepts are expressed verbally in terms: e.g., the word "tree". Concepts can be arranged into more complex units called judgments wherein one concept is related to another (for example, the concept "green" might be related to the concept "grass" in the judgment, "The grass is green"). Verbal expressions of judgments are called propositions. Finally, judgments can be arranged into groups of three or more which involve reasoning. These groups when expressed verbally are called syllogisms.

14

For Aristotle the doctrine of logic revolved around the study of concepts, judgments, and syllogisms. The highest form of reasoning was expressed in the latter. Syllogisms in turn could be either demonstrative or probable. In the first case, demonstrative syllogisms had both certain (that is, as opposed to merely probable) premises and certain conclusions. Probable or "dialectical" syllogisms had premises that were only probable, not certain: hence the conclusion was also only probable. Of these two types of syllogisms, demonstration was clearly superior for Aristotle.

It was pointed out in the previous section that Plato's ethics paralleled his theory of the soul and his theory of the State. This is also true of Aristotle's theories of ethics, the soul, and the State. But there are again some great differences from Plato's theory.

For Aristotle, the soul is related to the body as form is to matter. But matter and form, as was pointed out before, are inseparable in reality. There existed only one object composed of body and soul. This strongly suggests that when the body dies, so does the soul. And in fact, this seems to have been Aristotle's view, though he is not very clear on the subject.

In any case, Aristotle's emphasis in the realm of ethics was on the full development of the individual. Certainly wisdom or reasoning was the highest state of the human mind, but the human being was more than merely a mind. Hence virtue included the development of both action and thought. Aristotle often employed the doctrine of the mean whereby the best ethical action is that which lies between two unacceptable extremes. Aristotle's ethic, then, was more practical and this-worldly than Plato's.

His theory of the state (polis) followed suit. Essentially Aristotle felt that human perfection occurred naturally in the state: social life is part of ethics, not incidental to it. But what kind of organization is best for society? Aristotle argued that a moderate government by a property-owning and voting middle-class was the safest and best kind of society. He thus sought to avoid the extremes of tyranny and democracy.

A few words must be said about Aristotle's theory of God. Aristotle argued for the existence of Perfect Act understood in terms of a Prime Mover whose function was to explain how all things began their movement. This Prime Mover/Perfect Actuality was also a Perfect Mind (nous). God, for Aristotle, was entirely non-material in nature, simple, perfect, eternal, and good. God's mind eternally contemplated itself. He was both the Beginning (as Prime Mover) and End (as Final Cause) of the universe. Yet since God contemplated only himself, it seems that Aristotle's God was

15

not as concerned with human individuals and the universe generally, as was the Christian God. This element of Aristotelianism later met with some resistance among Christians whose faith rested on the notion that God had very specific and knowledgeable relations with the created universe. It has been pointed out that it is difficult to pray to an Aristotelian God. But Aristotle's God was posited to explain various features of the universe, and not to satisfy the demands of piety.

Main works: The Organon, consisting of 6 works on logic (Categories, De Interpretatione, Prior Analytics, Posterior Analytics, Topics, De Sophisticis Elenchis). Three works on natural science (Physics, De Generatione et Corruptione, Meteorology). Five works on the biological sciences (Historia Animalium, De Partibus Animalium, De Motu Animalium, De Incessu Animalium, De Generatione Animalium). Works on psychology (De Anima and Parva Naturalia which includes a number of smaller treatises on a variety of subjects). Metaphysics. Poetics. Rhetoric. Politics. Two works on ethics (the Nicomachaean Ethics and the Eudemian Ethics). Virtually all these works were for use in his school, and were lecture notes, probably revised in places.

CHAPTER 2

PHILOSOPHY IN THE PERIOD OF THE ROMAN EMPIRE

A. INTRODUCTION

Almost all of the movements to be discussed in this chapter actually have their beginnings with the Greeks. Rome produced few original thinkers of her own, and even these were far inferior to the Greeks. This was true not only of philosophical development but also of cultural development as a whole. Roman culture is more to be remembered for its highways and governmental structure than for its artists and thinkers.

Nevertheless the consolidation of the Western world under the rule of the Roman emperors had profound implications for later thought. Perhaps the most important overall feature was the tendency toward cosmopolitanism and humanism. The central question for the Romans was this: how should one live and attain happiness? The emphasis was clearly not on questions of physics and science, though developments in this area also occurred. Philosophers came from (by and large) the middle and upper classes, and tended to reflect the latter's concerns about how to live in a world of diverse cultures and values.

Besides cosmopolitanism and humanism, there was also a strong tendency toward eclecticism. Both the Peripatetic School (the followers of Aristotle) and the Academy (Plato's school) borrowed ideas from one another and from other sources as well. Few of their philosophers were of central importance. In addition, there were thinkers who reflected a variety of schools and yet belonged to none: Cicero was one such very famous eclectic whose rhetorical skills far outweighed his philosophical originality.

But there were other important developments during the era of the Roman Empire. Two of these developments are singled out for attention here: the rise of Christianity and the emergence of Neoplatonism. The relation between philosophy and Christian thought was, and is, many-faceted; only the most basic issues are discussed here. Perhaps the culmination of their early relationship can best be glimpsed in the theology of Augustine of Hippo.

The final centuries of the Roman Empire were marked by a growing concern for spiritual questions, and by a growing disillusionment with political life. Besides Christianity and other religions of the time, one prominent philosophical development in this direction was Neoplatonism, whose prime exponent was the mystic Plotinus. If philosophy in the period of the Roman Empire began with the legacy of the Greeks, it ended by planting the

17

seeds for the development of medieval thought.

B. STOICISM

Perhaps the most popular school of this period was Stoicism. Stoicism originated around 300 B.C. with the teachings of Zeno (no relation to Parmenides' disciple!). The school itself lasted well into the third century A.D. It included among its adherents and popularizers Cleanthes of Assos, Poseidonius of Apamaea, the Roman author Seneca, the slave Epictetus of Hierapolis (50? A.D.-138 A.D.) and the Roman Emperor Marcus Aurelius who ruled from 161-180 A.D.

The Stoics' fundamental teaching was to "follow Nature" and thereby achieve happiness. It is necessary first to see what they meant by "Nature", and secondly what they understood by "happiness".

The Universe as a whole is finite and is in the center of an infinite Nothingness. This world of finite things is constituted by two kinds of principles present in each thing: Matter, which is purely passive; and Fire which is purely active and intelligent. This Fire is called Logos or God. God, as Fire or Logos, pervades all things and thereby enlivens matter. Yet Fire is itself a material reality. The Stoics never subscribed to any theory of the spirituality of God or the soul.

Each thing has within it a seed of God or Fire which is called a logos spermatikos or "seeding logos". From this seed, the particular thing develops in a law-like way into its perfection. That each thing develops according to this law of Nature is a function of the nature of the universe itself and its relation to the Logos.

The Stoics believed that at the very periphery of the cosmos there was an envelope of fire which periodically—every 28,000 years to be exact—burnt up the Universe, after which the process of development would begin once again. The development of the Universe, however, was entirely determined beforehand in the nature of the Fire or Logos. Thus the development of the Universe is as law-like as the development of every individual thing in the universe.

This theory combined the Logos theory of Heraclitus with the theory of Matter and Form of Aristotle. It was materialistic and pantheistic, not entirely self-consistent, and somewhat fantastic in its speculation.

But the Stoic theory of the universe was only a stage-setting

18

for the most important element in their philosophy--the attainment of human happiness. To be happy, humanity must imitate Nature. Now the development of being occurs in accordance with the presence of Logos or fire within each thing. In man, Logos or Fire is Reason. Thus to be happy is to be rational. Further, since rationality is internal to man, man's external actions were essentially indifferent. Ethics is concerned basically with intentions, not with actual behavior.

Yet the Stoics did hold to some principles of human behavior based on their notion of rationality. First, it is rational to love oneself and to preserve oneself. Second, it is rational to love others. With regard to the second point, the Stoics posed as their outward ideal the brotherhood of all humans.

But being rational was as much a negative state as a positive one. To be rational meant to be non-emotional. Indeed the Stoic ideal was a-patheia, or non-feeling (our word "apathy" derives from this). Apatheia was not so much a state of boredom as it was a state of the elimination of all passions and desires. Only when humanity has achieved the ideal of apatheia can it be both tranquil and genuinely self- and other-loving. Love is the expression of this apathetic state, not an emotion or a passion of any kind.

Since the Logos or fire determines the development of all things, the Stoic ideal of apatheia also includes giving assent to the determination of all things. Thus for the Stoics, as later for Spinoza, freedom is the recognition that all things are determined.

Main works: The Live and Opinions of the Eminent Philosophers, by Diogenes Laertius (written in the 3rd century A.D.; the section on Zeno is the best source on early Stoicism); Hymn to Zeus, by Cleanthes (331-232 B.C.); On Tranquility, by Seneca (after 49 A.D.); The Discourses of Epictetus, by Arrian (after 100 A.D.?); The Manual of Epictetus, by Arrian (after 100 A.D.); Meditations, by Marcus Aurelius (d. 180 A.D.).

C. EPICUREANISM

If, as has often been remarked, Stoicism was the philosophy of the Roman middle classes, Epicureanism seems to have been the philosophical outlook of the aristocratic classes by and large. It was the only serious philosophical rival to Stoicism and had an equally long span of popularity. The school is named after its Greek founder Epicurus (341-271 B.C.), and its most important Latin exponent was T. Lucretius Carus (91-51 B.C.) in his work De Rerum Natura (On the Nature of Things).

Epicureanism, like Stoicism, propagated both a theory of nature and an ethical theory. While the Stoics owed their theory of nature to Heraclitus and Aristotle, the Epicureans borrowed their cosmology straight out from Democritus.

There are three kinds of realities: material atoms (an infinite number), space (which is empty), and the movement of atoms in space. Only in their theory of movement did the Epicureans differ from Democritus. In the beginning, they argued, the atoms were all falling downward, their paths of motion being entirely parallel to one another. The formation of the present universe began when one of the atoms spontaneously, randomly, moved sideways and disturbed the path of another atom. This began a chain reaction in which the movement of atoms began to vary, such that the atoms arranged themselves in diverse ways to form this universe, as well as (in fact) an infinite number of other universes. Each of these universes was separated from the other by vast spatial voids. In these empty spaces there resided the gods who were themselves composed of perfect atoms, but who had no knowledge of one another nor of our universe in particular.

Given this state of affairs, how did humanity come to have knowledge? The Epicureans replied that the surfaces of all bodies gave off a radiation of atoms which travelled at a high velocity and struck the atoms in our sense organs. It was this that caused sense perception. As such, sense perception could not be false—only judgments about sense perceptions could be false, and these only when certain objects were so far distant that radiating atoms struck our sense organs weakly. Concepts arose in the mind only so that our souls (composed of atoms) might anticipate possible errors in our judgment and correct them accordingly.

The guide to an ethically virtuous life is to be found in our feeling, however, not in our reason. Feelings are either pleasurable or painful. They are pleasurable only when the good is perceived; painful when evil is perceived. The pleasure of the soul is mental; the pleasure of the body is physical—and both types of pleasure are to be cultivated and balanced. All excessive pleasures must be avoided, since they lead to pain. Pleasure is the mere absence of pain, or the presence of peace.

An important aspect of mental pain is fear. Epicureans exhorted their followers to free themselves specifically from three kinds of fears. First, one should liberate oneself from the fear of fate. Fate is not to be feared because the origin of all movement in the universe is pure chance. This obviously contrasts sharply with Stoicism. Second, one should liberate oneself from the fear of death. For since there is no life after death, nothing need be feared on that count. Further, death often liberates us from the pain of dying, and thus is not to be feared.

20

Finally, one should liberate oneself from the fear of the gods. Epicurus did not deny the existence of the gods, as we have seen, nor did he urge anyone to forego outward religious practices. However, he did insist that such outward practices were quite useless since the gods were unaware of them and were in any event incapable of eliminating evil.

Pleasure, as we have seen, is simply the absence of pain; it is not, in any case, restricted arbitrarily to pleasures of the body. While the Epicureans were unquestionably hedonistic, they were not extreme in their practices. It is somewhat unfortunate and misleading that the noun "epicurean" has come to signify one who pursues merely bodily pleasures.

Main works: Principal Doctrines, by Epicurus (3rd century B.C.); On the Nature of Things (De rerum natura), by Lucretius (1st century B.C.).

D. SKEPTICISM

This school was far less popular than the other two previously discussed, yet it had some influence in the modern and contemporary periods. The only figures of any importance in this school are Pyrrho (365-275 B.C.)--hence the term "pyrrhonism" which means skepticism--and Sextus Empiricus (2nd century A.D.). Cicero also admired skepticism, and it was the latter's version of skepticism which inspired David Hume's 18th century skeptical attack on metaphysics.

The skeptics developed a number of arguments which were designed to refute any theoretical philosophical position. Thus they argued that anything that can be affirmed can also be denied; anything that appears to be true, may not be, and so forth. As a result, they urged a renunciation of judgment on all theoretical or philosophical questions. Indeed, their feeling was that philosophical theories were all so mutually opposed and contradictory that the listener was apt to become confused and thus troubled. The solution to this kind of unhappiness was suspension of judgment. As a consequence, peace of mind, tranquility, and happiness lay in simply doing those things which are customary in society, and making no judgments about the ultimate goodness or evil of anything, since all such matters are beyond human knowledge. Skeptics were thus inveterate social conservatives in their own style of life.

Main works: Sextus Empiricus, 4 volumes, tr. R. G. Bury ("Loeb Classical Library", Cambridge, 1933-1953).

E. NEOPLATONISM

Beginning in the second century A.D., the Roman Empire began to undergo great economic and social stresses. The Stoic and Epicurean schools steadily lost ground especially after 300 A.D. The Roman religion also lost ground to many of the Eastern religious sects that appeared, including Christianity. Increasingly, the Romans felt the universe and the human race to be bound up in misery, and began to look to those religions or philosophies which offered some escape or salvation from this present life. Philosophically, two thinkers were of pre-eminent importance toward the end of the Roman Empire: Plotinus the Neoplatonist, and Augustine the Christian. In this section we shall examine Plotinus, and in the next two the rise of Christianity and St. Augustine.

Plotinus (203-269 A.D.) was born in Egypt, but ended up in Rome in 243 A.D. where he lived until his death. In Rome, he opened a school and expounded his own thought which he believed to be merely a commentary on Plato. He was, however, something more than a commentator, although scholars still disagree to this day just how much of Plotinus' system can be laid at Plato's doorstep.

For Plotinus, all things come from The One (or The Good). It is called The One because in it there is no trace of multiplicity or parts. It is called The Good because it is that toward which all things strive. The One or The Good is beyond Being, beyond act and potency, beyond consciousness and thought. It is difficult to say anything at all about the One: only negative language is truly appropriate. The silence of mystical union is the best expression of it.

The One or The Good emanates or gives birth to what is called Being or Mind (Nous). This is less than The One or The Good, though it is still very close to perfection. Nous is simultaneously the Perfect Knower and the Perfectly Known. The latter, the object of knowledge, is the Platonic Forms in their essential unity. It will be noted that this conception of Nous is reminiscent of Aristotle's God who contemplates himself, the difference being that the object of knowledge is here said to be the Forms of all things. Thus Plotinus' Nous is a combination of Aristotle's Unmoved Mover and Plato's Forms, a thinker whose thought is within the mind.

Mind or Nous gives birth to a reality less than itself called Soul or Psyche. Soul also knows the Forms in Nous. But unlike Nous, Soul does not know the forms all at once or perfectly, but rather one at a time, or imperfectly. Soul is itself divided into a higher soul, whose function is to contemplate the forms one by one, and a lower soul whose function is to guide, direct, and give life to things in this material world. From the Higher Soul other

22

souls freely though mistakenly choose to break away. These individual souls have fallen into this world and are the souls of us
humans.

It should be noticed that Soul in many ways resembles Plato's
notion of the Demiurge or God, who both contemplates the Forms and
gives life to the material world. Further, these three
divinities--The One, Nous, and Soul--resemble the Christian theory
of the Trinity. Indeed some of the Christian Church's language in
speaking of the Trinity (e.g., in the Nicaean Creed) was borrowed
from Plotinus.

If Soul has created the material world, it could do so only
because of its metaphysical shadow, so to speak--namely Matter.
Matter is evil, almost pure non-being. The physical world is
partly made up of this Matter, and partly of Soul. Matter itself
actually exists at a level below the material universe, however.

If all things come from The One, they must also return to it.
Human souls, having left their unity in the higher Soul, are now
tied to bodily concerns in this world, and have thus forgotten
their origin in the eternal world. The return to the higher realm
is both a question of knowledge and a question of virtue, since
knowledge and virtue are in fact identical for Plotinus (as they
were for Plato). Plotinus was only concerned for the Soul's
ascent to the next world; he offered little or no insight into how
best to live in this life, except insofar as this life is a
preparation for the next. His tendency was to reduce ethics to an
aspect of the spiritual journey of the Soul to The One, and to
ignore political and social philosophy altogether.

There are three steps in the return of the Soul to The One.
First, the Soul must purify itself of the body and its concerns.
It can best do this by reestablishing a unity with the higher soul
in its contemplation of Nous. Secondly, it must come to identify
itself with the objects of Thought, that is, the Forms, and thus
become Nous or Mind. Finally, it must achieve a mystical union
with The One. This may actually occur in this life, but more
likely in the next life. Plotinus achieved this union with The
One at least four times in his life, according to his disciple
Porphyry. This road back to The One is one which passes through
knowlege itself to that which is beyond knowing and knowledge
altogether.

Plotinus' influence has proved to be very great. Augustine's
conversion to Christianity occurred only after his reading of
Plotinus had freed him from Manichaean materialism. Further,
Plotinus had an indelible influence on later Christian mystics.
Finally, he provided the medieval world with an outline of a basic
world view within which all thought and Christian revelation

could find rest. The structure of St. Thomas' Summa Theologiae parallels Plotinus' vision of all things proceeding from the One and ascending back to the One.

Main work: The Enneads.

F. THE RISE OF CHRISTIANITY

Christianity began as a small sect within Judaism. Neither it nor its mother religion were religions of philosophers, though Judaism had by the first century spawned at least one important philosopher in Egypt—Philo Judaeus (40 B.C.-40 A.D.) who may have had some indirect influence on Plotinus.

The question to be dealt with here centers on the attitude of Christians toward philosophy. This is a very controversial problem. Certainly, many passages from the Old Testament (such as the Creation account or the Wisdom literature) invite philosophical or metaphysical elaboration. Further, the Christian beliefs that God became man in the person of Jesus, and that Jesus rose from the dead suggest a need for elaboration and explanation.

At the outset, the Christian reaction was perhaps ambiguous. On the positive side, we have St. Paul's extraordinary speech to the Athenians recorded in Acts 17:16-34. Paul preached in both the synagogue and the market place: in the latter there were many, especially Epicureans and Stoics, who pressed him for an account of his beliefs.

So Paul, standing in the middle of the Areopagus, said: "Men of Athens, I perceive that in every way you are very religious. For as I passed along, and observed the objects of your worship, I found also an altar with this inscription, 'To an unknown god'. What therefore you worship as unknown, this I proclaim to you. The God who made the world and everything in it, being Lord of heaven and earth, does not live in shrines made by man, nor is he served by human hands, as though he needed anything, since he himself gives to all men life and breath and everything." (Acts 17: 22-25) [The Oxford Annotated Bible with the Apocrypha: Revised Standard Version, ed. by Herbert G. May and Bruce M. Metzger (New York: Oxford University Press), 1965]

This passage clearly portrays the Christian message not only as an alternative to other philosophies, but as itself the True Philosophy.

But St. Paul elsewhere offers another diametrically opposed view. In I Corinthians we read the following:

24

For Christ did not send me to baptize but to preach the gospel, and not with eloquent wisdom, lest the cross of Christ be emptied of its power.
For the word of the cross is folly to those who are perishing, but to us who are being saved it is the power of God . . . Has not God made foolish the wisdom of the world? For since, in the wisdom of God, the world did not know God through wisdom, it pleased God through the folly of what we preach to save those who believe. For Jews demand signs and Greeks seek wisdom, but we preach Christ crucified, a stumbling block to Jews and folly to Gentiles . . . (I Corinthians 1: 17-23) [The Oxford Annotated Bible with the Apocrypha: Revised Standard Version, ed. by Herbert G. May and Bruce M. Metzger (New York: Oxford University Press), 1965]

And again in Colossians:

See to it that no one makes a prey of you by philosophy and empty deceit, according to human tradition, according to the elemental spirits of the universe, and not according to Christ. (Colossians 2:8) [The Oxford Annotated Bible with the Apocrypha: Revised Standard Version, ed. by Herbert G. May and Bruce M. Metzger (New York: Oxford University Press), 1965]

These two passages seem to indicate a sharp separation between Christian faith and human or secular thinking. There is no attempt in these passages to portray Christian faith as a true philosophy; rather, Christian faith is seen as opposed to all human philosophy and wisdom whatever.

The point in raising a question about the attitude of Christianity toward philosophy is to make clear that the Christian community had some ambivalent feelings about the significance of philosophy from the outset. Recognizing this may help explain later divergencies among Christian philosophers on this very point. It is not the intention here, however, to suggest any particular answer to the problem raised, nor to comment on the adequacy of the interpretations of Scripture given above.

After 100 years or so of existence, the Christian community found it necessary to elaborate its faith in greater detail and precision in order to maintain its identity among the growing number of sects superficially similar to Christianity. Further, as persecution of Christians increased, and as converts among the Roman intelligentsia increased, more attention was paid to the use of Greek and Roman philosophy in the defense of Christianity before the Roman educated classes.

St. Justin Martyr (d. 165 A.D.), for example, taught that whatever good or truth could be found in Greek philosophy was borrowed in fact from the Old Testament. This had the net effect of baptizing philosophy for Christians. Minucius Felix (c. 180) wrote a dialogue called Octavius in which the virtues of paganism were argued and debated, and in which one of the debaters admitted defeat and sought to be converted to Christianity. Thus, philosophical argument is seen as a prelude to conversion.

Other theologians were not so appreciative. For example, Tertullian (160-220? A.D.) coined the now famous phrase, "Credo quia absurdum"—I believe because it is absurd. This indicated a rather negative attitude toward the value of philosophy and reason. (Despite this, Tertullian relied on philosophy more than a little in his theology.)

One of the great Christian theologians before Augustine, perhaps the greatest, was Origen (185?-253 A.D.). Origen himself was a most devout Christian, but his theology frequently relied on theories borrowed from other, especially philosophical, sources. For example, Origen sharply separated the three persons of the Trinity (much like Plotinus); he held to the theory of reincarnation (possibly obtained from Plato); and he argued philosophically against the existence of hell at the end of time. All of these eventually brought him under deep suspicion and condemnation.

Main works: Dialogue with Trypho by St. Justin Martyr; Apology, by Tatian; Octavius, by Minucius Felix; Adversus Haereses, by St. Irenaeus of Lyons; Protrepticus, Paedagogus, and Stromata by Clement of Alexandria; Contra Celsum and De Principiis, by Origen; Apologeticum, De Praescriptione Hereticorum, and Adversus Marcionem, by Tertullian.

G. ST. AUGUSTINE (354-430 A.D.)

St. Augustine's life is one of remarkable interest, and it is told with magnificent insight and vividness in the Confessions. He progressed through a series of philosophical and religious beliefs to his conversion to Christianity; later, he became one of the foremost Catholic bishops of his time. His great work, The City of God, was occasioned by the arrival of Roman refugees in his African diocese, after the sack of Rome in 410. Augustine died as barbarians stormed across Africa, burning his episcopal city of Hippo to the ground within a year after his death.

Augustine's intellectual activity was triggered by his encounter with the writings of Cicero, who was an eclectic and a skeptic. Later Augustine became involved with the Manichaeans, a

26

dualistic sect who believed that this world was a battleground
between the forces of Light and Darkness. Eventually he was
introduced to a Latin translation of Plotinus' works, and this
freed him decisively from his other materialistic beliefs. Only
three months later, he was converted.

Augustine was not a philosopher. He made no clear separation
in his writings between philosophy and theology. For him,
Christian faith was the true philosophy; more specifically, Faith
seeks Understanding. He borrowed freely from philosophy in order
to explicate his faith. It is thus difficult to separate philosophy and faith in his writings. Only a few topics of relevance to
philosophy will be discussed here.

Augustine's life was a search for truth. It is not surprising then that his approach to God was always colored by this
experience of God as Absolute Truth. Initially Augustine was
taken in by skeptical arguments that nothing could be known for
certain. But to say, "I am uncertain" entails saying, "I am,"
since the former is impossible without the latter. The act of
doubting everything presupposes the act of existing, and the act
of knowing that existence. Thus the mind discovers truth and
overcomes skepticism.

But the discovery of truth is not the manufacture of truth.
Where does this truth, indeed any truth come from? Surely not
from the realm of sense perception since things are not always
what they appear to be; surely not merely from the human soul
which is capable of making error. Ultimately all truth and all
knowledge of truth is only possible because of the light that the
Truth of God sheds on our existence. Thus all wisdom comes from
an illumination of Divine Truth.

Besides the certainty of the soul's existence and the knowledge of such, there is a third element as well: love. For
Augustine the very nature of the human person is love. For in
seeing the soul's existence, and in knowing it, the soul cannot
help loving itself. But love never seeks merely the finite; it is
never satisfied until it rests in God, the infinite. So Augustine
understands a twofold path to God: through the pursuit of Truth,
and through Love.

This love ascending back to God is reminiscent of Plotinus.
However, Augustine was quite independent of Plotinus' thinking on
other matters. First of all, God for Augustine was Perfect Being,
Perfect Mind, and Absolute Goodness. In identifying these three,
Augustine clearly parted company with Plotinus who separated Being
from The Good.

Furthermore Augustine, like all other Christian theologians,

27

believed in the creation of the universe out of nothing by God's absolute power. This theory of creation was at odds with the Neoplatonist belief that the universe was eternal and simply emanated from God according to some kind of divine law. For Augustine, there was nothing necessary about the existence of this universe; rather, it was thoroughly contingent upon God's will for its existence.

Augustine was very troubled by the problem of evil. At first he had simply assumed that evil was some material substance (due to the Manichaean religion). But with his reading of Plotinus and his rejection of materialism, his theory of evil changed markedly. Everything that existed insofar as it existed owed its existence to God and was therefore good. It would be impious to suggest that any substance whatever was evil by nature, since this would taint God with evil. Evil, rather than being a substance or a being, is defined as a lack of being, as some kind of non-being. There was no evil among natural things in the universe, as such: only if some event or thing (such as an earthquake) was isolated from the whole of the world or from God's plan or providence could it be counted as lacking in any way. But when seen as part of a whole, such natural evils turned out not to be evils at all.

But humans also are a source of evil, specifically moral evil. Such evil is possible by reason of the freedom of the creature: indeed evil without a prior choice is inconceivable. God allows such evil so that it will bring forth some good in the end. He does not cause such evil, however, even though he knows from all eternity what specifically evil choice the individual soul will make. Augustine affirms the compatibility of God's foreknowledge and human freedom to do evil.

In The City of God, Augustine postulated the existence of two societies, that of God and that of Man separated from God. He did not identify these as The Church and The State, however. Indeed he says quite explicitly that both the Church and the State are peopled by both societies. Nevertheless, Augustine was generally critical of the State, and argued that at best it was inferior to the Church, since its aims were secular. At one point he even advocated the Church's employment of the state for punishing heretics. Augustine's practice, as much as his theory, was to have much influence on the Middle Ages and beyond.

The City of God is notable also for its grand attempt to synthesize secular and sacred history, the history of Rome and Greece with the history of salvation. Augustine's attempt at a theology of history is certainly one of the most significant of all time, and had a remarkably long-lasting influence on Christian thinkers.

Main works: Against the Academics (386); On the Happy Life (386); Soliloquy (386); On the Magnitude of the Soul (388); On the Teacher (389); On the True Religion (391); On Free Choice of the Will (395); Confessions (401); The City of God (427).

CHAPTER 3

THE MIDDLE AGES

A. INTRODUCTION

Between Augustine's death in 430 A.D. and the 13th century (in which St. Thomas, St. Bonaventure, and Duns Scotus all lived) there were few significant philosophers whatever. As the Roman Empire collapsed, the Catholic Church fell into the role of preserving law and order at the local level. There was a brief resurgence of culture and thought during the short-lived reign of Charlemagne (768-814). But it was not until the time of the Crusades that the cultural situation improved in any significant respect.

The Medieval Period is often called the Age of Faith; and while that is accurate enough, it can be very misleading. For one thing, the Age of Faith was not an age in which intellectuals simply repeated the opinions of religious authorities and never asked questions. To the contrary: when medieval thought finally blossomed with the establishment of universities (and even before then), intellectuals were audacious and bold in their thinking. That their thinking took place within the parameters of their faith is not to say at all that those parameters were prison bars for the mind. What one finds in the medieval period is a surprisingly refreshing concern with questions of logic, epistemology, metaphysics, politics, and with the thought of philosophers regarded with suspicion by church authorities. The general question that pervades medieval thought is not whether the Christian can philosophize, but how far that philosophizing can go. For most it went rather far, sometimes too far in the mind of some spiritual leaders and bishops. But intellectual timidity was not a fault of the medieval world.

One important trend was toward the separation of philosophy and theology. This trend was probably in the back of many controversies of the period, and it was quickly accelerated after the important work of Thomas Aquinas. The implications of this separation were favorable at the time for both theology and philosophy, though the significance of this was not to be seen until the Renaissance and after.

B. JOHN SCOTUS ERIUGENA (C. 810-877 A.D.)

After the time of Augustine, the Church's theologians were philosophically indebted to Augustine's form of Platonism, and to the not so orthodox influence of Plotinus. An example of the

31

latter occurred in the 9th century philosopher Scotus Eriugena, whose principal writing De divisione naturae (On the division of nature) was ultimately condemned by the Pope in 1125 and was the inspiration for a number of other less than orthodox theologians and philosophers.

Scotus Eriugena's main philosophical notion is that of the division of nature. The division of nature signifies the act by which God expresses himself and makes himself known in a hierarchy of beings which are less than he. There are four divisions of Nature:

(1) Nature which creates and is not created. This refers to God as the principle of all things whatever.

(2) Nature which creates and which is created as well. This refers to the Ideas or Platonic Forms in the Mind of God. These forms are creative in that they are exemplary causes of all things inferior to them.

(3) Nature which does not create and which is created. This refers to the visible, physical world.

(4) Nature which does not create and which is not created. This refers to God as the Final Cause or as The Good. When all things have re-ascended back to God, God shall no longer create.

This system of nature comes very close to pantheism, however, for Scotus Eriugena denies that creation means anything like "making". Rather, creation means simply the presence of God in all things as their essence. Involved with this is a theory that each creature is a theophany, revelation, or self-appearance of God in some limited fashion. This notion of beings as revelations of God was to have considerable influence later in the Renaissance.

Main works: On the Division of Nature (De divisione naturae) (c. 866); On Predestination (De praedestinatione) (c. 850).

C. ST. ANSELM OF CANTERBURY (1033-1109)

St. Anselm's thought was heavily indebted to St. Augustine's in many respects. He, like his predecessor, emphasized God as the Truth of Being; and he expounded on the theory of knowledge as illumination from God. In expressing this relationship between soul and God, Anselm posed a most unusual, indeed novel, argument for the existence of God.

Anselm begins with the Augustinian statement that Faith seeks

Understanding. Now Anselm's faith tells him that God is that than which nothing greater can be thought, in other words, God is the most perfect imaginable being. Now if this idea of a most perfect being were merely an idea in my mind, it would not be the most perfect being possible since I could well imagine this greatest possible being existing in reality, and not just in my mind. Thus since the real existence of God is more perfect than God's existence merely in my mind, and since God must by definition be the greatest possible being, it follows that God must exist.

This argument (which is called the "ontological argument") has intrigued scholars for hundreds of years, and there is still much debate about it. Its critics have suggested that the argument proceeds from a definition to a reality without advancing any evidence; one might just as well argue with this logic that a perfect island exists as that God exists. But Anselm, who was confronted with this objection in his own lifetime, responded that only with the notion of God does this reasoning hold true; one cannot argue to the existence of perfect islands, but one can argue to the existence of a perfect Being.

St. Anselm's Augustinianism represents a more "orthodox" development than Scotus Eriugena's. More important than this, however, is the fact that St. Anselm's approach is always through careful logical distinctions. This concern for logic marks Anselm as one of the earlier "Scholastics" of the medieval period before the emergence of the "schools" or "universities" in the 13th century.

Main works: <u>Monologion</u> (1076); <u>Prolosgion</u> (1078); <u>De Grammatico</u>; <u>De Veritate</u>; <u>De Libertate</u> (between 1080 and 1085); <u>Why God Became Man</u> (<u>Cur Deus Homo</u>) (1098).

D. THE PROBLEM OF UNIVERSALS AND PETER ABELARD

A second manifestation of the concern for and interest in logic is the dominant focus on what has come to be called "the problem of universals." The problem, which was inherited from ancient Greek philosophy in a rather odd and circuitous fashion, was this: was the redness of an apple, for example, more or less real than the apple itself? Does redness exist beyond all apples or in each apple? Is redness simply an idea in the mind? In essence, this problem was concerned with how one should conceive the relation between a particular thing and its qualities which are universal. Several positions emerged:

(1) Realism held that the universal pre-existed the particular thing and was more real than the particular. (Thus, the redness of the apple referred to a universal redness, presumably

33

in the mind of God.)

(2)   **Moderate realism** held that while the universal might be
in the mind of God, it was more sensible to think of the universal
as a constitutive element in each particular.   Thus the universal
is _in_ each particular thing.

(3)   **Nominalism** held that particulars were more   real   than
universals,   and some nominalists even questioned whether the mind
had ideas of universals at all.

The   "received" Platonic tradition was realistic;   a few inclined   toward nominalism but were roundly rejected   as   heretics.
What is of interest,   though, is the gradually accelerating debate
among   intellectuals about the defensibility of a moderate realist
or nominalist position.   That is, the dominant tendency of thought
in   the   medieval   period   was   away   from   realism   and   toward
nominalism.   This   tendency was especially helped out by the   influence of   Aristotelianism on Thomas Aquinas and others   in   the
13th century.

But   nearly a century and a half before that,   Peter   Abelard
(1079-1142)   had   raised the standards of logical thought   in   his
attack on several of his teachers, the one a nominalist, the other
a realist.   The public debates he engaged in were among the great
intellectual events of the period, and earned him the wrath of St.
Bernard of Clairvaux (1090-1153),   among others,   who detested the
importation   of logic into religious matters.   Abelard may have
been   the intellectual "black sheep" of the 12th century,   but   in
most   respects he anticipated the general direction of thought   in
the 13th century.

Important   works: The   Metalogicon, by John   of   Salisbury
(1159); Dialectica, by Peter Abelard.

E.   ARABIC AND JEWISH PHILOSOPHERS

Within   several centuries after the Dark Ages,   there was   an
enormous   infiltration into the West of the writings of Aristotle.
To   understand   this and the impact of St. Thomas,   it   is   first
necessary to look beyond Western Europe.

The   writings of Aristotle were largely unknown to   Europeans
from the time of the fall of the Roman Empire.   They remained   in
Greek and were known primarily to Arabic speakers.   The growth of
Islam,   like   that of Christianity,   necessitated both theological
and   philosophical apologetics,   which made use   especially   of
Aristotle   and   the writings of Plotinus.   Beginning in the   9th
century,   Islamic theology and philosophy developed rapidly--until

its virtual demise at the hands of the theologian Algazel in the late 11th and early 12th centuries. The only 12th century Islamic philosopher of any consequence for the West was Averroes, who lived in what is now Spain.

Of the five Islamic thinkers discussed here, two generally reconciled Islam with Aristotelianism in a careful manner, while two others tended toward a more unabashed Aristotelianism. The first two were Alkindi (d. 873)--the first Islamic philosopher of note, and Averroes (1126-1198). Averroes' genuine position was largely misunderstood in the West. The views that are discussed here are those that were imputed to Averroes, not necessarily those that he actually held. The second two philosophers, who were much more enthusiastically Aristotelian, were Alfarabi (d. 950) and, perhaps the most radical of all, Avicenna (980-1037). (Views imputed to Averroes by Western thinkers were similar in fact to those of Avicenna.) A fifth philosopher, Algazel (1037-1111), was an ardent opponent of Aristotelianism.

A belief common to many of these philosophers (though not all) was that the world was eternal and that God's knowledge did not extend to the particulars of this universe (which would deny any notion of providence). Avicenna also emphasized the notion that the world was created necessarily by God who is the Necessary Being, because the only way a necessary being can create is--necessarily. Thus, while none of these thinkers was a pantheist in the classical sense, their views did tend to obliterate any metaphysical "distance" between God and the universe.

Another of the doctrines, imputed to Averroes especially and to some of the others, was that of the Agent Intellect. It will be remembered that Aristotle divided the intellect into the passive and the active, or Agent, Intellect. The latter was the metaphysical ground which made possible knowledge of concepts derived from the phantasms of sense-perception. Averroes reputedly held that the Agent Intellect is itself immortal and one and the same for all humans. Further, it exists somewhere in the heavenly bodies (near or in the moon). Each individual person here has only his or her passive intellect which perishes at death. Averroes' philosophy, such as it was understood, was clearly at odds with Islamic and Christian religious beliefs.

Averroes was also thought to have proposed a theory about truth which would modify or qualify the truthfulness of religious faith generally. This theory is that of multiple truth. The people, it is said, rest their beliefs on simple faith lacking in reason altogether. The theologians rest their case on mystical interpretations which also lack certainty. Only the philosopher achieves the true meaning of religious belief by using syllogistic or scientific demonstration. Each type of truth is valid in its own way, but only the philosopher achieves scientific under-standing.

Within Islam itself, the success of the philosophers, espe-cially Alfarabi and Avicenna, eventually caught up with them in the form of a powerful theologian named Algazel (1037-1111). Algazel argued that all rational proofs for the immortality of the soul were useless; that the notion of the eternity of the world was a contradiction in terms; and that the authority of the Koran was higher in all matters than the rationalism of Aristotle. Algazel's arguments rested often on skepticism, but a kind of skepticism directed at philosophers and in the service of Islamic theology. His criticisms were so effective that there were no major thinkers in the East after him. Only Averroes in Western Spain antedates Algazel's brilliant attack.

There were a number of Jewish philosophers in the Medieval period, often with a good understanding of developments in Islamic philosophy and theology. The most famous was Moses Maimonides (1135-1204), whose influence especially on St. Thomas Aquinas was considerable. Maimonides' approach to Aristotle was enthusiastic but cautious, and in any case always at the service of his under-standing of the Jewish faith. Thus Maimonides held that the world was not eternal, as Aristotle and the Arab philosophers believed. Yet he agreed that God knew only himself and other men, and no-thing of the external world. And while he believed in one sepa-rable Agent Intellect, he claimed that the passive intellects of the just are immortal. Maimonides accepted Aristotelianism but modified it to accord with his Jewish religious faith.

Main works: As-Sifa, by Avicenna; Destruction of the Philosophers, by Algazel; Revivification of the Religious Sciences; The Destruction of the Destruction, by Averroes; Guide of the Perplexed, by Maimonides.

F. ST. THOMAS AQUINAS (1224-1274)

In the late 12th century and early 13th century, Western European philosophers began to obtain Latin translations of the Greek and Arabic philosophers, and especially Aristotle. The impact was more than a little disturbing. Christianity had by that time become the only important religion in the West, and it had long since been dominated by various forms of Platonism and Neoplatonism. Aristotle appeared to many as a purely secular philosopher who emphasized this world too much and whose God seemed less than personal.

Hostility rapidly developed between Augustinians and Aristotelians. Some of the Aristotelian factions were indeed

36

radical and were soon condemned. But the Dominicans under the intellectual leadership of Thomas Aquinas sought to synthesize Aristotle and the Christian faith, without doing any injustice to the latter. The result was in the long run an incredible success, but in his own time Thomas' project was regarded by conservatives as avante-garde, to say the least. The Catholic Church met the incoming Aristotelianism with suspicion and occasionally outright hostility; it was not until the encyclical Aeterni Patris of Pope Leo XIII in 1879 that Thomism became the official philosophy of the Catholic Church.

Thomas argued that the philosopher and theologian, like reason and faith, must utimately agree with one another in the end. The approaches of each are different; the philosopher relies on the natural light of reason, the theologian relies on the authority of revelation. It is even possible that they both arrive at the same truth materially while using different methods. The ultimate argument for the unity of faith and reason is that the God of revelation is ultimately a rational God.

St. Thomas' theory of matter and form, potency and act, is very much that of Aristotle's. He adds one further distinction which he took over from the Arabic philosophers: that, namely, between essence and existence. This distinction is that between what a thing is (essence) and that a thing is (existence). Only in God are essence and existence identical. In other beings, they are logically distinguishable. Existence is the act of something whereby its essence is given some actuality. The principle of existence explains how some essences are real beings, and others are not.

Thomas felt that proving the existence of God was necessary as a preamble to faith. His proofs are not original particularly, and are not elaborated extensively: however, they are among the most discussed passages of his writings. Basically, Aquinas insisted that all proofs for the existence of God had to involve some rational argument in which one progressed from certain features of the created world to the existence of God. Thus he rejected St. Anselm's ontological argument since it involved a priori knowledge of God's existence.

Four of Aquinas' five proofs (proofs 1-3 and 5) for the existence of God are similar to Aristotle's. The first argument is that all things are in motion; that everything moved must be moved by something else; and that an infinite series of movers is impossible. Thus there must be a Prime Mover of all moved things.

The second argument is that there is a series of efficient causes and effects; that an infinite series of efficient causes is impossible; and that thus there must be a First Efficient Cause.

The third argument is that some beings have contingent existence, that is, that they are not necessary or might not have existed; that since they are contingent they could not have existed for all time; that at one time either something must have come into existence from nothing without a cause, or that there is a Necessary Being which created all the other contingent beings; and that since the first possibility is absurd, the second—the existence of a Necessary Being—must be true.

The fourth proof is more Platonic than Aristotelian. It is simply that there are degrees of perfection, goodness, truth, etc., in the things of this world, by virtue of which we can say that "this is better than that". But "better" always implies a "best"; indeed the "best" causally accounts for the "better". But perfect goodness, perfect truth, etc., are all the same, not different. There is, thus, only one Best or Perfect Being—namely God.

The fifth proof is that all inorganic things act with an end or purpose. Such an end is not known to the things themselves since they have no knowledge; and they cannot achieve such an end by chance alone. Therefore there exists some intelligent being which is the cause of the ends of all things.

The first three proofs are often lumped together and called the cosmological proof. The fifth proof is sometimes called the teleological proof. The fourth proof is generally regarded as the least compelling, perhaps because it is reminiscent of Anselm's ontological proof.

Having proved the existence of God, the next question Aquinas asks is this: just how much, besides existence, do we know about God? Indeed how is it possible for the human mind to know anything at all about God's nature, even if we do know that he exists? Essentially, Thomas admits that most of our knowledge of God is negative not positive: we know that God is not this, is not that, etc. Yet, we can and do know that God possesses certain qualities which are essentially good: for example, life, goodness, wisdom, etc. But is God good or alive in the same sense that John Jones is good and alive? Thomas answers this question negatively. Our knowledge of God is analogical: that is, God's wisdom bears a resemblance to ours, but is infinitely different (that is, God is infinitely wise). Thus Aquinas is reasonably cautious in stating just how much we know of God's nature.

Aquinas kept within the bounds of Christian theism in affirming that God created the world freely. Yet he also argued that the eternity of the created world was philosophically possible, though clearly not the case because of the content of

Christian faith.

Aquinas argues for the immortality of the individual soul, insisting that there is not just one agent intellect in all human minds. Thus he rejects Averroes very strongly, all the while maintaining his Christian belief that the soul is immortal. But the reader may ask: is not this immortality of the individual human soul clearly at odds with the Aristotelian belief that soul and body, as an instance of form and matter, are logically inseparable? Aquinas answered that yes, soul and body are logically inseparable, though it is possible for the two to be metaphysically separate; and yes, the soul is immortal. But he added that since the soul was naturally inseparable from the body, the immortal soul could not be separated from the dead body forever. Consequently, it follows that the body must be rejoined with the soul at some future time. In this most unusual way, then, Aquinas arrived through philosophical reason at the notion of the theological doctrine of the resurrection of the body, precisely by holding on to a crucial Aristotelian doctrine.

Aquinas' moral theory is centered on the notion of man's end in the supernatural--that, is, the vision of God. Virtue arises from using reason to obtain this end. There are two laws that are of relevance here. The first is natural law which is to be found in the very nature of man. Natural law is that law by which a man's nature is naturally perfected. In this respect, the natural law is perfectly rational and its basic precepts are unchangeable. Secondly, man must also follow the divine law, in which natural law is grounded. This divine law has been revealed especially in Scripture and the tradition of the Church. But this revelation is not irrational; rather it is entirely reasonable since it has been commanded by God who is purely rational. Thus, like the relation between faith and reason, divine law and natural law are both true simultaneously and cannot conflict with one another.

Aquinas' theory of the state is closely related to Aristotle's and shows a more positive appreciation of that phenomenon than Augustine's views. Aquinas argued that man's nature is social, and that the state arises out of that very nature, and is thus not simply a punishment for original sin. However, Aquinas favors constitutional monarchy as the best form of government. While monarchical authority derives ultimately from God if it is properly and rationally exercised, the State is still subject to the Church for all practical purposes. Thus Aquinas would not have favored any ultimate separation of Church and State, for the same reason he did not favor any ultimate separation between faith and reason.

Main works: On Being and Essence (De Ente et Essentia); Disputed Questions on Truth; Summa Contra Gentiles; Summa

39

Theologiae; On the Eternity of the World (De Aeternitate Mundi).

G. REACTIONS AGAINST ARISTOTELIANISM AND THOMISM

Perhaps the most avid opponents of Aristotelianism were the Franciscans, whose order was founded in the early part of the 13th century. The Franciscans were intellectually indebted both to St. Augustine and St. Anselm, but were also increasingly associated with a certain tendency toward empiricism. We shall examine here three very great thinkers, each of whose contributions is equal to the Thomistic synthesis of thought, but none of whom ever received the same ecclesiastical recognition.

1. St. Bonaventure (1221-1274)

Of all the Franciscans, St. Thomas' own contemporary St. Bonaventure was the most conservative. He read and appropriated some of the Aristotelianism of the day; but he was fundamentally an Augustinian mystic.

Bonaventure accepted the Aristotelian arguments for the existence of God on the basis of causality, but there were especially two other ways that were more significant for him. First, he took as axiomatic the Augustinian notion that "Our hearts are restless until they rest in Thee, O Lord." Thus, the human heart tends naturally toward God. Secondly, our very idea of God as Perfect Being or Perfect Truth requires that he must exist. This was, of course, St. Anselm's ontological argument which St. Thomas rejected.

Bonaventure also accepted the notion that the human soul is related to the body as Aristotelian form to matter. However, he qualified this in such a way as to better defend the real distinction of the two, as an Augustinian or Platonist would desire. Thus, the soul, he argued, is not only form to the body; it has also within it something called spiritual matter whereby it is individually distinct from the body. The question, of course, is: what precisely is "spiritual matter"?

One of the more famous disagreements between Bonaventure and Aquinas concerned the question of the eternity of the world. Both were agreed, of course, that the creation had a beginning in time, since Scripture so indicated. But Thomas, as has been seen, defended at least the possibility that the creation could have been eternal or everlasting. Bonaventure, on the other hand, argued that this was not possible at all. For example, he suggested that if the creation were everlasting, then an infinite time had already passed up till the present time. But more time would then remain to be added on: time would not have yet come to

40

an end. Now nothing can be added to an infinite period of time:
this would be absurd, since an infinite already includes everything. Therefore creation cannot be eternal or everlasting.

Main works: Commentary on the Sentences of Peter Lombard;
Breviloquium; On the Reduction of the Arts to Theology; Journey of
the Mind to God.

2. John Duns Scotus (1265-1308)

Duns Scotus was another Franciscan, whose philosophy was unquestionably one of the more complex elaborated in the Middle
Ages. He was renowned for his exceptionally subtle distinctions.

Scotus, like Bonaventure, was well acquainted with
Aristotelianism and accepted some of its doctrines. But while he
was even more critical of it in some ways, he often relied on
Aristotelian logic in ways that Bonaventure did not.

Aquinas had argued that our knowledge of God was analogical:
that God's existence was like or similar to ours, but different in
some profound ways as well.   Scotus suggested that unless there
was something that God and creatures shared in commmon, humans
would remain agnostic with regard to the knowledge of God. Scotus
thought that the notion of being or existence was just such a
logical concept that applied univocally to both God and creatures.
In this way, Scotus hoped to salvage the theory of analogy by
giving it a firmer foundation.

Scotus rejected Anselm's ontological argument as no more than
probable. He was also skeptical of the first two of Thomas'
proofs for the existence of God.   His favored proof was an expansion of St. Thomas' third proof based on the contingency of things
in this world.

If Scotus was reasonably close to Aquinas in his argument for
the existence of God, he was considerably more removed in his
discussion of how much humans know of God's nature.   He is quite
clear in his insistence that we cannot prove God's omnipotence,
his omnipresence, his justice, his mercy, and to some extent his
providence on the basis of reason alone.   This indicated a
sharpening of the distinction between philosophy and theology--a
distinction which would widen into a gulf or abyss later on.

Scotus argued that the human soul does not have a perfect
intuition of its own nature in this lifetime.   He bases his
reasoning on the notion of original sin, and quotes Augustine
approvingly on the matter. If the soul cannot be intuited in this
life, however, no conclusive argument for the immortality of the
soul can be given: for all such proofs rest on assumptions about

41

the spirituality and individuality of the soul.

It should be pointed out here that Scotus' skepticism in philosophical matters was no indication of his true beliefs. As a Christian he most certainly accepted belief in immortality of the soul, as well as belief in God's omnipotence, justice, mercy, and so forth. The point was that Scotus did not believe these could be demonstrated philosophically: they were to be accepted on faith, however.

Main works: Ordinatio or Commentaria Oxoniensia; Quaestiones Quodlibetales; Tractatus de Primo Principio.

3. William of Ockham (c. 1280-1349)

Perhaps the most radical Franciscan of all, however, was Ockham. Ockham's theological vision dominated his philosophy. His Christian faith rested upon acceptance of the primacy of God's absolute power and freedom. On this faith, he advanced arguments which seriously weakened the claims of many philosophical positions which had come to be assumptions of some theologians.

One of Ockham's most radical theories was the denial of essences. Ockham argued that the nature of horse, or the form of horse, existed only in the minds of humans: strictly speaking there were no forms in the real horse (as Aristotle would have it) nor in the mind of God (as Augustine would have it). Thus only individual things exist; forms do not exist—they are, rather, our way of thinking about individual things as groups.

Ockham's theory of knowledge was empirical for the most part. One of his axioms was that logical principles should not be multiplied when not necessary. This principle is called Ockham's razor. Ockham himself used this principle especially against the all too subtle distinctions of his predecessor Duns Scotus. Later philosophers have used the principle as a banner in the struggle of scientists against metaphysical entities. But Ockham himself did not use it for this purpose, at least not in any systematic way.

Ockham accepted the Aristotelian doctrine of the four kinds of causality, but placed the greatest emphasis on efficient causation—an emphasis which was to be a cornerstone of later scientific thought. Indeed he suggested that we only know that A is the efficient cause of B because it is regularly associated with B. This emphasis on the regular experience of the sequence, A-causes-B, marks a step away from the older theories of causation which were more preoccupied with singular instances, and which were more concerned with final than with efficient causes.

Ockham accepted Scotus' theory that being was univocally predicable of both God and creatures; but he went further than Scotus in attacking Aquinas' theory of analogical predication. He argues in effect that our knowledge of God is either univocal, or equivocal; analogical predication being reducible to one of these two kinds.

Ockham was extremely critical of all philosophical proofs for the existence of God. He gave a sort of half-hearted approval to one form of argument that the universe needs some being to conserve or preserve it in its existence: but he added he was not sure whether such a preserver was the Christian God or not.

As one might expect, Ockham insisted that there were no proofs possible to show that the soul was immaterial, incorruptible, and thus immortal.

Ockham's ethics rested essentially upon divine authority. While he did defend reason as the immediate norm of ethical action, he insisted that the ultimate norm of morality was God's will: and God's will was not subject to anything whatever. Thus it is entirely conceivable that God could have commanded humans to commit adultery or even hate God. The emphasis for Ockham is as much on obedience to the will of God as anything else.

If Ockham widened the gap between faith and reason, theology and philosophy, he also widened the gap between Church and State. He insisted that the authority of temporal rulers derived from God through the people, and not through the Church or the Pope. Ockham also suggested that the Church attempt to limit the authority of the Pope through the establishment of a General Council. Thus, Ockham's political sentiments seemed to have been more "democratic" than his predecessors.

Main works: Summa Logicae; Summulae in Libros Physicorum; Quaestiones Super Libros Physicorum; Ordinatio; Reportatio; Tractatus de Praedestinatione et de Praescientia Dei et de Futuris Contingentibus; Dialogus Inter Magistrum et Discipulum; Tractatus de Imperatorum et Pontificum Potestate.

43

CHAPTER 4

THE RENAISSANCE AND REFORMATION

A. INTRODUCTION

There are many misconceptions about the notion of the
"Renaissance". The first centers on its origin and the second
centers on the myth of the "Renaissance man".

The conventional view is that the Renaissance occurred
roughly between 1400 and 1600 and was a revival of Platonist and
Neoplatonist thought. To some extent the present work accepts
these confines, but not without some words of qualification.
First of all, there is every reason to believe that the revival of
learning came with the first influx of Aristotelianism in the 12th
century. The Renaissance proper can only be understood in terms
of its continuity with the earlier achievements of Aquinas and
Ockham. There were, of course, distinctive differences; perhaps
the most indicative is the shift from the universities to the
small philosophical academies, from subtle abstract concepts to
literary and humanistic concerns. Nevertheless the expertise of
the university was not wasted on the humanists; and increasingly
the Renaissance began to devote its inheritance of logical abstract thought to its revered Plato.

If the Renaissance cannot be understood first except in the
context of its medieval inheritance, it also cannot be understood
in isolation from the flowering of philosophical thought in the
17th and 18th centuries. The modern period of philosophy from
Descartes to Kant is in many respects a more uncluttered repetition of those trends of thought first developed in the 13th and
14th centuries. But the humanism of the Renaissance had in the
meantime been wedded to philosophical concerns, and the result was
that philosophy in this modern period is both independent of
theology and marked by its scholastic precision. Not until the
19th century is there a sense of having moved into an intellectual
milieu strikingly different from that of medieval thought.

The notion of the Renaissance man is also misleading. While
many figures of this period were masters of many different fields,
few if any of them in philosophy were really first-rate theorists.
Indeed one way to characterize the Renaissance is that it was a
group of fascinating ideas in search of a theory. The full theoretical development of these ideas had to wait for the modern
period. This is not to underestimate the contributions distinctive to this period. For the primary benefit of this age was its
desire to incorporate larger provinces of thought--especially
ancient thought and contemporary science--within the overall

45

vision of Christianity. This incorporation demanded in the short run, however, a distancing of secular learning from Christian theology, especially that of Thomas Aquinas. Yet such distancing proved to be most beneficial to the development of an independent philosophy in the long run.

Because the thought of this period can be better grasped in terms of groups of ideas than of individual thinkers, this section will be organized around five topics: 1) the development of scientific and empirical thought; 2) the development of humanism; 3) the development of political thought; 4) the development of theology within neoplatonist mysticism; and 5) the impact of the Protestant Reformation.

B. THE DEVELOPMENT OF SCIENTIFIC AND EMPIRICAL THOUGHT

It should be clear that Ockhamist tendencies were more clearly positive for the growth of the scientific spirit than Thomist tendencies.

Several examples of this can be indicated from Ockham's own lifetime. Nicholas of Autrecourt (1300-c. 1350), for example, suggested that there was only one standard of certainty, namely that of the logical principle of non-contradiction (A = A, not-A = not-A). Syllogisms are certain only if the conclusion is reducible to this form: A = A. However, no proposition about the causal connection between object A and object B can be so reduced. Therefore all knowledge of causal relations is at best only probable, not certain. This argument sounded a death-blow to Aristotelianism, which rested in part on the assumption that causal relations were necessary and not probable. Nicholas drew the conclusion from this that arguments for the existence of God based upon the notion of causality could never be more than probable. We shall see this train of reasoning pursued more dramatically with David Hume's skepticism in the 18th century.

Main works: Letters to Bernard of Arezzo and Aegidius; Exigit ordo executionis.

Further developments threatened other aspects of the traditional Aristotelian understanding of the cosmos. John Buridan (d. 1358), for example, emphasized the notion that an object once set in motion continues in motion until it encounters resistance. This theory clearly minimizes the importance of final causes, crucial to Aristotelianism. Further, Buridan pointedly suggested that this theory of impetus (as he called it) explained motion both in the heavens and on the earth, and that movement in both is of the same kind. And this again was at odds with with the sharp separation in Aristotelian theory between the movement of the heavenly bodies and that of earthly bodies.

Main works: <u>Questiones</u> <u>super</u> <u>libros</u> <u>quattuor</u> <u>de</u> <u>caelo</u> <u>et</u> <u>mundo</u>; <u>Quaestiones</u> <u>super</u> <u>octo</u> <u>libros</u> <u>physicorum</u> <u>Aristotelis</u>; <u>In</u> <u>metaphysicen</u> <u>Aristotelis</u> <u>quaestiones</u>; <u>Summulae</u> <u>logicae</u>.

<u>Nicholas Oresme</u> (d. 1382) went a step further, and suggested that it is entirely possible that the earth rotates on its axis. But, of course, the crucial step in this development was taken by the Polish monk <u>Copernicus</u> (1473-1543) who first developed a reasonably consistent theory of heliocentrism, the view that the sun, not the earth, was the center of the universe. Not only did this contradict Aristotelianism, it also seemed to contradict a number of passages in Scripture. But the conflict with the Church over this question did not develop until later.

Main works: <u>Le</u> <u>livre</u> <u>du</u> <u>ciel</u> <u>et</u> <u>du</u> <u>monde,</u> by Oresme; <u>De</u> <u>revolutionibus</u> <u>orbium</u> <u>coelestium,</u> by Copernicus.

An equally important development was the general realization that the universe was itself thoroughly mathematical or measurable in nature. Few advanced this view so forcefully and persuasively as <u>Leonardo da Vinci</u> (1452-1519). Such a view was profoundly at odds with Aristotelianism, and reflected instead a Platonic or Pythagorean view of the universe.

Main work: <u>The</u> <u>Literary</u> <u>Works,</u> Leonardo da Vinci, ed. J. R. Richter.

<u>Galileo</u> (1564-1642) formulated an outline of a consistent scientific world-view. Galileo admitted that knowledge from sense-perception was merely probable; the goal for the scientist was to find those natural laws that obtained behind the world of appearances. Now the laws of nature are thoroughly mathematical: God, in fact, is a geometrizing God, whose creation perfectly obeys the laws of number, geometrical figure, and quantitative function.

This search for mathematical laws of nature had certain implications for Galileo that were of immense importance. First, any search for final causes or essences is pointless, since none of these esoteric realities can be mathematically quantifiable. Secondly, Galileo pointed out that the qualities we perceive in our sense-perceptions (namely, those of taste, odor, color, sound) were also irreducible to mathematical realities, and hence were entirely subjective, not objective, in their reality. These sub-jective qualities came to be called secondary qualities. Primary qualities were henceforth those qualities of an object that were entirely reducible to mathematical equations, such as size, figure, motion, and so forth--those qualities, in other words,

47

that were fully real in a metaphysical sense. Galileo's views, and especially his advocacy of the heliocentric view of Copernicus, brought him into direct opposition with the Church, and he was subsequently tried in the Inquisition.

Main works: Discourse on Bodies in Water; Controversy on the Comets of 1618; Dialogue Concerning the Two Chief World Systems; Dialogues Concerning Two New Sciences.

A contemporary of Galileo's, Francis Bacon (1561-1626) formulated a critique of contemporary errors and false opinions, in order to lay bare a true and adequate philosophy of nature. Bacon divides the errors of his day into four types, each of which has a distinctive name. The "idols of the tribe" are those erroneous beliefs that our nature or sense-perception or emotion inclines us toward. Without more careful thought we are inclined to read things into nature that are not there.

The "idols of the cave" refer to those individual biases in our mental "caves" which tend to color our outlook on objective things. Such idols arise from our own private temperament, education, inclinations and so forth.

The "idols of the market-place" are the words that we use to hide the real world: Bacon's point is that we must not let words dictate to us what exists and what doesn't.

Finally the "idols of the theater" refer to the various philosophical schools of thought which entertained mankind more than they explained the real world.

Bacon emphasized the crucially important role of induction or experience in the development of knowledge of nature. Unfortunately, he minimized the role of mathematics. In spite of this, he contributed greatly toward the emergence of an empirical scientific philosophy.

Main works: The Advancement of Learning (1606); De sapientia veterum (On the Wisdom of the Ancients) (1609); De dignitate et augmentis scientiarum (1623); Novum organum (1620); Sylva sylvarum; New Atlantis.

The final chapter in the development of a non-Aristotelian scientific world-view came with Newton's (1642-1727) great laws of motion, which reduced all movements in the universe to three basic laws. The gap between the heavens and the earth was closed once and for all.

Main works: Mathematical Principles of Natural Philosophy (1687); Papers and Letters on Natural Philosophy, ed. I. B. Cohen.

C. THE DEVELOPMENT OF HUMANISM

The attack on Aristotelianism came not only from more empirical quarters, but also from the literary disciplines. Petrarch (1304-1374) exhorted readers to abandon secularistic Aristotelianism and once again seek man's end in God, which end had best been formulated by Plato, Cicero, and Augustine. Later the Catholic thinker Erasmus (1467-1536) urged a return to Scripture and ancient writers, and sharply criticized prevailing philosophies and theologies for being too concerned with the abstruse and too little concerned with humanity.

Main works of Petrarch: On the Remedies of Good and Bad Fortune (1366); On the Secret Conflict of My Worries (1358); On the Solitary Life (1356); On His Own and Many Other People's Ignorance (1367).

Main works of Erasmus: The Praise of Folly (1509); Colloquies (1518); On Free Will (1525); Hyperaspistes (1526).

Two writers especially made this revival of Platonism and Christian humanism concur with their call for a new philosophy centered on humanity. The first was the Italian John Pico della Mirandola (1463-1494), whose Oration on the Dignity of Man (1486) placed humanity squarely at the center of the universe. First, every human being is complete as a microcosm of the universe: for each person contains in his or her nature something of everything in the entire universe. Humans are part angel, part brute, part plant, part mineral. Secondly, the human person is incomplete in that he or she is free to shape his or her life as it pleases. It was Mirandola's hope that this vision of humanity as microcosm and as free would become the center of a new kind of Christian humanism.

Main works: Oration on the Dignity of Man (1486); Apologia (1487); Heptaplus (1489); On Being and Unity (1491).

In much the same kind of vein, the German scientist-philosopher Paracelsus (1493-1541) urged the simultaneous study of humanity and nature in order to bring both back to God. This indeed was the chief ethical mission of humans: to bring creation back to God. To do this one must study nature as though it were humanity writ large; and humanity as nature writ small. Thus all study was study of humanity: the purpose of such study was to better unite all things in the love of God.

Main works: Archidoxis (c. 1524); Opus Paragranum (c. 1529); Opus Paramirum (c. 1530); Philosophia Sagax (c. 1536); Labyrinthus Medicorum (1538).

If Platonism or Neoplatonism was involved in the development of humanism, Aristotelianism also was present. Pietro Pomponazzi (1462-1525) wrote a short work entitled, On the Immortality of the Soul (1516) which began with the thesis that the soul is not immortal. This was very likely the original view of Aristotle, though that is not certain. In any case, Pomponazzi argued that the soul is not spiritual but material in nature, requiring a body to supply the materials for knowledge. As a consequence, the soul is immortal only to the extent that it comes into contact with, or participates in, a higher reality (i.e., God); but of itself it is not immortal or spiritual. The goal of humanity is not intellectual contemplation so much as it is practical or moral virtue. Thus the end of humanity is quite finite and this-worldly. Though Pomponazzi did not deny the importance or the reality of the supernatural realm in human life, he did sharply separate it from the usual philosophical doctrine of the soul and from the pursuit of virtue.

Main works: On the Immortality of the Soul (1516); Apologia (1518); Defensorium (1519); On Incantations (1520); On Fate (1520).

D. THE DEVELOPMENT OF POLITICAL THOUGHT

Marsilius of Padua (c. 1285-1343) adopted Aristotle's notion of the State as the perfect community whereby humanity is perfected at the natural level. However, he went well beyond this theory in attempting to deal with the crucial problem of Church-State relations. He insisted that the Church had no right to temporal power at all, since this conflicts with the clear example of Jesus in the New Testament. Further, the Church was subject to the State in all temporal matters whatever; it was absurd to believe that temporal rulers received their power from the Papacy.

Marsilius was deeply disturbed by the intrusion of the Vatican States into the temporal life of citizens, and the consequent wars, corruption, and so forth, that he witnessed in his own lifetime. Although he was not radically democratic, he insisted that the legislative power of the State ultimately resided not in the Church or the State itself, but in the people or citizens. The function of the leader or prince is simply to direct the community according to the norms of that community. Marsilius did not argue for elective offices, though he seems to have preferred such to hereditary monarchies.

Niccolo Machiavelli (1469-1527) carried this separation of Church and State to even greater lengths. Machiavelli considered all interference by the Church, and even moral law itself, to be potentially contrary to the interests of the state. In his work entitled The Prince (1513) Machiavelli advocated an entirely amoral conception of a society governed by leaders whose primary consideration was how to maintain power. The Prince must put on an outward, indeed genuine, appearance of being compassionate, trustworthy, humane, honest, and religious; but when dealing with foreign governments, Machiavelli suggests that deceit may be advantageous. Machiavelli thus advocated a sharp separation between political theory and ethics, and clearly placed the former above the latter.

Main works of Machiavelli: The Prince (1512?); The Discourses (1517); A History of Florence; The Art of War.

E. THE DEVELOPMENT OF THEOLOGY WITHIN NEOPLATONIST MYSTICISM

The period of time between the 15th and 17th centuries was one of a succession of mystical philosophers and theologians, orthodox and unorthodox. Although their importance during this period was not overwhelming, they did contribute significantly to the ongoing Neoplatonist tradition whose fruition did not really come until modern and 19th century philosophy. All of these mystics were heavily indebted to Plotinus and especially Scotus Eriugena; none of them was terribly orthodox and some of them met with more than little resistance.

Meister Eckhart (1260-1327) was an original thinker and mystic whose thought in some ways is indebted to Neoplatonism. Eckhart maintained that the distinction of Persons in God was not the ultimate reality in God: indeed the Being of God was not ultimate either. Rather Being and the Trinity presuppose God's understanding or mind which is in fact the real absolute unity in God, the "God above God". The theory did not advocate two Gods, but rather delineated a notion of the unity of God logically transcending his plurality in the Trinity. Plotinus placed The One above Being, and Eckhart reflects this point of view here. But Eckhart identifies this Unity with Intelligence, unlike Plotinus.

Main works: Quaestiones Parisienses; Opus tripartitum.

Nicholas of Cusa (1401-64) was a Cardinal of the Church, deeply interested in its reformation and in the unification of Western and Eastern Churches. His philosophy and theology are unique for their use of mathematical examples to illustrate his unusual theories. He held that all knowledge begins with the admission that the human mind does not fully understand either the world or God. He called this theory of knowledge a theory of "learned ignorance." The reason why the mind could not fully understand the world or God was that both appeared to the mind as

51

the unification of opposites or contraries. Thus God is seen by the mind as the coincidence or unity of the maximum and the minimum. The same logic that tells us that God is the greatest possible being also tells that God is the least posssible being; the one implies the other. In the same way Nicholas describes God as the coincidence of the greatest actuality and the greatest possibility.

The world, by contrast, is the coincidence of relative actuality and relative possibility. The universe is a concretization of God, a finitization of the infinite. Thus the universe manifests in its own way this coincidence of opposites found in God. All things in the universe reflect God and God is the absolutization of the universe. This is not to identify the two; but it does bring God and the universe into a close metaphysical relationship. As such the universe's center can only be God: all things in the universe are relative to God and one another. With this, Cusa dismisses the Aristotelian geocentric theory.

Main works: On Learned Ignorance (1440); De coniecturis (1440); De Deo abscondito (1444); De quaerendo Deum (1445); De Genesi (1447); Apologia doctae ignorantiae (1449); Idiotae libri (1450); On the Vision of God (1453); De possest (1460); Tetralogus de non aliud (1462); De venatione sapientiae (1463); De apice theoriae (1464).

If Cusa had no trouble with Church authorities, such was not the case with Giordano Bruno (1548-1600). Bruno was burned at the stake by the Inquisition for his unorthodox pantheism, which had been inspired in part by the theories of Cardinal Cusa. Bruno held that God was the absolute identity of Matter and Form, the absolute Substance. The Universe appears as a plurality of things when the mind views this matter and form as relative or limited instead of infinite. The difference between the universe of space and time and God is one of perspective, not metaphysics. Bruno admitted that God appeared as the cause of the universe, and thus distinct from the universe, when the universe was regarded as composed of many diverse or finite things. When the universe was regarded as an infinite whole with no limitation, however, God was the principle of all things, not the cause of them. In this respect, God and the universe are immanently one. The goal of humanity, indeed the goal of creation, is the recognition of divine determination of all things, and the perfection of the love of God based upon this recognition or understanding.

Main works: Thirty Seals; The Ash Wednesday Supper (1584); De la causa, principio e uno (1584); De l'infinito, universo e mondi (1584); Spaccio de la bestia trionfante (1584).

The Protestant mystic and cobbler Jakob Boehme (1575-1624)

was also deeply influenced by this kind of thinking, though he, like Eckhart, was a man of deep piety first and foremost. Boehme argued that God in himself is beyond all distinctions whatever, and as such is the ground of all things. All things arise as part of the process of this Primordial Unity manifesting itself to itself. God manifests himself within himself. God's will wills his own mind and from this self-discovery there arises a power of life uniting these two. Will, mind, and life are the three movements whereby the Trinity or persons within God are constituted. Clearly Boehme's belief that the unity of God preceeds that of the three persons parallels that of Eckhart: but Boehme is more like Plotinus than Eckhart in subordinating mind to the unity, rather than the reverse.

Main works: The Works of Jacob Behman, 4 volumes, tr. by Ellistone and Sparrow.

F. THE IMPACT OF THE PROTESTANT REFORMATION

In all of the preceeding sections we have seen that the Renaissance was in part a time of growing disillusionment with the Aristotelianism of medieval Christianity. Perhaps the most symbolic historical event in this regard is the revolt of a large segment of Christianity away from the organized Roman Church. This revolt—led at first by Martin Luther (1483-1546), then broadened by Calvin and Zwingli—initiated a cry for a return to Scripture as the sole authority of the Christian faith, and an insistence on faith as a direct and unmediated relationship between the individual and God. Only thereby could the Christian soul be freed from the theological and philosophical encumbrances of the ages.

The impact of this on the history of philosophy is of some importance. The emphasis upon Scripture as the new authority in matters of faith was bound to lead to a generally non-philosophical explication of Christian faith. That tendency, of which one finds remnants in Kierkegaard and among some fundamentalists today, accounts for a certain residual hostility between theology and philosophy. Martin Luther's vehement denunciation of Aristotle as "the devil's whore" set the stage for this development. But Luther himself had been indirectly influenced by the thought of Ockham, which had driven a wedge between faith and reason several centuries previously.

While this was not a favorable omen for the development of a Christian philosophy, other tendencies were. The emphasis upon Christian freedom founded in a faith-relationship with Christ unencumbered by external intermediaries (such as the organized Church) did lead to a greater, freer use of philosophy in the

53

attempt to intellectually explicate this faith-relationship. A clear example of this sort of thing occurs in the thought of Jakob Boehme, discussed above. Since Protestantism never instituted anything like an Inquisition or even a central religious body to judge the orthodoxy or unorthodoxy of writings, it was largely free to develop whatever philosophy the individual Christian felt was compatible with his or her faith. As a consequence, Protestantism, besides its long history of fundamentalism, also has a long history of liberal theology and philosophy. The most important philosopher-theologian of this latter tendency was Hegel, whose impact is still being felt in both philosophy and theology.

The reaction of Catholicism to all this is to be noted briefly. The Catholic Church was forced to use Aristotelianism in its defense of the faith and the sacrality of tradition against the Protestant's exclusive emphasis upon Scripture and individual faith. Although Thomism was not officially endorsed until centuries later, it was unofficially the Church's philosophy after the Council of Trent (1545-1563). There were many Thomists of some competence after the 13th century. Perhaps the finest mind of all, and one of the most influential of the 16th century, was Francis Suarez (1548-1617). Suarez consolidated Thomism in a careful way, taking account of Scotist and Ockhamist objections, and elaborating his own defense of a number of points. The result was a more systematic elaboration of Thomism, whose impact on modern philosophers such as Descartes and Locke was significant.

Main works of Suarez: Disputationes Metaphysicae (1597); Varia Opuscula Theologica (1599); De Legibus ac Deo Legislatore (1612); Defensor Fidei (1613).

CHAPTER 5

MODERN PHILOSOPHY

A. INTRODUCTION

As was mentioned before, this period is in many ways a kind of rational recapitulation of the philosophical development of the late middle ages and Renaissance. It is a development that took place largely outside theology, however, unlike that in the previous period. Indeed, one of the defining characteristics of this period is precisely the sharp separation between philosophy and theology.

It was during this period that the great systems of philosophy were written. Perhaps the most classical of all in this respect was Spinoza's Ethics which was written in the style of a rigid geometry textbook.

All these philosophers were pre-eminently concerned with the question of knowledge: indeed the tone of the period was set by the question Descartes asked of himself: what is it that I can know for certain? This question was to have profound consequences for the very possibility of metaphysics. Indeed, by the end of the period, classical metaphysics of all sorts had been rather thoroughly put into question.

Many of the European governments during this time became absolutist, especially France and Prussia. Significantly, philosophy on the continent was heavily rationalistic in orientation: Descartes continued the Augustinian and Anselmian tradition, while Spinoza developed various aspects of Neoplatonism.

By contrast, England developed a more empirical and materialist school of thought which was more in keeping with its tolerant political and social views. English thinkers were profoundly important in developing the classic framework of the scientific, anti-metaphysical world-view.

But it was the Germans, not the English, who set the tone for the 19th century; and it was Kant specifically who marks the transition from the modern period. Kant's philosophy was an attempt to set rationalistic metaphysics on a new ground after it had fully confronted British skepticism. Kant's achievement was not long-lasting, but it was monumentally influential in spite of that.

55

B. CONTINENTAL RATIONALISM

1. René Descartes (1596-1650)

Descartes resolved to set aside all his ordinary, everyday beliefs and thoughts to ask whether there was anything whatever whose truth could not be doubted. Doubting was methodical for Descartes, unlike previous thinkers who had often overlooked the role of doubt in finding truth. First, he doubted the existence of the objects he found in his sense-perception: he might, after all, be dreaming or hallucinating. Further, the existence of his own body was no more certain than that of the table in front of him. Was God known for certain? No again: for there may be some evil spirit who deceives Descartes even in this supposed knowledge. Is skepticism the only alternative in the end, then? Or is there something the human mind cannot possibly doubt?

The answer to this last question is yes: for Descartes insists that every act of doubt involves an "I" that "thinks". Thus universal doubt implies a thinker that thinks and that exists, since it would be quite impossible for something to think or doubt without existing. This is the origin of Descartes' famous maxim, Cogito ergo sum: I think, therefore I exist. Now this "I" is clearly not the same thing as my material body, whose existence remains uncertain: it is thus a spirit which lacks extension in space. Further, the very nature of this "I" or "ego" is thinking, such that it is best termed a res cogitans or thinking substance. This argument is reminiscent of St. Augustine's argument against skepticism, although it is not known for certain whether Descartes borrowed from him or not.

Descartes did not stop with this discovery of the certainty of the thinking substance. He points out that this mind has within it many ideas, most of which it has been admitted could not be known for certain. But there is at least one idea whose existence could not be conjured up by a mere finite mind: namely the idea of God. Now I am certainly not God, since my own existence seems to be dependent upon something else. Further, nothing finite in the world could be the source of something infinite and perfect, since the world has neither of these characteristics within it. It follows that the only possible source of my idea of God is the most perfect being which we call God.

If the cogito ergo sum reflects Descartes' Augustinian indebtedness, this argument reflects his indebtedness to St. Anselm's ontological proof which it is modelled after.

Having established the existence of God, Descartes returns to the material world: how much of it can I be said to know for certain? After some elusive argumentation, Descartes concludes that the knowledge of nature can only be decided on the basis of its clarity and distinctness in the mind. Now with regard to nature, only mathematical ideas are clear and distinct. Hence only to the extent that nature is ultimately mathematical or made up of res extensa (extended substances) can I be said to know that material or extended substances exist certainly. My own sense-perception may well deceive me, since mathematical qualities (primary qualities) are not revealed in it. Within the realm of secondary qualities, such as sight, touch, taste, and so forth, doubt inevitably remains.

Two points should be made about this system of thought. First, Descartes has here codified the foundations of traditional metaphysics: they are res extensa, res cogitans, and God. Thus, the primary divisions of modern philosophy were understood to be the Philosophy of Nature, the Philosophy of Mind, and the Philosophy of God. The second important point is that the order of knowledge is quite specific: all knowledge of God and Nature presupposes self-knowledge. Thus Descartes placed the thinking Ego at the very heart of modern philosophy, which has given the latter a "subjective" tinge ever since. ("Subjective" here means "as opposed to objective"; it has nothing to do with either relativism or arbitrariness.)

One significant and profound problem remained for Descartes, however: given the absolute distinction between mind and body, how was it possible to account for the experiential unity of the two? Descartes admitted openly the unity of the human person; unfortunately his theory left the nature of that unity in considerable doubt.

Main works: Rules for the Direction of the Mind (1628; published 1701); Discourse on the Method (1637); Meditations on First Philosophy (1641); Principles of Philosophy (1644); The Passions of the Soul (1649).

2. Spinoza (1632-1677)

Spinoza's philosophy was the first attempt at a rigorously stated pantheism. In its main outlines it owes much to the entire tradition of Neoplatonism. But in several respects Spinoza was also indebted to Descartes' philosophy or Cartesianism, as it is usually called.

Spinoza began with the assertion that there could be only one substance, since a substance was defined as that which is conceived or understood through itself, that is, without reference to anything else. This One Substance was God or Nature. Now God has an infinite number of attributes, only two of which humans are aware of: thought and extension. Thought is not a res or

57

substance (as it was for Descartes), nor is extension; rather both are conceived as attributes of God.

This understanding of the attributes of God creates an unusual problem: if God has extension as an attribute, is God not defined spatially and temporally? Spinoza rejected this possibility, however, insisting that extension in God is the principle of extension, rather than extension as we know it in this universe. But this makes it unclear just what God's extension is like.

Now God emanates from his nature an explication of himself within certain modes. Modes are defined as those things which are only understood as being in another thing. Modes are rather like Aristotelian accidents. This universe is made up of two modes, each of which is infinite: mind and body. Neither mind nor body is a substance. Human minds are simply ideas, not substances distinct from the body. But how are my mind and my body so apparently unified? Doesn't Spinoza divide humans up in the same analogous way that Descartes does? What is the connection between the mental mode and the physical mode? For Spinoza, there is no connection. It just so happens that the series of events in the mental mode are correlated with the events in the physical mode. The reason Spinoza can say this is that both modes are ultimately God in their essence.

What is the goal of human life then? Spinoza finds that the human mind is beset with confusion and a lack of clarity. Specifically, the human mind imagines that bodies and minds are substances, distinct from God who is also imagined as an individual substance; that while our bodies are determined in the physical order, our minds are free and can change our bodies. These confusions are the source of unhappiness. For Spinoza, all happiness stems from the love of God. Now we are God in our essence: our own sense of self-affirmation is precisely the self-affirmation of God. The cultivation of reason allows humans to see that only God exists, that minds and bodies are not substances, and that there is no freedom except in the recognition of the divine determination of all things. With this recognition, blessedness or peace of soul comes to man. In the end, philosophy is man's salvation for Spinoza; he was, in fact, very critical of the traditional doctrines of religion—doctrines such as miracles, prophecy, revelations, divine creation, and so forth. For this reason he was largely regarded in his own time as an atheist, though that name is not particularly accurate.

Main works: Tractatus Theologico-politicus (1670); Ethics; Tractatus de Intellectus Emendatione.

3. Leibniz (1646-1716)

Like Descartes, Leibniz was a brilliant mathematician as well as philosopher. Leibniz' atomistic philosophy was formulated as an intense rejection of the absolute monism of Spinoza. However, this atomism was most unlike that of the Greeks, such as Democritus or the Epicureans. For Leibniz' atoms, which were called "monads", were far from being like little dead billiard balls knocked around helplessly in the cosmos. Rather, each atom or monad was alive. Its very essence was its thinking and feeling. Leibniz postulated an infinite number of such monads, each of which was eternal and immutable. What is especially interesting about this was Leibniz' belief that the nature of a monad was identical with its entire history of feelings and thoughts. In this way, time or history or development was introduced into the very nature of an entity.

Each monad was different in terms of its perfection; and its perfection was measured in terms of its clear or unclear perceptions. The monads which constitute ordinary rocks, for example, have extremely dull perceptions. Certain monads have such clear thought that they are called "souls". Each human person has one monad called a soul; while the body is made up of many other more physical monads.

One curious feature of the monad, however, raises significant problems: Leibniz insists that each monad is a world unto itself: it has no "windows" whereby awareness of any reality beyond it can originate. How, then, can the soul-monad know anything of its body? Since it is clear that there is knowledge of the body, it follows that such knowledge must be a priori; indeed, for Leibniz, all knowledge is ultimately a priori, a posteriori knowledge being quite impossible. The soul's knowledge is imprinted on it by God. Primordially God creates soul-monads and the monads of the body such that they are like previously wound clocks, each striking the hour together, but neither causing the other to do anything. There are no causal relations between monads of any kind.

All monads are created by the supremely perfect Monad--God. Leibniz argues that the universe is fully rational, and thus requires some necessary Being whereby it may be explained. God's creation is done out of perfect freedom--it is not a requirement of his nature at all. Further, God, who cannot act in a manner unworthy of his perfect nature, can only have created the best of all possible universes. (This view was attacked unmercifully, but with great humor, by Voltaire in his Candide).

The virtue of Leibniz' metaphysics of the monad (his "monadology") is that it avoids Descartes' dualism of thinking and extended substances. However, Leibniz' rationalism led him to believe that each monad was a world unto itself: consequently, just as Descartes could not explain the relation betweeen mind and body, so Leibniz could not explain the apparent relation between one monad and the other. Both philosophers relied on God rather arbitrarily to solve their metaphysical dilemmas.

Main works: Discourse on Metaphysics (1686); New Essays (1704; published in 1765); Theodicy (1710); "The Principles of Nature and of Grace", 1718); Monadology.

4. Jean-Jacques Rousseau (1712-1778)

Rousseau's early works centered on the contrast between what humans are by nature and what society has made them. Contemporary civilization (Rousseau was thinking of the upper crust of French society) was creating a society of greedy egoists, who no longer were aware of genuine human needs. Compounding this problem was the emergence of vast inequalities of both power and wealth among people. All of this is contrasted by Rousseau with humans in the hypothetical "state of nature" who were equal with one another, who knew how to satisfy their needs because they knew what genuine happiness was.

Rousseau came to the conclusion that a new kind of education and politics, rooted in our nature, were needed if society's inequalities and aritifices were to be overcome. In his great educational tract, Emile, Rousseau suggests that education should take place away from civilization in a rural area, and that the child should be educated at his own rate of learning. Children should be encouraged to learn not from books, but from the book of nature itself. The only book Rousseau allows the child to have is Defoe's Robinson Crusoe, that being because of its emphasis on self-reliance. Yet self-reliance, while basic, culminates in a society composed of isolated individuals. Self-reliance is not enough to explain why or how there can be society.

Rousseau seems to posit two principles to explain the origin of society. The first is that of natural passion. Yet if passion creates social bonds and social dependence, it does not create society itself. For society cannot be founded upon mere passions, however natural. For beyond mere passions are the virtues, those obligations we all have toward one another. Virtues are certainly not a function of passions alone. Rather, virtue is founded on the very nature of society insofar as it is a political reality. This theory is worked out in what is perhaps the most significant political work of the 18th century, the Social Contract.

Rousseau held that society must be based on right, not on force or might. And right is founded upon freedom. Hence any legitimate or rational society is founded upon and fully respects

60

the freedom of each person.   Indeed, one is only a moral being to
the extent that one is free.   Any society which denies this freedom denies the individual's humanity.

Yet each person must freely give up his rights if there is to
be a society at all, a society, that is, as opposed to a group of
individuals: and this leads Rousseau to make a distinction between
the will of the individual and the general will. The general will
is that objective condition which embodies every individual's
moral nature.   Only by giving up one's own individual will for the
sake of the general will can the individual become fully moral and
virtuous.   All political sovereignty rests with this general will;
and all government is simply an agency of the general will and its
sovereignty.   The sovereignty of government rests upon that of the
people and its general will. And only with the recognition of the
general will can the philosophical principle of the equality of
all humans find its proper explanation.   For that equality is
founded upon the rational nature of each person.

Rousseau the rationalist seems to be a long way from Rousseau
the portraitist of intimacy and the emotional life.   Yet the two
do fit together into a complex whole.   For Rousseau pitted both
nature and reason against 18th century social life, which he found
wanting in both respects.   For this reason, his thought is basic
both to later Romanticism and its preoccupation with the inward,
as well as to later liberal and radical political philosophies,
especially those of Kant and Marx.   Such is Rousseau's ambiguous
legacy.

Main works: <u>Discourse</u> <u>on</u> <u>the</u> <u>Arts</u> <u>and</u> <u>Sciences</u> (1750);
<u>Discourse</u> <u>on</u> <u>the</u> <u>Origin</u> <u>of</u> <u>Inequality</u> (1755); <u>Emile</u> (1762); <u>Social</u>
<u>Contract</u> (1762); <u>Confessions</u>.

C. BRITISH EMPIRICISM AND MATERIALISM

1. Thomas Hobbes (1588-1679)

Hobbes was a contemporary of Descartes, and while he agreed
with Descartes as to the possibility of a mathematical science of
nature, he disagreed with him on just about everything else.

Hobbes was an atomist and materialist, believing that all
atoms are material in nature, and that all change in the universe
is a change in physical movement.   The qualities of things, such
as the redness of the soil, are merely the effects of some other
causes. All things whatever are completely and rigidly determined
in the natural course of causes and effects. The soul is merely a
rarefied bit of matter, not intrinsically different from other
bits of matter, and just as subject as other atoms to local

61

changes or causes and effects. Thus a universal science of motion should be able to explain all such movements of atoms in the entire universe; and this would include the movements of the human body and soul, since these are both material in nature.

Hobbes denied all Aristotelian and Platonic notions of forms, substances, final causes, and so forth. He sought to explain the universe as a giant machine whose parts were perfectly determined and predictable once the laws of motion were understood.

Human knowledge begins with sense perceptions which travel along nerves to the brain where they are converted to ideas. Consciousness is merely a stream of ideas; reason is the association of various ideas with one another. There are no abstract ideas at all; but there are general words or names. And it is these names or words or language that are the object of philosophy. For philosophy or science is the knowledge of the consequences of one word as related to another word. This emphasis upon language anticipated trends in 20th century philosophy by several centuries.

If human minds are merely bundles of ideas, human bodies are bundles of passions or desires seeking some good. The human good rests primarily on the satisfaction of various desires to which human beings are subject.

What each man desires is the satisfaction or pleasure that comes with the end of passion or desire. Now this implies that each man seeks his own pleasure, not the pleasure of another. Thus Hobbes holds to a belief in psychological egoism, which entails that all love is self-love. If this is the case, each person is in actual conflict with every other person; a potential war of one against all emerges and each individual stands in danger of losing what he has to another.

To avoid absolute annihilation, humans make an agreement among themselves to give up their rights to a sovereign monarch of some sort, whose absolute rule allows peace and prosperity to emerge. Obviously religion is also subject to the rule of the monarch, since otherwise it would endanger the peace that comes with the perfectly unified state. But Hobbes takes great pains to spell out his own view of religion. He argues that God is best understood as a Supreme Despot who commands humans to give him due worship. Religion is precisely this obedience rendered to God. Thus God, the prime mover of the mechanical universe, is simultaneously made in the image of the sovereign ruler of the state. Hobbes may well have been hoping to avoid any conflict between the worship of a good God and the worship of a state sovereign who may or may not have been good. By emphasizing God as a Despot, the power of religion to confront the state was considerably lessened, and its similarity with the secular order greatly increased. Thus Hobbes' emphasis on religion stemmed from his political preoccupations, and not from any traditional religious sentiment. Hobbes was universally recognized as an extremist, even by royalist aristocrats. But his philosophy has been taken as one of the most consistent statements of the bourgeois view ever developed.

Main works: Human Nature (1650); De Corpore Politico (1650); De Cive (1642); Leviathan (1651); De Homine (1657).

2. John Locke (1632-1704)

Locke was the first of the great English empiricists of modern times. Although his writings have inspired generations of empiricists, they are not always free from inconsistencies and tendencies toward rationalism.

His great work, An Essay Concerning Human Understanding (1690), is quite complex, but unmistakable in its general thrust. He begins with a prolonged attack on the theory of innate ideas and rationalism. He argues that the foundations of logic (the so-called principles of identity and contradiction) are not known apart from actual experience. Similarly, knowledge of my own self as identically the same from birth to death is not a priori but given with experience. Finally, the knowledge of God is thoroughly dependent upon experience; and this is proven by the differences of beliefs that people actually have about God.

All ideas come from either sensation of the external world or reflection upon my own thinking or body. Ideas may be simple (for example, the color red, or the idea of volition) or they may be complex. Complex ideas are made by the combining, comparing, or separating of simple ideas. There are many different kinds of complex ideas but perhaps the most important is that of Substance.

Locke held that our sensations were composed of a number of simple ideas: for example, the table in front of me is brown in color, rectangular, and so forth. Now Locke, like his contemporaries, distinguished between the primary or objective qualities of an object (those qualities that were mathematically measurable and hence scientifically significant) and secondary or subjective qualities such as color, taste, etc. (which were not so mathematical). Now each of these simple ideas is united with all the others into a concrete empirical whole. This whole includes all the qualities of the object previously mentioned. But such qualities must reside in something. This "something" or "I-know-not-what" Locke called Substance. And the substance is itself a complex idea, not directly included among the perceived qualities of the object. This theory of substance began with empirical considerations; but ended somewhere beyond experience. It is in

63

this respect especially that Locke's empiricism was to be sharply challenged by later, more radical empiricists.

Another theory that transcended Locke's own empiricism was his notion of abstract or general ideas. Locke held that the mind was able to derive from several instances of the same object an abstract idea of that object. He is somewhat unclear about the nature of this abstract idea, but he seems to have held that it contained two components. First of all the abstract idea, for example of redness in itself, referred to all particular instances of red qualities. But secondly, he seems to have believed that such an abstract idea of redness also had a kind of meaning of itself, such that redness referred to the species of particular red qualities, and not to the particular instances of redness themselves. This theory of an abstract idea of the species was also potentially at odds with his empiricism, and other philosophers were quick to take note of that fact.

Locke's theory of the soul reflects his empiricist method. The question that he asks is this: how do I know that the "I" of the present moment is the "I" of two years ago? Certainly my body has changed in that time. But is my mental substance, directly perceivable at the present moment, the same as previously? Locke answered that this question of identity of the mind can only be answered with a sense of probability, not certainty. Locke did not deny the existence of an enduring mental substance; indeed he thought it fairly probable. But he did claim that certainty could not be had on the question.

Locke's attempt to prove the existence of God rests on the observation that I myself cannot have existed from eternity, and that something must have caused both me and the universe of which I am a part. This First Cause is what is called God. Once again, experience is used to argue to something which, strictly speaking, is beyond experience. Locke also attempted to show that Christianity was a thoroughly reasonable religion, and that the moral views it upheld were also thoroughly reasonable. Despite this, Locke's influence was primarily on the development of deism, an emasculated view which acknowledged the existence of a God who was otherwise unconcerned about the created universe.

Locke, as much as Hobbes, was the great political theorist of early capitalist England. He distinguished between a "state of nature" in which men lived together under the rule of natural law or reason and the present-day universal society or community of humankind. In the state of nature, each individual has a right to life, liberty, and property, and a right to judge and punish those who violate such rights. This right is tempered by the natural equality of humans in this state. Unfortunately, this state of nature is marked by human want and scarcity. This gives rise to human labor and property. The individual's labor or work is the foundation of the right to property; but as soon as human wants become satisfied generally by this labor and by the consequent accumulation of private property, the state of nature comes to an end. Civil society emerges precisely to help individuals preserve their right to private property. With this emergence of civil society, there is the development of publicly known laws, of a legal system, and a state that has the right to punish infringements of such laws.

The establishment of civil society requires the creation of a central political power. All individuals of the society agree to forego some rights in order to help preserve private property. Political power resides primarily in the people as a whole but government is established with the consent of the governed. If a government becomes oppressive, a revolution is permissible in order to reestablish the function of government, i.e., the preservation of private property. Locke's influence upon subsequent political theorists, including theorists of both the American and French revolutions, is well known.

Main works: A Letter Concerning Toleration (1689); An Essay Concerning Human Understanding (1690); Two Treatises of Government (1690); Some Thoughts Concerning Education (1693); The Reasonableness of Christianity (1695).

3. George Berkeley (1685-1753)

Berkeley was an Anglican bishop whose brilliant mind was largely unappreciated in his own lifetime. Berkeley's philosophy was a cogent attack on Locke's (so-called) empiricism precisely in the name of empiricism. Yet Berkeley's fundamental aim was far from skepticism or atheism. For Berkeley, the chief sin of the age was the belief in material substances existing in a world external to the mind, and hidden beneath primary and secondary qualities. The true worship of God was only possible if this belief in material substances could be shown to be false.

One of the foundations of Berkeley's philosophy is his attack on abstract ideas. Locke held that the mind was capable of abstracting ideas from particular objects or qualities. These ideas referred both to the individuals and to something abstract, namely the species. Berkeley admitted that we do have ideas of things that referred generally to individual things. But he vehemently denied that we have an abstract idea apart from particulars. Thus the idea of redness that I have is no more and no less than all the particular qualities of red than can be perceived, not some essence of redness which transcends every particular whatever.

Berkeley then directed his attention toward the problem of

65

material substance, which he regarded as resting on the doctrine of abstract ideas. According to Locke's almost classical view, one could distinguish between secondary qualities, such as color and taste, and primary qualities, such as figure, size, etc. The former were subjective, present only in the human mind; the latter were objective, found in the external world. These primary qualities in the external world inhered in a substance which was an "I-know-not-what". Berkeley first pointed out that it was impossible to imagine something red that was not extended in some fashion; that is, primary and secondary qualities always occur together, and could never occur separately. Both are ideas in the mind. Neither is any more "objective" than the other. But most importantly, Berkeley insisted that there is no "substance" in my ideas at all. A substance, by Locke's own definition, could not be perceived—only its primary or secondary qualities—and therefore, Berkeley concluded, there was no way in which the existence of any substance could ever be proven. Something that can never be perceived cannot "support" primary or secondary qualities. The idea of substance is nothing else than the idea of something beyond particular qualities minus any particular qualities. But this is nothing more than an abstract idea; and abstract ideas Berkeley will not allow as reliable guides in the search for what can be known. The mind's "furniture" consists essentially of ideas of particulars found in sense perception, or general ideas which refer to classes of particulars. But abstract ideas refer to objects that are never given in sense perception—in this case, the abstract idea of substance refers to something beyond all particular qualities. It follows from all this that the abstract idea of material substance refers to nothing at all. Berkeley concludes that the "objective natural world" exists as ideas in minds, and not beyond all minds whatever.

Berkeley's own metaphysics is itself an essay in simplicity. Existing things are of two types: ideas and minds or spirits. There are many spirits or minds besides my own, God being the highest of all. Ideas can be created out of my own imagination; but most ideas are caused by God. Thus the cause of my idea of this table in front of me is God, not some occult material substance standing behind the ideas. By seeing the cause of my ideas of the world in God rather than in material substances, Berkeley hoped to eliminate the destructive materialism of the day.

One might ask: how did Berkeley know there were other minds or God? Basically, Berkeley argued that I associated other minds with certin bodies, because I associate my mind with my body (it should be recalled that for Berkeley "my body" is a set of ideas in my mind, and does not refer to some "material substance" outside my mind). Knowledge of other minds is based on analogy. The existence of God is known by the order and law-like behavior of those ideas not caused by my own mind. Thus, Berkeley claimed that my mind has some kind of notion or intuition of other minds, and, in the case of the Divine Mind, some kind indirect knowledge based on evidence found in sense perception. But this is not consistent with his other claims at all: for why not claim the mind to have a notion or intuition of material substance as well? Berkeley's philosophy was as riddled with inconsistencies as Locke's, and it was the great skeptic David Hume who was finally able to unravel these problems.

Main works: An Essay Towards a New Theory of Vision (1709); A Treatise Concerning the Principles of Human Knowledge (1710); Three Dialogues Between Hylas and Philonous (1713); De Motu (1721); Alciphron (1732); The Analyst (1734); A Defence of Free-Thinking in Mathematics (1735); Siris (1744).

4. David Hume (1711-1776)

Hume was the most brilliant and incisive of all the British empiricists: he was also perhaps the most articulate skeptic who ever lived.

Hume began, like other theorists of this period, with a simple, even elegant, theory of knowledge. All ideas come from impressions. Impressions are from two sources: sense-perception and sentiments such as love, hate, desire, etc. Impressions are lively and forceful, while ideas are less so: this in fact is the only difference between the two. Now, Hume says, if one wishes to discover whether or not we know something, all we need do is break the knowledge down into its component ideas, and ask whether the ideas come from identifiable impressions. If they do, then knowledge is at least a possibility; if they do not, then we can have no knowledge because the ideas cannot be derived from impressions. Hume invites his opponents to find some idea which cannot be traced back to an impression, but which they know to be true.

Hume recapitulates Berkeley's critique of material substance. Material substance is not an idea for which any impression can be found; therefore it cannot be known to refer to anything. But he goes on: I have no idea of a mind or mental substance either; for nothing beyond my ideas could be known to exist. Just as there are no material substances beyond the impressions of their qualities, so there are no mental substances beyond the flow of ideas.

Hume's most distinctive contributions to skepticism, however, were his critiques of causality and God.

The traditional theory was that causality is a relation such that given cause "A" one and only one effect "B" could occur. Causal relationships, in short, were always necessary. But knowledge of causal relationships was supposedly drawn from experience, from sense-perception. Hume pointed out that all knowledge derived from sense-perception is probable, not certain. As such a necessary causal relationship between two objects in experience was a contradiction in terms: if it was in our sense-experience it could not be necessary.

How then could one account for our belief that things are in fact caused, that there is order and sequence in the universe? Hume was perhaps among the first to suggest that the scientific study of nature led to laws of great probability, not certainty. The reason I believe that "A" causes "B" is that I have previously experienced "A" causing "B" an indefinite number of times, and I have never experienced "A" causing anything but "B". The more often I experience "A" and "B" together, the greater the probability that "A" and "B" will be repeated together in the future, and the more I will be inclined to speak of a "necessary" relation between the two. But for Hume, no necessary relation actually exists, or could exist, since it is always conceivable that something other than "B" could follow "A".

Hume's concern about the existence of God was lifelong. While he was thoroughly respectful in his treatment of the subject, his conclusions were resoundingly skeptical. Arguments like those of Anselm and Descartes, he points out, assume that the mere idea of something is sufficient ground to conclude that it exists. But this is absurd. Ideas alone cannot substantiate the existence of anything. The case for the existence of God must rest upon evidence.

What evidence, then, is there for the existence of God? Hume acknowledges the order of the universe, though he points out that order is not absolute and not intrinsic to the universe. Now order can just as well occur by chance as by design. The only way in which one could know a given instance of order to have been designed is to have had previous experience of a designer: for the notion of order, unlike that of design, does not presuppose that of an Orderer. But if this is all true, then order cannot prove there was a designer of the universe; and design in the universe, which automatically presupposes a designer, has not been proven.

Other problems arise as well. For the universe needs to have as its maker not a fully intelligent, nor even a perfectly good maker. The postulated cause should not be any greater than the effect. But the effect, while showing many signs of order and goodness do not indicate absolute intelligence or absolute goodness. At best, then, one could only argue for a rather limited deity on the basis of the evidence.

But one final step removes even this possibility. All arguments from effects to causes, Hume points out, depend for their

force on a large number of instances. One instance is not enough
to make any judgments at all. If we had at hand a large number,
or even an infinite number, of universes, we could assess the
evidence in all of them, and come to some reasonable conclusion
about God as the cause of all of them. But there is only one
universe in fact. Any argument, therefore, about the cause of
this one effect, and about the nature of that cause, is wasted
effort and fruitless.

Hume draws two conclusions from all this skepticism. First
of all metaphysics, which rests on belief in material and mental
substances, causality, and God, must be rejected in the name of
empirical scrutiny. But secondly, Christianity remains possible
for those who acknowledge that its beliefs are totally and wholly
anti-rational in nature. Clearly, Hume was not a Christian; but
it was not so much his endeavor to rule out Christian belief, as
to demonstrate its total opposition to reason.

Main works: A Treatise of Human Nature (1740); Essays, Moral
and Political (1742); Enquiry Concerning Human Understanding
(1748); Enquiry Concerning the Principles of Morals (1751);
Political Discourses (1752); Four Dissertations (1757); Two Essays
(1777); Dialogues Concerning Natural Religion (1779).

D. IMMANUEL KANT (1724-1804)

Kant's philosophy is both the summation of the modern period,
as well as a brilliant effort to transcend the limitations of
previous thinkers. He remains one of the most important thinkers
to be reckoned with after Plato and Aristotle.

Kant was trained in the classically rationalist tradition of
Leibniz and Descartes, and to some extent he never abandoned that
background. However, as he himself notes, he was less than
critical as a philosopher, until he happened to read the work of
David Hume. By that time he was well into middle age. One could
hardly imagine a person changing significantly his or her mental
outlook at such a time. Yet Kant did just that: indeed all his
brilliant works, including the great Critiques of Pure Reason, of
Practical Reason, and of Judgment, were written and published in
his later years.

Kant was simultaneously concerned with a number of crucial
problems, at the center of which stood the resoundingly convincing
skepticism of David Hume. Hume had postulated that all knowledge
of the natural world was probable, not certain, causality being
the prime instance of this. Now Kant was absolutely convinced
that Hume was wrong in the end. The question was: how was he
wrong? Why was he wrong?

Kant classified propositions as either synthetic or analytic, and as being either a priori or a posteriori. A <u>synthetic</u> proposition was one whose predicate was not logically contained in the subject; thus, "this wall is green" is synthetic because the predicate "green" is not contained in the subject "wall". An <u>analytic</u> proposition is one whose predicate <u>is</u> so contained in the subject; thus, "every bachelor is an unmarried man" is analytic because "unmarried man" is contained in the subject "bachelor". A proposition is <u>a priori</u> if its source is independent of experience: thus "2 + 2 = 4" is a priori since it is known to be true independently of any experience. A proposition is <u>a posteriori</u> if its truth is only known through experience: thus, "some cats are white" is only known by experience.

There are thus four conceivable kinds of propositions:
    (1) analytic a posteriori
    (2) synthetic a posteriori
    (3) analytic a priori
    (4) synthetic a priori

Three of these four kinds of propositions can readily be accounted for. Everyone agrees that there are no analytic a posteriori judgments; thus all a posteriori judgments are synthetic in form. Further all agree that the basic propositions of logic (A = A) are analytic a priori. But what of synthetic a priori judgments?

Hume had suggested that all knowledge of nature, scientific or not, was a posteriori and synthetic in form. If this was the case, then Newtonian science, which rested on the existence of necessary connections between causes and effects, was seriously undermined. Kant, attempting to defend Newton's view of the science of nature against Humean skepticism, opted to defend an interpretation of the science of nature that was thoroughly at odds with Hume's. Kant argued that a science of nature was possible, contrary to Hume, and that such a science was founded upon propositions which were synthetic, to be sure, but which were <u>a priori, not a posteriori</u>. But how could this be?

Traditionally, the source of certainty with respect to natural objects, space, and time had been taken to reside in the external world. Hume had triumphantly shown that such certainty could not exist with respect to the external world. The world had been said to be rose-colored, and Hume pointed out that it wasn't.

But Kant had a fascinating insight. Perhaps the rose-colored world got its rose-coloring not from the world itself, but from the person perceiving it. Perhaps the mind itself contributed the certainty that was thought to stem from the real world!

70

Kant then launched a highly technical defense of an absolutely certain science or metaphysics of nature. It is far too complex to discuss in detail. Only the essential steps are recounted here. Traditional theorists distinguished between sensibility and the understanding, but discussed the content of the ideas in each as though they were determined from the outside. Kant discussed each, however, in terms of the way each shaped or formed knowledge. Kant was certainly convinced that there would be no knowledge at all without input from the outside world. But he was also convinced that there is in knowledge a component not derived from the external world, a formal element contributed by the very structure of sensibility and understanding.

Thus sensibility was structured so that all things that were perceived were in space and time. Space and time were the two forms of sensibility. Geometry and mathematics were both derived from these structures of sensibility, not from knowledge of the external world. As such, they were both composed of synthetic but a priori judgments. Today, many philosophers reject this theory altogether and hold that geometry and mathematics are analytic and a priori. But Kant felt a judgment like "24 + 53 = 77" was not immediately known to be analytic by the mind since its components had to be arranged in a certain way in order to arrive at the conclusion.

Kant also discussed the understanding as it shaped or formed knowledge. The 12 Categories of the understanding shaped or formed all perceptions. One of these categories was Causality. Causal relations were built into the mind: the mind inevitably had to understand the real world as necessarily caused. And Hume was right: if we look beyond our minds for the source of our knowledge of causal relations, we will find nothing.

Kant's theory did not stop with a metaphysics of science, however. For he realized that the questions about traditional metaphysics were in need of some illumination. Once again, his method, sometimes referred to as his "transcendental turn", put new light on the matter.

Beyond the understanding, consciousness has created three very important ideas: those of God, the World, and the Soul. These 3 ideas of pure reason are of things-in-themselves. So far, Kant had only dealt with the way things appeared when organized by understanding and sensibility. But what lay beyond appearances? The metaphysics of nature was concerned with the certainty of the Appearances or Phenomena of the world and the self. But traditional metaphysics was concerned with Noumena or Things-in-themselves. If knowledge of the former was possible, was knowledge of the latter? Kant's reply to this was in the negative. No theoretical knowledge of God, of the soul, or of the realm of material substances was possible. Our minds had knowledge only of what was in experience. Any attempt to form judgments about those things beyond experience inevitably led to puzzles, paradoxes, and contradictions--in short, no knowledge at all.

But once again, while Kant was agreeing with Hume's skeptical conclusions, he did not stop there. The question that Kant raised was this: why, if traditional metaphysics is not possible, was the human mind so intent on its pursuit? Part of the answer was the fact that the mind simply wanted a complete intellectual picture of reality. Yet part of the answer as well was that the mind was not simply a <u>knowing</u> mind but a <u>moral</u> mind as well. The question of traditional metaphysics was then raised within the context of Kant's moral theory to which we shall now turn.

For Kant the basic fact of practical or moral reason is the experience all persons have of being morally obligated. What is involved in this obligation? Kant assumed that all moral law was purely rational, and that the moral law itself was promulgated by will itself. This will is in itself holy or perfectly good. It is precisely this will to which humans are subjected when they feel morally obligated. The human sense of duty is founded upon obedience to a holy and good will. This will is one and the same for all rational beings, indeed is their will.

What is the content of this moral law? Kant calls the moral law the categorical imperative: it is essentially the "Golden Rule". But Kant points out several features of this. First, all moral duty must be performed for its own sake. Action done for some other purpose is not moral at all. Secondly, the golden rule regards each person as an end-in-itself, not as a means to an end. All morality is antithetical to the use or manipulation of human persons for some purpose. Finally, the moral law treats each person as a member of a kingdom of ends. The goal of moral action is to bring this kingdom into being. Any action done out of pleasure, out of utility, or out of mere obedience to another is de facto not a moral action. A moral action is done for its own sake, not for any other purpose.

Kant adds at the end of his discussion of the moral law that such a law presupposes certain postulates for its truth. These postulates are freedom, immortality, and God (which correspond to the three ideas of pure reason mentioned previously). Thus, Kant's solution to the problem of metaphysical ideas of things-in-themselves is that they are presupposed by the fact that we are moral beings. Kant insists that we do not know any more theoretically about such ideas by their being so postulated by practical reason--only that their postulation is inevitable. As a consequence, traditional metaphysics which was ruled out on theoretical grounds was in fact let in the back door on moral or practical grounds.

Kant broadened this ethical theory into a rather idealistic political philosophy founded on the notion that each person is an end-in-itself. In doing so, Kant attempted to provide a more scientific foundation for the political philosophy of Rousseau which he greatly admired.

To conclude: Kant's impressive synthesis combined both rationalistic and empiricist elements into an impressive whole. Yet nagging doubts remained about the connection between morality and knowledge, between noumena and phenomena. Within a generation almost all German philosophers had abandoned Kant's moderate dualism in an attempt to resolve those doubts. But by the late 19th century German thinkers generally began to reconsider Kant's perspective, and his fame has grown steadily since then.

Main works: Critique of Pure Reason (1781); Prolegomena to Any Future Metaphysics (1783); Foundations of the Metaphysics of Morals (1785); Critique of Practical Reason (1788); Critique of Judgment (1790); Religion within the Limits of Reason Alone (1792); Perpetual Peace (1795); Metaphysics of Morals (1797); Anthropology (1798).

CHAPTER 6

19TH CENTURY PHILOSOPHY

A. INTRODUCTION

The period of modern philosophy, which began with the rationalism of Descartes and the empiricism of Locke, came to a
critical culmination in the thought of Immanuel Kant. Kant attempted to show the limits of empiricism on a rationalistic foundation; and in so doing, the subject of knowledge became the
foundation of all knowledge. Yet Kant had also attempted to come
to terms with metaphysics, agreeing with the empiricists that such
non-empirical knowledge is invalid, and yet agreeing with ratio-
nalists that metaphysics does have some kind of foundation in our
ethical nature.

Nineteenth century idealism proceeded on the assumption that
metaphysics could only be justified in terms of the standpoint of
the subject. Yet German thought in the wake of Kant repeatedly
attempted to go beyond Kant's critique. This was done generally
by simplifying the realm of things-in-themselves to one absolute,
and by grounding all appearances in this absolute. In this way,
Kant's dualism was overcome by a monism based upon an ego that
stands at the base of all egos whatever. But the way in which
this idealist project was carried out varied considerably.

Two thinkers in particular symbolize the reactions to Kant
among German idealists in the 19th century: Hegel and
Schopenhauer. Hegel's endeavor was to find a rational foundation
for all thinking and experience in the Absolute Mind. The result
of his quest was a historical vision of God and humankind in a
dynamic, rational unity, progressing from a belief in plural
realities and dualistic divisions to a perfect or absolute knowledge of the unity of all things in God.

Hegel's vast cosmic vision brought the question of human
relationships into philosophy in a decidedly important way. No
longer could the history of humanity remain outside the philosophical vision. For history was the progression of mind toward
absolute knowledge.

By contrast, Schopenhauer's philosophy capitalized on the
notion that knowledge is not inherent in the Absolute. If so,
then the Absolute is the ground of being, not by knowing, but by
willing. And the willing of the Absolute is blind. For
Schopenhauer, history has nowhere to go. It is rather inherently
tragic; the goal of life is, if anything, to escape from life in
some way, rather than to see life and history continue to produce

evil and suffering.

Hegel's thought emphasized the progressive development of knowledge through history; while Schopenhauer's thought emphasized the pursuit of aesthetic contemplation in an indifference to history and its suffering. While Hegel overwhelmed the first part of the 19th century, Schopenhauer's influence on Wagner and Nietzsche dominated the latter part of the 19th century. Both thinkers continue the emphasis on subjectivity begun with Descartes. The significance of German idealism consists in how it attempted to overcome the metaphysical "distance" between subjectivity in its human form and the absolute, a distance which had been taken as the norm with but few exceptions (Spinoza being one of the exceptions).

The 19th century began with a series of impressive idealistic "systems of thought"; it quickly developed antithetical reactions, especially in Marx, Kierkegaard, and Nietzsche; and it continued into the latter part of the 19th century in Great Britain (and many other parts of Europe and America), when German thought became the rage. Earlier in the century, the tradition of British empiricism continued with J. S. Mill, but even he had been influenced to some extent by a preoccupation with history. And with the emergence of Darwin's theory of evolution in the 1870's, a more "scientific" approach than Hegel's to the philosophy of history was created by Spencer. But for all the advances of the sciences in the 19th century, it was in many respects an age of romanticism, of the arts, of history, and of grand thinking on a scale rarely attempted in the history of philosophy.

B. THE DEVELOPMENT OF GERMAN IDEALISM

1. J. G. Fichte (1762-1814)

Of the early German idealists Fichte was perhaps the most closely bound to Kant; indeed his early Critique of All Revelation, published anonymously, was taken by the public as a "fourth critique" from Kant himself.

Fichte was always the political and moral radical, advocating republicanism, and even fighting in the struggle against Napoleon in 1812. Fichte's philosophizing began with the Kantian insight that moral activity is prior to all other concerns, and he set out in his later writings the assumptions of his rigorously moral views. Fichte believed that moral action is the ground of our experience of duty and of our knowledge. The experience of duty, he argued, presupposed a human community and a world in which that duty is to be carried out. Moral action is a spiritual reality which creates that duty by positing out of its own subjectivity the other and the world in which that duty is to be carried out. That which acts morally is ultimately an Absolute Ego. This Ego, which transcends the world of appearance, posits in its consciousness a non-ego; and this leads to a modification of the positing of the ego, and so on and so forth. The condition of our finite existence emerges out of the self-defining creative activity of an unlimited absolute ego.

The empirical ego, that is, the ego as it appears to others, and the world of nature are to be understood as posited by this divine Ego. The human vocation, Fichte argues, is to recognize the inner nature of this divine Ego, and to will in such a way that every other person, every other ego, is willed as free. Fichte was convinced that history marked the advance of the empirical ego's awareness of the nature of ethical duty, and of the responsibility it has to further freedom.

Fichte became a champion of German nationalism and of German economic self-sufficiency. Fichte's moral idealism had much influence later on in Great Britain. But his philosophy was overshadowed in his own time by Hegel's in particular.

Main works: Critique of All Revelation (1792); On the Concept of the Science of Knowledge (1794); Groundwork of the Complete Science of Knowledge (1794); The Science of Ethics as Based on the Science of Knowledge (1798); The Closed Commercial State (1800); The Characteristics of the Present Age (1806); Addresses to the German Nation (1808).

2. F. W. J. von Schelling (1775-1854)

Schelling's early works reflect Fichte's idealism, and in many respects it was Fichte's system of idealism that Schelling spent much of his life modifying or qualifying. His thought underwent several different phases, and it is difficult therefore to describe it as a unified whole.

Schelling's earlier contribution, and that which made him famous in the years before the publication of Hegel's major work The Phenomenology of Spirit in 1807, centered on the philosophy of the sciences and of the arts. Schelling emphasized, in his interpretation of Fichtean idealism, the difference between spirit and nature, even as he understood nature to be posited by spirit. But the reality and objectivity of nature had not been appreciated fully by Fichte, and so Schelling set forth a vitalist account of nature, emphasizing the idea that force, as the essence of life, pervades all of nature, and that nothing in nature is simply passively inert. This is because, in the end, the vital force in nature is the same as the vital force or creativity of spirit itself. Knowledge of nature was a function of the self-activity of spirit: thus the highest knowledge was of spirit as that which wills all nature, while the lowest knowledge is of spirit as determined by sensation. That is to say, spirit experiences nature in its greatest otherness as that which impinges on spirit; but it is only as a morally active and creative being that spirit experiences how it is itself the true foundation of nature. It is not surprising that Schelling found art, the experience of aesthetic creation, to be the most revelatory of the true spiritual nature of the ego, higher than any science or philosophy which merely contemplates the world passively.

Schelling proposed what has been called a "philosophy of identity" as an attempt to spell out more clearly the nature of God, perhaps in response to his emphasis on the difference between nature and spirit. At this time, he was attracted to the rigorous geometrical method of Spinoza, and his fundamental belief--that the unity of nature and spirit was to be found in the absolute self-identity of reason in all its manifestations--was clearly inspired by Spinoza. This absolute self-identity, expressed in the fundamental tenet of logic that A = A, is the nature of God and expresses both what God is and how God differs from everything else. In short, the philosophy of identity was a form of Spinozistic pantheism, but unlike Spinoza's system, Schelling insisted that nature was fully alive and vital.

In his later phase, which began around 1809 and lasted for the rest of his life, Schelling adopted what amounts to a kind of existentialism--a view which had little influence until the 20th century. Schelling came to be critical of his earlier emphasis on reason, and began to consider the idea that the fundamental problem of philosophy is not the absolute so much, as the situation of human existence, not reason so much as symbol. The meaning of human existence is to be found especially in the history of religious myth, and the task of philosophy is to heal the wounds in human existence which are so often spoken of in these myths. Schelling's "existentialism" has had some influence on Ernst Cassirer, Jaspers, Scheler, Heidegger, the Protestant theologian Paul Tillich, and many others.

Main works: Ideas Toward a Philosophy of Nature (1797); On the World-Soul (1798); First Sketch of a System of the Philosophy of Nature (1799); Preface to a Sketch of a System of the Philosophy of Nature (1799); On the True Concept of the Philosophy of Nature (1800); System of Transcendental Idealism (1800); Statement of My System of Philosophy (1801); Bruno, or Concerning the Divine and Natural Principle of Things (1802); Lectures on the Method of Academic Study (1803); On the Relation of the Fine Arts to Nature (1807); Philosophical Investigations on the Essence of Human Freedom (1809); The Ages of the World (1811; published posthumously); Introduction to Mythology, Philosophy of Mythology, and

78

Philosophy of Revelation (all three published posthumously).

3. G. W. F. Hegel (1770-1831)

Neither Fichte nor Schelling had anything like the influence that Hegel did. The latter's great masterpeice, The Phenomenology of Spirit, was published in 1807, only three years after Kant's death, and at the height of Fichte's fame and Schelling's philosophy of identity. Yet there is a world of difference between Hegel and all these other philosophers, however much they may have in common.

Like many other forms of idealism, Hegel's system was reminiscent of Spinoza's. Hegel called the Absolute "God" or "the Idea" or "Absolute Knowledge" or "Absolute Spirit". This Idea was absolute because it included all other ideas and realities whatever as part of its nature. Thus the universe was a part of God for Hegel; indeed, the universe the matter, the traditional notion of God the form, and the totality was one Being composed of matter and form: this Absolute Idea being God. Hegel's notion of God included the traditional Christian notion, such that the latter was "superseded" by the former: thus the truth of theology was superseded by Hegel's philosophy. Surprisingly, many Protestant intellectuals warmed up to this and remained dominated by it until the 20th century.

Yet, having said all this, it is not yet clear how Hegels' system was any different from Spinoza's; and whatever else it was, it was most certainly different. What was new about Hegel's pantheism? Spinoza's universe was a rather static affair, discussed primarily under the two divine modes of mentality and extension. There is no feeling or sense that for Spinoza the temporal development of the universe was of any importance.

But for Hegel the very essence of the universe, and hence of God, was temporal development. By including time within the nature of Being, Hegel's God resembled one of Leibniz' monads on a grand scale. Much of Hegel's discussion in the Phenomenology consists of analyses of various events of history. There have been few in the history of Western thought who contributed as much as Hegel did to the very idea of History. For Hegel, all history was the history of mind in its various activities--Philosophy, Religion, Politics, Art, Morality. To understand, say, the notion of God, one must understand its historical development, for it is only through this historical development that there is any knowledge whatever. It is much like the fact that without my own personal history, the idea of myself is simply an empty abstraction; and by studying my own personal history I come to understand just what it is that I am. Being, history, and time cannot be separated from one another. The nature of their relationship is

79

to be found in what has come to be called "the dialectical method". Dialectic is simply a name for the law-like way in which spirit actualizes itself in time, and for the analysis of these manifestations by spirit itself in the process of coming to know itself.

Dialectic involves three moments when analyzed. The first is the positing of something; this is called the Thesis. The second is the negating of the Thesis: this is called the Antithesis. The third is the overcoming of the separation between Thesis and Antithesis by the recognition of the truth and falsity of both: this is called the Synthesis. This sounds quite abstract, so it may help to give an example.

In The Phenomenology of Spirit Hegel analyzes the relation between masters and slaves as one moment in the development of the mind. The Thesis, one might say, is the Master, with his asserted superiority, laying claim to the work and labor of another human being, the Slave. The Master is free, the Slave is not. But, ironically, the Master depends on the Slave for his livelihood; without the Slave's labor, the Master would be helpless. The Slave realizes that, in fact, the Master is not free; and furthermore that the Master cannot control the slave's internal mind and thought. Thus the Slave comes to believe that the Master is outwardly unfree, and the slave is inwardly free. This is the moment of Antithesis. The final stage comes with the recognition that the whole master-slave relation, beset with the contradictions just enumerated, must give way to a situation of genuine freedom, both external and internal, so that the full nature of freedom for both Master and Slave may be realized. Thus the moment of Synthesis is the realization of a community freed from the Master-Slave relation.

The whole point of this theory of dialectical analysis is to explain how and why change occurs. For Hegel, all change represents the inherent instability of the contradictory. If reality is marked by the mutual presence of thesis and antithesis, it must give way to a synthesis in which contradictions are reconciled in some fashion. In this sense, all change is logical and law-like by nature.

Hegel's use of dialectic is sometimes profound and enlightening (the analysis of the Master-Slave relation is one of his best and most famous), and sometimes neurotically obsessive-compulsive (especially in his later writings). Dialectic is omnipresent in everything he wrote. One finds that the main structures of his works are in three's or groups of three's; that subdivisions are the same; and that even discussions within subdivisions are broken down once again into three's or their multiples. It is clear that Hegel's faith in the dialectic may have been greater than his ability to apply it meaningfully.

It should be noted that each synthesis in the dialectic is a new thesis, and thus that dialectical development continues indefinitely. The question arises, is there an end to this development? For Hegel, there is, and it is important to realize some of the different portraits he made of his "final states of affairs". Thus, in the religious sphere the final state of affairs is the Absolute Spirit in the Christian community. Hegel strongly emphasizes the way in which individual and community are reconciled in Christianity--and this because each is a revelation of the Absolute, though the community is a more truthful revelation than the individual. The same is true of the political sphere where the family (thesis) is opposed by civil society (antithesis) and finally reconciled in bureaucratic government (the State). These analyses of the Christian community and the Prussian state would be influential later on in shaping the thought of both Kierkegaard and Marx.

There is another answer to the question about the end of the development of spirit. For Hegel, the end of dialectic, the synthesis of all syntheses, is Absolute Spirit. But God or the Absolute only knows through the human spirit which is in its essence divine. God's consciousness is our own reason. In that sense, our development of mind is a development or revelation of God to Himself, the gradual realization of the "Kingdom of God" on earth. There is a sense of optimistic urgency in Hegel, grounded in the knowledge both that we are already God and that absolute knowledge must be pursued, so that God may truly be "all in all".

Main works: Phenomenology of Mind (1807); Science of Logic (1812-6); Encyclopedia of the Philosophical Sciences in Outline (1817); Philosophy of Right (1821). Posthumously published: Lectures on Aesthetics (1835-8); Lectures on the Philosophy of History (1837); Lectures on the Philosophy of Religion (1832); Lectures on the History of Philosophy (1833-6); Early Theological Writings.

4. Arthur Schopenhauer (1788-1860)

Perhaps Hegel's most implacable contemporary foe was Schopenhauer. Schopenhauer found the Hegelian system to be guilty of crass optimism, of covering over and rationalizinag away the great evil in the universe. Schopenhauer's own system of thought owed much to Kant and to, of all things, Buddhism.

Schopenhauer sharply distinguished between the realm of phenomena and the realm of noumena. In most respects, Schopenhauer's treatment of the realm of phenomena is a close reflection of Kant's views, though Schopenhauer made a number of

81

simplifications, probably to Kant's benefit. But Schopenhauer's genuine originality lay in his view of the noumenal realm. Schopenhauer argued that there is in human consciousness a certain intuition of the will as the ground of the realm of appearances. He based this on introspective observation of the subordination of knowledge to the will, a subordination also noted by Fichte and Schelling.

For Schopenhauer, the notion of multiplicity only made sense within the realm of phenomena, not noumena. Hence, instead of three ideas of reason (as in Kant), for Schopenhauer there is only one noumenal reality: Absolute Will. Absolute Will is beyond appearances and thus beyond knowledge, since knowledge is only of appearances. Absolute Will is thus the ground of both knowledge and appearances. This Will, since it is beyond knowledge, is blind. Every individual thing in the universe is an embodiment of this blind will; and each thing blindly seeks its own pleasure, and thereby comes into conflict with other individual things. The world is a scene of vast meaningless conflict, and of horrendous evil. One can now see why Schopenhauer was so opposed to Hegel. For Hegel the ground of being was God, and God was good; for Schopenhauer the ground of appearances was Will, and this Will was the cause of all evil and suffering. For Schopenhauer existence in this world was itself an evil to be eradicated; for Hegel it was a good to be affirmed.

Did Schopenhauer advocate suicide? No, he did not; he claimed in fact that the desire to kill oneself was one more effect of the Will. There were only two ways Will could be annihilated: aesthetic contemplation of art, which was only temporary; and religious asceticism, which involved the extinction of desire. The latter concern led Schopenhauer to a study of Buddhism, which is similarly concerned with the extinction of desire.

One may ask, how could that which is created by Will have the power to overcome it? Schopenhauer is not too clear about this, but he does insist that nature has over-endowed humans by in effect giving them more intellectual abilities than they need. It is this intellectual "reserve" that becomes the human's last solace. For when an individual and his or her mind perishes at death, there is nothing else.

Schopenhauer's extraordinary pessimism had much influence on the great German opera composer Richard Wagner. But his most important influence was on Friederich Nietzsche, who will be discussed later.

Main works: On the Fourfold Root of the Principle of Sufficient Reason (1813); The World as Will and Representation

(1818); <u>On</u> <u>the</u> <u>Will</u> <u>in</u> <u>Nature</u> (1836); <u>On the</u> <u>Two</u> <u>Fundamental</u> <u>Problems</u> <u>of</u> <u>Ethics</u> (1841); <u>Parerga</u> <u>and</u> <u>Paralipomena</u> (1851).

C. REACTIONS TO HEGEL: THE DEVELOPMENT OF SOCIALISM

1. Ludwig Feuerbach (1804-1872)

One of the more radical followers of Hegelianism was Feuerbach. He has the irony of being an atheist whose entire life was spent writing about religion and especially Christianity. His knowledge was vast; his theories simplistic, yet sometimes powerful. His influence has been felt deeply in the theological community, perhaps even more than in the philosophical community.

The first dialectical stage of religion is simply a stage of alienation from the gods. Human nature is separated from the source of reality and being. Now this separation is not real, of course--to the contrary it is entirely in the mind. But the mind persists in calling this abstracted human nature "God". God is real, we humans are much less than God. In God's sight, humans are mere nothings. Thus primitive or natural religion is basically crippling to man.

Christianity, the second stage of dialectical development, overcomes natural religion. It does this in two important ways. First of all, in Christianity God--or perfect human nature-- becomes man again, in the person of Jesus. But Jesus leaves the earth, and once again man's nature is alienated from himself. So while the Incarnation promises an end to alienation from human nature, it negates it fundamentally. And this is not all: Christianity also believes that God is three persons in one substance. These three persons are essentially a veiled theoretical statement of human nature. The trinity idealizes the relation between two persons ("I and Thou") bound together by Love. Human nature, as revealed covertly in the Trinity, is intrinsically social and infinite in its capacity to use Reason and Will in bringing about Perfect Love. But as long as this Trinitarian God remains in human imagination, happiness will elude the human condition and the full potential of human nature will remain unrealized. So neither the Incarnation nor the doctrine of the Trinity deliver what they promise: the realization of an end to alienation.

The final dialectical stage, then, must be the reduction of theology to anthropology. Feuerbach's life-long project was to show how every doctrine of religion and of Christianity in particular was about the development of human nature, but never overtly recognized as such. To reduce theology to anthropology was to literally show how talking about God was the same thing as

83

talking about human beings. Only through such a reduction could humans be liberated from enslavement to their own imaginations. Philosophy is anthropology; and anthropology is the key that will unlock human unhappiness and the lack of love in real life.

Main works: <u>Thoughts on Death and Immortality</u> (1830); <u>The Essence of Christianity</u> (1841); <u>Principles of the Philosophy of the Future</u> (1843); <u>The Essence of Religion</u> (1846); <u>Theogony</u> (1857).

2. Pierre-Joseph Proudhon (1809-1865)

Proudhon is given credit as the "father of anarchism". He was a self-taught man, whose absorption of Hegel and Feuerbach and others was often somewhat simplistic and superficial.

In his early works Proudhon attacked the institution of private property and championed a kind of "back to the country-side" solution to economic problems. Marx found the attack on private property, at least, quite attractive, and for a time the two radicals were considered allies, if not friends. But by the mid-1840's Marx had become disillusioned with Proudhon's theories, and this led to a life-long bitter struggle between the two men, who together dominated the radical political movements of the day.

Proudhon in his earlier works had postulated a kind of Hegelian triad to explain the development of history. That development was from the institution of private property, which was the cause of inequality, to the phenomenon of communism, which implied an authoritarian government and an end to individual freedom. Proudhon believed that out of this contradiction would emerge finally the state of freedom for all, in which individuals would organize themselves into collective communes for the production of goods. Each commune would then set up relations with other communes, and thus a kind of federalism would hold society together externally, without the presence of an authoritarian government.

In his later years, Proudhon continued to champion many of these ideas, but he was less certain that history was inevitably going to some given point. He saw his role as being the incessant critic of private property on the one hand, and authoritarian government on the other. In time, his insistence on the evils of government would lead him and other anarchists into direct conflict with the Marxists, who held that a state might still be necessary, temporarily at least, in the transition from capitalism to communism.

Main works: <u>What Is Property?</u> (1840); <u>System of Economic Contradictions</u> (1846); <u>Philosophy of Progress</u> (1853); <u>Confessions</u>

84

of a Revolutionary (1850); General Idea of the Revolution in the Nineteenth Century (1851); On the Federal Principle (1863); On Justice in the Revolution and in the Church (1858); On the Political Capacity of the Working Classes (posthumously published in 1865).

3. Karl Marx (1818-1883)

Marx was a disciple of both Hegel and Feuerbach, and while influenced by both, disagreed with both. First of all, Marx found Hegel's notion of the Absolute swallowing up the real world to be turning the world on its head. For Marx, Hegel patently ignores the primacy of the real material world. Yet Marx borrowed much from Hegel. For example, Marx insisted on the basic truth of the dialectical theory, which in his hands became "dialectical materialism" (see below). Secondly, Marx felt that Hegel was quite right in seeing the central importance of history in all knowledge.

Hegel had ended his political philosophy with the assumption that the Prussian state of the 1830's was the final embodiment of Absolute Spirit. Marx knew that to be absurd. For Marx, Hegel had not really understood that political life is a function of economic life, and that economic life had yet to become fully developed dialectically, which is to say that capitalism's inner contradictions had not yet become fully apparent. In this re- spect, Marx posited Medieval Feudalism as the historically condi- tioned economic Thesis; Modern Capitalism as the economic Anti- thesis; and suggested that a synthesis would arise out of capitalism. This synthesis was Communism, the abolition of pri- vate property, and the beginning of an utopian economic existence for all.

In effect Marx argued that economic development occurred with the development of contradictions. Now the collapse of feudalism came with the growth of the free towns in the midst of the feudal kingdoms. The latter were agricultural; the former were urban. In time feudalism gave way to the free towns, to the burgers or bourgeoisie. These bourgeoisie exercized economic power at first by the manipulation of finances in the banking industry, and then later by the development of manufacturing. With this latter, there came into being an entirely new kind of economic relation in history: the bourgeoisie who owned the means of production (the factory , as well as the products made) and the proletariat who owned nothing but their labor. This relation between the bour- geoisie and the proletariat is rather like that between Master and Slave (to recall Hegel's analysis), and in time the contradictions inherent in this economic relation will give rise to a world in which all humans are truly free. Communism is the name of a society that is truly free for Marx. That perfectly free community will no longer require a state, since the state was invented for the purpose of aiding oppressors. Marx was aware of course that the existence of a state might be necessary for an intermediate period of time after a revolution and before the full blossoming of communism; but he is quite clear that in the end the state will "wither away". With this development, history as such would come to an end, since the perfect community, and thus human nature, would have been fully realized.

Marx also criticized Feuerbach for not being concrete enough in his reduction of God to humanity. For Feuerbach seemed unmindful of the economic bases of the belief in God, which for Marx were crucial in explaining why humans had come to believe in God at all. For Marx, religion was an ideology designed by a master class to keep an oppressed class enslaved. For example, belief in the hereafter focused human attention away from this life, and specifically enjoined an ethic that prevented the faithful from changing their lot in life. Religion was an opiate designed to alleviate the pain, not remove its source; it was not in itself the cause of the oppression, only its symptom and necessary accompaniment. Given this analysis, it is clear why Marx thought the arrival of the perfect community founded on communism would imply the end of religion. For when the source of the pain is removed, there will be no more need for an opiate.

There are several misconceptions of Marx' thought that are commonly encountered. First of all, Marx believed that the transition from capitalism to communism would be peaceful in some cases, violent in others. He did not believe violence or revolution was inevitable. Secondly, he insisted that revolution would occur in the most developed capitalist countries first, and would probably not occur in countries still in the "dark ages", so to speak. Thus he predicted Britain and Germany and France would be the first to turn communist; he was rather dubious about Russia and other outlying non-capitalist countries. Finally, dialectical materialism is not to be identified with the theory that all things whatever are material, that is with common materialism. Marx, in an early work, rejected the materialism of Epicurus and Democritus. While he was an avowed atheist, Marx held that some aspects of reality, such as culture, ideas, and so forth were "spiritual"; but his point was that they were determined entirely by the economic base of a given society. Dialectical materialism has more to do with economics, for Marx, than with any claim about the metaphysical nature of reality.

Main works: Economic and Philosophic Manuscripts of 1844 (posthumously published); The Holy Family (1845) (with Engels); The German Ideology (1846) (with Engels); Poverty of Philosophy (1847); Communist Manifesto (with Engels) (1848); Das Kapital (Vol. I—1867; Volumes 2 and 3 published posthumously); A

86

<u>Contribution</u> <u>to</u> <u>the</u> <u>Critique</u> <u>of</u> <u>Political</u> <u>Economy</u> (1859).

4. Friedrich Engels (1820-1895)

It is frequently difficult or impossible to separate Engels' from Marx' contributions in a given work that was jointly authored. But Engels, who was Marx' lifelong friend and companion, wrote a number of works apart from Marx which had a significant influence on later communists.

Perhaps the most significant was a work entitled <u>Dialectics</u> <u>of</u> <u>Nature,</u> written in the 1870's. In this work, Engels attempted to broaden Marx' theory of dialectical materialism. The latter was primarily an economic theory deriving from Hegelian metaphysics, and Marx had not sought to expand it to a full-fledged philosophy of nature. Engels attempted to do just this, and he used Darwin's theory of evolution as a kind of framework. In essence, his argument was that dialectical materialism, the theory that human development progressed or changed through inherent contradictions, also explained the progress of nature itself, a progress which was from the inorganic to the organic, and from the merely biological to the fully human. Dialectical materialism, Engels argued, was unlike previous forms of materialism because of its close relation to the modern sciences; whereas the traditional form of materialism, being a metaphysical theory, was hostile to the development of science. One of the more curious results of Engels' emphasis was the tendency to identify dialectical materialism with scientific positivism, at least among some Marxists. This is a "curious" result, because positivism is rather foreign to Marx' own outlook, which derived rather exclusively from Hegel, and was not much indebted to modern natural science. Marx was well aware of Engels' interest in these matters, but appears not to have said much about them. It is of some interest that Marxists in the Soviet Union have generally sided with Engels; while European Marxists have often tended to champion Marx over Engels.

Main works: <u>Anti-Duhring</u> (1878); <u>Dialectics</u> <u>of</u> <u>Nature</u> (published posthumously in 1925); <u>Ludwig</u> <u>Feuerbach</u> <u>and</u> <u>the</u> <u>Outcome</u> <u>of</u> <u>Classical</u> <u>German</u> <u>Philosophy</u> (published posthumously in 1934); <u>The</u> <u>Origin</u> <u>of</u> <u>the</u> <u>Family,</u> <u>Private</u> <u>Property</u> <u>and</u> <u>the</u> <u>State</u> (published posthumously in 1902); <u>Principles</u> <u>of</u> <u>Communism</u> (published posthumously in 1919). For works written with Marx, consult the section on Marx.

D. REACTIONS TO HEGEL: INDIVIDUALISM

1. Max Stirner (1806-1856)

Stirner was not so much a great, as an interesting, thinker whose major work was virtually his only work: The Individual and His Property (1845).

Stirner praised Feuerbach for freeing humankind from the tyrannical Hegelian God that alienated humans within themselves. But Feuerbach substituted for this mythical God another myth--the myth that humankind has a social essence. This myth of a social human nature must in turn be destroyed, precisely so that the most concrete reality of all may emerge--the individual ego.

The individual concrete existing self is thus the philosophical starting point for Stirner. This Ego is utterly self-reliant, and it exists to preserve itself from other egos and to enhance its own existence. This enhancement entails the creation of the ego's own "world" of things, persons, morals and religion (if desired). The general name for this self-created world of the self-reliant ego is "property". All that can be said to exist is this ego and its property, in company with other egos and their property. Such a society of radical egoists is the only genuine society possible.

Stirner's influence on contemporary Hegelians and later existentialists was significant. Marx criticized Stirner, suggesting that a society of radical egos was a middle-class bourgeois society, and not a classless society.

2. Soren Kierkegaard (1813-1855)

Another similar but more Christian reaction to Hegel along these lines was the philosophy-theology of Soren Kierkegaard. Kierkegaard was horrified at the philosophy of Hegel which he regarded as an attempt to intellectualize Christianity out of existence. In his later years, Kierkegaard launched a personal protest against the Danish Lutheran Church (he was a member himself), which had become heavily oriented toward Hegel's thought. He, like Luther, attacked Christendom in the name of Christianity.

Kierkegaard regarded the Hegelian dialectic as the heart of the problem. For with the dialectic one could think one's way into heaven; faith was forever being transcended by philosophy.

Kierkegaard discussed three spheres of human existence: First, there was the aesthetic sphere, where many people spend their lives. This sphere is personified by the myth of Don Juan. It is marked by the desire for sensual immediacy which, since it is intrinsically unsatisfying, ends in despair. Humans may or may not transcend the aesthetic sphere: there is no dialectical magic that suggests that they must or that they will.

Some, in any case, rise to the ethical sphere. The model for this sphere is Socrates, the man who claimed ignorance as to the nature of virtue, but was in fact a virtuous man. The ethical sphere involves the free decision to do those things commanded by the moral law. The state of marriage is the fulfillment of this sphere (as well as that of the aesthetic sphere), and is the highest goal of a purely human existence. But the highest goal of human existence transcends the purely human.

For the very few there is a higher goal, the religious sphere. Here the model is Abraham. Characteristic of the religious sphere is an absolutely passionate, inward state of the individual which is called faith. Faith takes place when the individual confronts the infinite gap between himself (the finite) and the infinite God. With faith he can leap across this gap. Yet faith is not inevitable—perhaps only a few have that courage. In faith, the individual is radically separated from all others— becomes most an individual—becomes least a thinker—in confronting the infinite. Faith and philosophy are radically opposed. The moment of faith is not only not undertood, but is radically absurd to the philosopher.

In this curious way, a Christian took up Hume's challenge. It will be remembered that Hume concluded that Christianity and rationality were violently opposed. Hume himself chose to be rational, of course. But Kierkegaard argues the same position in his own way. Christian faith and philosophy have nothing to do with one another; and Kierkegaard chose to be a Christian.

Main works: Either/Or (1843); Fear and Trembling (1843); Philosophical Fragments (1844); The Concept of Dread (1844); Stages on Life's Way (1845); Concluding Unscientific Postscript (1846); The Sickness Unto Death (1849); The Attack Upon "Christendom" (1855).

E. THE DEVELOPMENT OF FRENCH AND BRITISH THOUGHT

1. Jeremy Bentham (1748-1832)

Bentham was fascinated with the state of the system of jurisprudence in his own day, and ended up devoting his life to a project of reforming the law and morals. Bentham rejected the current practice of law at the time as based on numerous and pointless obscurities and illogic. Just as Descartes had proposed a philosophical reformation based on clear and distinct ideas, so

89

a reform of the law based on clear and distinct ideas was needed.

Bentham attacked what was called legal intuitionism, the belief that certain actions were legally proscribed simply because the legislator didn't like them, even if no one was harmed by them. He called this the fallacy of "ipsedixitism" (literally "he himself speaks", meaning "this action is not allowed, or this one is, because the legislator has said so, and for no other reason"). Against intuitionism, Bentham proposed Utilitarianism, the view that all legal obligations shoul rest not on arbitrary moral principles, but on the greatest happiness of the greatest number of people.

To that end, Bentham suggested establishing a hedonic calculus, by which the amount of pleasure associated with any given action could be assigned a mathematical quantum (a value on a scale of, say, 1 to 10). Let us say that of all the things I do, listening to music gives me the greatest pleasure, reading somewhat less, doing the dishes much less. I might assign, on a scale of 1 to 10, a value of 10 to the first, 8 to the second, and 3 to the third. Now the general happiness of all can be calculated by simply measuring the relative value of all the pains and pleasures any given action will have for all members of society.

It should be noted that Bentham's theory ignores any qualitative distinction between pleasures; one of his more infamous remarks was that "quantity of pleasure being equal, pushpin is as good as poetry." The principle of the greatest happiness of the greatest number has been accused not so much of fostering egoism or hedonism, but of denying both in the name of the greatest happiness of the greatest number. It is not entirely surprising that Benthamism tended toward the modern welfare state in its political programme.

Bentham rejected Locke's contract theory of the origin of government and argued for a fully utilitarian view, based on the calculation of pleasures and pains for society as a whole, and rejecting any kind of authoritarian natural law theory. He also argued vociferously against the doctrine of natural rights as proclaimed in the French Revolution, arguing that all rights are founded upon law, and thus presuppose the existence of a government.

Bentham wrote little on metaphysics, but did write a number of incomplete essays on logic which are extraordinarily interesting. He argued that all sentences should be reduced to combinations of words which refer to real entities. This was to avoid all reference to fictitious entities (the kind of thing that the law did quite often!). Thus terms like good, duty, right, etc., should ultimately be translated into terms which refer to

concrete situations.   In this way, ordinary language can be carefully corrected by logic, and metaphysical speculations can be
eliminated.

Bentham lived a very long life, and attracted many political
disciples, who became known as the Benthamites or Radicals, and
who had enormous influence on the political directions of Great
Britain in the early 19th century.   Among early converts to Benthamism were James Mill and his brilliant son John Stuart.

Main works: A Fragment on Government (1776); Introduction to
the Principles of Morals and Legislation (1789); Anarchical
Fallacies; Being an Examination of the Declaration of Rights
Issued during the French Revolution (written in 1791; first
published in French in 1816); Traite des preuves judiciares
(1823); The Book of Fallacies (1824); Rationale of Judicial
Evidence (1827).

2. Auguste Comte (1798-1857)

Comte, like Hegel, was fascinated with the history of
humanity.   But Comte understood history rather differently from
Hegel.   Comte argued that knowledge passes through three stages.
The first stage is that of theology, where the causes of natural
events are hidden by the postulation of personal deities.   The
second stage is that of metaphysics, where the cause of natural
events is said to be some abstract personified principle.   The
third stage is the Scientific or Positive stage (hence the name
Positivism).   In this stage the explanation of natural things is
to be found within and among the natural events themselves.

Comte went on to arrange all the sciences in a hierarchy of
importance.   He began with astronomy and physics.   But his final
science, the queen of sciences, was the study of society, which he
called Social Physics.   All sciences began and ended in their
service to humanity. Comte, the founder of the science of sociology, also promoted a bogus Religion of Humanity whose goal would
be the worship of humankind by humankind.   Though Comte's involvement in this "religion" marked him as a strange eccentric, his
thought had considerable influence on John Stuart Mill.

Main works: Cours de philosophie positive, 6 volumes, (1830-
42); Systeme de politique positive, 4 volumes (1851-4); Catechisme
positiviste (1852).

3. John Stuart Mill (1806-1873)

Mill was trained and educated in a rather cold, calculating,
rational way by his father who was a devoted disciple of British
empiricism and a friend of the social reformer Jeremy Bentham.

91

Mill contributed to the development of empiricism in a number of ways, primarily through his enlargement upon the problem of causality and scientific method in Hume, as well as by his suggestions for a psychology based upon Humean principles.

Mill held that the mind was just a bundle of ideas and sensations; and that thinking was the process of associating various kinds of ideas with others. But Mill advanced beyond this basically Humean belief when he dealt with the question of the notion of the external world or matter. The question, of course, went back to Berkeley; yet Mill suggested a totally psychological explanation for the origin of this notion. He said, in effect, that belief in an external world was merely a belief that certain sensations would be perceived if I did such-and-such. My belief that the TV is still in the front room is simply a belief that if I go into the front room I will perceive a certain rectangular object in the far corner that I call a TV. Now this is what one might call a pragmatic theory of knowledge: it suggests that a certain belief is true psychologically when it gives rise to X, Y, and Z kinds of sensations. This was to have influence on the development of Pragmatism in the 20th century.

Mill was somewhat enthusiastic about Comte's Religion of Humanity largely bcause he felt that it provided an emotional and religious framework compatible with scientific empiricism, but dismally lacking in the latter. Mill admitted, unlike Hume, that there is some evidence of a God finite in power and (perhaps) intelligence who created this world. But this belief, like that of immortality, was only based on possibility. The heart of true religious belief should be the worship of humanity. It is to Mill's credit that his enthusiasm about this sort of thing was considerably less than that of Comte, who actually became a High Priest and celebrated appropriate religious services in honor of humanity.

Mill's theory of morality, which is a modified version of Bentham's Utilitarianism, was also of some importance. Mill argued (against Kant) that the highest moral principle of all is the greatest amount of happiness for the greatest number of people. Moral duty or obligation might be part of that happiness, but Mill strongly rejected Kant's assertion that morality began and ended in duty. Happiness was the fundamental criterion of morality. Those things which were truly useful toward this end (hence the name utilitarianism) were those things which ought to be done morally. Mill regarded justice as a component of happiness, and political freedom within a representative democracy as essential. His radical support for individual freedom--individual freedom of thought, the freedom to be different--is among the most spirited of all writers. He also championed the rights of women and universal suffrage.

Main works: System of Logic (1843); Essays on Some Unsettled Questions of Political Economy (1844); Principles of Political Economy (1848); On Liberty (1859); Dissertations and Discussions (1859); Considerations on Representative Government (1861); Utilitarianism (1863); An Examination of Sir William Hamilton's Philosophy (1865); Auguste Comte and Positivism (1865); The Subjection of Women (1869); Autobiography (1873).

4. Herbert Spencer (1820-1903)

Spencer is noted for his synthesis of a Darwinian theory of evolution with English empiricism, taking into account some fundamental distinctions borrowed from Kant. Spencer's evolutionism, in fact, was not strictly indebted to Darwin, but at times embraced variants of Lamarckianism. Thus Spencer sometimes suggested that the use of a given biological organ could cause a modification in future generations—a thesis Darwin was at pains to reject. But Spencer is primarily remembered for his philosophical popularization of Darwin.

Spencer held that the most fundamental principle of evolution is likewise the most fundamental principle of reality insofar as the latter is knowable. That principle is that everything whatever in the universe begins in a stage of relative simplicity, in "indefinite, incoherent homogeneity," and progresses through the simultaneous dissipation of motion and integration of matter to a stage of "definite, coherent heterogeneity". The direction in evolution is from a situation where things are relatively alike to one where they are different from one another and arranged in an articulated order. Spencer proceeded to apply this principle to a wide variety of phenomena.

Some of the more interesting of his applications were to the field of sociology, to which Spencer made substantial contributions. Spencer argued that the dominant concern of human life was survival, and that human intelligence and emotions were very much to be understood in those terms. Thus the difference between a creature that merely senses and one that both senses and knows is the difference between a creature that cannot plan for the future, and one that can. Intelligence allows for a better chance of survival. In the same way, society which is founded on human cooperation and feelings of sympathy functions solely for the sake of individual survival, and assures the latter much better than if such feelings did not exist. Because of this interpretation of society as a means to the end of individual survival, Spencer was sharply critical of any attempt to make the state of paramount importance in human life. Spencer was a committed individualist in his ethics and his politics, and opposed almost any kind of attempt to use the State for the purpose of modifying the course of evolution. Spencer's own ethical theory was a version of utilitarianism borrowed from Mill and others.

Spencer granted to Kant the fact that science is concerned with appearances. But he argued that Kant's edifice of forms of sensibility (such as space and time), and the categories of the understanding were all quite mistaken. What we know of space and time, for example, we know because of our organismic interaction with reality. In the end, Spencer granted that beyond the realm of what is known and knowable (science), there is the Unknowable. This distinction roughly corresponds to Kant's distinction between phenomena and noumena. But Spencer was adamant that beyond science we know nothing at all; the utlimate nature of reality is beyond the capacity of any mind. Hence Spencer is quite agnostic about all religious doctrines, even atheism, and he was generally rather critical of the impact of Christianity, except in ethics, since Christianity has largely impeded the development of science.

While Spencer has not been perceived as a very profound philosopher, it is undeniable that his influence was significant.

Main works: Essays on Education (1861); First Principles (1862); Principles of Biology (1864-7); Principles of Psychology (1870-2); Principles of Sociology, 3 volumes (1876-96); Principles of Ethics (1879-1893); Man Versus the State (1884); The Study of Sociology (published posthumously).

F. FRIEDRICH NIETZSCHE (1844-1900)

Just as Schopenhauer launched a rather lonely and isolated protest against Hegel in the first half of the 19th century, so Nietzsche launched a rather lonely and isolated protest against Schopenhauer. Nietzsche learned much from Schopenhauer; yet in the end, like the world-weary music of Wagner, Schopenhauer's philosophy struck him as a symptom of the disease of the age, a disease whose roots stretched back into the history of Western civilization.

Nietzsche's view was dominated, like Schopenhauer's, with the realization that all reality is will. Nietzsche added: the will-to-power.

This will-to-power is a constant becoming, a constant strife and conflict. With respect to this will-to-power, there are two types of human beings: the first are the Masters or Uebermenschen, the second are the Slaves. The Masters are those whose wills say Yes to Life in an ecstatic self-affirmation; the Slaves are those who say No to life. The Masters are physically and intellectually superior, not by reason of race or genetics, but by the will-to-power. The slaves are those who are physically weak, exhausted with life itself.

Because they are exhausted and weak, slaves naturally must band together into "herds" for their own self-protection. They become paranoid of all outsiders and of all who seem to be stronger than they. Their gut reaction to the strong is one of revenge. This revenge or hatred manifests itself in two culturally important ways.

The first is the notion of an otherworldly God who has created heaven for the weak and hell for the strong. Before this God all are equal. Nietzsche holds thus that religion is an invention of the lower or weaker elements in society to topple the stronger or higher elements. This theory is diametrically opposed to Marx!

Nietzsche proclaimed that God was dead. It was not that he (Nietzsche) was anxious to promote atheism, but that he felt no one really believed in God anymore. He found that most members of his society continued going to Church every Sunday without really considering the vacuum in their hearts and minds.

Even though Christianity and God were culturally dead, Nietzsche knew that the Slaves still held on. The second form of revenge against the strong was the notion of morality. Morality itself had originated in Judaism and Christianity. Yet it continued to linger on even among so-called atheists. Morality is a system of beliefs whereby life is condemned for what it should have been and wasn't. Closely related to the survival of morality is the spread of egalitarianism and democracy. All of these phenomena threatened to obliterate the true masters from the face of the earth.

But who are these Masters? The Master is one who affirms Life, even to the point of willing that everything that has happened should happen again and again, an infinite number of times. This eternal repetition Nietzsche called the doctrine of the Eternal Recurrence, and it was an explicit attempt to revive a pagan conception of time drastically opposed to the Christian conception of time as a straight line, with a beginning, middle, and end.

The Master is one who creates his own values, and does not submit to the values of others. Love is one of the highest values, but has nothing to do with the Christian version of it. Christian love is a desire to satisfy someone else's need and thereby embarrass and humiliate them; or it is a desire to find someone else to satisfy one's own need. In either case,

Christianity assumes that love is founded on need, and therefore weakness. By contrast, Nietzsche understands love as a gracious outpouring to another, not based on anyone's need to love or be loved.

Nietzsche offers a curious verbal portrait of the Master. He says that he has the appearance of Caesar with the soul of Chist. It was in this way that he attempted to portray the absolute goodness and absolute power of the Master. Nietzsche's philosophy affirmed the will triumphantly, in a way that would have sickened Schopenhauer. Nietzsche considered Schopenhauer the last of the Christians, entirely preoccupied with hatred of this life. Yet Nietzsche always paid great homage to the man who had taught him the primacy of the notion of will.

Main works: The Birth of Tragedy (1872); Thoughts Out of Season (including "David Strauss, The Confessor and Writer"; "Of the Use and Disadvantage of History for Life"; "Schopenhauer as Educator"; "Richard Wagner in Bayreuth") (1873-6); Human, All-too-human (1878); The Dawn of Day (1881); The Gay Science (1882); Thus Spoke Zarathustra (1885); Beyond Good and Evil (1886); On the Genealogy of Morals (1887); The Case of Wagner (1888); The Twilight of the Idols (1889); The Antichrist (1895); Nietzsche contra Wagner (1895); Ecce Homo (1908); The Will to Power (selections from Nietzsche's notebooks).

CHAPTER 7

20TH CENTURY RUSSIAN AND EUROPEAN PHILOSOPHY

A. INTRODUCTION

There is a well known Chinese curse that says: "May you live in interesting times!" The 20th century, now coming to an end, has proved to be unusually interesting. A number of developments have occurred which have driven almost everyone to more and more radical stances.

The extraordinary developments in science and technology are certainly important. We are all quite familiar with the rapid advances in medicine, biology, and physics. Philosophically, two things are noteworthy: the first is the challenge to the familiar conception of matter, and of the universe generally. Almost overnight, the world was forced to drop the view that matter consisted of small atoms moving about in absolute space and time. We now think of the universe as energy, as more like a fluid or an ether, than like so many billiard balls. If absolute space and time gave way to relativity, so also did the time-honored view that matter was a determinate phenomenon enduring through through time. Einstein and Heisenberg changed the mind-set of a generation, and we are still feeling the shock-waves nearly 80 years later. A second noteworthy development is the expansion of the sense of time and history. The history of the our solar system, which is already known to be incredibly long, is only a small part of a much larger history—the history of a cosmos unbelievably old. The old conception of time, with a beginning, middle, and end, seems to have been set aside in favor of a sense of time which is an indefinite "middle."

The changes in science, and especially in electronics, have forced philosophers again to re-examine the time-honored questions: what do we know, and how do we know it? Even as the nature of the physical universe became increasingly a matter of metaphysics, much to the regret of empiricists everywhere, the nature of the human mind was being probed and to some extent duplicated in computers. And that too has forced us to ask with much greater urgency than Descartes: how do I know that I am not a mere machine? For that matter, how do I know that the machine is not human?

The arts underwent analogous revolutions at the beginning of the century. The music of Debussy and Stravinsky and the painting of Picasso forced everyone to reconsider not just new styles of music and painting, but just what music was, just what art was. The art of this century is philosophically provocative in a way that previous art only rarely was. Art, it seemed, is suffering from the same kind of profound anxiety that science is suffering from--the anxiety that comes when one experiences not only something genuinely novel, but genuinely disorienting.

Perhaps the most stunning development has been the progress of political life and death in this century. The century began with a war whose carnage still staggers the imagination; and it proceeded to a period of totalitarian governments whose shadow has forced everyone to reconsider the value of freedom, and the significance of the philosophies that made those experiments in terror possible. At the same time, the world has suffered the unifying impact of a planetary tendency toward mass culture and mass society, making the world a safer place for Western capitalists, in any event. In just several generations, the technology and communications potential of the Western world has rapidly spread, and been foisted upon what has come to be known as the Third World. Peoples whose life style was very remote from anything Western have been compelled to wear shoes, suits and ties, drive automobiles, and generally begin to lose their sense of cultural self-esteem, and with that their identity. The turmoil set off by the imperialistic Western economic structure may be centuries in coming to an end.

It is easy in the face of this to see only tragedy and decline. But the intellectual thought of this century has been rich and multi-faceted. After all, periods of declines are usually also periods of transition to a different world. We may have been cursed to live in a period of decline; but we have been blessed to live in a period of transition.

It may be this transitional character of the 20th century that explains why contemporary philosophy seems so fragmented, why communication among philosophers seems so impossible and unlikely. But communication takes time. It will be a while before the dust begins to settle.

The number of philosophers discussed in both this and the next chapter far exceeds that of any previous chapter. That does not necessarily mean that this is a better century for philosophy; only that (a) the reader is perhaps more likely to have run across these philosophers than others; and (b) it is just about impossible to narrow a list of 20th century philosophers, since that demands the kind of intellectual distance impossible for a contemporary to possess. It is hoped that the unwieldy length of these final chapters is balanced by their usefulness for the reader.

The 20th century philosophers discussed in this and the next chapter have been arranged into the following cultural or national groups: Russian, German, French, Southern European, British, and

American. There is no significance intended in the order. It has also been difficult to know how and where to classify certain authors. Sometimes language has been the deciding criterion, sometimes intellectual interests, sometimes geographical impact. The reader will have to bear with the present classification. The author is aware that it suffers at times from an inevitable arbitrariness.

B. RUSSIAN PHILOSOPHY

1. Introduction

The history of contemporary Russian philosophy is dominated by the impact of the Russian Revolution in 1917, and subsequently the emergence of Stalinism. Russian thought at the beginning of the 20th century was a remarkably varied and fascinating phenomenon. With the revolution, both Marxism and Russian philosophy took new directions, and many non-Marxist thinkers were forced settle in Europe or America. Some freedom of thought remained within Marxism until the advent of Stalin's Reign of Terror. Since Stalin's death in 1953, philosophical studies have been somewhat freer. But overall, Marxism has become an orthodox religion in the Soviet Union, and alternative forms of philosophical thought have not been encouraged.

2. Peter Kropotkin (1842-1921)

Kropotkin was known as the "Red Prince", because of his close connections with the aristocracy and with the Czar, and because of his subsequent espousal of what is called anarcho-communism. Besides all this, Kropotkin was one of the finest geographers and natural scientists of the 19th century, and was known as a gentleman and conscientious scholar.

Kropotkin was converted to anarchism in 1872, served time in prison, then fled to Europe where he was active in anarchist circles. Eventually he fled to England where he lived until after the Russian Revolution, when he returned to his homeland for the final time. Kropotkin initially supported the Russian Revolution, but became dismayed by what he felt were tendencies toward authoritarian domination by party and state--tendencies which the anarchists had all along felt had compromised the development of the Marxist movement.

As an anarchist, Kropotkin stressed a kind of communism based on free distribution of all produced goods. While Kropotkin wrote much to defend this kind of communism from Marxist attacks, his most famous contribution came in his attempt to show that cooperation, not competition, is the method by which the human species

99

has advanced. Humans, he argued, have always cooperated historically in helping one another to survive; and capitalism which stresses individual competition completely misreads the historical record. Kropotkin's theory was an explicit attempt to counter the individualistic interpretation of Darwinism found in writers like Spencer, and to provide a scientific foundation for anarchism, which has been the chief political alternative to Marxism in radical circles.

Main works: Paroles d'un revolte (1885); The Conquest of Bread (1892); The State, Its Part in History (1898); Fields, Factories and Workshops (1898); Memoirs of a Revolutionist (1899); Mutual Aid (1902); Modern Science and Anarchism (1912); Ethics (1922).

3. Leon Shestov (1866-1938)

Shestov was an together different kind of thinker than Kropotkin. He turned to philosophy only when he was about 30 years old. He did not leave Russia until 1922, and he spent the remaining years of his life in Europe, generally in Paris.

Shestov's position is similar to Kierkegaard's, though it was worked out independently of knowledge of the latter. Shestov is most famous for the title of his major work: Athens and Jerusalem. These two eternal cities represent two profoundly different turns of the human spirit. Athens, on the one hand, represents the triumph of theoretical reason, of the tendency to understand everything, and thus to justify everything--including evil--in rational terms. Reason can only deal with necessity, with the whole, with what is already given, and thus with what is essentially lacking in life.

By contrast, Jerusalem represents the triumph of individual human existence, the triumph of individual human creativity and freedom. The reality of evil can only be discerned in terms of this spirit, for the discernment of evil presupposes one's existential involvement in a given situation.

Shestov drew from this view a kind of religious existentialist ethic which resembles Nietzsche's in certain ways. Fundamental to this ethic is the denial of the dominance of reason in human life, of order in human life. Ethics is founded on freedom, and freedom in turn means the denial of the possibility of any complete order in things. The choice, then, is between death and life, rationalism and existentialism, Athens and Jerusalem. Shestov champions the latter alternative in each case.

Main works: The Apotheosis of Groundlessness: An Essay in Undogmatic Thought (1905); In Job's Balances (1929); Athens and

Jerusalem (1938).

4. Nicolai Berdyaev (1874-1948)

Berdyaev is one of the more famous Russian existentialists who, like Shestov, found himself quite uncomfortable with the new Soviet government and fled in 1922. And, again like Shestov, he spent most of his remaining years in Paris.

Berdyaev's views were sometimes idiosyncratic, and often syncretic. He began as an influential Marxist, but eventually converted to Russian Orthodoxy. His views were independent of Orthodox thoeology, as much as Marxism, however much he may have been influenced by either.

Berdyaev's metaphysical views were derived especially from the neoplatonist tradition. He held that a kind of division between the ultimate principle of reality and God as Creator was necessary to maintain. The ultimate principle was the Divine Nothingness, the sheer potentiality out of which all things emerge into creative existence (similar perhaps to Plotinus' notion of The One beyond Being). Besides this Divine Nothingness, there is God the Creator of being, who has absolute power over the universe (similar perhaps to Plato's Demiurge). Now this theory explains the dualistic split in human nature. On the one hand, humans are free, and in their freedom, they experience the depth of indeter- mination or Divine Nothingness. On the other hand, humans are free to create, and in that freedom learn the difference between good and evil, which is created by God. But just as God aims to create even beyond morals, so humans must learn to seek the ground of good and evil, which is God. The original sin, Berdyaev argues ironically, was not a fall away from God, but a fall toward God through the knowledge of good and evil.

Three kinds of ethics are distinguished: (a) the Ethics of Law. This is an ethic of primary use for the masses, the herd. It is an inevitable reality, but it is the lowest form of ethic. Second (b) there is the Ethics of Redemption. This is an ethic based upon the grace of God. Such an ethic participates in God's grace, and is thus aristocratic and strong. It thus transcends the herd. (There are clear overtones here of Berdyaev's indebted- ness to Nietzsche). Finally (c) there is the Ethics of Creative- ness. Creativeness rests upon freedom, but transcends the ethic of grace. Its goal is to create a community through love as a kind of radiating energy. The goal of such a love is not merely the good, but the beautiful. Thus an emphasis upon individuality is balanced off with an emphasis on the community. The former element Berdyaev attributes to Nietzsche and to Christianity; the latter to Russian orthodox theology, which lays great emphasis upon the community.

101

The primacy of the community led Berdyaev to denounce both capitalism and Marxism. Capitalism and Marxism both champion the ownership of property; they differ only on the question of whether ownership should be private or public. But all ownership is contrary to the ethic of Creativeness, for Berdyaev. His argument is simply that all things belong to God, not to humans. Christian socialism is the only view consistent with this fundamental thesis. Christian socialism entails the abolition of the Hegelian and Marxist and Capitalist Master-Slave relations. It is not, for all that, an ethic which levels society to the lowest common denominator. The Ethic of Redemption resists just such a levelling. So in the end, Berdyaev's Christian socialism was an uneasy mixture of radical egalitarianism, and Nietzschean individualism. It is easy to see why his views did not please the ideologues. Despite this, he was very influential on the development of existentialism in Europe and America.

Main works: The Philosophy of Freedom (1911); The Meaning of Creativeness (1916); The Philosophy of Inequality (1923); The Meaning of History (1923); The Destiny of Man (1931); The Self and the World of Objects (1934); Spirit and Reality (1937); Solitude and Society (1938); Man's Slavery and Freedom (1939); An Essay in Eschatological Metaphysics (1947).

5. N. O. Lossky (1870-1965)

Lossky stayed on in Russia after the revolution, but he was finally expelled in 1922 because of his religious beliefs. He emigrated to Czechoslovakia; then emigrated again in 1946 to New York City where he lived until his death.

Lossky's philosophy is a strongly religious metaphysics, much influenced by Bergson and especially Leibniz. Lossky argues that the foundations of knowledge are discovered in the phenomenon of intuition. There are essentially three kinds of intuition, which correspond to three types of objects. There is, first of all, sensory intuition of other material bodies in space and time. Second, there is intellectual intuition of such phenomena as relations between things and mathematical qualities. Third, there is mystical intuition of the Absolute or God.

Lossky finds that each of these different kinds of intuition discloses a different realm of being and suggests some important aspects of being. In the first place, each kind of intuition discloses a relation between subject and object. Secondly, the disclosure of material objects reveals that each object is a monad unto itself, causally distinct and unrelated to any other object or subject. But third, each material object reveals an immanent presence in the subject. The latter is especially revealed by

102

intellectual intuition, through which all objects are discovered to be united by universal relations and mathematical qualities. Finally, each subject is revealed to be united with all other subjects in sympathy and love, bound together in a community of mutual presence.

The mystical intuition of the Absolute or God is an intuition of that Being whose creative power accounts for this ultimate unity of things in plurality. Lossky's conception of God is classically theistic, emphasizing God's otherness, which is essential, he argues, to any notion of freedom. But God is not merely transcendently other; he is also immanent to the universe as the source of being and creative energy.

Lossky's ethics centers on the purposive use of human freedom to achieve an ideal nature. Thus for Lossky sin and evil arise primarily when one loses creativity, that is, when one turns in freedom away from God, from the unity of the world, and the community of human spirits. All creativity presupposes independence; but simultaneously it seeks to realize perfection by creating a self that is bound by love to others.

Main works: The Fundamental Doctrines of Psychology from the Point of View of Voluntarism (1903); The Foundations of Intuitivism (1906); The Intuitive Basis of Knowledge (1919); The World As an Organic Whole (1917); The Fundamental Problems of Epistemology (1919); Freedom of Will (1927); Value and Existence (1931); Sensuous, Intellectual and Mystical Intuition (1938); The Conditions of the Absolute Good (1944).

6. The Development of Russian Marxism Before the Revolution

Marxism's early development before World War I is enormously important in explaining especially the development of Russian Marxism as a movement. Marxism had been dominated by its German founders, and remained largely German until the war. Marxists had generally argued that if a war broke out, it would be a war among European capitalists, and they therefore concluded that it would be in the best interest of the workers everywhere to join together and to refuse to fight. This did not happen. The radical left collapsed in the face of war, in part because of persistent internal bickering and disagreements in the years preceeding the outbreak of hostilities. The first and second "Internationals"-- essentially European workers' parties--had been dominated by Germans. The third International would be dominated by Russia, and with that, Marxism as a movement changed significantly. While open disagreement was common before the Russian Revolution, the Marxist movement became increasingly intolerant as time went by.

Two early thinkers helped pave the road toward a properly

103

"Russian" Marxism—Plekhanov and Lenin.

Georgii V. Plekhanov (1856-1918) joined other Russian radicals in his early years. With time, Russian radicals began to split into a multitude of various groups, ranging from the most extreme Marxists to others who were simply reformists. Plekhanov became associated with Lenin in the foundation of the Russian Social-Democratic Labor Party. When this party began to disintegrate into Bolshevik and Menshevik factions, Plekhanov supported the latter. Over the years he moved closer to Lenin for a time, then broke permanently with the revolution.

Plekhanov's philosophical contribution lay in attempting to show how Marxism was a consistent philosophical system, clearly superior to previous philosophical systems. Plekhanov argued that dialectical materialism is the only position that can avoid the pitfalls of both materialism and idealism. However, Plekhanov became famous for his assertion that matter existed outside the human mind, and that a certain philosophical "faith" was required for this. This view was sharply attacked by Lenin for its "Humean" overtones.

Plekhanov also tried to illumine the relation between matter and spirit. He proposed several theories, the last of which was that spirit was simply the subjective or internal process of matter in motion.

Plekhanov's defense of dialectical materialism tended toward the metaphysical at times, but his discussion of these and other issues, despite his break with Lenin, often became the locus classicus for further discussion among Russian Marxists. His popularity has wavered in the Soviet Union, but he is still regarded as the "father" of Russian Marxism.

Main works: Socialism and the Political Struggle (1883); Our Disagreements (1885); Anarchism and Socialism (1895); In Defense of Materialism: The Development of the Monist View of History (1895); Essays in the History of Materialism (1896); Criticism of Our Critics (1906); Fundamental Problems of Marxism (1908); From Defense to Attack (1910).

V. I. Lenin (1870-1924) was at first sympathetic with general leftist trends in Czarist Russia. It was only in 1890 that he read Marx and Plekhanov. His involvement with the movement increased, and finally he was arrested and exiled to Siberia in 1897. From 1900 to 1917 he lived abroad. From 1903 onward, he was the leader of the Bolshevik faction of the Social Democratic Labor Party. It should be remembered that the Bolsheviks assumed power in 1917 after the Mensheviks had taken control of the government.

Lenin's earliest writings were defenses of Marxism against Russian populism. One of his most important early works is What Is To Be Done?, written in 1902. In that work, Lenin emphasized the importance of a centralized, disciplined party membership, as opposed to the usual Marxist view of a group of intellectuals supporting a labor movement in the attempt to take power in a revolution. The turn here is very significant. Marxism, up until this time, had been largely a workers' movement, in effect a kind of international labor union. The taking of power was envisioned as the workers' taking of power from the elite. Lenin changed all this. The reason for Lenin's viewpoint is clear: there was little development of capitalism in Russia at that time, and hence few proletariat in the modern sense. The result was that, practically speaking, if there was to be a revolution, it almost certainly could not be carried off by Russian workers. (It should be remembered, of course, that Marxism denied the peasants any meaningful role in the revolution, since the revolution was dictated by contradiction within capitalism, and the peasants are a hold-over from feudalism.) In any event, the centrality of the Communist party, its distinctness from the workers, and the conception of a revolution in terms of a small closely-knit group of revolutionaries, was novel in Marxism, and was undoubtedly Lenin's major contribution.

Lenin also wrote tracts analyzing European imperalism and the role of the state in the revolution. Lenin was clear that a dictatorship of the proletariat would last for a brief period of time during the transition from feudalism to Marxism. A short time after the revolution, there would remain no government but only "the administration of things"—or bureaucracy, as some have interpreted it. Lenin's actual rise to power demonstrated how unrealistic these claims were. As we know now, the "dictatorship of the proletariat" had to create the proletariat, indeed had to create an industrial society. The withering away of the state has not happened, though the state has become enormously bureaucratic.

Lenin also wrote on more abstract matters, his Materialism and Empirio-Criticism and his posthumously published Notebooks being of chief interest. The first work, in particular, was directed against all forms of scientific positivism in an attempt to show that Marxism was realistic and materialistic in its metaphysical commitments.

Lenin's work was based heavily on the writings of Engels and of Marx' later works. Marx' early writings, which show such extensive dependence on Hegel, were not available to the public at this time. The publication of those early writings later in the 20th century would change the interpretation of Marx considerably outside the Soviet Union. The result is that, today at least,

Marx as understood within the Soviet Union, and Marx as understood in Europe and America, are two different matters.

Main works: What Is To Be Done? (1902); One Step Forward, Two Steps Back (1904); Materialism and Empirio-Criticism (1909); Imperialism, the Highest Stage of Capitalism (1916); State and Revolution (1918); Philosophical Notebooks (1914-6; published posthumously).

7. Heterodox Marxism Before Stalin

Two philosophers in particular well demonstrate the range of Marxist thought in the early years of the Revolution.

A. A. Bogdanov (1873-1928) was one of the philosophers that Lenin had attacked in his Materialism and Empirio-Criticism. Bogdanov had been heavily influenced by Kant, and argued that the characteristics of physical objects were in effect collectively defined by the mind. Space, time, and causality were structures of the collectivity by which the objective physical world was organized. Bogdanov did not doubt the reality of the physical world; but his point was that objective knowledge of that world was a function of collectivity, and not of private individual experience.

Bogdanov distinguished, as did Kant, between categorical moral imperatives and hypothetical or instrumental imperatives. Kant had argued that only the former were genuinely moral or ethical. Bogdanov showed that the "fetishism" of categorical imperatives was a function of the capitalist mentality, and that under socialism all imperatives are hypothetical or instrumental. If one asks what the ultimate goal of humankind is, the goal which is to justify all hypothetical imperatives, Bogdanov replies that it is the integrity, the "wholeness" of the human species.

Main works: Empiriomonism: Articles on Philosophy (1904-6); A Philosophy of Living Experience (1912).

A. V. Lunacharski (1875-1933) was a self-styled "Nietzschean Marxist." He served as the Commissar for Education between 1917 and 1929. Lunacharski argued for a distinction between macrophysical individualism and microphysical individualism. The former conceives the Nietzschean Overman as a collective person living beyond morality, as the subject of artistic creativity, as supremely free. The latter conceives the Overman as an individual with the same characteristics. The latter view is, of course, Nietzsche's, while the former is the heart of Lunacharski's interpretation of Socialism.

Lunacharski also attempted to interpret this macrophysical

106

individualism in a way which was compatible with the Russian orthodox emphasis on the religious value of the community. Thus Lunacharski argued that the macrophysical individual is the basis for the creation of a new religion--the final religion to replace all others. This new Religion of Humanity demands that every socialist "build God"--that every socialist recognize the interconnection of all things, the profound importance of the future, and the religious demands placed on the individual socialist. In this way, Lunacharski hoped for an emerging socialist culture which would rival previous religions.

Main works: "On the Question of Valuation" (1904); "The Problem of Idealism" (1903); Fundamental Principles of Positive Aesthetics (1904); R. Avenarius: "Critique of Pure Experience" (1905); "The Future of Religion" (1907); "Once More on the Theater and Socialism" (1909).

8. Philosophy Under Stalin

Beginning in 1929, various Soviet cultural institutions and the government under Stalin's direction tightened its grip on intellectual life. It was formally declared that while philosophical truth may be a function of the interests of the proletariat, for all practical purposes only the party, and more particularly the Central Committee, knows those interests, and hence philosophers should serve the aim of proclaiming the truth of the party. As Stalin began to purge and subsequently destroy even the party itself, it became clear that truth was a function of Stalin himself, not even of the party.

The result was predictably devastating. Many philosophers were declared enemies of the people for so-called "deviations" that are difficult for anyone then or now to understand. An example will suffice. One of the most famous of the philosophers in the early years of the Revolution was A. M. Deborin (1881-1963). Deborin had at one time been a Bolshevik, then a Menshevik. In 1917, he changed his mind again, and in 1928 he was accepted into the party. Deborin was a mediocre philosopher; his chief contribution was an attack on mechanism and positivism. He insisted that Marx' philosophy was rooted in Hegelian dialectics, and that the "heresies" in question were non-dialectical. All of this was quite orthodox Marxism and Leninism. However, under Stalin an attack on mechanism and positivism was deemed "un-Marxist", and Deborin was labelled a "Menschevizing idealist"--whatever that means. The effect was that Deborin, in order to survive, became an orthodox Stalinist. After Stalin's death in the early 1950's, Deborin returned to his previous views, this time unhampered by the government. The rejuvenation of philosophical studies after Stalin has been widespread, though the tendency is always toward the orthodox line. Originality of thought is lacking, but there are many who have contributed toward Marxist interpretations of Western philosophers, and many of the latter--including the works of Hume and Kant for example--have been translated into Russian for the first time.

C. GERMAN PHILOSOPHY

1. Introduction

German philosophy in the twentieth century has been dominated by two markedly original thinkers: Husserl and Wittgenstein. The former developed phenomenology as a philosophical method; the latter developed first logical positivism, then later philosophical or linguistic analysis. It is significant perhaps that the influence of Wittgenstein has been largely in Britain and America, while that of Husserl has been dominant on the Continent. Both philosophers were deeply dissatisfied with previous philosophy; but where Wittgenstein sought to "let the fly out of the bottle" or untie philosophical knots, Husserl seemed more concerned with tieing up knots that had been left loose. Husserl's project was to save philosophy, while Wittgestein's was to avoid it. But it was perhaps typical of the Germans that whatever they ultimately thought about philosophy, they took it very seriously. In many respects German philosophy has been as fruitful in this century as in the last.

2. Edmund Husserl (1859-1938)

Husserl began his training as a mathematician, and only came to philosophy later. The sciences, it seemed to him, provided no ultimate certainty. For science dealt with natural objects and their relations, or with the "natural" ego (as in the science of psychology)--and all of these were contingent in nature. No absolutely certain knowledge could be had about contingent existence. A source of absolute certainty had to be found, in which all science could be grounded. Husserl was obsessively concerned with developing this perfect science, which he called phenomenology.

Husserl proposed a method for procuring this absolutely certain knowledge. This method is called "epoche" or "bracketing". The ordinary natural contingent existence of a thing must be bracketed out or put into parentheses, as it were, and consciousness must focus attention on the essence of the object. In this way consciousness changes its standpoint with regard to the object and thus reduces it from its natural state to its essential state.

Now the essence of an object has meaning; but the meaning of something is always something posited by some mind or ego. Thus

108

one should say that essences are posited or intended by consciousness. The notion of the "intentionality" of consciousness simply refers to the fact that consciousness intuits or constitutes the essential meanings of the object.   As a consequence the essences of objects are within consciousness; natural objects are, by contrast, beyond or outside the natural ego.

What is it that knows these essences?   Obviously it is not the natural ego.   What must be done is to perform the "epoche" or "reduction" on the natural ego; the result is what Husserl calls the "transcendental ego". The transcendental ego is to the natural ego what essences are to natural objects.   The transcendental ego differs from essences in that the former actively constitutes the latter, but the reverse cannot be said to be true.

Husserl hoped to establish a science of essences within the transcendental ego or consciousness. In many ways, this resembles previous forms of idealism (recall Plotinus' notion of Mind or Nous), except that it is proposed here as a method rather than as a dogmatic assertion.   In his later years, Husserl proposed that this science of essences would be founded upon a community of transcendental egos; and he became more concerned with the roots of the phenomenological quest in an understanding of history itself.

Husserl applied the method of phenomenology to a number of different problems.   But he always expected that his students would do most of the actual application, while he would remain largely concerned with the theoretical elaboration of the method itself.   Some of his finest students, however, turned out to be less than faithful to his methodology, as will be seen.   In any case, phenomenology has proven to be a strong philosophical movement in the 20th century.

Main works: Philosophy of Arithmetic (1891); Logical Investigations (1900-1); Ideas--General Introduction to Pure Phenomenology (Volume 1, 1913; Volumes 2-3 published posthumously); Formal and Transcendental Logic (1929); Cartesian Meditations (1950); The Crisis of European Sciences (1954).

3. Max Scheler (1874-1928)

Scheler was for a time the most famous phenomenologist after Husserl.   However, Scheler's interests and temperament were quite different from those of the founder of phenomenology, and this became more evident in Scheler's later years.

Scheler's early interest in phenomenology was primarily put to use in formulating a comprehensive theory of ethics. He argued that values were the grounds of emotion or feeling, and were thus a priori. A value is the object of every aspiration; the end of humankind is the realization of values, not some particular material content such as pleasure or knowledge. A value by nature is always found in the end of human aspiration. The end is to be distinguished from any imagined aim or purpose; for the end is inherent in the aspiration, whether it is consciously thought or not. In any event, having demarcated the realm of values, Scheler goes on to use a version of phenomenology for classifying and studying their essences and their various interconnections. His investigation yields a hierarchy of values, from those of mere sensibility (the values of pleasantness or unpleasantness) to those concerned with what is holy.

Scheler was much influenced by Nietzsche and wrote several works, one on Ressentiment and the other on The Nature of Sympathy, that combine his Nietzschean perspective with his phenomenological concerns.

Scheler's interests increasingly turned away from phenomenology and toward a sociology of knowledge and eventually a kind of ontology. His last work, essentially unfinished, was Man's Place in Nature, and in it he outlined the foundations of this ontology. He distinguished a number of levels of human existence. There is (1) the undifferentiated vital impulse or drive, unconscious by nature. This vital impulse is marked by its totally outward orientation, and by its lack of inwardness. This vital impulse is the source of all other human energy. (2) There is that behavior of the organism which is purposive for the whole organism, and which operates to help the species of that organism to survive. This purposive behavior is instinctual. (3) The third level of human existence is that of associative behavior, or memory. This is made possible by the separation of the sensory system of the organism from the motor system. (4) There is the level of practical intelligence, of spontaneous problem solving. (5) Finally there is the level of spirit, whose ontological status is intrinsically different from the previous four levels. Spirit, in essence, is free from nature; is fully conscious and thus capable of objectifying the world; is capable of abstracting essence from existence, and thus of performing the phenomenological method; and most of all spirit is personal.

Spirit's very life energy depends on the vital impulse. Yet spirit uses this energy to say no to life and the world, by distancing itself from both. Thus spirit is both dependent on nature and relatively independent of it.

Earlier in his career, Scheler had been strongly committed to Christian theism. However in this last work he proposed a rather different viewpoint. He argued that the goal of history is the growing interpenetration of spirit and life, and that that interpenetration would create God.   This process is one of self-deification, and it was a truth, Scheler believed, which only the courageous could bear. The religious mind, he argued, objectified God into something finished, and thereby promoted passivity and childishness.   His view of God, by contrast, demanded that humans courageously seek to spiritualize nature, and thereby realize the highest values.

Main works: Ressentiment (1912); Formalism in Ethics and the Material Value Ethics, 2 vols. (1913-6); On the Eternal in Man (1921); Toward a Sociology of Knowledge (1924); The Place of Man in the Cosmos (1928); Philosophical Perspectives (1929); The Nature of Sympathy (1931).

4. Martin Buber (1878-1965)

Few works have had more widespread influence on what has come to be called "existentialist" thought as Buber's 1923 I and Thou. The latter work certainly has the "feel" of an application of phenomenology, but in fact it was conceived quite apart from Husserl's philosophy.

Buber emphasized a more poetic form of thinking about reality than was ordinary in traditional philosophy.   Essentially there were two kinds of "words" spoken by humans, that is, two ways of thinking about reality.   There is the word "I-Thou" spoken by a whole being in relation; and there is the word "I-It" spoken by a fragmentary or partial being, distanced from other beings.   The "I" of each of these is distinctly different. The "I" of "I-Thou" is in relation to the other, while the "I" of "I-It" is an ego which is either experiencing or using the "it" or "object".   The "I-Thou" inevitably degenerates into an "I-It"; but Buber's em-phasis was on the former because modern civilization is built on the "I-It" and threatens to deny the very possibility of genuine relation with the other.   Traditional philosophy and metaphysics centered almost entirely on the "I-It" relation; only in the poetic-religious experience of the Thou does one realize that true being is in relation, not in a subject or an object.

Buber understood that each of these two "primal words" could be spoken between (a) humans and nature; (b) one human and another; and (c) humans and the divine.   He thus emphasized re-covering a sense of Nature as a Thou; and he pointed out how religion often ends up being concerned with a relation between the ego and God conceived as an infinite Object.   Again, any genuine relation with God must be founded upon the "I-Thou" relation. Relations among humans always degenerate into the "I-It", but the latter alone is not enough for a truly human life. When the other person becomes an "It", the other becomes a "he" or "she" who is experienced as an object, and thus available to be used for some purpose or other. If one comes to believe that the other is just an "It", it is possible to end up either defending a kind of radical individualism which denies the existence of any Thou, or a kind of radical socialism which denies the existence of an "I" outside the "I-It". Buber came to espouse a kind of religious socialism, consistent with his "I-Thou" perspective, and reminiscent of the spirit of the Jewish kibbutzim, which he very much admired.

Main works: I and Thou (1922); Paths in Utopia (1949); Eclipse of God (1952); Good and Evil (1953); Between Man and Man (1955); The Knowledge of Man (1965).

5. Karl Jaspers (1883-1969)

Jaspers' philosophy represents an attempt to translate Kantianism into the language of existentialism. Jaspers began by giving a kind of universal name to the totality of being or reality: "The Encompassing". The Encompassing is experienced as (a) what we are; and (b) what the world is. Furthermore, The Encompassing is experienced as within experience, that is, as immanent; and it is experienced as extending beyond experience, that is, as transcendent. The distinction between the immanent and transcendent aspects of experience are reminiscent of Kant's distinction between appearances and things-in-themselves. But there are some important differences in Jaspers' philosophy.

If we look first of all at our experience of the Encompassing insofar as we are identical with it, we realize that there are a number of different levels that must be distinguished. Jaspers argues that one may live at the purely natural level, where everything is a means to the end that one is. A second way of living is by an orientation toward "consciousness in general", that is, toward the foundation of all science and morality in the consciousness of the human species. A third way is through Geist or Spirit, which is the source of the free organizing creativity that makes thought possible and which is the source of all social organization and wholeness.

Each of these three modes of life represents a fundamental option, and there is no necessary movement from one to another. All of this resembles Kierkegaard to some extent. But all three of these modes of life are immanent within the Encompassing. Only with the mode of life called "Existenz" is the Encompassing experienced as going beyond the determinations of life as it appears. "Existenz" refers to the moral center of the individual. It is experienced in ultimate situations, or as a result of a breakdown in existential communication. The notion of "Existenz" is very similar to Heidegger's notion of authenticity, but Jaspers was preoccupied with the centrality of the moral task in his

112

conception of "Existenz", whereas Heidegger's authenticity was conceived as more fundamental than morality. It is of some importance that after World War II, Jaspers changed his emphasis from "Existenz" to "Reason", partly in response to the accusation that existentialists were guilty of the same kind of nihilism that was promoted by the Nazis.

The Encompassing is also experienced as the world (immanently). In this regard, the study of the way in which the world appears is what is called science. But the world is also experienced as pointing beyond itself. To that extent one may speak of "Transcendenz" at the horizon of the world; that is, there is the persistent experience that what is extends beyond in some vague way whatever the world appears to be, and thereby gives the world its meaning. This is, of course, by analogy with "Existenz", which has a similar role with respect to human life. Another name for "Transcendenz" is God. In the nature of the case, there cannot be any proof for the existence of God; but the reality of the Divine expresses the fact that the world is more than can be spoken of scientifically.

Main works: General Psychopathology (1913); The Psychology of World-Views (1919); Man in the Modern Age (1932); Philosophy, 3 volumes (1932); Existenzphilosophie (1938); Truth and Symbol (1947); The Perennial Scope of Philosophy (1948); The Origin and Goal of History (1949); Reason and Anti-reason in Our Time (1950); The Way to Wisdom (1951); Tragedy Is Not Enough (1952); Reason and Existenz (1955); The Future of Mankind (1957).

6. Martin Heidegger (1889-1976)

Heidegger · was closely associated with phenomenology in his earlier years, and was largely regarded as one of Husserl's more promising students. Yet Heidegger remained independent of Husserl's emphasis on method. The one question that dominated Heidegger's entire philosophy was this: what is the meaning of Being? While Heidegger never really answered that question, his approach to the question underwent some profound changes.

His great work, Being and Time (1927), was ostensibly an application of phenomenological method to the meaning of human existence. Heidegger says at the outset of this work that the meaning of Being can only be discussed if one first asks about the meaning of the human being and the beings in this world. A human being is fundamentally a being-in-the-world. This world is constituted with objects for use and objects merely "present". Heidegger argues that objects for use are more primordial in our experience of the world, than objects that are merely "there". All worldly objects are originally part of a network of meaning and purposes relative to being-in-the-world; whereas the

113

experience of a mere object that is "just there" is of something that has been wrenched away from this primordial network.

Another component of human existence is being-with-others and being-with-oneself. Being-with-others can be ordinary, everyday-like, inauthentic; or it can be authentic, extra-ordinary. For the most part living with others is inauthentic, however. The same can be said of being-with-oneself--it may be authentic or inauthentic. To be-with-oneself authentically is a function of one's encounter with one's own death, which is experienced as that possbility which outstrips all other possibilities. If the essence of human being is to care for a world, for others, for oneself, then the basis of care is precisely the fact that we exist facing our own death. In this relation toward death, we have a clue to the nature of human existence: it is temporality, time--not the inauthentic clock-time of science, but the authentic, lived, meaningful time of the human being, that makes human nature to be that of care. For to experience death is only possible if the past and the future and the present are "ecstatic"--reaching out toward one another in a unity of experience. By contrast, the usual or scientific notion of time is of moments each of which is disconnected from the next.

In the mid-1930's, Heidegger's outlook underwent considerable change, influenced in part by his examination of the philosophy of Nietzsche. The question of the meaning of Being remained overwhelmingly important: but he came to criticize the method of approach he had chosen in **Being and Time.** That approach, and the approach of much of the history of philosophy, was too much indebted to the Nietzschean will-to-power. This same will-to-power stood behind contemporary science, technology, and philosophy. The meaning of Being cannot be uncovered until this will-to-power is renounced. But this is difficult since Western philosophy has from its beginning been infected by this will-to-power, by a conviction that human being or reason or will is at the center of the interpretation of being.

Heidegger claims that Being is again "turning toward" humanity today; and that humanity must abandon all "calculative" ways of thinking and learn to let Being speak through language. Poetic language that thinks is the authentic approach toward Being, not technical metaphysics. Heidegger, in emphasizing the unusual and the non-ordinary modes of speech, stands diametrically opposed to Wittgenstein's philosophy of ordinary language. For Heidegger, not all language is ordinary at all. And all ordinary language receives its meaning from poetic language.

Heidegger emphasizes more the correct approach to Being than he does any final answer to the question about the meaning of Being. Indeed, his later writings, which have often been labeled

114

"mystical", never answer the question. Heidegger apparently thought it enough that he should raise the question in the proper way. For in his view, the entire course of Western civilization might depend on the answers given to the question.

Main works: Being and Time (1927); Kant and the Problem of Metaphysics (1929); What Is Metaphysics? (1929); On the Essence of Truth (1943); Letter on Humanism (1949); An Introduction to Metaphysics (1953); What Is Called Thinking? (1954); Question of Being (1955); What Is Philosophy? (1956); Identity and Difference (1957); Gelassenheit (1959); On the Way to Language (1959); The Question of the Thing (1962).

7. Gyorgy Lukacs (1885-1971)

Lukacs was an Hungarian philosopher, but he is included among the Germans since that was the language in which he wrote. Lukacs is perhaps the most famous and important Marxist of this century; but he is a curiosity in that the work for which he is most famous, History and Class Consciousness (1923), was repudiated by him and by the Soviet regime. It has had a considerable impact on Marxism in Europe, however.

Lukacs, almost a decade before the publication of Marx' youthful writings which show the latter's dependence on Hegel, offered an interpretation of Marxist dialectics which emphasized Marx' Hegelian connections. Lukacs, who was by training a literary critic, developed a theoretical perspective which would allow him to interpret works of art from a Marxist perspective.

Lukacs argued that dialectical theory presumed a standpoint where subject and object were ultimately identical. That is, dialectics rested on the premise of Totality, within which any "fact" must be understood. The insistence by naturalists, empiricists, and literary realists that objects, or nature, or facts simply exist apart from any reference to the totality is borne of the capitalist mentality whereby objects are subjectified (they become fetishes; e.g., the automobile) and subjects are objectified (the proletariat becomes a mere thing for the ends of the capitalist). In capitalist society, the true nature of either subject or object is veiled by reason of capitalist exploitation, and thus it is thought that subject and object exist independently of each other. This apparent independence of subject and object is what makes empiricism, naturalism, and literary realism possible, for all these latter phenomena presume that it is not necessary to refer to the totality of social conditions in order to explain or understand the phenomenon in question. Thus Lukacs criticizes empiricists who argue that facts exist independently of the human social consciousness; naturalists who argue that the natural world can be understood

115

apart from the social world, and that the social can be derived from the natural; and literary realists who believe that the function of art is simply to "represent" reality, where "reality" has no connection with human consciousness.

That subject and object are dialectically united is known primarily and solely through the consciousness of that class which is simultaneously both subject and object, i.e., the proletariat. The communist party is the chief representative of that class, and it is the duty of the intellectual to pay heed to the party. Lukacs generally remained in favor with the Communists, in part because he towed the party line rather carefully, even under Stalin. However, he did take part in the Hungarian uprising (which he survived); and he has endured the condemnation of his early works by the Soviet government, with which, of course, he claimed to have agreed. But it is perhaps significant that his best work may well be the one that he and the Soviet government would least like to remember.

Main works: History and Class Consciousness (1923); Studies in European Realism (1948); Existentialism or Marxism? (1951); The Historical Novel (1962); The Meaning of Contemporary Realism (1963).

8. Ludwig Wittgenstein (1889-1951)

One of the most curious figures in 20th century philosophy is Ludwig Wittgenstein, who by all accounts was ill at ease with academic life, and spent much of his life doing odd jobs quite unrelated to his talents. Yet Wittgenstein single-handedly changed the course of philosophy twice during his lifetime, a remarkable achievement given the rarity of his published works. Wittgenstein's philosophy, both the early and the later periods, centered around the problem of language; he was among the first to make language itself the key to the solution of all philosophical problems.

In his earlier work Tractatus Logico-philosophicus (1922), Wittgenstein elaborated his famous picture-theory of language. This theory assumed that language is made up of groups of propositions, ultimately composed of names. Language, like reality, was not infinitely divisible; the fundamental indivisible language-units or names referred to fundamental objects in the world. Propositions referring to objects had to be composed of such names arranged in a way that "pictured" the arrangement of objects being referred to—hence the "picture theory" of language. Any meaningful proposition, that is any proposition that could be verified or falsified, could ultimately be reduced to names which pictured reality. Any proposition which could not be so reduced was meaningless. The latter would apparently include both ethical and metaphysical statements. Wittgenstein's elegant defense of this view came to be known as logical atomism or logical positivism. Wittgenstein's views heavily influenced the so-called "Vienna circle"--a group of logical positivists which included (more or less loosely) both Carnap and Ayer--though Wittgenstein was never really very close to the group.

While the logical positivists were genuinely enthused about the Tractatus, they were rather distressed when Wittgenstein hinted near the end of the work that metaphysical, theological, and ethical propositions were not merely meaningless, but were in fact the "mystical" manifesting itself. Wittgenstein insisted, of course, that the realm of the mystical was that about which nothing could properly be said, and that silence was more appropriate than anything else. But what precisely did this mean? Wittgenstein's rather curious preoccupation with the "mystical" struck the other positivists as strange, to say the least. Wittgenstein at this point was almost certainly under the influence of philosophers who were not much appreciated by the positivists--notably Schopenhauer and Kierkegaard. It is the latter's emphasis, in particular, on the silence that obtains between the individual of faith and God, that may well have directly influenced Wittgenstein. (Wittgenstein's mysticism was almost certainly moral, not religious, however.) But in the Tractatus itself there is not a hint of what Wittgenstein meant by the "mystical"--all of which could only enhance his status as a "cult" figure of sorts.

In his much later, and equally well known, work, Philosophical Investigations (posthumously published in 1953), Wittgenstein subjected his Tractatus to much criticism, and in general took a rather different perspective on language. He complained that in his earlier Tractatus he had been dictating how language should be used, and not really describing how it was used. For ordinary language is like a game of chess, and words are like the pieces; to play the game, one must know the rules. There are many different kinds of language games: giving orders, describing an object, reporting an event, making up a story, guessing riddles, translating, praying, and so forth. We must learn how to play each of these: for the rules are different in each case. The model of language used in the Tractatus was essentially scientific description; but this is only one form of language, and a relatively unimportant one at that. Philosophical problems might best be unravelled not by the tactics announced in the Tractatus, but by seeing how they are generated by those who do not know the proper rules for the use of language.

If language is conceived as a kind of "play", it is even more fundamentally a form of life. Language helps people to live and specifically to live in different kinds of ways. Thus scientific language is one form of life, conversational language is another, ethical language is another. In this way, Wittgenstein hoped to resolve all the puzzles about metaphysical, theological, and ethical language that appeared in his earlier work. Needless to say, not all positivists or analysts were much taken with this point of view. Yet positivism has declined in importance since the 1950's, while Wittgenstein's later "ordinary language" philosophy, or "linguistic analysis", as it is sometimes called, has steadily gained in importance.

Main works: Tractatus Logico-philosophicus (1922); Philosophical Investigations (1953); Remarks on the Foundations of Mathematics (1956); The Blue and Brown Books (1958); Notebooks 1914-1916 (1961).

9. Rudolf Carnap (1891-1970)

Carnap began his philosophical career as a member of the Vienna Circle, under the influence of Bertrand Russell and Wittgenstein's Tractatus. Under pressure from the Nazis, he moved to the U.S. in 1935 where he remained for the rest of his life. Thus much of his work was published in English, but he is included here because of his connections with Wittgenstein, and because he is the sole German representative of the Vienna Circle chosen for discussion.

Carnap was first, last, and always a logical positivist. He held, on the one hand, to an empiricist theory of truth, and to a strong emphasis on the importance of logic and mathematics in the clarification of the meaning of sentences. The basic principle of logical positivism, as Carnap worked it out, was that any statement about some knowable object could be reduced to a statement about observable qualities (a scientific "protocol" statement), and then empirically tested for truth or falsity. Any statement that could not be so reduced and tested was meaningless, and therefore not about any knowable object. There are two aspects of this procedure: the first, a method of reducing one proposition to another more basic one; the second, a theory of the empirical meaning of sentences. The first is called the reducibility thesis; the second the verifiability thesis.

An example may help to clarify the matter. The statement, "The king of France is bald", if it is meaningful, should be reducible to some other more basic statement, such as, "There is one and only one x such that x is the King of France, and if x is the King of France, then x is bald." The major difference between the second and the first proposition is that the first proposition is logically misleading since it sounds as though there exists a king of France; the second proposition is much

118

clearer since it explicitly states that the connection between being the King of France and being bald is contingent upon their being a King of France in the first place. This method of reduction was first championed by Bertrand Russell; it is at the heart of Wittgenstein's Tractatus, and Carnap also championed it.

While Carnap also insisted on both the reducibility thesis and the verifiability thesis, the attempt to reduce statements through logic to forms which could be empirically tested was not altogether successful. Basically Carnap and the other positivists moved from a strict interpretation of both theses, to an admission that neither thesis could be taken narrowly without yielding absurd results. Some of the complications can be seen in the sentence given above. It is easy enough, more or less, to get an idea of how "bald" is reducible to a set of observations; but how would one reduce the phrase "the King of France", even assuming there is one, to such a set of observations? While it might not seem impossible in principle, it is almost certainly impossible in practice. The problems, in any case, plagued positivism throughout its philosophical heyday.

Carnap's belief was that philosophy was the logic of the sciences, and in his later works he turned more and more to semantics, the study of the general conditions of meaning and truth, to clarify the nature of logic. One of his most ardent beliefs was that logical positivism and its philosophical program could show how metaphysics, ethics, and the like were made up of propositions that were not meaningful or testable in any fashion. Thus philosophy could be purified of pseudo-problems, such as the relation between mind and body, or God and the world, in favor of clarifying the nature of scientific knowledge. Carnap and the Vienna Circle thus stood poles apart from the philosophy of Heidegger and existentialism, which Carnap attacked as incoherent nonsense masquerading as meaningful communication.

Main works: Der Logische Aufbau der Welt (1928); Logical Syntax of Language (1937); Philosophy and Logical Syntax (1935); Foundations of Logic and Mathematics (1939); Introduction to Semantics (1942); Formalization of Logic (1943); Meaning and Necessity (1947); Logical Foundations of Probability (1950); The Continuum of Inductive Methods (1952).

10. Recent German Philosophy

Contemporary German philosophy has been dominated by two outstanding thinkers: Hans-Georg Gadamer and Juergen Habermas. While there are certainly links between the two thinkers (notably Heidegger), they are generally divergent in their concerns, the first preoccupied initially with aesthetics, the second with politics.

Hans-Georg Gadamer's (1900-   ) Truth and Method (1960) is
one of the most important contemporary works concerned with what
has come to be called "hermeneutics". Hermeneutics is today that
discipline which is concerned with the interpretation of literary
texts. Gadamer's work was one of the first recent works which
undertook a full-scale theory of hermeneutics.

Gadamer's point of view is hinted at in the very title of
his book. Truth, which is the aim of a hermeneutical investigation, is set off against method. Every method, as applied to the
meaning of a literary text, is an attempt to determine beforehand
what shall appear as true, as meaningful. But what the literary
text really says can only be understood if one lets the text
appear as it is, and that implies the radical negation of every
methodical approach.

Gadamer is critical of the standpoint of modern aesthetics.
That standpoint emphasizes the distance between the subject confronting the text, and the text, or work of art, as the object.
This approach assumes that the truth or meaning of the work of
art is a consequence of the subject who approaches that work of
art. This, of course, makes the meaning of the work of art
fundamentally subjectivist. Gadamer opposes to this an aesthetics which relies not on the distance between subject and
object, but on the dialectical interplay between the two, such
that the truth or meaning of the work of art is never simply a
function of the subject confronting it.

The work of art, Gadamer argues, is a revelation of a world
in itself, inhabiting both its own place and its own temporality.
The meaning of the work of art distances itself both from the
subjectivity of the author of that work, and the intepreter of
that work. Gadamer acknowledges the possibility and need for re-
constructing the world of the author, out of which the art work
emerged. But he insists that this is a subordinate task in
hermeneutics, and not at the heart of it. For the meaning of a
literary text or work of art is not a function of the author--it
is always other than that, or more than that.

The relationship between the interpreter and the text is one
of dialectical questioning. The interpreter addresses or questions the text, and in a very real way the text questions the
interpreter. Each, as it were, brings its own historical tradition in which it stands to this questioning, and each is questioned by the other. Through this interplay of interpreter and
text, the truth of the text is allowed to emerge. The interpreter's task is to listen to the text, not to dictate to it.
This demands that the interpreter cease thinking of language
simply as a medium to be used calculatingly in order to get some

result. Rather, language must be understood primarily as a disclosure of the text. It is language which speaks through the text; and language creates the world in which the interpreter participates. Thus to understand or interpret the text one must be radically open to the text and to the historical and linguistic traditions which speak in it.

Gadamer's theory was not just a theory of aesthetic appreciation. For hermeneutics was at the heart of all understanding whatever, not just the understanding of works of art. It is for this reason that Gadamer's theory is of interest for philosophy generally.

Main works: Plato's Dialectical Ethic: Phenomenological Interpretation of the "Philebus" (1931); Plato and the Poets (1934); Folk and History in Herder's Thought (1941); The Problem of Historical Consciousness (1959); Truth and Method (1960); Kleine Schriften, 3 volumes (1967).

Juergen Habermas (1929-) is a good example of the transformation of Marxist thought outside the Soviet Union. Habermas' concerns generally fall within the Marxist tradition, but Habermas is extremely critical of some of Marx' most important theses--especially the belief in economic determinism. Indeed, for Habermas the chief crisis affecting the modern world is not the conflict between Marxist East and Capitalist West, but the conflict generated by the failure to develop a new form of culture based on communication.

Habermas distinguishes between rational-purposive behavior and communicative behavior. The former has been strongly emphasized as the key to understanding both capitalism and communism. The difficulty, for Habermas, is recognizing and understanding the limits of rational-purposive behavior. For human beings demand not just rational control and power in order to realize human potentiality; they also need a political arena in which a maximum of communication makes possible a revelation of the interests of each individual. The fundamental limit of rational-purposive behavior, then, is communicative behavior. The latter is needed both by capitalist and non-capitalist societies; the crisis is not merely one that is felt by the proletariat, a typical Marxist claim, by one that is perceived throughout all contemporary industrialized societies.

Much of Habermas' writing is concerned with unmasking those social and cultural conditions which impede the development of communicative behavior. In this respect, it is important to note the social and cultural context of all communicative behavior, which Habermas says occurs in speech acts. Speech acts convey more than merely what is overtly said; for speech acts are also said in a certain way, in a certain cultural context. The full meaning of the speech act includes more, then, than simply an account of the spoken words. No scientific account of language or of speech acts offers a viable way of interpreting communication. For in the nature of the case, every speech act varies from one situation to another, and so no universal laws of meaning can ever be specified.

That which impedes communicative behavior most sharply in modern society is not just distorted communication, but systematically distorted communication. One of the most important aspects of the latter is ideology, science being one of the most important ideologies of our time. An ideology is by nature a belief system which distorts reality. Science does this by accepting uncritically a distinction between facts and values, and then ruling out the significance of asking about this very distinction. But communication is not possible unless one asks about the connection between this set of "facts" and the values of those who perceive them.

Thus Habermas points to a new epoch in history, an epoch determined by the existence of an ideal speech community, a community wherein communication is facilitated by the recognition of the limitations of rational-purpose behavior and ideology.

Main works: Toward a Rational Society: Student Protest, Science, and Politics (1970); Knowledge and Human Interests (1971); Theory and Practice (1973); Legitimation Crisis (1975); Communication and the Evolution of Society (1979); The Theory of Communicative Action, 2 volumes (1983).

D. FRENCH PHILOSOPHY

1. Introduction

French philosophy in the first part of the 20th century was dominated by an interest in the phenomenon of evolutionary change. Few thinkers were so honored as Henri Bergson, who combined elements of Nietzscheanism and Darwinism into a philosophy based on the primacy of life, viz. "vitalism". An interesting off-shoot of this vitalist philosophy was the political thought of Georges Sorel.

Contemporaneous with this development was the emergence of two of the more important Catholic philosophers of the century: Maritain and Marcel. Both were influenced, in varying degrees, by Bergson, the former negatively, the latter positively. But both represented an important attempt to discuss and elaborate a kind of religious philosophy compatible with Catholicism on the one hand, and accessible to contemporary concerns on the other. Within Catholicism Maritain was regarded as the more traditional thinker, Marcel as more idiosyncratic.

Twentieth century French philosophy has virtually been identified in recent years with "existentialism", a philosophy which stresses the centrality and dynamics of human existence. Sartre, de Beauvoir, Camus, and Merleau-Ponty have all been of extraordinary importance.

Recent French philosophers have turned away from Sartre and de Beauvoir to some extent and turned toward Nietzsche and toward the structuralism of social thinkers such as Durkheim and Levi-Strauss. These developments have some points of comparison with recent German philosophers such as Gadamer and Habermas, though the French are considerably more independent in their thinking.

2. The Vitalists

Two philosophers will be discussed under this heading: Henri Bergson and Georges Sorel. Bergson was one of the most respected philosophers in the Western world in the first part of the century, but his fame has declined steeply since then. Sorel was not superficially concerned with the same sorts of issues as Bergson, but his political philosophy was deeply indebted to Bergson.

<u>Henri Bergson</u> (1859-1941) was a gifted writer as well as philosopher. He attempted to resolve many of the traditional philosophical problems (e.g., realism vs. idealism, mechanism vs. teleology) by situating them within the context of evolutionary biology. Bergson argued that the fundamental philosophical category was not some kind of static reality, such as unchanging being, but life. Life by nature is marked by an <u>elan vital</u>, a movement toward greater external complexity (the metaphysical principle of matter) and a movement toward greater internal concentration (the metaphysical principle of mind). In the human species, two mental faculties testify to two very different metaphysical interests: intellect which is oriented toward the static concept of being, toward matter, and space; and intuition which is oriented toward the dynamic reality of becoming, toward life, and time. While traditional philosophy had assumed that intellect was superior to intuition, Bergson insists that intellect's function is entirely pragmatic, not theoretical; its function is to help us survive. By contrast, intuition is the only cognitive function by which we are able to get a glimpse of reality for what it is. And what is revealed in intuition is constant change, duration. Human freedom is related not so much to intellect as to intuition. Bergson understood the foundation of science to be intellect, while the foundation of philosophy

was intuition.

Bergson formulated an ethical and religious theory based more or less on this distinction between intellect and intuition, between the static and the dynamic. According to Bergson, there are two types of moral systems. A closed moral system functions to preserve the social status quo, even at the cost of the individual, and to preserve the social group, even at the cost of all humankind. In this respect, closed morality is a morality of the group, and is neither individual nor universal. By contrast, an open morality is founded upon the principle of life, of creative love and freedom. It is intensely inward, and constantly seeks to see universal humankind beyond the group. For Bergson, the crucial question was not which morality one would live with, but which was more fundamental. It is clear that open morality is superior to closed morality. The reader should note the evident relation between this theory and Nietzsche's belief in a morality of masters vs. a morality of slaves (or the herd). Nietzsche, in fact, was a major source of Bergson's overall intepretation of philosophical issues.

Bergson's theory of religion is quite similar to this ethical theory. He distinguishes again between static and dynamic religion. Static religion seeks to neutralize the intellectual activity of the individual by singing "lullabies" to the believer--lullabies in the form of intellectual myths. Such myths prevent the individual from thinking or developing. By contrast, dynamic religion is founded not on intellectual activity, but on dynamic mysticism. Mysticism is a phenomenon in which the individual is attuned to the life impulse; it occurs only in unusual individuals (again, this reminds one of Nietzsche's Overmen vs. the herd). It is the mystical experience which provides evidence for belief in God (no intellectual argument is possible) and for belief in immortality. Bergson came to believe that the founder of Christianity was a mystic in the sense in which he understood it, and that Christianity was the crystallization of mysticism.

Main works: Time and Free Will: An Essay on the Immediate Data of Consciousness (1889); Matter and Memory (1896); Laughter: An Essay on the Meaning of the Comic (1900); Introduction to Metaphysics (1903); Creative Evolution (1907); Mind-Energy (1919); Duration and Simultaneity (1922); The Two Sources of Morality and Religion (1932); The Creative Mind.

Georges Sorel (1847-1922) was a political theorist who claimed to be a Marxist, but who had more influence on the development of non-Marxist political philosophies. Sorel was an admirer of both Bergson and Nietzsche, and championed a Marxism freed of the corruption of intellectualizing party members.

Specifically, Sorel argued that many Marxists had succumbed to an interpretation of dialectical theory which led to determinism, and an interpretation of Marxism generally which emphasized its rationality. Sorel argued that Marxism was not a deterministic theory, and was not wedded to the canons of capitalist rationality. Rather, he opposed to the intellectualistic interpretation of Marxism an intepretation of revolutionary action as spontaneous, as founded on revolutionary myth, and as carried out by producers, not by the party composed of intellectual elite. In this respect, Sorel emphasized the importance of violence (his most important work is entitled Reflections on Violence [1908]), rather than planned action. In all of this one can see Bergson's emphasis on intuition and freedom as superior to intellection. Moreover, Sorel identified the proletariat as the Overmen predicted by Nietzsche. This meant that the revolution was not a revolution by the poor against the rich, by the have-nots against the haves, but by those producing social goods, who carry out the revolution for its own sake and not for some ulterior purpose.

Sorel had virtually no influence on Marxism, but he did influence Mussolini and the Fascists, as well as later anarchists, and political radicals such as Sartre and Frantz Fanon.

Main works: Essay on Church and State (1902); Introduction to the Modern Economy (1903); Reflections on Violence (1908); The Illusions of Progress (1908); The Decomposition of Marxism (1908); Materials for a Theory of the Proletariat (1919); On the Utility of Pragmatism (1921).

3. The Catholics

Catholic philosophy was stimulated into growth at the beginning of the 20th century by a number of factors, including the growth of what has come to be known as "modernism", and especially by the revitalization of Thomism in the wake of the papal encyclical Aeterni Patris (1879). Among the French, two philosophers have been of genuine importance in this regard: Jacques Maritain and Gabriel Marcel.

Jacques Maritain (1882-1973) championed a revitalized form of Thomism, and considerably expanded Thomist philosophy into relatively undeveloped areas. Originally it was Bergson's philosophy which had liberated Maritain from positivism and personal despair, in much the same way Plotinus had liberated Augustine from materialism many centuries before. But Maritain's acceptance of Bergson waned as he became more acquainted with Aquinas.

Maritain's chief criticism of Bergson (and of other modern philosophers) was the latter's distinction between intellection which was a servant of the senses, and intuition which was in-depedent of this. The difficulty with this was that it limited the intellect to the senses, and even worse, made intuition into something altogether non-rational. Maritain insisted that intuition at its highest was intellectual and did reveal a number of metaphysical principles, specifically those principles of being enuntiated by Aristotle and Aquinas—act and potency, causality, and so forth.

Maritain probably contributed more to a Thomist epistemology than to metaphysics. In his The Degrees of Knowledge, Maritain delineated two basic divisions of knowledge, rational and supra-rational. Both kinds of knowledge are again divided into a number of subdisciplines. Fundamentally, the distinctions among the rational disciplines arise by reason of the nature or degree of abstraction from the realm of material objects. Thus, knowledge of the material realm is of three types: direct knowledge of the objects of sense perception; knowledge of the world through mathematics, (since mathematics abstracts from the quantitative features of the physical object); and metaphysical or trans-sensible knowledge (which abstracts beyond even mathematics to pure being). Direct knowledge of the objects of sense perception is of two sorts: physical science in the modern sense, and the philosophy of nature, which has to do with the fundamental principles of science.

Maritain both emphasizes the importance of mathematics in the modern view of the world, and carefully qualifies its relevance. He also insists that in the past philosophy had unwarrantedly dictated scientific conclusions; the relation, by contrast, should be one of mutual cooperation and illumination. Metaphysical knowledge has, as its intuited object, being itself, and it is in metaphysical knowledge that the philosophy of nature is rooted, unlike experimental science. Now being is itself God, but God is known through intuition only through various analogates, i.e., the world. Thus metaphysical knowledge, while knowledge of God, is knowledge of God through the reality of the world.

Beyond rational knowledge there is suprarational knowledge. This realm is governed by Christian faith, and includes theology and mysticism, as well as the beatific vision of God in the next life.

Maritain's most original thought is contained in his various works on political philosophy and the philosophy of art, for neither of which Thomists had ever been noted. Maritain argued that the notion of sovereignty had come to be fundamental for modern political philosophy, and correlative to this was the notion of absolute property in capitalism. The first idea is rooted in the belief in human autonomy with respect to God, while the second denies the fact that only God has ownership of the things of this world. The first conception culminated with totalitarianism, the second with capitalism. Totalitarianism and Capitalism are both anti-humanistic, and against both of them Maritain pitted his notion of integral humanism, founded upon the recognition of certain fundamental Christian values. Maritain argued that both Marxism and Fascism had ended up with an anti-humanist cast, because neither acknowledged the possibility of the individual's supernatural dimension as essential to the common good. Maritain's political philosophy espoused a kind of social democracy based on the notion that political society should be based on the belief that every individual has a supernatural dimension which cannot be coopted by any state; and that therefore the power of the state should be minimal rather than maximal. Maritain's arguments were a giant step forward from the traditional monarchicalism espoused by Thomists, and he had considerable influence at one time on Latin American social democratic movements. His criticism of Marxist philosophy and his open praise for American democracy earned him the lasting enmity of many other French intellectuals, however.

Maritain had much to say about the philosophy of history, especially in reaction to Marx, to Bergson's view of evolutionary biology, and to the views of the Catholic theologian Teilhard de Chardin, who was much influenced by Bergson. All three of the latter believed that the future was immanent in the past, and that the outcome of history represented a progressive development toward an ideal of some kind. Maritain argued that, while human progress had been made in many areas, it was quite mistaken to believe that it was inevitable or universal. Fundamentally, all such views were deterministic, and denied the possibility of radical change, a possibility which is affirmed at the heart of Thomism.

Maritain wrote numerous works on the philosophy of art, in which he expanded on certain key passages from Aquinas, and constructed a full-fledged theory of artistic intuition and creativity. He also wrote numerous works of art criticism which show both an appreciation for modern art, as well as a sense of Aristotelian moderation in interpreting its significance.

Main works: The Bergsonian Philosophy (1914); Art and Scholasticism (1920); The Degrees of Knowledge (1932); The Dream of Descartes (1932); A Preface to Metaphysics (1934); Philosophy of Nature (1935); Science and Wisdom (1935); True Humanism (1936); Education at the Crossroads (1943); Existence and the Existent (1947); The Person and the Common Good (1947); Man and the State (1951); The Range of Reason (1952); Approaches to God (1953); Creative Intuition in Art and Poetry (1953); On the

127

Philosophy of History (1957); _Moral Philosophy, Vol. I: An Historical and Critical Examination of the Great Systems_ (1960); _The Responsibility of the Artist_ (1960).

A second French Catholic philosopher of this period was Gabriel Marcel (1889-1973). Marcel, unlike Maritain, had little use for Thomism, and his style of philosophizing could not be more different. Marcel was an active composer and dramatist, and his best philosophical works were often in the form of journal entries. It is only his later multi-volume work _The Mystery of Being_ which attempts some kind of systematic statement of his thought. Further, Marcel has no method to espouse. His thinking is rather personal, though never merely occupied with himself.

Marcel makes a clear distinction between the perception of being as a problem to be solved vs. the perception of it as a mystery to be lived. Modern society experiences being as brokenness, as distance between the self and the world. It is in this context that "solutions" are proposed to the problem--solutions which increasingly substitute technology for people, the impersonal for the personal, and which seek to alleviate the pain of existence by leveling everything to the lowest common denominator. It is only when being is experienced as a mystery that one can begin to seek some kind of healing for modern life. To experience being as a mystery is to experience a need for transcendence, for it is only when one transcends the brokenness of the world than one can experience its hidden unity.

Two types of reflection correspond to the two perceptions of being. Primary reflection is occasioned by the brokenness in the world itself. This kind of reflection tends to regard each element in the world as totally distinct from the other. It is analytical by nature. By contrast, there is secondary reflection in which it becomes possible to see to the unity of the world. Secondary reflection presupposes the experience of the mystery of being.

This distinction is important in Marcel's various meditations on bodiliness. The experience of a distinction between my mind and my body is a function of primary reflection; in this regard I am said to _have_ a body. But I experience myself as one with my body; and this experience is known through secondary reflection. In this regard I don't _have_ a body, I _am_ my body. In a similar fashion, primary reflection emphasizes the distinction between myself and others, while secondary reflection acknowledges my essential relation to others. It is also through secondary reflection that God's presence as the ultimate mystery is experienced.

The distinction between primary and secondary reflection has

128

some analogies with Bergson's distinction between intellect and intuition. And in fact, Marcel was favorably impressed with Bergson. But he too was critical of the optimistic evolutionism of Bergson, and of the latter's theological disciple Teilhard de Chardin. For Marcel the possibility of sin was very real, and the tendency of the world was, if anything, toward external and internal catastrophe. The reason was that the modern world was created by the slave mentality, and that mentality and its effects were spreading rapidly, leveling everything in its wake, and leading simultaneously to increased collectivization and atomization of the individual. Marcel's antidote to Nietzsche's prophecy about the spread of slave morality was an existentialist interpretation of experience based loosely on Christian faith grounded in an experience of being as mystery. His philosophical vision is thus very indebted to his religious convictions.

Main works: Metaphysical Journal (1927); Being and Having (1935); Creative Fidelity (1940); Homo Viator (1945); The Philosophy of Existence (1949); The Mystery of Being, 2 volumes (1951); Men Against Humanity (1951); Problematical Man (1955); Presence and Immortality (1959); The Existential Background of Human Dignity (1963).

4. The Existentialists

French existentialism and phenomenology were much influenced by Husserl and by Heidegger's early work Being and Time. Yet there is a strongly political and often radical cast of mind among the French intellectuals that is missing from the Germans. Though Sartre and Camus quarreled about politics, both of them, as well as de Beauvoir and Merleau-Ponty, were decidedly to the left on most issues, and sometimes to the far left.

Jean-Paul Sartre (1905-1980), like Heidegger, began with a fascination for Husserlian phenomenology, but broke away from it at an early date. Husserl applied the phenomenological reduction to the natural ego and found a transcendental ego which posited the essence of objects. Sartre argued that there was no transcendental ego and that the essence or being of objects was not derived from any such ego. Sartre called the being of objects being-in-itself or simply the en-soi. This realm of being simply exists; its existence cannot be explained.

The human body, like other objects, is also en-soi. But the "I" of the human body is not an en-soi at all. We are conscious of our bodies, of other objects. This consciousness is itself freedom; and consciousness or freedom is what Sartre calls the pour-soi or being-for-itself. This pour-soi is nothingness. Nothingness is the desire to be en-soi, a desire which cannot be accomplished in any way without the annihilation of

129

consciousness.

Thus Sartre's phenomenological ontology is founded on this Cartesian dualism between being-in-itself, which cannot be other than what it is, and being-for-itself or consciousness, which only desires to be what it is not, and cannot be that.

Sartre uncovers many different ways in which consciousness strives to become en-soi. He analyzes sexual experience as precisely this desire of consciousness to be en-soi; and of course the experience is ultimately frustrating in this regard. That sexuality affords us such great pleasure and such great dissatisfaction are both grounded on the ambivalence of consciousness in its relation to the body of the other as being-in-itself.

All values, Sartre argues, are freely chosen by consciousness. Any attempt to identify values with real objects is an attempt to deny our own freedom in choosing such values. Such identification Sartre calls "bad faith". Several examples of bad faith should be noted. An attempt to explain one's values in terms of sociological determinations or economic determinations would be an example of bad faith. But so would an attempt to suggest that values are determined by God from all eternity. For Sartre, the prior existence of a God dictating all values beforehand is a grand example of bad faith and an attempt to deny one's own free choice of those values.

Sartre's theory of freedom presupposes absolute responsibility for everything; for every value in the world is subject to my choosing, and thus I am responsible for all. There is no escaping this; we are "condemned" to freedom and thus responsibility.

Another form of bad faith manifests itself in the attempt to deny the freedom of others. We are constantly guilty of this: for we very much like to categorize people by their outward behavior and actions. And we even come to expect that our friends should permanently manifest those behaviors and actions of which we approve or in which we take pleasure. But, much to our frustration, neither we nor anyone else stays the same because all of us are free beings. This is perpetually frustrating: we seek to reduce others to en-soi, but their freedom or pour-soi keeps us from doing just that. Sartre can truly say that "Hell is other people."

Like St. Augustine, Sartre admits that our hearts are restless until they rest in God; but Sartre adds that they will never rest in God without the annihilation of their freedom or consciousness. The very idea of God is the idea of perfect en-soi.

As such God is the object of all desire. To become God would entail the absolute annihilation of consciousness or pour-soi. Therefore human nature is essentially frustrated.

This notion of God, it should be pointed out, is not quite the same as the Christian notion. For this latter concept is one of a perfect en-soi endowed with absolute consciousness or freedom (pour-soi). For Sartre, this is a contradiction in terms: no such thing could exist. What Sartre calls "God", then, refers merely to the "en-soi" and not to this traditional Christian idea. Sartre remains thus an atheist.

Sartre's existentialist philosophy was worked out in his Being and Nothingness (1943). After that time his interests increasingly turned toward the political arena, and especially toward a philosophical account of Marxism which would at the same time do justice to his earlier existentialism. It was not until 1960 that the long-awaited Critique of Dialectical Reason appeared, however. In that work, Sartre attempted to surmount his prior existentialist framework, while relying on some of the same fundamental notions. Essentially, Sartre argued that the "ensemble" that constitutes society freeing itself from oppression is the proper aim of the individual, and that this liberating project is not at the same time an attempt to realize the pour-soi in a way which is impossible. The reason for this is that free political society is the only condition in which it is possible for the individual to know the limits of his or her own desire. The difficulty with capitalist society is that those limits—which are freedom—are constantly denied in fact, while upheld in theory. Only Marxism fully implies the liberation of all in both theory and practice, and thus the full development of existentialism is to be found in Marxism dialectically interpreted, that is, interpreted according to the subject-object categories that Sartre borrowed from Hegel for Being and Nothingness. Many Marxists have rejected this interpretation as gutting the whole understanding of economic determinism and dialectical materialism; and some existentialists have claimed that Sartre's notion of political society simply contradicts his earlier existentialism. But many are convinced that it effectively bridges a gap between a philosophy noted for its individualism and one that is inherently socialistic.

Main works: The Transcendence of the Ego (1936); Nausea (1938); The Emotions: Outline of a Theory (1939); The Psychology of Imagination (1940); Being and Nothingness (1943); Existentialism and Humanism (1946); Anti-semite and Jew (1946); No Exit (1947); The Flies (1947); Situations (1947-9); The Devil and the Good God (1952); Saint Genet: Actor and Martyr (1952); The Critique of Dialectical Reason (1960).

Simone de Beauvoir (1908-1986) was Sartre's life-long companion and friend. Her primary works in philosophy were an early essay on The Ethics of Ambiguity, and her later works The Second Sex and The Coming of Age. All of these rely on Sartre's existentialist position as worked out in Being and Nothingness, but all reveal a perspective distinctly different from Sartre's. Whereas Sartre emphasized the inherent frustration of the human situation, and the fundamental desire to be God—a desire which is impossible to realize, de Beauvoir emphasized the necessity of reconciling on the one hand the tendency to treat others as end-in-themselves, and on the other hand the tendency to use the other as a means to an end. In this lies the ambiguity of the human endeavor, which is at the heart of the ethical perspective she develops. Always she insists that human freedom recognize the freedom of others, no matter what action is taken; and thus there can be no attempt to evade responsibility both for what one does as well as what one does not do.

In The Second Sex de Beauvoir applied this understanding of ethics to an interpretation of the male-female relationship. She argued that women had been relegated to virtually a distinct caste, understood only as the object of male desire. Freedom for women would mean first that women themselves would have to awaken to their own freedom, and secondly that men would have to recognize that women are not merely other, not merely the object of desire, but in essential respects just as free as men themselves. The ground of this is the fact that all are free, and that every human project is one of liberation by nature. The relation between male and female is thus analogous to all other relations of oppression; and the task in this case is the same as it is in all other such relations. If women are to become free they must become like men—both subjects and objects; and thus what women are will change for men.

Main works: Pyrrhus and Cineas (1944); The Ethics of Ambiguity (1947); L'Existentialisme et la sagesse des nations (1949); The Second Sex (1949); The Coming of Age (1972).

Maurice Merleau-Ponty (1908-1961) is perhaps less well known to the public than the others discussed here, but his philosophy has had a notable impact, among phenomenologists because of its brilliant clarity. Merleau-Ponty shared many of the same sympathies as Sartre and de Beauvoir, but unlike them was concerned his entire life with the writings of Husserl.

Husserl, according to Merleau-Ponty, had insisted that the phenomenological method begin by bracketing the real world so as to allow consciousness to recognize the true essences of things. Merleau-Ponty, like Sartre, distrusted Husserl's tendency toward idealism, the tendency, that is, to seek for a foundation of the possibility of the phenomenological method in a transcendental ego of some kind. Sartre, it will be recalled, had found the source of consciousness in the world itself, in the object. Merleau-Ponty was also convinced that consciousness was inherently related to the world, and specifically to nature. But unlike Sartre who emphasized simple consciousness, Merleau-Ponty felt that what was required was an elaboration of the very structure of perception, since it was perception, that is, the body as the center of the life-world, which was the bridge to the natural world more generally. Several of his early works from the 1940's deal with the "primacy of perception" in a phenomenological account. Perception is neither simply a matter of "pure" consciousness, since all consciousness is in-a-world-through-a-body, and never pure; nor is it so many sense perceptions or sense data, as the English would have it. For perception's unity can never be explained on the basis of perceptual atoms. Rather, the unity of perception is discovered, not invented, and it is discovered as the meaning of the perceived. Meaning is not objective in a scientific sense, but it is inherent in any account of perception as lived experience.

Perception thus seems to have features of both bodiliness and consciousness, while it is neither in itself. Merleau-Ponty felt that an analysis of perception was crucial to a phenomenological account of any other human phenomenon, such as consciousness or freedom or society. His account of freedom, for example, is at the foundation of his radical Marxist beliefs; and that account stresses the ambiguity in freedom, the ambiguity in the fact that all freedom finds itself already in a situation, and thus never "pure". And every act of freedom has consequences for which one must be responsible, and this too takes away from any notion of "pure" responsibility, where the individual claims to take responsibility but denies the consequences of his or her own act.

Toward the end of his life, Merleau-Ponty shifted his concerns from perception to history and especially language, as "bridges" between consciousness and nature. Further, he suggested in the posthumously published The Visible and the Invisible that phenomenology needed to be grounded in some kind of ontology, that the distinction between perceiver and perceived needed to be rooted in some understanding of Being. But this position was not extensively developed.

Main works: The Structure of Behavior (1942); Phenomenology of Perception (1945); Humanism and Terror (1947); Sense and Non-sense (1948); Eloge de la Philosophie (1953); Adventures of the Dialectic (1955); Signs (1960); The Visible and the Invisible (1964).

Albert Camus (1913-1960) was perhaps more of a novelist than a philosopher, but his non-fiction works have had some influence over the years. Included among these latter works are The Myth of Sisyphus and The Rebel. The first is concerned with the moral problem of suicide, the second with murder. Camus considered these two questions to be the central questions of the 20th century.

Camus proposed a philosophy of the absurd in The Myth of Sisyphus. That philosophy is founded on the perception of a lack of relation between humans and their world. That is to say, human life is an experience of not being able to find ultimate meaning or happiness, when one expects to. Now to experience the absurdity of this situation it is necessary to be alive to affirm it. It follows that any attempt to deny the "lack of a fit" between human expectation and the world is an attempt to repudiate the very conditions of meaning. Suicide is one method of denying the absurd; it does this by denying life itself, and in denying life one denies the possibility of knowing the absurd. Camus concludes that suicide cannot be justified precisely because human life is absurd; suicide is the attempt, one might say, of giving meaning to life by insisting that it shall have none at all. But the philosophy of the absurd rests on the assumption that there is some meaning in life, just not any ultimate meaning. Camus even suggests an analogy between suicide and the essential tendency of the religious spirit which posits a God only to alleviate the pain of human existence. Camus' ironic reply to those who would argue that if there is no God, one should kill oneself, is that if there is no God, one should not kill oneself; and indeed that believing in God is logically closer to suicide than is atheism.

In the late 1940's and early 1950's Camus entered into a famous debate with Sartre over Marxism. Eventually that drove Camus to publish The Rebel, an attempt to criticize Marxism from the perspective of the philosophy of the absurd. Camus argued that the great historical debate with Marxism centered on the supposed justification of murder in the name of the Russian revolution. The whole point of the revolution was to make everyone free; but in the name of the revolution many were murdered, and Stalin's purges marked the acme of all this. Sartre's position was that the fundamental choice was between the Soviets and the Americans, and that however bad the Soviets might be, their aim was good, and that could not be said for the Americans. Camus replied that Marxism itself marked the advent of a philosophy which justified the rational killing of others for the sake of some end in the future. Now murder, like suicide, is an attempt to end domination or oppression, the latter being an important part of the absurdity of human life. For absurdity is experienced not just in the individual's life, but in other lives

134

as well. Murder can no more be justified than suicide, because
both violate the very nature of the condition of human absurdity.
The only proper political stance in this day is to renounce
murder, even as one continues to fight against all oppression,
political and economic, and that means renouncing Marxism, as
well renouncing all forms of capitalism. Thus Camus maintained
that the philosophy of absurdity was a philosophy based on the
value of life itself implied in the experience of absurdity, and
that value was shared by all humans. If there is no God, then
life does have a value, and one must therefore draw the line at
murder.

Camus' arguments, though engagingly formulated, have been
roundly attacked as somewhat muddy, however well intentioned.
While his general position struck some as founded upon a basic
human decency, other French leftists found his position senti-
mentalist and impractical. But the debate between Camus and
Sartre is one of the most interesting of the post-WW II era.

Main works: The Stranger (1942); The Myth of Sisyphus
(1942); The Plague (1947); The Rebel (1951); The Fall (1956).

5. Recent French Philosophy

French philosophy has, since the decline of Sartre's popu-
larity, been much under the influence of Heidegger and especially
Nietzsche, as well as sociologists such as Levi-Strauss.
Foucault and Derrida represent a new generation of French
thinkers, a generation that is rather difficult for many non-
French to understand.

Michel Foucault (1926-1984) was much influenced by French
structuralism. He took as his point of departure the understanding of social discourse, or rather, the unravelling of the
various layers and levels of meanings in social discourse. There
is no privileged social discourse: the writings of the criminal
and the sex deviant are as relevant in understanding modern
society as those of the psychiatrist and the philosopher.
Indeed, Foucault's procedure was often to illuminate the latter
with the former. Foucault's point is that no form of discourse
is self-justifying; and more generally, that every discourse that
claims to be privileged can be challenged by other forms of
discourse.

Foucault, in his various studies on the history of madness,
of medical clinics, of prisons and jails, and of sexuality,
sought to explore how since the 16th century there has come to
exist an enormous shift in the discourse concerning criminals and
the insane, among others. This shift, to put it roughly, is
toward the "idea of man", that is, toward a supposedly

135

self-justifying rational discourse, first made explicit in the Enlightenment, and now found everywhere in modern society. The purpose of this "knowledge" is to exercize control or power over others. Thus the emergence of this new "knowledge" is the emergence of newer and more effective systems of control. The object of control is defined as that which must be repressed, and repression has now become essential for the "idea of man" in its modern fulfillment.

Foucault arrived at the general position that privileged forms of discourse serve to hide from all concerned the existence of power and the use of that power to control others. What threatens power is desire; and thus it is not surprising that the modern world has been especially preoccupied with sex, which as desire threatens the established rule of power. Foucault does not believe that there is some kind of innate equilibrium between the forces of power and those of desire; to the contrary, repression of desire has become an obsession in the modern world, and with that the true nature of power has been concealed behind a mask of reason. Modern society is much more "rational", and therefore much more "anarchical", than any previous society.

Foucault's thesis was developed through a careful analysis of often obscure historical materials (not untypical of the so-called Annales school of historical research). While Foucault's "philosophy", consisting of a theory of language and a vision of the nature of society, often rises beyond his empirical evidence, some of his works address theoretical issues more directly. Foucault, it should be noted, often spoke in "millenarian" terms, expecting the West to collapse under the weight of its obsession with the repression of desire. He sides with the victims of society, but his point is not to celebrate madness. This puts him in the general position of being a leftist, but he is very far from ideological Marxism, which, like Freudianism, is too much part of the problem, and not enough of the solution.

Main works: Maladie mentale et psychologie (1954); Madness and Civilization (1961); The Birth of the Clinic (1963); The Order of Things (1966); The Archaeology of Knowledge (1969); 'I, Pierre Riviere, Having Slaughtered My Mother, My Sister and My Brother. . .' (1973); Discipline and Punish (1975); History of Sexuality (1976-   ).

Jacques Derrida (1930-   ) is one of the strangest of recent philosophers, and it is not an easy task to say just what it is he is up to. Derrida's philosophy is much influenced by the tendency toward "hermeneutical theory" in Heidegger. But Derrida takes hermeneutics one step further. That next step is called deconstruction.

Derrida's deconstruction is aimed at the literary text. One of the most fundamental claims made in the history of philosophy is that vocal speech is more fundamental than written language, in that speech provides written language with its meaning, which consists of its being expressed by speech. Speech, in turn, receives its meaning ultimately from some metaphysical foundation which guarantees its truth. Heidegger, Derrida argues, had turned attention away from the subject and toward Being in his deconstruction of philosophical texts. But Derrida wants to cut all philosophy off "at the pass", as it were, by arguing that any attempt whatever to "point to" something beyond the text cannot possibly succeed. For such pointing is itself part of a text. The meaning of any text is thus not to be found outself the realm of textuality generally. Any attempt to found the meaning of the text on the philosophical subject or object, or on something like "Being", is metaphysical by nature and inherently a delusion.

If this is the case, then the distance between philosophy and literature, for example, is no longer anything like what it has always been taken to be—and Derrida writes about both in the same way. Further, the meaning of a text is never simply in any given word. For the meaning implies metaphors which constantly point to other texts, and they in turn do the same.

Derrida's deconstruction of the truth of the text has a certain resemblance to remarks of Nietzsche which suggest that all meaning is relative because it is bound up with metaphors, analogies, and the like. Derrida has capitalized on Nietzsche's remark that truth is a woman, and used this, sometimes in a bizarre way, to show how a deconstruction of Nietzsche's texts reveals the lack of any foundational truth in Nietzsche's writing. This is by contrast with Heidegger's reading of Nietzsche, which finds in Nietzsche a theory of Truth in the sense of a theory of Being. Thus Heidegger's reading turns into metaphysics, while Derrida relentlessly wages war on such readings.

Main works: La Dissemination (1972); Marges de la philosophie (1972); Speech and Phenomena, and Other Essays on Husserl's Theory of Signs (1973); Glas (1974); Of Grammatology (1977); Writing and Difference (1978); Spurs: Nietzsche's Styles (1979); Positions (1981).

E. SOUTHERN EUROPEAN PHILOSOPHY

1. Introduction

It would be quite incorrect to think that philosophy in the 20th century was exclusively the province of northern Europe.

The development of intellectual life in southern Europe was intense, even as it often was deeply influenced by currents from the north. This is not to say that southern European philosophy was a simple consequence of the other: it was not. It would be more true to say that distinctive Spanish and Italian currents intermeshed with an emphasis on Hegel and Marx and Nietzsche, for example, and produced a synthesis that was peculiarly "Mediterranean".

2. Italian Philosophy

Benedetto Croce (1866-1952) was the most important Italian philosopher of the opening years of the 20th century, and certainly one of the most important of all in Italian history. Croce's philosophy was in part a product of Hegel's philosophy, which was having an enormous impact generally throughout Europe in the latter part of the 19th century, and in part a product of the tendency toward an emphasis on history due to the 18th century Italian philosopher of history Giambattista Vico.

Croce set forth an epistemology that was fairly simple and straight-forward. There were two ways by which the mind could grasp reality: it could grasp the individual as such, or it could grasp the relations or universals that obtained among individuals. The former was called intuition, the latter conception. Croce adds to this the distinction between two possible kinds of spiritual activity--theoretical and practical. Thus four divisions of knowledge or activity are possible: (1) theoretical intuition or art; (2) theoretical conception or logic; (3) practical intuition or economics; and (4) practical conception or morality.

Art is concerned with intuition of the sensuous particular, but because it is "theoretical" in nature it is simultaneously a synthesis of form and content. Further, the mere apprehending of theoretical intuition triggers a spiritual desire for expression. Thus Croce's philosophy of art is an attempt to balance an emphasis on both form and content. Croce's work on the theory of art has been the most frequently studied and translated of his various works.

By logic, Croce refers to the spirit's unification of subjects nad objects in propositions or judgments. Croce explores the various kinds of judgments that are possible--judgments that lie at the foundation of the sciences, of empirical knowledge, and of metaphysics and religion. Croce distinguishes between empirical knowledge per se, and modern scientific knowledge. The former deals with the objects of sense perception, which are empirical approximations, that is, more like universals than individuals in the logical sense (e.g., "cat" only approximates to the creature I perceive at the window). The latter deals with abstracted concepts that have no content (mathematics and geometry being examples). All of this leads Croce, an Hegelian, to champion a kind of positivism—perhaps one of the few to reconcile these two movements. Croce thoroughly rejects the possibility of metaphysics, since metaphysics rests on a claim to have propositional knowledge about individuals and their relations which are beyond what we could know in principle. Croce also rejects the religious mentality, which rests on myth and falsehood.

Croce's exploration of economics is strongly oriented toward the individual as the economic unit, and emphasizes utilitarian considerations as essential. Croce had been strongly influenced by Marxism in his early years, and though not orthodox, his economic doctrine is decidedly liberal.

Morality is concerned not with the individual, but with the individual's relation to the whole of society. The foundation of morality cannot be utilitarianism, for in the end the justification of the moral act must itself be grounded, and utilitarianism cannot do this. Morality, in the end, must stem from a will that is both free and conditioned. It is conditioned in that it arises out of various conditions which it cannot change; it is free insofar as through creative activity it can transcend whatever was and produce what is not.

It is with the foundation of morality that Croce turns to a fifth discipline, called simultaneously philosophy and history—the two names being used interchangeably. The movement of spirit in its theoretical and practical activities is the movement of spirit as the unity of subject and object, and as the dialectical interplay of the individual and the universal. This interplay is grounded, not in the future as Hegel might have it, but in the present. Yet the present is always aiming toward some future, a future which is not fully understood. Spirit is the name of the entire process of reality in its eternal evolution. That process aims at something, but the nature of the goal is not known. Thus Croce will not speak of an absolute spirit as Hegel will; for if absolute spirit exists, then the goal of history is known. But history is process, and philosophy is the inward knowledge of this process. History and philosophy are thus two names for the same unfolding process of the spirit.

Main works: Historical Materialism and the Economics of Karl Marx (1900); Aesthetic (1902); Logic (1905); What Is Living and What Is Dead in the Philosophy of Hegel (1907); Philosophy of the Practical (1909); History—Its Theory and Practice (1917); The Conduct of Life (1918); Politics and Morals (1922); History as the Story of Liberty (1938).

If Croce's spiritual mentor was Hegel, that of Antonio Gramsci (1891-1937) was Karl Marx. Gramsci was originally much influenced by Croce's neo-Hegelianism, but became critical of Croce as Gramsci's own commitment to Marxism became more important. Gramsci, in the years after WW I, became involved in economic and political unrest that eventually brought Mussolini to power. Gramsci himself became the head of the Communist party in Italy, or at least that section of the leftists which gave their allegiance to Lenin's new revolution in Russia. While Gramsci was away in Moscow, Mussolini took over. For a time Gransci was stranded in Russia, but then, by reason of being elected to the Italian parliament, was able to return. However, Gramsci was eventually arrested in 1926 and imprisoned until 1934. He remained in poor health, and died a few years later.

Gramsci's philosophical contribution rests on his notes during his years of imprisonment. Although Gramsci was a supporter of Lenin, his own philosophical leanings were original. Gramsci approached Marxism not from the angle of science (a la Engels) or evolution, but from the aspect of history. All knowledge, Gramsci argued, even knowledge of nature in physical science, was a branch of human history—not the other way around. Gramsci interpreted Marx as a humanist, not as a Darwinian, and thus put human history , rather than natural history, at the center of his vision of Marxism. Gramsci rejected the idea that socialism was scientific, if that latter term entailed a metaphysical commitment to materialism. For humanism, not materialism, is the heart of Marxism.

Gramsci was critical of the tendency by Marxist intellectuals to regard true doctrine as something to be instilled in the workers. Marx' philosophy entails the unity of knowledge and practice in the proletariat. This means in the first place that the source of knowledge in the Marxist movement must be in the workers. It was the task of intellectuals to give voice and shape to this knowledge, but not to assume that only intellectuals had such knowledge.

Gramsci's emphasis on the proletariat and the workers also led him to reject the notion of a revolution being waged by the party alone. A true Marxist revolution which culminates in the withering away of the state could only occur, he argued, when the revolution is itself waged not by the party but by the workers, organized into workers' councils. Ironically, Gramsci accepted Lenin's writings, but came to be more and more opposed to developments in the Soviet Union. It is no accident that Gramsci's thought has had no influence on the official Russian view of Marxism, but has had considerable influence, especially since WW II, on European and Italian communism.

140

Main works: Selections from the Prison Notebooks of Antonio
Gramsci (1971); Letters from Prison (1973); History, Philosophy
and Culture and in the Young Gramsci (1975).

3. Spanish Philosophy

There can be no doubt that Spanish philosophy in this century has been dominated by one genuinely outstanding thinker:
Ortega y Gasset (1883-1955). Ortega's thought was much influenced by the trends of his time, especially by Nietzsche. But
his philosophy was distinctively original.

Ortega was both a vitalist and a forerunner of existentialism, yet he differed from both because of his emphasis on
reason. He argued that the ultimate metaphysical category was
life, and that life by nature strove for self-realization. Now
the foremost appearance of life is human life, and that life
tends toward self-realization not in some random or hit-and-miss
way, but through a realization of its own unique perspective and
integrity.

As applied to a theory of human existence, Ortega's vitalism
entailed a denial of human nature and an extraordinary emphasis
on human history. For it is only in time, in history, that
humans become what they may. Human freedom is premised on the
lack of a pre-determined end. Ethics is grounded not on a theory
of essence, but on the authenticity with which one devotes oneself to a full self-realization.

Ortega distinguishes in his most famous work, The Revolt of
the Masses, between the individual and the social. The individual person, who is united wth others through friendship and
love and thus is not isolated, is one who takes seriously this
vocation toward self-realization. The vast majority of people—
the masses—are lazy and do not care to realize such a vocation.
Thus there is a radical inequality in society between the aristocratic individuals of talent and ambition, and the plebeian
masses who drown themselves in passivity and the chains of cus-
tom. It should be clear that the masses do make gains, that the
general tendency toward socialization is not unequivocally evil.
But those advances constantly threaten to submerge the aristocratic individuals with false ideas and ideals, and thus submerge
their higher ambition. And this must, of course, be resisted.

Ortega argued that, based on this distinction between the
individual and the social, there were fundamentally different
types of philosophy in history: the philosophy of realism and the
philosophy of idealism. Whereas in his earlier writings he
sought to transcend both, in his later work he emphasized the

141

inherent superiority of idealism over realism. The natural allies of realism—empiricism and the tyranny of common sense—are
all ways of knowing which are inherently passive and plebeian.
By contrast idealism recognizes that knowledge is essentially
active, and only the best aristocratic natures are capable of
such knowledge. All knowledge, as created by an active mind, has
a fundamental nature of being concerned with what is a priori,
with what is produced by freedom, not by sense experience. Thus
philosophy is more like a game to be played than a tedious method
of knowing the truth about reality through sense perception.

Main works: Meditations on Quixote (1914); Invertebrate
Spain (1922); The Modern Theme (1923); The Dehumanization of Art
(1925); Man and Crisis (1933); On Love (1939); Concord and
Liberty (1941); History as a System (1941); Man and People
(1957); What Is Philosopohy? (1957).

CHAPTER 8

20TH CENTURY BRITISH AND AMERICAN PHILOSOPHY

A. INTRODUCTION

Both British and American philosophy were deeply influenced by Hegelian philosophy in the 19th century, and both reacted against that influence in the opening years of the 20th century. However, idealistic currents have been dominant in some form or other in the U.S. throughout this century, while British thought has witnessed a resurrection of its long defense of a scientific empiricism. Perhaps the most important development is the later philosophy of Wittgenstein, which continues to exercise a remarkable influence on all English speaking philosophers.

B. BRITISH PHILOSOPHY

1. Francis Bradley (1846-1924)

Bradley's philosophy was part of a general wave of enthusiasm for all things Teutonic that swept over Britain's intellectual life during the heyday of the Victorian era. Bradley's position utilized elements of Hegelianism in a critique of empiricist and utilitarian views, especially those of J. S. Mill. In his major metaphysical work, Appearance and Reality, Bradley set out to show that the world of appearances, of space and time, movement and relations, was a world which was logically self-contradictory; and that only reality, lying beyond appearance, could possibly be self-consistent and thus fully real. One of Bradley's more famous arguments was against the existence of real relations. In the world of appearance, there are things which are really related to one another. Thus we say that my fingers are really related to the keyboard as I type. Let's call my fingers A and the keyboard B, and the relation between them C. Now if C is real, then A must be related to C in a real way, and B must be related to C. Let's call the relation between A and C "D", and the relation between B and C "E". But then A must be really related to D, as is C; and B must be really related to E, as is C. The reader can see where this leads. If there are real relations, then there are an infinite number of such relations, and that is tantamount to saying that there is no final relation by which one thing is related to another. And this suggests that neither of the "things" one began with are related to one another; and since they are not related they must be identical. Thus the world of apparent relations, consisting of many things each different from the next, is shown to be logically self-contradictory. Bradley's conclusion was that only a whole exists, and that any attempt to describe parts as

143

independent of that whole, and as bound together by real relations, ends up in self-contradiction.

Bradley's emphasis on the "whole" underlies his ethics as well. He argues against the individualism of Mill and others that no one can be understood apart from the society of which they are a member, and that each "individual" is in fact an expression of the whole of society. It follows that my "individual" duties are duties which derive from the whole of society and its needs. Thus morality is inherently social, not individual.

Main works: Appearance and Reality (1897); Principles of Logic (1922); Ethical Studies (1927).

2. The Reaction Against Idealism

Three figures dominated the reaction against idealism in British philosophy of the 20th century: Russell, Moore, and Ayer. What have come to be known as analytical philosophy and logical positivism emerged from this intellectual milieu.

G. E. Moore (1873-1958) was closely associated with Bertrand Russell in his earlier years, and the two of them together were the foremost exponents of this method. Moore's genius is perhaps best seen in his early work on ethics entitled Principia Ethica (1903). One of the most important points in that work is the exposition of what Moore calls "the naturalistic fallacy". Moore points out that most ethical theories traditionally have been based on some statement of the form, "The good is pleasure", "The good is reason", "The good is utility", "The good is following the moral law", and so forth. Moore argues that a statement of the form "The good is X" is not an analytical statement, where the predicate is logically contained in the subject. Rather it is always a synthetic judgment. Consequently any attempt to analytically define the good commits a logical fallacy, since there is nothing whatever with which "the good" is logically identical. The fallacy of identifying the good with any naturally observable quality is called the naturalistic fallacy. By implication the good is always something non-natural.

The question may be asked: if goodness is a non-natural quality, where is it? How is it perceived? Moore insisted that goodness was objective, and that it was discerned by what was apparently an intellectual intuition of some kind. While this theory was much criticized, it should be noted that it is remarkably similar to Plato's theory. For Plato argued that the Form of the Good was the highest of all forms and metaphysically distinct from everything else in the universe. Moore, however, did not postulate that goodness was a Platonic form or that it resided beyond or outside of this physical world.

144

Moore defended common sense realism against Bradleian idealism. He argued that "to perceive X" can mean both "to perceive an object named X", and "an act of the mind whereby X is perceived". Now the idealist assumes that these two meanings are identical. Obviously they are not identical, but different. It follows that one cannot reduce statements of perception to statements of mental acts without ignoring an essential part of the meaning of the statement. Bradley's whole philosophy rests on just such an error, according to Moore.

Moore's method amounted to careful logical analysis of claims about things. His approach is marked by rational precision, and the method of logical analysis has, in one form or another, had enormous influence on philosophical style of the English speaking world.

Main works: Principia Ethica (1903); Ethics (1912); Philosophical Studies (1922); Some Main Problems of Philosophy (1953); Philosophical Papers (1959).

Bertrand Russell (1872-1970) was an early associate with Moore in the reaction against idealism. Russell's claim to fame was largely made in the mathematical foundations of logic. It was during his most productive years just before WW I that he co-authored the Principia Mathematica with A. N. Whitehead, a work which is unquestionably one of the most important in the history of logic and mathematics. The fundamental aim of this work was to show how it was possible to reduce mathematics to logic. This meant, for example, seeing that whole numbers, such as "2", refer to classes of things, in this case to the class of all classes each of which has one thing and some thing else not identical with the first. The point of this is to show how "2" does not refer to some mystical platonic form called "twoness" but refers to classes of classes of things. In this way, one avoids any embarassing ontological questions, such as, "where in the universe can one find twoness"? Russell's tendency was always to de-mystify talk about ontologically "strange" things, such as numbers or classes. His logical theory of types is related to this effort. Thus, according to the theory of types, paradoxes result if one attempts to predicate a class of itself. The class of all white things is not itself white. To presume that it is is to treat the class of things as itself an object of some kind. Classes are made up of objects, but are not themselves objects.

Russell and Whitehead's logical system is the foundation of much of what is taught as symbolic logic today. That system is founded upon an enormously powerful symbolic notation, with a great many developed methods for translating ordinary sentences into that notation. Briefly, it was possible to symbolize (1)

145

relations of implication (if a then b, for example) whose basic units are propositions, and this part of the logic is called the propositional calculus. It was also possible to symbolize (2) the relation of quantified subjects ("some cows", for example) with predicates ("are black", for example) within a proposition (for example "There are some apples in that basket"), and this part of the logic is called quantification. An important technique within the latter is called the theory of descriptions. This theory is simply a method for reducing propositions of the form "The so-and-so" to another more fundamental form. The difficulty with propositions such as "The king of France is bald" is that one is tempted to suppose that every time one refers to "the king of France" one is referring to some kind of entity, even if there is no king of France. To avoid positing platonic forms in order to explain what is referred to when one refers to non-existent objects in the world, the theory of descriptions reduces "the king of France"--which Russell says is a description of something, rather than a name for something--to a proposition such as: "There is one and only x such that x is the King of France and x is bald." This latter sentence means the same thing as the former sentence. But it has the advantage that it clearly expresses the logical fact that the phrase "the King of France" describes some x or other, and does not name or refer to an object directly.

The logic in the Principia was intended to show how relations of implication could be reduced to relations between propositions, and how propositions could be reduced, through the theory of descriptions among other things, to statements referring to sense data, the things to which the x's and y's ultimately refer. This logic, reductionist in spirit, was taken as an indication of the nature of reality. When translated into a world-view or ontology, the theory is called logical atomism, and Russell subscribed to some version of it most of his life. According to this theory, the fundamental elements of knowledge are acquired through direct acquaintance, and these fundamental elements are the foundations of our empirical knowledge. The latter, of course, involves more complex perceptions, that is perceptions made up of various sense data. Thus we experience cows and tables as wholes made up of simpler sense data (this shade of color coupled with that given shape, etc.). These wholes, which are physical objects, are to be understood as constructed out of the more elementary sense data of which they are composed. Russell argues that both physical objects and minds are so constructed. If any proposition is to be understood ultimately, it must be reducible to these basic elements of sense data. In the end, language, whose ideal structure is announced in the logic of the Principia, is isomorphic with the world. Or more precisely, the structure of language is ismorphic with the structure of the world: for not everything that is expressible in language corresponds to anything in the world. What is needed is some technique of reduction whereby complex propositions can be ultimately reduced to sense data. That is, what is needed is an empiricist criterion of the meaning of propositions. The theory of descriptions, and the whole reductionist spirit of the Principia, are aids in attaining this epistemological goal.

With regard to ethics, Russell early on subscribed wholeheartedly to Moore's analysis of goodness in the Principia Ethica, which entailed that goodness was a non-natural property of things directly intuited. However, in time, Russell abandoned this theory for a clearly subjectivist position. He came to think that if Moore was right, ethical propositions were propositions about facts (goodness being as much a fact as tables and chairs). Now ethical propositions are really evaluations of facts, or better, expressions of emotion about various facts. Thus ethical propositions are never true or false in themselves. Most controversies in ethics are not about basic ethical propositions, but about the means one should take toward a given end, and in this respect ethics can entail rational disputes and are about facts.

Russell's social and political views underwent many changes over the years. He began as an advocate of British imperialism, but as a result of a personal quasi-religious experience in 1901, he became a moderate pacifist. He opposed British entry into WW I, and for his views he was jailed for 6 months. He favored entry into WW II, however, since Nazism was, he thought, a genuine threat. Russell advocated democratic socialism, but he was very critical of socialism in Russia after the revolution.

Russell also achieved notoriety for his moral and religious views. He rather shocked his contemporaries by advocating in Marriage and Morals the possibility that sex before marriage might not always be bad and that homosexuality should not be treated as a felony. He was constantly harassed in the U. S. in the early 1940's because of his expressed views, and he lost several positions as a result. Russell was for all practical purposes an atheist, though he usually termed himself an agnostic. His position was that the possibility of the existence of the Christian God was on an equal footing with the possibility of the existence of any other god in any other religion. It was, in short, very improbable that God should exist. He did not believe in human immortality, and he thought that on the whole religion had had a negative influence on human life and development, and that it would be a good thing if religion would eventually die out.

Main works: Philosophical Essays (1910); Principia Mathematica (1910-1913); Problems of Philosophy (1912); Our Knowledge of the External World (1914); Mysticism and Logic (1918); The Analysis of Mind (1921); The Analysis of Matter (1927); Freedom and Organization 1814-1914 (1934); Religion and

Science (1935); Power: A New Social Analysis (1938); An Inquiry Into Meaning and Truth (1940); A History of Western Philosophy (1946); Human Knowledge, Its Scope and Limits (1948); Authority and the Individual (1949); New Hopes for a Changing World (1951); Human Society in Ethics and Politics (1955); Why I Am Not a Christian (1957).

A. J. Ayer (1910-   ) was associated both with Russell's logical atomism, and with Carnap, Wittgenstein, and the so-called Vienna Circle. Ayer championed logical positivism, an attempt to combine Russell's logical discoveries with a strong orientation toward seeing philosophy as the logic of science. Perhaps Ayer's most famous work is the early Language, Truth, and Logic (1936).

Ayer says flatly that all propositions are either meaningful or meaningless. Meaningful propositions are either empirically verifiable, in which case they may be either true or false, or they are "tautologous" or "analytical." An example of the latter would be "2 + 2 = 4", or "A bachelor is an unmarried man." To use Kant's terminology, all meaningful propositions are either synthetic a posteriori or analytic a priori. Ayer vehemently rejects all synthetic a priori propositions as contradictions in term.

The vast majority of all ordinary propositions are either synthetic or analytic. But what of a metaphysical statement such as "The Absolute is neither black nor white"? While the terms "black" and "white" have meanings, it is not clear that the term "Absolute" has any meaning at all. The entire proposition must be either analytical or synthetic. Analytical propositions are always definitions or tautologies, Ayer says; but this proposition is not a definition of anything. Further "Absolute" does not refer to anything in experience, and so any statement about an "Absolute" cannot be verified as either true or false. It follows that this proposition is meaningless.

All theological propositions and metaphysical propositions containing terms which have no empirical reference are either arbitrary definitions or meaningless. Since everyone denies that they are mere definitions, it follows that theological and metaphysical propositions are meaningless.

But this is not all. All ethical propositions containing evaluative or ethical terms such as "good", "wrong", "evil", "ought", "should" and others—all such propositions are inherently meaningless since the terms have no empirical reference, and since they are clearly not intended to be definitions (it would make no sense to say that the proposition "Stealing is not good" is a definition of stealing).

Ayer admits that theological, metaphysical, and ethical pro-

148

positions have another function besides their cognitive meaning:
namely, to help an individual to emote or feel something. In
saying that such propositions are emotive Ayer is not saying that
they are propositions about emotions (since this would make them
cognitive once again), but that they are themselves expressions of
emotion and thus only pseudo-propositions.

Main works: Language, Truth and Logic (1936); The Foundations
of Empirical Knowledge (1940); The Problem of Knowledge (1956);
The Concept of a Person (1963)

3. British Realism and Idealism

Two British philosophers perhaps best characterize the
philosophical tradition that remained independent of the attack on
traditional metaphysics stemming from Russell and Ayer: Samuel
Alexander and R. G. Collingwood. Both were of importance especially in the years between the first and second world wars,
though Collingwood is more read today than Alexander.

Samuel Alexander (1859-1938) is known almost solely for his 2
volume study Space, Time and Deity (1920). This work was in the
"grand" style, inspired in part by science, and especially by
evolutionary theory. Metaphysics, whose possibility Alexander
defended, differed from science only in terms of its breadth, not
its methods. The purpose of metaphysics was to lay bare the
essential or categorial features of the world. These features
were the constants of the universe, while all other features were
variable. Alexander insisted that both the constants and the
variables were a matter of empirical discovery, and he rejected
any Kantian attempt to locate the constants in the human mind.
Thus Alexander was a metaphysical realist.

The world was fundamentally understood as composed of point-
instants, which are an abstract expression of the smallest unitary
phenomenon at a given point in space and a given instant in time.
Each point-instant is the center of a perspective, the latter
being the way in which other point-instants can be ordered or
perceived with reference to the given point-instant. Implied in
this account is the difference between the way the world appears
to a given perspective and what it actually is.

The world of material bodies that we are aware of is a world
composed of complex arrangements of point-instants--arrangements
in which all the point-instants in a spatial or temporal group
share some quality or universal characteristic. The qualities
that a given organization of point-instants can assume are conditioned in part by the complexity of the structures. But fundamentally, the world is in process, and this means that new qualities emerge which could not have been previously predicted--there

is genuine novelty in the world. These new qualities are called "emergents", and they exist in various grades of complexity throughout nature. Thus the various degress of life, sensibility, and intelligence in the plant and animal kingdom are all instances of more and more complex and unpredictable emergents. Mind is essentially a complex arrangement of point-instants: it is matter with certain emergent properties.

But this is to look at mind from an external point of view. As the center of a perspective, mind unifies the world into an historical continuity, in which our past and future are unified by reason of the present. There is, then, a close relation between mind and time, and indeed more generally between time and creative process.

Alexander's theory of Deity is also novel. Deity can refer to one of several phenomena, indeed to both. Deity in one sense simply refers to the totality of spatio-temporal reality. This would make Alexander into a pantheist, and he was not adverse to the suggestion. But a second meaning of Deity is also possible: Deity refers to the next highest emergent quality in the process of evolution. In this sense, God is about to come into existence, and this is the significance of religious experience which is more about the future than about the past or the present.

R. G. Collingwood (1889-1943) was much influenced at first by idealism, especially by Benedetto Croce and Hegel. That influence can be easily perceived in his early work Speculum Mentis (1924), which examined five types of experience for the kind and degree of truth present in each: art, religion, science, history, and philosophy. Only philosophy, in which the the subject of knowledge becomes simultaneously its object, attains anything like absolute truth. Curiously, Collingwood insisted that philosophy had no formal content: it was more like the necessary standpoint from which or by which all other pursuits of knowledge could be examined and judged. On this viewpoint, history, along with the other types of knowledge, could only attain relative truth.

Around 1928, Collingwood had a change of heart about his early work, and he began a series of historical studies, most notably the Idea of History (1946), which explored a new conception of history and philosophy. For a time he embraced a classically idealist conception of philosophy, arguing that philosophy did have a content. But more important was his revision of the task of history. Collingwood argued that his earlier judgment that history could not attain certain truth was mistaken. In judging a past historical act, one is not condemned to mere external knowledge. History has as its task the need to understand the internal thinking involved in a given historical act, so that the act can be fully understood. Now this attempt to "get inside the agent's mind" is not doomed to impossibility or to arbitrariness. Every act is involved in some historical context, and one cannot make sense of that act except by constructing the one understanding of the agent's mind that fits with all the other elements in that context, both spatial and temporal.

Collingwood's understanding of metaphysics changed once again in his later work entitled Essay on Metaphysics. Here he argued that metaphysics is founded on presuppositions which are absolute with respect to propositions derived from them, and which are not, therefore, either true or false. For one can ask about everything except presuppositions, and this implies that presuppositions are beyond questioning, and thus beyond any verification. Presuppositions do change, but they change for largely unconscious reasons. History can of course study the sequence of these changes, and relate them to the larger social context in which they occur. But it is not possible to go beyond these presuppositions to more ultimate reasons.

With this shift in his account of metaphysics, it is not surprising that Collingwood also changed his understanding of the nature of mind. For whereas he had asserted in Speculum Mentis that philosophy was grounded in the mind's ability to know itself, in his last work The New Leviathan Collingwood suggested that the mind never has itself as an immediate object, and that all knowledge always involves some kind of separation between the subject and the object. Collingwood also suggested the possibility that the whole discussion of the mind-body dualism was based on a misconception, and that a careful analysis of the language used suggested that talk about mind and talk about body revealed no conflict whatever. These views seemed to have been deeply influenced by linguistic analysis, which had come to be popular at about this time.

Collingwood's theory of historical understanding has had considerable influence. His philosophy of mind and metaphysics reflect an increasing input from not only linguistic analysts, but from logical positivists as well. Yet unlike the latter thinkers, no matter how much he was driven away from any Hegelian idealism, he never ceased thinking of history as being on an equal footing with philosophy, and in this respect he remained under the influence of Croce his whole life.

Main works: Speculum Mentis (1924); Essay on Philosophical Method (1933); The Principles of Art (1938); Essay on Metaphysics (1940); The New Leviathan (1942); Idea of Nature (1945); Idea of History (1946).

4. Recent British Philosophy

Recent philosophy in Britain has been heavily influenced by the later thought of Wittgenstein. It is very much a reaction against logical positivism, and to a considerable extent a reaction against Russell's emphasis on logical atomism. What is central in the newer tendencies is the reliance on an analysis of language in order to uncover the source of philosophical dilemmas.

The philosophy of Gilbert Ryle (1900-1976) is a notable example of this tendency. In the early 1930's, Ryle published one of the most famous papers of the linguistic analysis movement: "Systematically Misleading Expressions." In this paper, Ryle suggested that philosophical perplexities arise because of the misconstrual of the grammar of certain expressions. Thus, to give a simple example, it might be easy to think that the word "exercizing" refers to the same thing in both of the following sentences: "Exercizing is good for you"; and "Exercizing is not an adjective." Ryle suggests that many of the traditional puzzles of philosophy (for example, the mind-body dualism) arise from misconstruing the grammar of several sentences which seem identical but which are grammatically very different. In the example above, one might mistakenly think that the second sentence is grammatically identical with the first, that therefore the word "exercizing" which in the first sentence refers to some bodily activity refers to some abstract reality--such as a Platonic form--in the second sentence. The mistaken assumption is that the word "exercizing" in both cases refers to something, the truth being that reference is integral only to the first sentence.

The implications of this way of looking at the origin of philosophy in the confusion over certain grammatical structures is worked out in a striking way in what is certainly Ryle's most important and enduring work in philosophy, The Concept of Mind (1949). In this work, Ryle emphasizes especially one type of misleading expression, a type which he calls the "category mistake." Suppose a visitor from another planet asked me just what the words "city of Chicago" referred to. I proceed to show the individual the major buildings in the dowtown area, the city hall, the residential areas, the shopping malls, and so forth. But the visitor might well protest at the end of the sight-seeing trip that while many different buildings and people had been seen, the city of Chicago had nowhere been seen. This would suggest that the visitor thought that the phrase "city of Chicago" referred to something in the same way that "Napoleon" referred to a particular French leader. It is to suppose, in other words, that "city of Chicago" belonged to the same logical category as "Napoleon". In short, the visitor had made a category mistake.

One of the most famous examples of a category mistake ex-

plored at length in the Concept of Mind is that of Descartes'
distinction between body and mind. This category mistake leads to
what Ryle has called "the dogma of the ghost in the machine", the
belief that our bodies are machines inhabited by ghostly minds,
whose relations with the body are inexplicably strange. Ryle
proceeds to show that a wide range of mental phenomena can be
explained without invoking the existence of an entity called
"mind" or "soul". Basically, Ryle relies on the notion that mentality is really a kind of disposition or ability to do certain
sorts of things, and that dispositions are dispositions toward
certain behaviors. This of course is a kind of psychological
behaviorism, and Ryle's contribution goes a long way toward defending a behaviorist account of mind which avoids the pitfalls of
Cartesian dualism.

Main works: "Systematically Misleading Expressions" (1932);
The Concept of Mind (1949); Dilemmas (1954).

Another philosopher much associated with linguistic analysis
was J. L. Austin (1911-1960). Austin's published work was minimal, but his influence in Britain and America was signifiant. In
Sense and Sensibilia Austin launched a strong attack on the sense-
datum theory of logical positivists, the theory that sentences
ultimately referred to sense data. Against this view, Austin
championed the notion that language did not primarily have as its
function referring to sense data at all, and he proposed developing a science of language as a way of avoiding this and other
kinds of philosophical mistakes.

In How To Do Things With Words, Austin suggested an important
distinction between various kinds of speech acts. Some speech
acts clearly have as their intention referring to something or
other, and these are called locutionary acts. But much more
important in our language are illocutionary acts: these are acts
such as warning or informing--speech-acts whose intention is not
to refer to something, as to do something, the doing occurring
precisely in the speech act itself. Finally, there are perlocutionary acts whose meaning is to be found in what is brought about
by the saying of something, whether this is intended or not. Thus
to persuade someone is a perlocutionary act whose result may or
may not involve changing someone else's mind. It should be apparent that Austin's quarrel with formal logic was that it assumed
all too conveniently that language was fundamentally locutionary,
and it ignored the possibility that the statements actually made
in ordinary language often have little to do with truth or falsity, because their meaning has nothing to do with referring to
something. With Austin, the tension between the new philosophy of
language, and the older philosophy of language assumed by Ayer,
Carnap, Russell, and the early Wittgenstein, becomes very evident.

Main Works: Philosophical Papers (1961); Sense and Sensibilia (1962); How to Do Things with Words (1962).

A third philosopher who defended a similar position for a time was P. F. Strawson (1919-   ). In his early work Strawson attacked an idea central to Russell's theory of descriptions--namely that statements which are meaningful are either true or false. Strawson argued that a sentence such as "The king of France is bald" is meaningful, but any given statement of this in practice will be neither true nor false because the presupposition of the statement--that France has a king--does not hold. Strawson held that presupposing something was not the same as asserting that it exists or does not exist. The statement in question could only be true or false if it in fact asserted one way or the other that there was a king of France. It does not do this, so it is neither true nor false.

Strawson went on to propose a theory of language which was even more radical than Austin's. Austin had insisted on the defensibility of locutionary acts of speech--those acts which could be said to refer to something or other, despite the fact that Austin considerably downplayed the importance of such acts. However, Strawson attacked Austin even on this point, by arguing that if one analyzes the way in which the word "true" is used, one will discover that it is always used in illocutionary contexts, and thus that statements that are said to be true or false are speech acts whose meaning has to do with some activity involved in the speech act itself. Truth is not a property of a statement when that statement describes something; rather, saying that a statement is true is a linguistic convention whose meaning is to be found in that very convention.

Strawson's most famous work is called Individuals (1959), and it marks a shift away from his earlier preoccupation with linguistic philosophy. Strawson continues to write as though he was still doing linguistic analysis; but the work in question is committed straightforwardly to the defense of a certain metaphysical view of things. Strawson distinguishes at the outset between metaphysics which seeks to revise our views of reality, and metaphysics which seeks to merely describe our actual perception of reality. Generally metaphysical systems have been a mixture of both, but the classical systems of Descartes and Spinoza, for example, have been preoccupied with prescribing how we should think, rather than actually informing us how we do think. Strawson's work is explicitly descriptive, not prescriptive and thus he hopes to inject new life in the very traditional project of metaphysics even as he divorces himself from that tradition to some extent.

Strawson's metaphysical views are that there are two basic

154

particulars that constitute the world required by language: material objects enduring in space and time, and persons. The concept of a person, he argues, is that to which consciousness and physical properties can be ascribed (thus a person includes both states of consciousness and a material body). Yet persons are not "minds" as understood in classical metaphysics, and this for several reasons. First of all, a mental substance in classical metaphysics could not have as one of its properties having a material body. Secondly, a person is not a substance at all, and is not some composite substance consisting of both mind and body. Rather, the concept of a person is a concept required by our speech, which presupposes certain basic particulars (our bodies), but also presupposes certain states of consciousness. The concept of mind is thus much simpler than the concept of a person, and the latter is more fundamental than the former. Needless to say, this is one of the most discussed of Strawson's theories.

Main Works: Introduction to Logical Theory (1952); Individuals (1959).

C. AMERICAN PHILOSOPHY

1. Early Twentieth Century Philosophy

Two thinkers, each overlapping the 19th and 20th centuries, are of great importance for the development of American philosophy: Royce and Peirce. Both were influenced by German thought, the first by Hegel and the second by Kant. And both influenced one another to a degree.

Josiah Royce (1855-1916) was the foremost American idealist of the late 19th and early 20th centuries. Royce argued that the central problem of philosophy is the explanation of the connection between Being and Thought. He shows that traditional metaphysical theories such as realism and Kantianism, as well as "mysticism", fail to clarify the nature of knowledge, though each has important elements to contribute to a true account of how knowledge is possible. In the end, knowledge occurs when an idea seeks out or intends its individual object. Every idea is inherently purposive, and never merely passive: and each idea is true only if it corresponds with the one determinate individual which will make it true. Now this seemingly simple statement of the matter leads to perhaps unexpected conclusions. First of all, no idea, and for that matter, no judgment, can ever be understood in isolation from all other ideas and judgments. The sum total of all ideas and judgments that are true constitute infinite thought. Secondly, the individual object that each idea seeks can only be that determinate object which is understood precisely in relation to all the actual objects to which it is related. Thus the subject of knowledge, if there is to be knowledge at all, is an infinite knower; and the object of knowledge is infinite reality, which is determinate.

Royce insists that knowledge is not mere contemplation at all. Rather it is an active interpretation of the meaning of signs. This suggests that at the core the act of knowing is an act of willing, and Royce's general position has been described as voluntaristic.

Royce subscribed to the view that the infinite actuality was a fully determinate individual reality, and that it was made up of a plurality of individual things and persons. Royce argued strongly against Bradley's insistence that plurality is self-contradictory and that only unity characterizes reality. Royce argued instead that reality was both one and many, and that the many were required as an expression of the one.

Royce's metaphysics was closely related to his religious concerns, and the two were delicately interwoven in The Problem of Christianity. Royce championed the notion that the heart of Christianity was to be found in the doctrine of the ideal community, a community of intepretation, of love, and of loyalty. Royce did not understand the community to be static, but to involved in an on-going process of increasing intepretation or understanding, increasing love, and an increasing loyalty to the cause of the great community. Royce's ethics centered on the notion of loyalty to a cause or goal. More specifically, it was important for each in the community to not only have loyalty, but to be loyal to loyalty itself. Loyalty is founded upon free choice, but it involves the self-transcendence of the individual toward the community. Thus loyalty is the ethical equivalent of intepretation in the theory of knowledge. This theory of loyalty was taken up later by Gabriel Marcel, who was much impressed by Royce.

Main works: The Religious Aspect of Philosophy (1885); The World and the Individual (1901-2); Philosophy of Loyalty (1908); The Problem of Christianity (1913).

A second philosopher, of extraordinary to importance to the development of pragmatism, was Charles Sanders Peirce (1839-1914). Despite his usual classification as a pragmatist, Peirce was an original thinker who is not easy to classify. He was fundamentally a logician and epistemologist, and his studies of logic led him to Kant, to Duns Scotus, and to Aristotle. His development was complex, and what is summarized here is the philosophy of his mature position.

Peirce attempted to revise and systematize the categories of logic, that is, those fundamental classifications of reality that are presupposed in all judgment. He proposed three such categories, originally based on Kant's three kinds of noumenal realities (matter, mind, God). Peirce's categories were Firstness, Secondness, and Thirdness. These three categories are three kinds of possible relations between things. Peirce held that each of these three kinds of relations, which really are monadic, dyadic, and triadic relations, are irreducible to the others. Firstness or monadic relations refers to the mere perceived quality of an object as given phenomenally. Secondness refers to what Duns Scotus had called haecceitas or "thisness". Thus while Secondness refers to what is in effect the principle of individuation in reality, Firstness is by contrast general and abstract.

Thirdness, the most complex of the three categories, refers to all combinations of things, each combination presupposing minimally two things and a relation between them. Thus Thirdness includes the relations indicated in the copula of a proposition whereby subject and predicate (Secondness and Firstness) are joined in a variety of ways. These relations are objective, yet not of the same order as what is denoted by Firstness and Secondness. This suggests a close relation between Thirdness and Mind, since the essence of reason has to do with the understanding of relations. But relations are objective, not merely subjective; they are in the world, just as much as they are in the mind which makes judgments about that world. It follows that in some fashion there is an ideality to the world which is akin at least to mind. It is for this reason that Peirce's stance has been called objective idealism, or, to use Peirce's own term, "synechism", which is a position holding for the reality of relations outside the mind. To say that relations are real and objective is to say, among other things, that relations are not particulars, but general. The usual belief among nominalists has been that outside the mind there are only particulars; thus Peirce's theory is strongly anti-nominalistic.

Peirce was concerned in the end with explaining not just the types of realities, but also how the mind comes to know reality. He was deeply influenced, as were so many in the late 19th century, by Darwin and Spencer, and by the general framework of an evolutionary cosmology. Now the survival of an organism is dependent on its having certain habits that insure a successful interaction with the environment. Peirce held that the general direction of the human mind is from doubt to belief. A belief is a simply a matter of knowing how to interact with the environment; a doubt leads to belief, and the whole direction of the pursuit of scientific knowledge is toward those mental habits that represent succesful habits of the organism in its attempt to survive. It is in this regard that Peirce proposed what amounts to a pragmatic theory of the meaning of terms. That theory is simply that what is indicated in the concept of an object is the sum total of all possible habits or behaviors with regard to that object.

Peirce suggested that scientific inquiry, that is, the resolution of doubt into belief by a pragmatic delineation of the meaning of terms, was a kind of model for the development of the universe as a whole. That development went from a state of pure feeling without thought (chaos) toward a state with thought and order. Two principles governed this process: tychism (the principle that there is chance in the world) and synechism (the principle that the world is not pure chaos, but consists of individuals really related in some orderly fashion). The general tendency of evolution was from a state of undifferentiated chance events to one of increasing order. Related to this was the development of the human mind from individual unpredictability to a scientific community of inquiry possessing those habits of belief which reflect the real order of things. Chance and chaos could never be eliminated; but the direction of history and evolution was toward order and reason.

Main works: <u>The Collected Works of C. S. Peirce</u>, 8 volumes.

2. The Pragmatic Tradition in American Thought

If Peirce is often accounted the founder of pragmatism, it is William James and John Dewey who will forever be associated with this movement in the minds of most people. While its heyday was in the earlier part of this century, it continues to exercise great influence on American thought. It is for this reason the single most important movement within American philosophy as a whole.

<u>William James</u> (1842-1910), the brother of the great novelist Henry James, proposed the first extended philosophy of pragmatism in his early work, <u>The Principles of Psychology</u>. This work clearly reflects James' own preoccupation with psychological questions, but also demonstrates interests that are more fundamental than psychology in any narrow sense. James regarded metaphysics as an extension of science, and thus as a posteriori, based on experience. This claim meant that any given metaphysical belief had a meaning in terms of the consequences entailed by that belief within experience. It should be clear that experience is a fundamental category or reality for James, and that experience consists in the process of coming to know what things mean by tracing their meaning in the consequences and actions that are tied up with that belief. Every belief, no matter how apparently abstract, is a function of an experience which is always aiming at something, and always has certain interests at heart. Thus a belief that thoroughly stands apart from all practice is a contradiction in terms. Finding the meaning of a such a belief may not be easy, but there

158

is simply no other way of speaking or thinking about the meaning of a belief.

James called his theory radical empiricism, and contrasted it with both traditional empiricism and with rationalism. Rationalism, of course, rested on the notion that the meaning of fundamental metaphysical beliefs could be known apart from any practical experience at all. James could not agree with this; but neither could he accept the traditional empiricist rejection of metaphysics on the grounds that metaphysical beliefs could not be reduced to components found in sense experience. This latter approach rests on the assumption the meaning of beliefs is determinate and easily calculable in terms of sense perception. By contrast, James argued that most beliefs, especially those that are of any importance, are invariably indeterminate and forever concerned with phenomena that may be more complex than mere sense perception. James situated the pragmatic theory of belief within an evolutionary framework, and argued that those beliefs which "worked" or which were "successful" were those whose meaning was to be understood as having a function in the scheme of evolution.

James argued that the fundamental elements of human consciousness could be understood as the fundamental elements of the universe. The theory of radical empiricism was thus consistent with some kind of panpsychism, and with the view that the universe is causally indeterminate (since humans were free and not fully determined—the denial of this view being incompatible with experience). Many of these suggestions for a metaphysics based on a radical empiricism were taken up by Whitehead.

James was especially troubled by the question of religious experience, and attempted to give an account of it along pragmatic lines. He argued that religion differed from morality, and that the difference was both good and troubling. Religion reminded us of the limits of morality, of the need to get some perspective on our moral endeavors; but at the same time, it tended to weaken our commitment to moral ideals because it aimed at a reality beyond this life altogether. James was always very careful in his estimate of religious experience, and not given to simple judgments about the significance of such experience. But in the end, a religious belief's meaning can only be understood in the way any other belief is understood—in terms of its consequences within experience.

Main works: Principles of Psychology, 2 vols. (1890); The Will To Believe (1897); The Varieties of Religious Experience (1902); Pragmatism (1907); The Meaning of Truth (1909); A Pluralistic Universe (1909); Essays in Radical Empiricism (1912).

Perhaps the single most famous American philosopher of all,

and certainly one of the most prolific, was John Dewey (1859-1952). Dewey began his philosophical career as an Hegelian, but soon abandoned this for a philosophy based upon the experimental canons of scientific method. He often criticized Hegelianism, as well as other kinds of philosophical idealism, as too concerned with the human intellect as opposed to human action, and not sufficiently attuned to the importance of scientific experimentation.

Dewey's philosophy was called instrumentalism or experimentalism. Humans find themselves in problematic situations, situations that are experienced as questions and which drive them to seek resolutions to those questions. It is in this context that hypotheses and theories are developed, then publicly tested and developed. After testing, the hypotheses and theories are revised as necessary, then further testing is done. All theory is to be understood in this context; and so it is not surprising to find Dewey condemning any philosopher who seeks to remove theory from the context of pragmatic experimentation in order to determine the meaning of the theory. Theory which is cut off from practice leads to belief in an eternal reality having nothing to do with the world of change and becoming. The tendency of philosophers toward otherworldliness is thus rooted in a mistaken conception of the nature of theory. It is not surprising to find Dewey strongly critical of traditional religious beliefs for their tendency to block scientific inquiry because of convictions that are thought to take precedence to all practice and experimentation.

Dewey emphasized the importance of the community of scientists in the acquisition of knowledge. In this regard, he was much closer to Peirce's emphasis than to that of William James, whose pragmatism Dewey regarded as somewhat individualistically conceived and thus intellectually capricious.

Dewey consistently emphasized the development of logic within the context of scientific method, and disparaged the old Aristotelian logic as largely irrelevant to the process of inquiry. The same emphasis on scientific method also dominated his understanding of ethics. Dewey had no sympathy for a transcendental ethics, which gave as the reason for doing something that "it was God's will". All ethical valuations which are of the form "The good is X" should be empirically tested, and the resulting experiences compared and analyzed. Out of this experiment a new theory about ethical value might be formulated, and this could again be tested for its experiential consequences, and so forth. Ethics, in short, arose in problematic situations where values clashed head-on. The only way to resolve ethical problems was by operationalizing the values involved and then seeing which course of action resulted in a state of affairs that was more preferable. Dewey thus ridiculed the notion that ethics was simply a matter of applying values out of thin air: instead, he insisted that ethical discussion and problems arose out of troubling situations, and that the only way to resolve a situation of conflicting values was through experimentation.

It was Dewey's hope that this approach would set ethics on a new foundation and avoid certain extremes. Those extremes were that ethics was concerned with strictly eternal values, and that ethics was concerned with very transitory values (such as pleasure or enjoyment). Ethics was both rational and non-rational; non-rational insofar as it involved subjective experiences, but rational insofar as it involved the application of scientific method to the discernment of what was truly good. No final good could be reached by using this method, since every new hypothesis was capable of being refuted. Yet every hypothesis was closer to the truth than its predecessors.

Dewey's commitment to scientific inquiry pervades his theories of education and his social and political philosophy. Always he is concerned to avoid extremes, and to avoid especially the tendency to ground either the good of the classroom or the good of society in individuals as such. In both cases, Dewey emphasizes the centrality of social inquiry and experimentation for both a successful form of education and for a rational interpretation of democracy.

Main works: The School and Society (1900); Studies in Logical Theory (1903); Democracy and Education (1916); Reconstruction in Philosophy (1920); Human Nature and Conduct (1922); Experience and Nature (1929); Art as Experience (1934); A Common Faith (1934); Logic: The Theory of Inquiry (1938).

Few philosophers have had as much an impact on psychological and sociological theory as G. H. Mead (1863-1931), who developed the most elaborate pragmatist theory of the self. Mead assumed that a self was a product of the interaction of the biological organism with the environment. His account of the emergent self is in the broadest sense behavioristic. However, Mead was generally critical of those behaviorists whose analysis excluded all mentality, introspection, and purposive behavior. Rather, Mead sought to show just how mentality originated within the interaction of organism and environment.

The self, according to Mead, is organized around actions, which begin in the privacy of the organism and terminate in the environment, whereupon the process is reversed, and the consequences of the original action in the environment impede on the originating center of action in the "I". Every human action is not only an interaction with the natural environment, however, but with the social environment. It is because of this that human action is always symbolic and gestural, and never merely a passive response to an external stimulus. That an "external" action can have "internal" meaning is only possible when the self has become an object to itself. Mead carefully analyzes the various stages of the development of the self that has become an object to it-self. The "I" which is experienced directly by the organism is coupled with a "Me" which is the way "I" am perceived by some other. While the "I" is the principle of the initiation of action, the "Me" is the principle of the modification of the aim of the action in light of the perception by others. The highest point of development is when this modification is made on behalf of what Mead calls the "generalized other", that is when the other is the entire community itself.

Thus Mead's account suggests that the self presupposes both an unobservable starting-point (the "I") and a a set of behaviors that are quite observable and which have meaning both to myself and to others (the "Me"). The self is both what I do, as well as what I do.

Mead suggests that self-consciousness is a function of the development of reflexive thought, and that reflexivity in turn is a function of this interaction with the social environment, and the gradual formation of the "Me". In this way the self, and its self-consciousness, is genuinely emergent and novel, and is a function of the nature of the interaction between the organism and the environment. Of great significance to the development of self-consciousness is temporal awareness. Thus Mead points out that the self, which is rooted in the present, constantly re-evaluates its past and its future. Without this constant orientation toward time, every purposive aim at some consequence in action would lack symbolic depth and social significance. Many have found certain points of similarity between Mead and the phenomenologists and existentialists on the subject of the temporality of the self. Mead's theory also had considerable influence on Whitehead and process metaphysics.

Main works: Philosophy of the Present (1932); Mind, Self and Society (1934); Movements of Thought in the Nineteenth Century (1936); The Philosophy of the Act (1938).

C. I. Lewis (1883-1964) attempted to provide a more coherent outline of a pragmatist theory of knowledge than James had. Lewis was an eminent logician, and helped to develop the study of modal logic, which is concerned with the interrelationship of propositions of necessity and possibility—a study which was not much in favor in the period when Russell and Whitehead's Principia dominated the scene. Lewis' contributions to modal logic, which will not be discussed here, went a long way to making it an important area of study in recent years.

162

Lewis, like other pragmatists, understood knowledge to be a function of the relation of the organism to the environment. But whereas other pragmatists were captivated by the naturalistic overtones of this perspective, Lewis was first, last and always concerned with the logic of cognition. He understood that knowledge was always hypothetical and thus verifiable or confirmable. This presupposed a relation of activity between the organism and the environment, but it also presupposed some given, some sensation. Now the given which is presupposed is not itself a matter of knowledge, since there can be no error about it. Knowledge, which always involves the possibility of error and revision, presupposes a given; more particularly, it involves the relation between the concept and the given which is expressed in the variety of possible behaviors one might take with respect to what is expressed in the proposition. Thus the meaning of a given term can be found in the sum total of behaviors that one can take with respect to that term. The number of such judgments possible is indefinite, and thus there is no absolutely certain knowledge about anything beyond the given. While Lewis' position with respect to the given sounds somewhat like that of the logical atomists, the latter held that the given was known directly or immediately, while Lewis, as has been seen, denied just this point.

If knowledge always presumes a given, it involves the application of a priori concepts to experience. This application of a priori concepts is fundamentally a function of what Kant would call categories, but Lewis interpreted the doctrine of categories pragmatically. Thus a category was simply a set of behaviors whereby meaning could be given to some proposition; categories could and did change, and there was no reason to think that they were a priori or certain. Lewis did hold that there were a priori truths and disciplines concerned with these truths, but he did not think their relation to reality was automatic and absolutely certain.

In his later work An Analysis of Knowledge and Valuation (1946), Lewis went on to argue that the theory of knowledge was ultimately grounded in a theory of values. Lewis regarded values in much the same way he understood the perceptual given: values were intrinsic to experience (even if extrinsic to any propositional understanding of reality), and they were genuinely "objective", which is to say, an invariant associate of certain types of givens. Value judgments, which presuppose values, are always capable of confirmation, and are thus very much like propositional knowledge of the scientific variety. While his position is reminiscent of that of the logical positivists, Lewis always maintained that value judgments were capable of being evaluated by an appeal to experience, and thus that they had some kind of cognitive status.

Main works: A Survey of Symbolic Logic (1918); Mind and the
World-order (1929); Symbolic Logic (1932); An Analysis of
Knowledge and Valuation (1946); The Ground and Nature of the Right
(1955).

Willard Van Orman Quine (1908-   ) has not usually been considered a pragmatist, but some of Quine's most fundamental positions are much indebted to the pragmatist outlook. Quine studied
logic under Whitehead and C. I Lewis, and later associated with
Carnap and the logical positivists. With this varied background,
it was difficult for many to arrive at a clear estimation of his
own fundamental perspective until his first major book-length work
in philosophy, Word and Object (1960).

Quine first achieved fame by attacking several foundational
claims of the logical positivists and of empiricists generally.
In 1951 he published "Two Dogmas of Empiricism", which while not
abandoning a general empiricist orientation, levelled some important arguments against that very position. The first of the two
"dogmas" Quine attacked was that of the viability of the analytic-
synthetic distinction. This distinction, common from the time of
Kant to that of Carnap and linguistic philosophers such as
Strawson, was founded upon the claim that in some sentences the
predicates can be interchanged with the subject, while in others
they cannot. Quine argued that interchangeability could not be
the criterion of an analytic statement in any event, since it is
possible for two linguistic phrases to be interchanged without any
kind of identity in meaning. What is needed is some logical
criterion by which it is possible to say that this term and that
term have precisely the same meaning. Such a criterion of syn-
onymy could then be used to prove analyticity. But how would we
know that two terms are synonymous, then? The usual answer—that
they are synonymous if they are interchangeable in an analytic
statement—is clearly circular reasoning. It follows that the
distinction between analytic and synthetic statements cannot be
upheld.

The second dogma of empiricism is that the meaning of a given
statement can be reduced to sense data. Here Quine suggests that
it is quite impossible to divorce one proposition from the whole
set of propositions that constitutes philosophy and science, and
that in fact the meaningfulness of a given proposition is never
simply a function of this set of sense data.

Quine's pragmatist sentiments become more clear in his major
work Word and Object, which is in many ways an attack on
Strawson's Individuals, the latter being published only a year
before. There Quine continues and broadens his attack on the

164

analytic-synthetic distinction.　This is perhaps best seen in his theory of the indeterminacy of translation.　Quine argues that the attempt to translate the language of an isolated tribe, for example, into English can yield any number of translation guides. It is never really possible to be certain just what a given word means to the tribal speaker.　The reason for the indeterminacy of translation is, that translation involves showing how two terms are synonymous.　Now Quine had previously argued that it is quite impossible to do this without involving oneself in circular reason.　So the thesis of the indeterminacy of translation is simply another way of stating his rejection of the analytic-synthetic distinction.

Quine also addresses some broader issues in Word and Object. He argues in favor of a conception of philosophy which is sharply opposed to that of the logical positivists or traditional metaphysicians.　Philosophy, he argues, is inseparable from science, but differs from it chiefly by its breadth.　Further, it is quite impossible to distinguish between a purely descriptive metaphysics and a revisionary metaphysics, as Strawson attempts to do.　All metaphysics or ontology is "revisionary" in Strawson's sense.　And Quine, unlike the positivists, is not at all hesitant in proclaiming the inevitability of ontology as a philosophical discipline.　He holds that any particular way of speaking about the world entails certain ontological commitments, and that an ontically neutral system of language is not possible.　Further, there is no one language system or logic that fits the world exclusively: thus, Quine seems to accept a kind of ontological relativity, that is, a relativity with respect to the various ways of speaking about the world.

Main works: "On What There Is" (1948); "Two Dogmas of Empiricism" (1951); From a Logical Point of View (1953); Word and Object (1960); Ontological Relativity and Other Essays (1969); The Web of Belief, with J. S. Ullian (1970); Theories and Things (1981).

3.　American Metaphysics

George Santayana (1863-1952) was by everyone's account a man of contradictions: he was born in Spain, died in Italy, but spent the better part of his life in America; he was passionately opposed to the British and American interpretation of empiricism, but a great champion of naturalism and realism; an unbeliever critical of Catholicism, but an admirer of Catholicism all his life.

Santayana was an exponent of naturalism in his earliest years.　He understood that the human organism's mental life had to be placed in the context of a natural interaction with the

165

environment, within which the survival, the life and death, of the organism were determined. In his early 5 volume work, The Life of Reason, Santayana outlined the various activities of the human mind in its interaction with the natural environment. While he was clearly influenced by Hegel and Schopenhauer, he was adamant in this early work that he was not an idealist, since he regarded the mental as one aspect of the natural environment, and not as a fundamental principle of reality. Thus Santayana rejected any Hegelian notion that the mind's various experiences pointed toward some Absolute Idea grounding all knowledge and existence. Rather, Santayana kept a healthy respect for the pluralism of the mind's experiences, and for the notion that the human mind has no ultimate goal toward which it aspires.

Most distinctive was Santayana's understanding of the function of imagination, which lies at the base of phenomena such as art and religion. The human imagination is spontaneous and transcends the material world in its activity. However, the products of imagination in the conceptual world or the world of discourse have no innate guarantee of representing the world, that is, there is no inherent truth in imagination as such. Thus, when the imagination is unrestricted by a consideration of the real natural environment in which the human organism finds itself, it constructs an imaginary metaphysical underpinning to the world, which even provides a moral meaning to life. In this effort, religious myth is born. Religion, Santayana felt, was inherently problematic because it was a product of the mind unhampered by a consideration of the truth of the material world. Yet as a product of the imagination, religion tended of its own nature to further emphasize the importance of the imagination for human life, and in this respect religion was altogether praiseworthy. Thus one can see why Santayana, an unbeliever, persisted in his identification with Catholicism.

In his 1923 work Scepticism and Animal Faith and the works that followed, Santayana announced a new turn in his thinking, which many felt meant the abandonment of his earlier naturalism. Yet it can also be plausibly maintained that Santayana was only attempting to provide an adequate foundation for his earlier thought. The chief difficulty with the earlier position was the uncriticized belief in the existence of a material world. The question central to philosophy since Descartes had been how it was possible to know that the external world existed. The skepticism inherent in this question had to be answered, even if the human organism had a kind of "animal faith" that that world existed. But how was it possible for the human animal to even ask the question about the existence of the wo?

Santayana suggested a fourfold categorization of being: essence, matter, truth, and spirit. The realm of matter consists of those things in space and time which exist outside the human mind. Direct knowledge of matter is not possible; all knowledge is symbolic or indirect. The realm of truth is simply that realm of propositions which objectively describe the realm of matter as it actually exists. While truth is non-subjective in nature, it is also thoroughly contingent in character.

Presupposed by the notion of truth is not only a realm of material things, but a realm of essences. It is the discovery of a realm of essences, suggesting the influence of Husserl, that led many to believe that Santayana had abandoned his earlier naturalism. Santayana argued at this point that an essence is simply a general characteristic of something, and that, unlike Plato's conception, it has no moral or causal significance. Essences are instantiated in nature or matter, but as such they are timeless. The intuition of essence presupposes a transcendental consciousness which is distinct from any material reality. However, Santayana insisted that this consciousness, while at the summit of human life, is thoroughly dependent on matter for its power of intuition, such as it is. Thus Santayana's transcendental consciousness is far removed from any idealist understanding of consciousness, and there is a clear sense in which Santayana remained fundamentally a naturalist. In any event, Santayana's notion of essence and transcendental consciousness allow him to answer the question posed previously: how is it possible to doubt the existence of the natural world? It is possible because there is an ontological standpoint distinct from that natural world, that is, the standpoint of the transcendental consciousness; and because knowledge is immediately of essences which are timeless. Our knowledge of the material world is only possible because of our animal faith that there is such a world: not everything that we can intuit is true, and the only way in which truth can be known is through our interaction with the natural world.

Main works: The Sense of Beauty (1896); The Life of Reason, 5 volumes (1905-6); Scepticism and Animal Faith (1923); Realms of Being, 4 volumes (1927-1940); Dominations and Powers (1949).

A. N. Whitehead (1861-1947) was, like Santayana, born outside the U.S.; but like Santayana he had more influence on American philosophy than on European philosophy. And though Whitehead was several years older than Santayana, his influence was felt in America somewhat later than Santayana's. Whitehead first became well known as a colleague of Bertrand Russell, and coauthor with the latter of the Principia Mathematica. He was by training a mathematician, not a philosopher. Indeed Whitehead did not turn to philosophy until he went to the United States in 1924, though he had made earlier and substantive contributions to the philosophy of science and mathematics. His most developed philosophical work was Process and Reality (1929).

Perhaps the one philosopher whom Whitehead most resembles is Leibniz. Whitehead begins with an atomistic schema: he calls his atoms "actual entities" and like Leibniz' monads they are essentially living beings. Indeed, for Whitehead anything that exists must be an actual entity or some aspect of an actual entity. And just as Leibniz does not hesitate to suggest that God is a monad, so Whitehead insists that God must be understood in terms of the category of actual entity.

But beyond that, the comparison begins to fade. Leibniz' monads were windowless, self-contained beings whose relation with other monads was guaranteed only by God's priori arrangement. But Whitehead's system is based on the premise that all actual entities "feel" or "prehend" one another: indeed that that is their very nature or essence as living beings. Each actual entity begins by prehending many different features in its environment and organizing the felt data in more or less complex ways. Each actual entity has both a "mental pole" and a "physical pole", that is, a feeling of the physical data from the immediate past and a feeling of the abstract possibilities both inherent in those data and in some cases distinct from them. In this way Whitehead eliminates any distinction whatever between minds and bodies as separate entities, preferring to think of mentality and bodiliness as simply aspects of experience. In any event, some actual entities have highly developed mental poles: and these entities are especially those that constitute living organisms, animals, and human brains.

Whitehead's actual entity differs dramatically from Leibniz' monad in that, whereas the life-span of a monad is an eternity in length, Whitehead's actual entity lasts only an infinitely short bit of time. Indeed, Whitehead sometimes suggests that when actual entities "die" they create those moments by which time is marked. The sense of time is marked by the perpetual dying of entities from the immediacy of experience. Only when entities die can they become objects-to-be-felt by other entities. Thus what is felt by an actual entity is another entity which has already perished.

The only other major metaphysical notion in Whitehead's schema is something he calls "eternal objects". These are roughly something like the Platonic forms. Actual entities feel other actual entities who participate in these eternal objects: and sometimes (in those entities with more developed mental poles) eternal objects are felt directly apart from any nearby entity. This phenomenon is at the heart of human imagination, for example. Whitehead argues that these eternal objects, being ordered among themselves and infinite in number, must exist somewhere: and that

"somewhere" is God. God is that being in which the eternal objects reside. God often acts to increase the mentality of some
actual entities by providing certain possibilities or eternal
objects to be felt apart from the immediate environment. In this
sense, God stimulates creativity within the universe.

Some other points about God should be mentioned. Whitehead
emphasizes that God is finite insofar as God is a specific entity,
but infinite insofar as he contains within himself the infinite
number of eternal objects. More importantly, God's role in relation to the universe is not one of monarchical rule, but of an
artist or a shepherd. Whitehead claims that this philosophical
theology, while unorthodox, is more in conformity with the God of
Jesus, the God who suffers on a cross, than the traditional God
who resembles a Roman emperor.

The fascination that many thinkers in the scientific world
have had with Whitehead's philosophy is that he patiently explains
in considerabole detail how our universe of trees, animals, rocks,
and protons is built up of large groups of actual entities. Thus
his overall framework is one of an evolutionary scheme of great
detail; Whitehead was convinced that philosophy had as its task
the explanation of everything that is, and especially the connections between the concerns of the various branches of human
learning.

Clearly, Whitehead's metaphysics is one which emphasizes
massive change and constant process, with the perpetual tendency
toward the evolution of relatively permanent evolutionary traditions. It is a philosophy built on the notion of the many becoming one (that is, the world being unified in a subject of
experience), and the one becoming many (that is, the subject
perishing in order to become an "ingredient" to other entities).
This dialectical alternation between the one and the many is the
meaning of creativity, which Whitehead calls the "universal of
universals."

Main works: Principia Mathematica, 3 volumes, with Bertrand
Russell (1910-1913); An Enquiry Concerning the Principles of
Natural Knowledge (1919); The Concept of Nature (1920); The
Principle of Relativity (1922); Science and the Modern World
(1925); Religion in the Making (1926); Symbolism, Its Meaning and
Effect (1927); Process and Reality (1929); The Function of Reason
(1929); Adventures of Ideas (1933); Nature and Life (1934); Modes
of Thought (1938).

4. Recent Moral and Political Philosophy

American philosophy has always been preoccupied with moral
and political issues, and that trend has intensified in recent

decades, if anything. To choose philosophers for discussion here will inevitably appear arbitrary; I have opted to consider only three thinkers, who I believe represent some of the variety of perspectives that have been defended.

One of the most fashionable ethical theories in the 1940's and '50's especially was called emotivism, and it was in many respects allied with the logical positivist movement in Europe. Perhaps the best exponent of emotivism was the American philosopher C. L. Stevenson (1908-). Stevenson's theory centered around the linguistic nature of ethics: the question that he asked was not, what should one do in order to be happy, or in order to reach moral perfection—but rather, what is it that people do when they use terms like "right" or "good" in their linguistic behavior? The logical positivists had concluded that ethical terms had no cognitive import at all, and thus that ethical judgments, which use such terms, also have no cognitive import. Stevenson was sympathetic with this line of thinking, but also critical of it. He argued that ethical judgments had essentially two functions: they express a belief of some kind, and secondly they express an attitude toward something. Thus to argue that our present system of justice encourages crminality is to express a belief about our present system of justice, a belief which can be true or false, and to express an attitude with reference to that state of affairs—an attitude which one encourages others to take as well. It is in the latter respect that ethical judgments are emotive—they are ways of forcing others or persuading others to change their minds. Ethical disagreements can occur either because there is a disagreement with respect to belief, or because there is a disagreement with respect to attitude. The former can be resolved in principle by an appeal to relevant facts; the latter can never be resolved, because attitudes are non-rational in nature.

Main works: Ethics and Language (1944); Facts and Values, Studies in Ethical Analysis (1963).

One of the most interesting phenomena in American philosophy in recent decades has been the impact of German thought in the wake of the flight of many intellectuals from Germany under Hitler. Among those who have been influential, Herbert Marcuse (1898-1979) has been hailed by many as a kind of "spiritual leader" of the New Left of the 1960's.

Marcuse was loosely associated, at least in his early years, with the so-called Frankfurt School. One of the hallmarks of this group of intellectuals generally is a tendency to interpret Marx in very Hegelian terms. Marcuse argues that the Hegelian concept of reason, which is at the heart of Marxism, demands a transcendental critique of whatever exists, not with the presumption that there is any final or ultimate reality, but with the notion that the heart of philosophy is its "critical" function in society.

Opposed to this interpretation of reason as critique is positivism, especially in its American embodiment. Marcuse understands positivism to be a kind of fetishism of "facts", an attitude in which the factual is simply presumed, and left unquestioned. But the "factual" is itself a matter of selection, of values, of interests, and all of these are clearly conditioned by the class and bureaucratic structure of post-capitalist society. American society is essentially totalitarian because its culture forbids the questioning of the so-called "factual nature" of the "facts".

Marcuse also offers an analysis of Freud's pessimistic understanding of modern civilization. Where Freud sees a conflict between the pleasure principle and the reality principle, between the id and the super-ego, and the resolution of this conflict in terms of the suppression of the pleasure principle, Marcuse suggests that the solution to this conflict lies in the revolutionary change of society itself. Such change would bring about a release of sexual energies, without the abolition of sublimation which is essential for human society. Thus Marcuse opposes the general drift of psychoanalysis and psychology into a program for muting the need for social change because of their assumption that the cause of sexual frustration and unhappiness is to be found in the individual rather than in society.

The tendency to leave the present world unquestioned, a tendency present equally in positivism as in psychoanalysis, is founded upon what Marcuse calls the "one-dimensional" thinking of present society. Modern society is one-dimensional because it lacks an understanding of reason as that which criticizes the present order of things, whatever that order may be. The irony is that America prides itself on being rational, when in fact its rationality amounts to a worship of facts, and lacks any notion of a questioning, critical reason. Marcuse, like others associated with the Frankfurt school, did not confine his criticism to America; he argued that the Soviet Union was guilty of many of the same kinds of problems, though the latter country at least has the benefit of being open to a solution of its own problems, whereas the U. S. is quite closed. This of course was the kind of criticism that alienated Marcuse from orthodox Marxists, who saw the Soviet Union not as a shining light somewhere in the future, but in the present as well. Marcuse was not as enthused with the course of Russian Marxism as they, however.

Main works: Reason and Revolution (1941); Eros and Civilization (1955); Soviet Marxism (1958); One-Dimensional Man (1964); Five Lectures: Psychoanalysis, Politics and Utopia (1970).

An altogether different approach to ethics and politics than that of either Stevenson or Marcuse is represented by John Rawls (1921-), whose A Theory of Justice, published in 1971, has not only set off a flurry of controversy, but stimulated a number of first-rate counter-proposals in book-length form. Rawls' theory is an attempt to deal not with the language of ethics, nor with a Marxist theory of politics, but to deduce a priori the kinds of normative rules that should obtain in a society if there is to be justice. The approach is to some extent reminiscent of classical political theory before Marx, but the interest in distributive justice gives the theory a peculiarly modern flavor.

Essentially Rawls wants to argue from a hypothetical situation: if everyone in a given society were unaware of their talents, and unaware of their social position, and if everyone wanted to agree to rules that would foster justice, where the latter is understood as fairness and a lack of arbitrariness in decision-making, what kinds of rules would be agreeable to all? Rawls argues for two rules. The first rule would be that everyone is to have an equal right to the most extensive freedom compatible with that of others. The second rule is that all inequalities of a social and economic nature are to be founded upon two assumptions: first, that such inequalities will benefit all; and second, that such inequalities will be connected with those social institutions or positions which are open to all (a principle of equal opportunity). The first rule takes precedence over the second; thus Rawls wants to argue that the rule of freedom is essential to the notion of justice, and not the sort of thing that could be set aside in favor of economic injustice. Rawls argues the point very carefully, and does allow for very limited exceptions. The assumption that Rawls makes, of course, is that people will agree to these rules if we assume the "veil of ignorance" at the outset. They will tend not to assent to these rules if they have vested interests. What Rawls urges, then, is a kind of neutral non-subjective standpoint for making fundamental decisions about the rules that would best obtain in the search for justice.

Rawls' important work has contributed enormously toward turning both ethicists and political philosophers away from the mere concern with language, toward a rational understanding of the normative contexts in which ethical judgments are made. This would seem to be a fruitful move, though the study of ethical language is not without considerable merit.

172

CHAPTER 9

A BRIEF HISTORY OF INDIAN PHILOSOPHY

A. INTRODUCTION

Until modern times, Indian philosophy was almost entirely a product of the various religious traditions—namely, Hinduism, Buddhism, and Jainism—within that region of the world. That is not to say that philosophy there was simply a matter of religion—it was often relatively independent of it. But it did always take its origin from the various religious texts; indeed, one philosophical "school" differs from another largely in terms of which texts are chosen for comment. Philosophy in the West, though deeply influenced by religious elements at times, has always been to some extent secular and independent, due in large part to the origin of philosophy in Greece.

There is another important difference as well. The early development of philosophy in India was very much associated with "schools" of intellectuals, rather than with individuals. It is not until medieval times that many of the authors of various texts can be identified with certainty. Further, some authors achieved fame by contributing to several schools of thought, though their sympathies might lie with only one. As a consequence, it has been judged best to approach classical Indian philosophy (that is, until the advent of Vedanta philosophy in the medieval period) from the perspective of "schools of thought", rather than from that of contributing individuals.

The religion of Hinduism, which is older than Buddhism but probably not as old as Jainism, dates back to at least 2500 B. C. or so. It was a polytheistic religion of the invading Aryans, and elements in their language and religion are related, though distantly, to those of the Greeks and other European Aryan-speaking groups. The body of religious writings inherited from this early period includes four famous "Vedas": the Rg Veda, the Yajur Veda, the Sama Veda, and the Atharva Veda. The word "Veda" is related to the English word "wise" and the German "wissen", and means simply Wisdom: the Vedas are books of wisdom, therefore. Each of these Vedas has a fourfold structure: the Mantras or hymns; the Brahmanas, or documents on ritual performances; the Aranyakas, which are interpretations, allegorical or otherwise, of the religious rituals; and the Upanishads, which are philosophical meditations.

Of the four Vedas, the Rg Veda is by far the most important. The Yajur Veda is very much dependent on the Rg Veda and especially emphasizes the duties of the Brahmin priests. The Sama

Veda is largely a songbook of sorts. The Atharva Veda is a book
of incantations and the like, used to ward off evil spirits. The
Vedas, as we know them now, were arranged in their present form by
600 B.C. or so.

A somewhat later addition to this tradition are the great
Hindu epics, two of the most famous being the Ramayana and the
Mahabharata. The Ramayana is concerned with the conflict between
the invading Aryans and the previous inhabitants of India. The
Mahabharata is nominally concerned with a particular political
conflict, but its subject matter is quite broad. One part of the
Mahabharata is the Bhagavad-gita, one of the most famous works in
world literature. Produced around the same time as these epics
were the Code of Manu, concerned with social and political rules,
and the Artha-sastra, by Kautilya, written about 300 B.C., and
concerned with political and economic matters.

B. PHILOSOPHICAL TENDENCIES IN HINDU RELIGIOUS TEXTS

The texts mentioned above reflect an enormous variety of
concerns and interests, and a wide range of intellectual sophisti-
cation. One place to begin in characterizing the philosophical
tendencies in these documents is the notion of deity. The invading Aryans were polytheists. Many of the hymns and rituals in
the Vedas are concerned with individual deities. These deities
are often very closely related to some natural phenomenon. They
are not generally understood as transcendent to the world in the
way in which the Christian deity is.

These deities not only help keep the physical order of the
universe, they are also guardians of the moral order. In this
respect, the term rta is important; it indicates the belief that
the world is not only orderly in a general sense, but also that it
is subject to moral law.

There were tendencies toward consolidation of the growing
list of deities. One tendency was to identify one of the gods as
supreme, and to subordinate the other gods to the first. The
problem here was that no one god could find enough allegiance to
make this a viable solution. So one also sees another alternative
emerge--an alternative which is typically Indian, and which helped
to resolve the issue of polytheism, at least for the intellectuals. It was the tendency toward monism, as opposed to monotheism. Monism was the belief, religious or philosophical, that
all the gods were manifestations of one fundamental divine
reality. In some of the Upanishads, this one reality came to have
several possible names. One of those names was Atman, the other
was Brahman. The word "Atman" refers to what is essential about
something, and meant originally "breath of a living creature"--

174

rather like the Greek "psyche". The word "Brahman" meant originally "that which bursts forth", as in a prayer; the word was applied to all of nature, as that which "bursts forth" from the Divine. "Brahman" was a term designating all of reality outside the human subject, "Atman" for what was real in the very essence of the human subject. If the tendency was toward monism, it was toward the view, therefore, that all reality was one, that what was outside human subjectivity (Brahman) was the same thing as what was inside it (Atman). Thus we have the famous Upanishadic statement "That Thou art", where "That" refers to "Brahman" and "Thou" refers to "Atman".

Reality was thus one. But this did not mean that the world as perceived was ultimate reality. The Upanishads make clear that the ordinary things of the world have a rupa or specific form or nature, and a nama, a name by which the thing is symbolized in human discourse. To the extent that things have a specific form and name, to that extent they are not ultimate reality. It is only with respect to what they are essentially that they are ultimate reality.

This distinction between the apparent or empirical thing and its true reality is also applied to the human being. There we find a distinction between the body and the soul in some of its functions, and the soul in its highest function. The soul or jiva is essentially concerned with breathing, but its other functions including experiencing and acting. Further, the soul is understood to have both unconscious and conscious activities. What is important to understand is that all the processes of the soul are connected with the processes of the body in some general way. Only when, through the proper spiritual training, the individual attains the dreamless state of turiya in which one knows Brahman, does the soul genuinely transcend the body.

The ethical views of the Upanishads are closely related to this. The goal of life is moksa or liberation from the cycle of reincarnations and transmigration. An intermediate goal would be to attain a higher state of consciousness in the next reincarnation than in the present one. To achieve the end of moksa, which is sometimes understood as identification with Brahman, one must practice detachment (vairagya), and acquire knowledge (jnana). The acquisition of knowledge is done with the help of a guru, and aims at realizing the unity of oneself with the unity of the world. The possibility of degrees of liberation from transmigration is embodied in the caste system, where each caste represents those individuals at a certain level of salvation. The castes, which today number in the thousands, tended to follow class and occupational lines, with the central groups of ancient times being delineated in the Code of Manu as the Brahmin or priest, the Ksatriya or warrior, the Vaisya or tradesman, and the Sudras or

175

workers.

The connection of the famous Bhagadvad-Gita with the Upanishads is clear overall, but difficult in detail. The Gita was probably finished around 200 B.C. Its emphasis is first of all on the personality of the Divine, an emphasis which suggests that the Gita is in the theistic line devolving from the Upanishads. Closely related to this notion of a Supreme Deity is a distinctive understanding of ethics. Central to this is the doctrine of karma-yoga, a phrase which literally means a deed performed by means of self-application. The idea here is of an action done for its own sake without regard for consequences--that is, the idea of detachment as applied to ethical action. Thus the tendency for detachment to lead to philosophical contemplation is here changed so that detachment becomes an essential part of the active life. The doctrine of karma-yoga is thus an attempt to preserve the ideal of detachment while de-emphasizing the tendency toward religious passivity. It is closely related to the growth of the ideal of personal devotion to a personal Deity, as manifested in actions performed with detachment. It may also be that this ethic was more fitting and sensible for one of the warrior caste than the tendency toward contemplation among the philosophers. The central figure of the Gita, after all, is a princely warrior.

C. PHILOSOPHICAL ASPECTS OF BUDDHISM AND JAINISM

1. The religion of Jainism is very ancient, undoubtedly dating back in its origins to a period as ancient as the Hindu religion. Jainism underwent considerable growth and modification, especially after the systematization of its doctrines by Vardhamana who lived in the late 6th century or early 5th century B.C. While the earliest philosophical writings date from a much later period, it is believed that most of the doctrines of the Jains were formulated at a date contemporary with the formulation of the other major schools of Buddhism and Hinduism (yet to be examined).

The Jainist religion is founded upon the veneration of 24 teachers (of whom Vardhamana was the last chronologically). Jainism is a religion of self-salvation, premised upon a rejection of the authority of the Vedas. It is for the latter reason that Jainism, like Buddhism, is regarded as "heretical" by Hindus.

As a religion Jainism is noted for its two religious sects, one of which insists on radical detachment even from things such as clothes, while the other is more accomodating to the frailties of humans. But this religious division is not of particular philosophical importance.

176

The religious aim of Jainism is liberation (moksa) from bondage to the body and its cycle of reincarnations. Jain philosophy is preoccupied at the outset not with any Supreme Being or God, but with the situation of the human soul. Indeed, the Jains are notorious for their atheism (where theism is understood as belief in gods outside the material universe). Jain philosophy argues strenuously against any notion that the world is created or produced or made by a Deity which exists outside that world. The Jain religion focuses on the liberation of the soul from matter, and that liberation does not require grace from on high, but reformation from within.

Essentially liberation is premised on three kinds of rightness: right trust with regard to the fundamental teachings of the 24 masters; right knowledge with regard to the details of those teachings; and right conduct, which consists of the control of passions and ultimately of the body itself. These three goals are closely interconnected. But what is presupposed in this understanding of knowledge and conduct?

The Jains proposed an elaborate metaphysics as a foundation for their understanding of liberation. The world is made up of substances and their various characters. The characters of a substance are infinite in number, and can be divided into two general categories: essential and non-essential. The Jains argue that while the non-essential characters of a substance may change often, the essential characters are more or less permanent. Their view in this regard is reminiscent of Aristotle's in the West, and is certainly more moderate than the metaphysical views of the Buddhists.

Substances are either living (jiva) or are inorganic (ajiva). There are five kinds of inorganic substances: (1) matter (pudgala) which is ultimately atomic in character; (2) space (akasa), which is the place of substances or the place surrounding substances; (3) time (kala) which is not extended in space, but makes all change and movement possible; (4) dharma, a substance whose presence is the necessary condition for movement; and (5) adharma, a substance whose presence is the necessary condition for non-movement. All of these five, except for time (kala), are understood to be extended substances. Although time is a substance it lacks spatial extension. Since time has no spatial extension, it has no internal divisions, and is therefore pure and whole. Divisions of time having a beginning and an end are conventional and arbitrary; time in itself is always an eternal present.

Besides inorganic substances (ajiva), there are a number of different kinds of living substances (jiva). The degree of life is a function of its consciousness; and the latter is a function

177

of a variety of factors, most of which are due to the lack of the inhibiting infuence of matter in one form or another. There are souls in the elements (earth and water, for example), in vegetables, in all animals, and in humans. At the lower range, the degree of consciousness is determined by the possibility of movement; at the middle range by the number of senses; and at the higher range by the achievement of liberation or moksa. The human soul is a substance distinct from the body, eternal, capable of occupying space (and thus finite), and having an infinite capacity for knowledge of objects (that is, potentially omniscient). What prevents omniscience is the influence of karma and of matter generally. Omniscience is founded upon immediate knowledge of an object with its infinite qualities. The Jains formulated an interesting epistemology and logic based on the notion of a partial judgment or mediate knowledge. They regarded all judgements (naya) as relative to the one judging and as partial with respect to the object judged. Disagreements arise because this double relativity of judgments is ignored or forgotten. This led the Jains to insist that all true judgments must be prefaced with some phrase to indicate their relativity. One does not say "The sun is shining today", but rather "Somehow, or in some respect, the sun is shining today".

Main works of Jainist philosophy: Acaranga (possibly 4th century B.C.); Sutrakrtanga (possibly 4th century B.C.); Sthananga (1st century B.C.); Bhagavati or Vyakhyaprainapti (later than 1st century B.C.); Uttaradhyayuana; Dasavaikalika; Niryukti on the Dasavaikalika by Bhadrabahu (possibly 1st or 2nd century A.D.); Tattvarthadhigama Sutra, by Umasvati Acarya (after 3rd century A.D.); Nyayavatara, by Siddahasena Divakara (6th century); Pariksamukha-sutra-laghuvrtti, by Anantaviryya (11th century); Yogasastra, by Hemacandra (1088-1172); Syadvadamanjari, by Mallisena (13th century).

2. Buddhism is a much more complex religion than Jainism, and its philosophical tradition has been much more varied than the latter. Yet Buddhism shares with Jainism an official rejection of the authority of the Vedas that makes it an "outsider's" religion in Hindu society.

Gautama Buddha, the founder of the religion, was born in the 6th century B.C., and was very likely a contemporary of Vardhamana, the last of the 24 sages of Jainism. There are three canonical works of the religion, called the Tripitakas (literally "three baskets"): the Vinayapitaka, which deals with rules of proper conduct; the Suttapitaka, which contains the sermons and dialogues of Buddha; and the Abhidhammapitaka, which contains philosophical discussions. It is the latter two books which are most important in evaluating the philosophical tendencies of very early Buddhist thought.

178

Buddha counsels against pointless philosophical pursuits. He is concerned, first, last, and always, with enlightenment and with the problem of human action. The central portion of his teaching concerns the so-called "Four Noble Truths". These truths are that there is suffering in the world, that it has a cause, that it can be prevented, and that there is a method for doing just that. Buddha's analysis of the causal nature of suffering is somewhat detailed; but the essence of it is that everything whatever is conditioned by the existence of something else, which is to say, that the cause of suffering, like the cause of anything else, is bound up in an indefinitely long chain of causal agents that extend into the past. It is possible to end this chain of suffering, that is to achieve a state called nirvana. When that happens the individual becomes an arhat or saint. Nirvana is not a state of inactivity or passivity; to the contrary, the arhat or saint remains active, but the action now is done with detachment, and hence does not involve the individual in the chain of suffering.

Buddha enjoins a complex method whereby nirvana may be reached. This method is a series of steps, each of which is necessary for the achievment of liberation or moksa. The first is obtaining correct knowledge--this being understood in terms of the Fourfold Path outlined above. The second is a resolve toward reformation of one's life. The third is correct speech (that is, not lying, etc.). The fourth is morally good action. The fifth is earning an honest living, where the emphasis is on honesty. The sixth is to maintain a constant effort or resolve with regard to the above. The seventh is to be constantly mindful and vigilant, that one does not slip back into old ways of thought. The eighth is right concentration, and it is subdivided into four steps: first, the achievement of a rational meditation on truths of knowledge; second, the enjoyment of the joy and peace that come from contemplation; third, detachment from the enjoyment of joy and peace; and fourth, the achievement of the state of nirvana beyond even the stage of conscious detachment. It is in this latter state that all suffering ceases.

Probably the two most important philosophical assumptions in Buddha's teaching are his understanding of the causal nature of all things, and his denial of the existence of the soul. Buddha believed that all things are involved in change, that is, that there are causes and effects, and that things are always coming to be. This causal framework, which denies the existence of permanent entities, is essential for understanding how and why liberation from suffering is possible. The theory, in short, is not proposed out of metaphysical curiosity, but out of a desire to understand that which keeps many from finding liberation.

179

The second philosophical assumption is that there is no soul. By soul is meant some kind of enduring substance. Buddha taught that there is a constant flow of consciousness, and that it is this flow which can be, and is, "reborn" in the great chain of suffering. After all, if there is a soul which transmigrates from one body to the next, we would all be experiencing salvation already, since the soul would not be subject to change, and would thus lie beyond the causal chain because of which there is suffering. But the existence of suffering and of universal change argues against the existence of anything unchanging in our natures.

While the growth of the philosophical schools within Buddhism will be examined shortly, it would be well at this point to say something about the fundamental <u>religious</u> divisions within Buddhism. These are two: the Hinayana and the Mahayana. While these names (which literally mean "the Lesser Vehicle" and "the Greater Vehicle") come from Mahayana Buddhists, suggesting the later appearance of the Mahayana, it is not entirely accurate to say that Buddhism was "Hinayanist" in the first several centuries, and then split up later. It is probably more accurate to say that tendencies toward both schools existed from the beginning, and it was probably not until the 3rd century B.C. that they crystallized as we now know them. In any event, the Hinayana was more individualistic in its interpretation of liberation and more tied to the original Buddhist scriptural canon. They were, in short, more "fundamentalist", to use a rather misleading term. By contrast, the Mahayana were more concerned with liberation for all, and they tended toward much more speculative metaphysical theories, among other things. Geographically, Hinayana Buddhism survived only in the southern part of India, and on the island of Ceylon. Mahayana Buddhism, being considerably more open, was strongly missionary and spread quickly into Nepal, Tibet, China and Japan. For our purposes here, it is important to remember that both Hinayana and Mahayana Buddhism gave rise each to literally dozens of philosophical schools. The development of a few of the more prominent of these schools will be examined shortly. The development of Mahayana Buddhism in China will be briefly examined in the following chapter.

D. THE AGE OF THE PHILOSOPHICAL SCHOOLS

1. The Development of Philosophical Schools in Hinduism

The period roughly between the time of Christ and about 500 A.D. was one of the growth of philosophical schools within Hinduism and Buddhism. These are only approximate dates in any event, and they are somewhat misleading in that one should not think that the foundations of these systems are that recent. In fact, the foundations for almost all these schools are much older, and were undoubtedly part of an oral tradition long before they were written down.

While the number of major philosophical schools in Hinduism is usually reckoned as six, only five will be discussed here: the Nyaya school, the Vaisesika school, the Sankhya school, the Yoga school, and the Mimamsa school. The sixth—the Vedanta school—received its formulation a little later than these five, and will therefore be discussed separately.

a. The Nyaya School

The Nyaya school has a long history, extending into modern times, and has undergone considerable development in its history. The school's preoccupation historically has been with what in the West is called epistemology. The founder of the school was Gotama (3rd century B.C.), but the most important early commentaries on the Nyaya system date from a much later period, and include most significantly the commentary of Vatsyayana (c. 400 A.D.). Later thinkers and contributors to the school include Uddyotakara (7th century), Vacaspati (9th century), and Gangesa (c. 1200). There was a strong tendency to combine the Nyaya school with the metaphysics of the Vaisesika beginning with Sivaditya (c. late 10th century), and then later especially with Annambhatta and Visvanatha (17th century). The discussion below emphasizes the Nyaya epistemology, but also deals briefly with its metaphysics.

The very term "Nyaya" means something like "correct reasoning or inference", and the name alone suggests that the school was preoccupied with largely epistemological and logical issues. According to the Nyaya school, there can be true knowledge of reality, and that true knowledge consists in a correspondence between knowledge and its object. There is such a correspondence when successful activity and satisfaction result from acting on given knowledge; there is no such correspondence when action results in frustration and a lack of satisfaction. But this is not a pragmatic theory, since practice only reveals and does not determine the existence of correspondence.

There are four sources of true knowledge of reality. The first is perception (pratyakasa), which is defined as a definite cognition of some sense object, caused by contact with that sense object, and which results in true knowledge. There are five external senses (touch, taste, sight, hearing, and smell), and one internal sense (mind or manas). The five external senses are made of the same physical qualities that are perceived. Thus the colors perceived by the eye are so perceived because those colors constitute the organ of the eye itself. The principle here is that of like knowing like. The internal sense of mind (manas) is not made of material elements, as are the external senses. Its function is the perception of psychological phenomena such as pleasure and pain, willing, desire, and so forth.

Perhaps the uniqueness of the Nyaya epistemology becomes clearer in the distinction drawn between ordinary (laukika) and non-ordinary (alaukika) perception. The difference is roughly that between immediate and mediate perception, the latter occurring when knowledge of something comes only through a non-ordinary medium.

There are three kinds of non-ordinary perception. The first is samanyalaksana or the perception of classes. The way in which one comes to know all cats is not by in fact knowing every single cat, which is impossible, but by perceiving the very essence of cat in various individuals. Knowledge of the class of cats is thus mediated by knowledge of the essence of a given cat. This is an instance of mediate perception (the perception of "cats" being mediated by the perception of the essence of cats), and thus of non-ordinary perception. It should be clear that "perception" has a much broader meaning in this philosophy than Westerners are used to assigning to it. Some interpreters argue that the term "intuition" may be more appropriate here than "perception".

The second kind of non-ordinary perception is called jnanalaksana or the perception of qualities. This refers to that phenomenon expressed in judgments such as "The chair 'looks' 'soft'", or "That oven 'looks' 'hot'". Such assertions attribute to the perception of sight qualities which are only appropriate to that of touch. The explanation by the Nyaya is simply that previous perceptions of touch are joined with the present perception of sight and this makes possible a kind of "non-ordinary" perception.

The third kind of non-ordinary perception is called yogaja, and it is a kind of intuitive perception made possible by meditation on all possible objects of knowledge.

There are also three kinds of ordinary perception. The first, nirvikalpaka, is an indeterminate perception of an object and its qualities such that the relation between the two is not apprehended. The second is savikalpaka which is the definite perception of an object and its qualities as related in some fashion or other in judgment. The third is pratyabhijna which is the judgment that the present cognition of some object and its qualities is the same as some previous cognition.

The second source of true knowledge of reality, besides perception, is inference (anumana). Inference is a process of reasoning involving in its simplest form three terms and three propositions (though the formal statement of an argument always requires five propositions in Indian logic). The Nyaya theory of inference is remarkably similar to the Western theory of the syllogism, which also possesses three terms and three propositions. But there are considerable differences as well. The Nyaya school holds that inference involves establishing a relation between a subject (paksa) and an object (sadhya) by means of a reason or third term (hetu). An inference is formally stated by giving the conclusion first, and then by giving the various premises (the order again being different from that in the West).

If one asks how inference is possible, or more precisely, what is the nature of the connection between the premises and the conclusion, the ultimate response is that such a relation is not possible on inductive grounds alone, but presupposes the possibility of perceiving the general essences of things, that is, what was referred to above as the first type of non-ordinary perception (samanyalaksana). In this respect, the Nyaya theory of inference bears a marked similarity to the Aristotelian theory, which also strongly emphasizes knowledge of essences.

One way of understanding an inference is to see it as a connection between cause and effect. By "cause" and "effect" the Nyaya understand an an invariant or necessary relation. Three kinds of inference from the properties of one object to those of another are thus distinguishable. A purvavat inference is an inference from a known cause to an unknown effect. A sesavat inference is from a known effect to an unknown cause. A samanyatodrsta inference is one based on a likeness between two things which are not causally related. The latter is thus an analogical argument.

The Nyaya held that all inferences are formally valid by definition, but that they can be invalid in virtue of their content or matter. In this regard, the Nyaya proposed an extensive classification of material fallacies, the details of which are too technical to consider here.

The third source of knowledge, besides inference and perception, is comparison (upamana). By comparison is meant the immediate relation between a word and its denoted object; thus comparison is quite distinct from that type of inference known as samanyatodrsta (inference by analogy). Comparison, as a source of true knowledge, occurs when one applies a name, whose referential significance has been previously learned, to a new object which has not been perceived before, and which is known to be related to the name in the same way that the previous object was. The Nyaya are alone in Hindu philosophy for maintaining both that this is not a form of inference, and in thinking it is a true source of knowledge.

183

The fourth source of knowledge is testimony or sabda. Testimony here explicitly means the verbal assertion of someone who is trustworthy. In this regard, the Nyaya have developed a theory of semantics and/or semiotics. The Nyaya hold that a verbal assertion is a sentence made up of words arranged in a meaningful way. A word can have meaning to the extent that it has a potency or possibility to refer to some object; and that potency is ultimately founded in the will of God. But the intelligibility of a given sentence depends on more than just the potential meaning of words. Specifically, if a sentence is to be intelligible, its words must be proximate in time and space, bear some kind of affinity for one another linguistically, avoid obvious incompatibilities of meaning, and the sentence as a whole must have some subjective intention which gives it meaning.

This complex theory of knowledge developed by the Nyaya is considered foundational for their understanding of the nature of reality. On most issues, the Nyaya metaphysics is similar to that of the Vaisesika which is discussed below. In general, the Nyaya hold to an atomistic understanding of the universe, believing that there are ultimately four kinds of atoms out of which all the world is composed: the atoms of earth, water, fire, and air. Each of these atoms is spatially finite, eternal and unchanging, and all the macrocosmic objects of human perception are composed of them. In addition to these atoms, the universe contains three other substances: akasa or the void; kala or time; and dik or space. Each of these three is infinite, by contrast with the four kinds atoms previously mentioned. Akasa is a physical substance, just as the four kinds of atoms. However both space and time are understood as non-physical substances which pervade the universe. The implication is that in some fashion (through an inference) the void can be perceived through the senses, while neither space nor time can.

The goal of Nyaya philosophy is, like that of virtually all Indian philosophy, liberation (mukti) of the self from the body. The Nyaya school elaborated a theory of the soul and a theory of God to support their interpretation of liberation of the self. In the first place, knowledge of the self is distinct from perception of mental qualities. Those qualities, such as desire, pleasure, pain, and so forth, are known as qualities of a substance. The self is essentially this eternal substance, distinct from all material atoms, infinite and independent of space and time. When liberation is achieved, all mental qualities, especially pain and peasure, disappear, but so also therefore does consciousness. Consciousness is inherently tied up with the standpoint of the subject which knows material objects; transcendence by the soul of the entire realm of material objects thus entails a transcendence of consciousness.

184

The early Nyaya school suggested that knowledge of my own soul may be direct, but most later members argued that for the most part such knowledge is inferred, as the existence of other souls is clearly inferred. If liberation is to be achieved, it is important that a correct understanding of the nature of the soul be found, and one can see why the Nyaya were so intent upon the logic of inference, which no doubt grew out of this practical religious concern.

The doctrine of God in the Nyaya was a relatively late development, coming only after the merging of the Nyaya and Vaisesika schools. Liberation can only be achieved if, in addition to a correct inferential knowledge of the soul, one has the grace of God. It is essential to understand, therefore, the nature of God.

The Nyaya argued that the existence of God was not so much a matter of direct knowledge as of inference. God was understood as the creator and destroyer of the physical and moral order of the universe. The universe and its atoms were, as we have seen, understood as eternal, and thus as co-eternal with God. But the world has an order which was created and which is maintained through time; and that order also includes a moral order whereby our actions bring about certain consequences (the doctrine of karma). God is ultimately the cause of the particular joys and sorrows that we experience as a consequence of our actions. Yet ultimately, it is through God's grace that we achieve liberation from this order. How then do we know that God exists?

The Nyaya proposed a number of arguments for the existence of God, which are quite similar to those proposed by theists in the West. One of the more famous of these arguments is that from causality. The world as we perceive it is clearly a combination of atoms. This combination suggests that the objects of perception are all ordered effects. But such ordered effects demand, as their proper explanation, some kind of intelligent cause distinct and separate from the non-intelligent material causes of those effects. That supremely intelligent cause of the ordered effects in the physical universe is God. Another argument emphasizes God as the supreme cause of the joys and sorrows, pleasures and pains, which come to us as a result of our actions. This moral order of the world is clearly not of our own making, at least to the extent that that order involves a causal connection between our actions and our subsequent emotional and mental reactions to those actions. It should be noted that neither of these two arguments—that from physical order and that from moral order—proves that God is the creator of the very existence of things—a point which the Nyaya do not maintain. They prove only a first cause with respect to order in some form. In this respect their doctrine resembles Aristotle's more than Thomas Aquinas'.

185

Main works of the Nyaya school of philosophy: Nyaya-sutra, by Gotama (3rd century B.C.); Bhasya on the Nyaya-sutra, by Vatsyayana (c. 400 A.D.); Vartika, by Uddyotakara (7th century); Tatparya-tika, by Vacaspati (c. 9th century); Tatparya-tika-parisuddhi, by Udayana (10th century); Nyaya-manjari, by Jayanta Bhatta; Tattva-cintamani, by Gangesa (c. 1200); Commentary on the Tattva-cintamani, by Vasudeva Sarvabhauma (c. 1500); Didhiti, by Raghunatha (16th century); Commentary on Tattva-cintamani, by Gadadhara (17th century); Sapta-padarthi, by Sivaditya (10th century); Tarkasamgraha by Annambhatta (17th century); Bhasa-pariccheda or Karikavali, by Visvanatha (17th century).

b. The Vaisesika School

The Vaisesika school of philosophy arose independently of the Nyaya, though eventually it was combined with it, as has been seen. The founder of the school was Kanada who lived sometime later than the 3rd century B.C. The actual origins of the Vaisesika school are thought to be older, however, than this and the Nyaya. One of the most important expositions of this philosophy was that written by Prasastapada (4th century). Later commentators belonging to this school include Vyomasiva, Udayana, and Sridhara (the latter two belonging to the 10th century). Many other philosophers contributed to the school in the period after its union with the Nyaya.

Just as the Nyaya school's very name ("correct reasoning") refers to its primary concern with epistemology, so the name of the Vaisesika ("individual difference") refers to its primary concern, which was with metaphysics. The Vaisesika was founded upon the principle of metaphysical pluralism. The teaching of the Vaisesika can be summarized in terms of a statement of the seven (originally six) metaphysical categories, and a doctrine of metaphysical change and becoming. Both of these will be discussed.

Briefly, the seven metaphysical categories of the Vaisesika are:
  a) Substance (dravya)
  b) Quality (guna)
  c) Action (karma)
  d) Generality (samanya)
  e) Particularity (visesa)
  f) Inherence (samavaya)
  g) Non-existence (abhava) (a later addition)

Substance (dravya) is understood as the substratum of qualities and actions, without which qualities and actions could not exist at all. There are nine kinds of substances. Atoms of earth, air, fire, and water, as well as akasa (the void) are the

186

physical substances. All atoms are eternal and unchanging; however, any object composed of such atoms is finite and temporal. The void (akasa) is understood through an inference about the nature of sound. The Vaisesika held that sound is not a quality of any atom whatever, though it clearly has to do with a relation between things. Sound must, as a quality, inhere in some kind of substance, and that substance is inferred to be the void. The existence of the four kinds of atoms, like the existence of the void, is also a matter of inference, since atoms are much too small to be perceived.

Besides the five physical substances there are four non-physical substances: space (dik), time (kala), soul (atma), and mind (manas). Since these substances are non-physical, they are all inferred, rather than directly perceived. Each of these non-physical substances is infinite or eternal and partless. Space is inferred in order to explain our perceptions of distance and proximity. Time is inferred in order to explain our perceptions of the past and the future. Thus we seem to experience space and time as made up of parts; but in fact this is not the case. Soul, which is eternal and infinite, is inferred from the existence of consciousness, though the latter is not essential to the former. There are two kinds of souls: individual souls and the Divine Soul. Mind is inferred from the existence of internal perceptions of phenomena such as desire or pleasure. Just as the external perception of an object presupposes an organ by which perception occurs, so the internal perception of subjective feelings presupposes an organ by which this occurs. This organ is called mind or manas. Mind is intermediary between the soul and the body, and is fundamentally the means whereby it is possible to acquire knowledge. At the same time it is that which limits our knowledge as well, and thus impedes liberation of the soul. Liberation is thus liberation from mind, among other things. Mind is both atomic and eternal, though it is not physical in nature.

The second category is Quality (guna). A quality is understood as that which depends on a substance for its own existence, and which can never be the efficient cause of anything, including another quality. There are 24 kinds of qualities, each of which the Vaisesika school maintains is non-reducible to any other quality.

There are first of all those five qualities perceived by the various senses—colors, tastes, smells, touch, and sounds. Each of these has various subdivisions (thus the color blue has many shades).

Next there are seven qualities which are of general metaphysical significance. These are: number (sankhya) or that which is referred to by mathematics; magnitude (parimana) or that by

187

which things are said to be large or small; individuality (prthaktva); conjunction (samyoga) which appears between or among several individuals; disjunction (vibhaga) which appears when a connection is broken or ended; and remoteness (paratva) and near- ness (aparatva) which can be either temporal or spatial in charac- ter.

Next are six qualities pertinent to the subject of conscious- ness. They are: true knowledge (buddhi); pleasure (sukha); pain (duhkha); desire (iccha); aversion (dvesa); and effort (prayatna), which includes willing or striving of various kinds.

Finally, there are six qualities that are generally more specific in application than the above. These include: heaviness (gurutva) which causes physical objects to fall; fluidity (dravatva) which causes some physical objects to flow; viscidity (sneha) which causes various atomic particles to coalesce into a spherical shape (as in the drops which make up a body of water); tendency (samskara) which includes velocity, elasticity, and cog- nition which is instrumental in memory; and virtue (dharma) and vice (adharma) which lead either to the possession of happiness or misery respectively.

The third category of the Vaisesika school is that of action (karma). Action is understood as movement or change which always is rooted in some substance. Whereas qualities are entirely passive in nature, actions are not. Not all substances are capable of action. Only the four kinds of atoms or objects com- posed of them are capable of action. In addition mind (manas) is capable of action, though since mind is imperceptible its action can only be known inferentially. Action can not be imputed to any of the other four kinds of substances--namely, space, time, the void, and soul.

The fourth category of the Vaisesika school is that of generality or universality (samanya). The general or universal is the essence of a certain class of things. This essence (for example "catness") is found in each individual in that class, and accounts for why that individual is said to belong to that class. In Western terminology, the Vaisesika school is a realistic one in that the universal is thought to be real over and above the indi- viduals which participate in it. However, the essence of a class, which is one and eternal, cannot be said to exist in the way that substances, qualities, and actions exist. The highest universal is said to be being itself or reality, since all things whatever possess it; while a universal such as "substantiality" is less broad because it does not apply to things such as qualities or actions. While this notion of universality seems much like the Western or Platonic-Aristotelian notion of essence or idea, it is different in some respects. For one thing, the classical Western

188

notion of essence has been generally tied to the notion of a
biological species, that is, a natural grouping of things, whereas
the Indian notion of generality simply refers to any quality that
might pervade a given group of objects and constitute them into a
class.

The fifth category of the Vaisesika school is that of particularity (visesa). This category is a logical correlate of generality. But the notion of particularity or individuality must be
carefully understood here. In the first place, this category is
not required to explain how one composite thing differs from
another. For things which have parts are distinguished from one
another in terms of their parts. Composite things thus do not
require the metaphysical category of particularity. But those
substances which are inherently incomposite do require this category if they are to be distinguished from one another; otherwise
one substance would be indistinguishable from another, as would
space from time, and so forth. The very name of the Vaisesika
school derives from the emphasis upon this category.

The sixth category of the Vaisesika school is that of inherence (samavaya). The metaphysical category of inherence must be
carefully distinguished from the quality of conjunction (discussed
above). Conjunction is a temporary, non-essential, and always
reversible relation between two things. By contrast, inherence is
that category which is needed to explain how quality and action
are related to substance, and how generality is related to particularity. Specifically, quality and action are said to inhere in
substance, and generality to inhere in particularity. Thus inherence is eternal, not temporary; essential, not dispensable; and
always irreversible. Inherence is a categoreal requirement of
this metaphysical system, and distinctly different from the
quality of conjunction.

The seventh category of the Vaisesika school is that of non-
existence (abhava). It is almost certainly a later addition to
the above six categories. There are two fundamental kinds of non-
existence: the absence of something in something; and the fact
that one thing is not another. The former is called samsargabhava
and is expressed in the logical judgment "X is not in Y". The
latter is called anyonyabhava and is expressed in the logical
judgment "X is not the same as Y". There are three kinds of
samsargabhava. (1) There is first pragabhava or the relative non-
existence of something before it is produced. So we say that
before the television was assembled it did not exist—even though
its components did. (2) There is secondly dhvamsabhava or posterior non-existence of a thing after it has been destroyed. So
we say that the television does not exist after it has been destroyed. (3) Finally there is atyantabhava or radical non-
existence. Thus we say that squares never have been circles, and

189

never will be.

The Vaisesika account of the becoming and change of the universe as it is perceived is very closely connected with its metaphysics. Within the universe generally, one can distinguish between the eternal components--the atoms--and those objects which are made up of those components. Objects which are composite are either dyads, triads, or larger combinations. Dyads, like single atoms, cannot be perceived; but triads and larger combinations can be perceived. What we perceive as water, for example, is in fact a combination of many dyads and triads of water-atoms, the latter being unperceivable. The same is true of air, fire, and earth. Other objects are made up of combinations of these compounds or atoms.

To explain the creation of the universe is to explain both the beginning and ending of a phase of combinations of atoms. The creation of the universe takes place in time, and clearly there have been an infinite number of such creations. The time of the universe from beginning to end is called a kalpa or complete cycle, and there have been an infinite number of such cycles. This belief is endemic in Hinduism generally, of course.

The creation of the physical universe is always subservient to the moral order created by God. When the Supreme Lord creates a universe it is for the purpose of a given moral order, such that individual souls may experience the possibility of happiness and satisfaction through their actions. Through thought the Supreme Lord creates the macroscopic elements of air, water, earth, and fire (or light) composed of combinations of dyads and triads. At this point the universe is a kind of embryo which God animates by the presence of the world-soul or Brahma. The further work of creation is undertaken by Brahma or the world-soul, rather than by the Supreme Lord. The destruction of the world comes about after a long period of suffering and tribulation, and consists in a reduction of all combinations of things into their atomic components. Eventually the cycle begins again.

Main works of the Vaisesika school of philosophy: Vaisesika-sutra, by Kanada (3rd century B.C.); Bhasya, by Prasastapada (4th century A.D.); Vyomavati, by Vyomasiva; Kusumanjali and Kiranavali by Udayana (10th century); Kandali, by Sridhara (10th century); Upaskara, by Samkara Misra (17th century). See also the works by Sivaditya, Annambhatta, and Visvanatha, listed under "Main works of the Nyaya school of philosophy".

c. The Sankhya School

The Sankhya school of philosophy is usually allied with the Yoga school, though here the two will be treated separately.

Unlike the history of the association of the Nyaya and Vaisesika schools, however, which began as separate approaches and merged over time, the Yoga and Sankhya very likely began as a unified approach, and with time developed into distinct perspectives. Despite this, they are often still treated as one philosophy. Typically, the Sankhya school is preoccupied with metaphysics while yoga is concerned with psychology. Perhaps the most notable difference to appear between the two is over the doctrine of God, the classical Yoga position being theistic, while that of the Sankhya being atheistic for the most part.

The origin of the Sankhya school is attributed to Kapila whose existence is shrouded in legend, but who, if he lived, most likely flourished in the sixth or seventh centuries B.C. The earliest work of the school still extant is that attributed to Isvarakrsna, who lived sometime between the 3rd and 5th centuries A.D. Other commentators include Vacaspati (9th century), the anonymous authors of the Tattva-samasa and the Sankhya-sutra (the latter attributed to Kapila, but dating probably from the 14th century), Aniruddha (15th century), Vijnana Bhiksu (16th century), and Mahadeva Vedantin (18th century).

The Sankhya school, like all Hindu schools, begins with an interpretation of liberation from the body or mukti. Salvation is to be found in liberation from all pain, including that which results from either the body or the mind, from external factors of various sorts, and from supernatural beings such as demons. At the core of this analysis of pain is an understanding of reality as divided into the subjective and the objective, into self (purusa) and nature or the not-self (prakrti). There are in fact many selves, each of which transcends the realm of the bodily and the realm of the mental. For the self transcends the ego or the I which is the subject of moral activity and the center of the feeling of both pleasure and pain. The self is eternal and free because of this transcendence. It should be clear that if there is suffering, liberation can only come by recognizing or discerning that the self is not the ego and is not the body. The main block to liberation is ignorance (ajnana), and ignorance is non-discrimination (aviveka) between the self and the non-self. The achievement of liberation, therefore, does not imply any real change in the nature of the self; rather, liberation is more a matter of recognizing who one is. This recognition, transcending pain, must also transcend the emotions of joy and pleasure. It should be noted that the method of transcendence is generally taken to be the practice of Yoga, whose psychology is proposed in Yoga philosophy.

The Sankhya school commented extensively on the question of the sources of true knowledge as outlined in the Nyaya school. In essence, the Sankhya philosophers recognized perception, inference, and testimony as sources of true knowledge, but rejected comparison which they claimed could be reduced to other categories. Another important modification was the insistence that the ordinary testimony of trustworthy persons was reducible to perception in principle, and that by "testimony" one should understand here the testimony of the Vedas only.

The analysis of how knowledge occurs is also somewhat different from the Nyaya school. The Sankhya school argued that knowledge involved three elements: the subject (pramata), the object (prameya), and the means of knowledge (pramana). The Sankhya adopted a somewhat more complex psychology than the Nyaya or Vaisesika. The Sankhya claimed that besides the senses and the mind (manas) there is an intellect (buddhi) and beyond that the pure consciousness of purusa. Now knowledge, which is always a relation between purusa and the non-purusa, cannot occur in the purusa itself, since that would be to introduce the changing and the temporal into what is neither. Thus knowledge occurs in the intellect or buddhi, or rather the intellect is the means whereby the self knows an object.

The account of knowledge given by some Sankhya commentators is remarkably analogous to that given by medieval scholastics under the influence of Aristotle. A form is impressed upon the senses from the external world and it is that form which is in turn impressed on the intellect. But the intellect is by nature unconscious. It can only know the form of the object if the light of the self is allowed to fall upon it. In short, when the intellect (buddhi) reflects this light from the purusa, the intellect actually becomes "transparent" and knowledge occurs.

This account of knowledge provides the key for understanding the broader metaphysics of the Sankhya position. For knowledge is understood to be the effect of two very different principles: the conscious and the unconscious (purusa and prakrti respectively). It would be well to consider each of these principles separately.

The self or purusa has already been discussed to some extent. The Sankhya school holds to a plurality of such selves, each of which transcends the physical realm and is thus eternal; more specifically, the self is the subject of pure consciousness, that subject whose very essence is consciousness. That there is a plurality of selves seems obvious from the fact that there is a difference between what I consciously know and do, and what others consciously know and do. That there is such a self at all can also be proven in a number of ways. Thus it is argued that the world around us has as one of its subsets the class of artificial objects which by their nature are means to some end. That end does not reside in themselves or in any other material object, since neither of these have intelligence; and so it follows that since it must reside somewhere, it resides in pure consciousness. The same kind of argument can be given with respect to our moral and ethical actions, and to our various pains and pleasures. In all these cases some conscious self must be presupposed in order to explain the meaning of the phenomena in question.

Perhaps the most remarkable element in Sankhya metaphysics is the doctrine of prakrti. Prakrti, unlike purusa, is one in nature. The notion of prakrti or nature is the answer to the question: what is the cause of the world considered as a series of effects? Prakrti is the cause of material beings which pervades all those beings with something of its very nature. Prakrti is unconscious by nature, being opposed to the principle of purusa which is conscious by nature. Thus, as a cause of the world, prakrti is not aware of what it produces. And since it pervades the entire universe, and things are constantly being caused, it follows that prakrti is eternal and independent of all the effects produced by it. It is interesting to note that the Sankya theory of the causal relation between prakrti and the world of material bodies differs from that of the Nyaya-Vaisesika in that the former holds that the cause, in this case prakrti, contains the effect potentially within it, while the latter holds that cause and effect are entirely distinct.

In elaborating this notion that the cause potentially contains the effect, the Sankya school argued that the principle of prakrti was constituted by three gunas or essential constituents. These gunas are not be understood or translated as "qualities", as the term can be translated in other contexts; for if gunas were qualities, then prakrti would be substance, which the Sankhya school denies. In any event, these three gunas are sattva, rajas, and tamas. Obviously if prakrti is essentially one, these three constituents can only be understood as prakrti itself as it relates in various ways to the principle of purusa. In any event, it is the discussion of these three constituents that demonstrates how the world of physical bodies is contained potentially in its cause (prakrti).

The principle of sattva is the principle of the dynamic upward movement of light itself. The principle of tamas is the principle of passivity, obstruction, and downwardness. The principle of rajas is that of movement, of both moving and being moved. These three principles are relative to one another, and always belong together by nature. Yet while they are meaningless in separation, they can be in conflict with one another, or can exist in equilibrium even while constantly changing. Thus in periods of equilibrium it is said that either each guna will change within itself without affecting the others, or that two of the gunas will come to be dominated by the third. The former is typical of periods in which the world is undergoing dissolution, while the latter is typical of the birth of objects in the universe.

The Sankya, like the Vaisesika, offer an account of the evolution of the world. That evolution consists of contact (samyoga) between the principle of self (purusa) and the principle of nature or not-self (prakrti). The world itself cannot come to be without this contact of both principles, for either principle by itself would produce nothing. Purusa does not act, though it is intelligent; while prakrti acts unconsciously. It is clear that if the world is to be brought about, if, that is, there is to be intelligent action, both principles are required.

The beginning stage of evolution occurs when an equilibrium of the three gunas of prakrti comes to an end. This happens when the principle of rajas begins to vibrate (recall that rajas is the principle of movement!). A struggle among the gunas ensues, and eventually different combinations of the gunas come about in different objects.

The first product of this evolution is mahat or buddhi. This is the seed of the entire cosmos, and is present in each individual. The principle of the intellect or buddhi is that of knowledge of subjects and objects. The second product of this evolution is ahankara or ego, which is at the root of the sense of "I" or "mine". The ego gives rise to three subordinate phenomena, based on the three gunas present within it. The principle of sattva is associated with the 5 organs of perception, the 5 organs of action (the mouth, hands, feet, anus, and sex organ), and the mind (manas), which guides both the organs of perception and those of action. (It should be noted that while the Nyaya-Vaisesika school holds that the mind or manas is atomic and eternal, the Sankhya school insists that it is composed of two principles [purusa and prakrti] and temporal in nature.) The priniciple of tamas is associated with the 5 subtle elements (tanmatras) which are the unperceived "essences" of sounds, touches, colors, tastes, and smells. From these 5 subtle elements there arise 5 gross physical elements: namely, akasa or space from sound, air from touch, light or fire from color, water from taste, earth from smell. The principle of rajas is associated with the movement inherent in the previous two principles.

It should be noted that the progress of evolution is from buddhi or intellect to the gross elements, much in the same fashion that Plotinus' neoplatonist theory of emanation proceeds. In fact, the Sankhya theory is more concerned with the "devolution" of the universe than its evolution, at least in the modern sense of that word, which suggests progress. However, the Sankhya school maintains that this "devolution" ultimately helps the individual self to attain liberation, and in that sense there is a "progressive" element in this account.

Purusa and prakrti, buddhi or intellect, ahankara or ego, manas or mind, the 5 sense organs, the 5 organs of action, the 5 subtle elements, and the 5 gross elements constitute the 25 principles of Sankhya philosophy. However, it is the first two principles upon which all the others rest. For this reason the Sankhya philosophy is often called dualistic.

One final word should be added on the subject of God. The Sankhya school was never of one opinion about whether God existed or not. The earliest view may well have been theistic (as is the Yoga school); but in any event, the classical Sankhya position is thought of as atheistic. It is not difficult to see why belief in a Supreme Deity who is the cause of the material world would be difficult for the Sankhya position: for the cause of the material world is prakrti or nature, and while it is one by nature, it is also unintelligent. Purusa also cannot function as God, for this principle is multiple and inactive, though intelligent by nature. It is clear that the dualism at the foundation of the Sankhya system is inimical to the very idea of a supremely intelligent creator. A number of arguments against the existence of a creator God have been proposed by some members of the Sankhya school. Thus it is argued that the very idea of a God who acts to control the world is at odds with the notion of perfection which involves taking no action at all (the self liberated from the body is clearly the model of perfection). Further, the perfection, immortality, and eternity of each self implies that it is not created by anything; and so one either identifies God with the selves, which pluralizes God; or one makes the various selves parts of God, which is equally absurd. It follows that if selves exist, God does not.

Main works of the Sankhya school of philosophy: Sankhya-karika, by Isvarakrsna (between the 3rd and the 5th centuries); Commentary on the Sankhya-karika, by Vacaspati (9th century); Tattva-samasa; Sankhya-sutra (14th century); Sankhya-pravacana-sutra-vrtti, by Aniruddha (15th century); Sankhya-pravacana-bhasya and Commentary on the Sankhya-sutra, by Vijnana Bhiksu (16th century); Vrtti-sara, by Mahadeva Vedantin (18th century).

d. The Yoga School

The Yoga school of philosophy was reputedly founded by Patanjali (2nd century B.C.) who is said to be the author of the Yoga-sutra, the principal text of the school. However, the latter work dates from the 5th century A.D. Other thinkers included in this school are Vyasa (between 3rd and 5th centuries), Vacaspati Misra (9th century), King Bhoja (c. 1000), and Vijnana Bhiksu (16th century).

The Yoga school arose as an attempt to describe the yoga
method of attaining liberation from the body. It explains this in
terms of coming to awareness that the self (purusa) is not identical with the body, the mind, or even the intellect (which the
Yoga calls citta instead of buddhi, the latter being the Sankhya
term). It should be clear that the method is practiced by many
who do not necessarily accept all the philosophical details of the
Yoga philosophy. But for the most part even the Yoga philosophy
is widely accepted among Indian intellectuals.

All cognition occurs through citta and thus reflects both
prakrti and purusa. There are five states of citta: (1) pramana
or true knowledge—which, in agreement with the Sankhya, is subdivided into three kinds: perception, inference and testimony; (2)
viparyaya or false knowledge; (3) vikalpa knowledge which is
merely verbal or linguistic; (4) nidra or consciousness while
asleep; and (5) smrti or reproductive memory.

The fundamental difficulty is that the individual does not
recognize the difference between these various states of citta and
the true self or purusa. To do this it is necessary to transcend
the five kinds of suffering or distractions from contemplation
that the citta is subject to: (1) avidya or ignorance of the truth
about reality; (2) asmita or the mistaken belief that the self is
the buddhi (intellect) or manas (mind); (3) raga or the desire for
pleasure; (4) dvesa or the desire to avoid pain; and (5)
abhinivesa or the fear of death.

A somewhat more formal account of the various possible states
of citta is provided by the invocation of the theory of the three
constituent elements of prakrti—namely sattva (the light, upward
movement of things), tamas (the heavy, downward movement of
things), and rajas (the tendency to move or be moved). Since
citta or intellect is one of the products of prakrti, it, like
everything else, is possessed of these three constituents. Thus,
when the mind is under the sway of rajas and tamas, it is at its
lowest level, which is called ksipta. This is the stage of
dominance of the senses, especially where one pleasure leads to
another. The second stage is called mudha, and it is due to the
dominance of tamas. In this stage the intellect tends toward the
lowest state of moral and cognitive existence. The third stage is
called viksipta or temporary concentration on objects. Here the
principle of tamas has been left behind, but that of rajas or
movement continues. Thus the mind comes to concentrate on objects, but can lose that concentration through distraction. The
fourth stage is called ekagra or concentration, and it is the
first point at which yoga in the proper sense commences. The
object of concentration may be gross physical objects, subtle
objects (e.g., the tanmatras), the senses, and finally the ego.

196

This highest point of concentration still involves a recognition of difference between the self and the ego, and thus still involves something less than absolute happiness. Formally, the principles of tamas and rajas have been left behind, so that the principle of sattva dominates. The fifth stage of citta is that of niruddha. At this stage, thought ceases, there is no longer contemplation of an object, but rather the mind is thoroughly lost in the object. This is the point of liberation, of joy and happiness.

As a method, Yoga consists of 8 practices or forms of self-purification. The first is yama, which is restraint practiced with regard to thought, word and deed, including a renunciation of violence of all kinds. The second is niyama or positive observances of rules concerning good conduct in life. The third is asana or discipline of the body, which especially emphasizes good posture. The fourth is pranayama or the discipline of proper breathing, which is necessary for the attainment of prolonged concentration. The fifth is pratyahara which is control of the stimulation of perceptual organs. The sixth is dharana which involves steady concentration on some object. The seventh is dhyana or steadfast concentration without distraction. The eighth is samadhi or concentration in the pure sense which involves transcendence in consciousness of the subject-object distinction.

One element of the second kind of self-purification mentioned above (niyama) is meditation on God. It should be clear that the Yoga school and method seeks liberation from the body, but not identification with God. Devotion to God is part of the means of purification, but not the object of the method itself. It is for this reason that the Yoga school both defended the existence of God in opposition to the Sankhya school (and thus argues for 26, rather than 25, metaphysical principles), and yet did not find this point so substantial as to cause a break with the Sankhya school.

For Yoga philosophy God is understood as that being who is a model for the achievement of liberation, and who is understood as the cause of the world. In the first regard, the Yoga school argues that there must be a God because things of both the smallest magnitude and the largest magnitude must exist, and God has the greatest amount of knowledge and power. In the second regard, the Yoga school emphasizes the necessity of invoking a principle besides purusa and prakrti to explain how or why the two principles ever became associated. This association must not only be caused, it must be caused by an intelligent being who makes this association one that is orderly and which develops for the sake of a moral order.

Main works of the Yoga school of philosophy: Yoga-sutra,

ascribed to Patanjali (probably 5th century); Commentary on the
Yoga-sutra, by Vyasa (between the 3rd and the 5th centuries);
Tattva-vaisaradi, by Vacaspati (9th century); Commentary on the
Yoga-sutra and Yoga maniprabha, by King Bhoja (c. 1000); Yoga-
vartika and Yoga-sara sangraha, by Vijnana Bhiksu (16th century).

e. The Mimamsa School

The Mimamsa school of philosophy was one of the earlier ones
to crystallize in writing, its primary text (2nd century A.D.)
having reputedly been authored by Jaimini (1st century B.C.). One
of the most important commentaries on this work was by Sabara (c.
400). Other important commentators include Prabhakara (c. 650),
Kumarila Bhatta (c. 700), Bhavanatha, Parthasarathi Misra, Mandana
Misra, Madhava (c. 1350), Khandadeva (c. 1650), Apadeva (c. 1650),
and Laugaksi Ghaskara. It should be noted that Prabhakara and
Kumarila Bhatta were the founders of two distinct schools within
Mimamsa philosophy; however their differences will not be considered here.

The Mimamsa school of philosophy is founded upon that religious experience which it considers essential for liberation: the
experience of performing those duties enjoined by the Vedas. For
the Mimamsa, liberation from the body can only be achieved through
religious ritual done for its own sake, which is the kind of
motivation required by the Vedas. It is in the analysis of this
understanding of liberation that Mimasa philosophy developed.

The Mimamsa philosophy rests first of all on a conception of
religious duty performed for its own sake. Religious ritual is to
be performed because it is of the nature of such an obligation
that no external reason can be given for it. This means that
neither any consideration about the object of worship (God or the
gods) nor any consideration about the subject of worship (the
individual worshipper and his soul) is pertinent to the explanation of why worship is to be given. Liberation is achieved as a
consequence of the performance of religious ritual; but this
consequence is not the reason for performing it in the first
place. In the same manner, the ultimate consequence of liberation
is the attainment of heaven, which is stressed much more than any
kind of mystical transcendence of the body. Yet even here the
Mimamsa philosophy denies that the reason for performing the
ritual is the attainment of heaven.

Perhaps the oddest consequence of this notion of ritual was
the tendency of the Mimamsa toward atheism. While the earliest
Mimamsa texts have little to say about God, the later texts argue
against the existence of God, whether in the form of monotheism or
polytheism. The Mimamsa agrees that religious ritual is always
specific in addressing a particular god. But the reason for

performing the ritual lies strictly in doing what the Vedas command because they command it. The Vedas are themselves higher than any god. The inerrancy of the Vedas and the performance of religious ritual clearly dispense with the need for belief in God in any philosophical sense.

There are other consequences of this unusual view of religious ritual. One of the most important centers on the Vedas as sources of knowledge, and this in turn occurs within the wider context of the on-going discussion of the sources of knowledge in Hindu philosophy. The Mimamsa school recognizes six sources of knowledge. These are: perception, inference (<u>anumana</u>), comparison (<u>upamana</u>), authority (<u>sabda</u>), postulation (<u>arthapatti</u>), and non-perception (<u>anupalabdhi</u>). The Mimamsa understanding of inference is substantially identical with that of the Nyaya-Vaisesika. Since the most distinctive of these sources of knowledge for Mimamsa philosophy is authority (<u>sabda</u>), it is best to begin with it, and then consider the others.

The Mimamsa school understands testimony or authority (<u>sabda</u>) to be either from the Vedas, in which case it is impersonal authority, or from some other source, in which case it is personal. The Vedas are impersonal authority because no author of them is known. In fact, it is argued that the Vedas are eternal; and this in turn is based on the claim that words, insofar as they constitute the Vedas, and insofar as they have meaning, transcend transitory existence and are eternal. Now the Vedas provide a kind of knowledge that no other source of knowledge can provide: the knowledge of religious duty. Personal authority, by contrast, can conceivably be derived from other sources of knowledge, such as comparison or perception. So authority, and specifically the authority of the Vedas, has a standing that no other source of knowledge can have.

Another interesting feature of this interpretation is the distinction between statements about the things that exist and statements enjoining duties based on the former. The Mimamsa argued that existential statements are wholly subordinate to statements about religious duties in the Vedas. One can see why neither the existence of God nor the existence of anything else was of special importance for the Mimamsa school.

The Mimamsa school's interpretation of perception is also of some interest. The school argues that perception is a two-layered phenomenon, the most fundamental layer being that of an immediate indeterminate knowledge that things exist, and the second being that of a determinate knowledge of what things do in fact exist. One might say that perception is itself based on a complex apprehension of both indeterminate existence and determinate essence. Now despite this complexity, perception is reliable as a source of knowledge of the world. The world that is revealed in perception is fundamentally real and made up of a plurality of things.

The Mimamsa understanding of comparison (upamana) is rather different from other Hindu schools. Comparison involves a recognition that an object that has previously been perceived is similar to an object that is presently being perceived. In putting it this way, any reduction of comparison to perception is ruled out, for obviously the relationship itself is not a matter of perception.

The Mimamsa argue that another source of knowledge is assumption (arthapatti). What is meant by this is the cognitive need to assume a specific ground to explain something, even though what is assumed is not perceived. Now while it is obvious that arthapatti cannot be reduced to perception, what is not so obvious is why it cannot be reduced to inference. The Mimamsa argue that inference always involves some invocation of a universal connection between things, while assumption does not presuppose a universal connection, but only a connection that is necessary in this particular instance.

A sixth source of true knowledge, and one that is again distinctive to the Mimamsa school, is anupalabdhi or non-perception. This is simply the recognition of what is called negative facts (e.g., the nonexistence of my belonging to the French foreign legion derived from the nonperception of such). The Mimamsa school insists that non-perception cannot be reduced to either perception or inference. Non-perception of negative facts cannot be derived from perception; for what is not the case cannot be perceived. Further, non-perception of negative facts cannot be a kind of inference. If it were, it would again involve a universal connection between the non-existence of my belonging to the French foreign legion and the non-perception of it. But clearly there is no universal or necessary relation between these things. In any event, non-perception, like assumption, is always less than universal in scope, and thus not an inference.

This rather elaborate theory of knowledge may seem far removed from the Mimamsa's preoccupation with the religious rituals of the Vedas. But in fact it probably well serves it. For the overall theory of knowledge generated by the Mimamsa is one which allows for many different sources of knowledge, including knowledge which cannot be formally reduced to inference, and which especially emphasizes the notion that all knowledge is true unless proven otherwise. This conclusion, that truth is self-evident, is probably the most important way in which Mimamsa epistemology is connected with its religious preoccupations. The Mimamsa epistemology is unusually broad in what it admits within the boundaries of true knowledge; and this certainly prepares the way for the assertion of the eternal authority of the Vedas.

The metaphysical views of the Mimamsa are also distinctive, but probably not as extensively developed as other Hindu schools. The Mimamsa epistemology is exceedingly realistic, and it comes as no surprise to find that the metaphysics is similarly realistic. Some members of the Mimamsa school accepted Vaisesika atomism. However, God could not and did not function to create the order of things in the world, since of course the Mimamsa did not believe in the existence of such a God. Rather the world is maintained in both its physical and moral order by the presence of the force of karma. Now karma cannot be perceived, and is known only through the Vedas. How precisely does karma operate? The Mimamsa argued that karma was only possible because things possessed positive power to bring about a given effect. This power (sakti) is unperceived and resides within the cause. While this power can be obstructed by external causes, it generally tends to bring about its given effect. This metaphysical theory may well have been developed to explain how the performance of a given religious ritual brings about good effects later on. The theory holds that the religious ritual generates such a power in the individual soul which later bears fruit. Thus the theory of power in the soul (apurva) appears to be the reason for the theory of power in things generally (sakti). The physical order of things is explained in the same way that the moral order of things is explained.

The theory of the soul (atman) is like that of the Nyaya-Vaisesika, in that the soul is thought to be eternal and infinite, and that each body has a single soul. The soul is thought to be beyond consciousness as such. But the Mimamsa admitted that the soul did undergo change, even though it was eternal. In this regard they tended to be "realistic" in their interpretation of the nature of the soul. And this is fully in accord with their unusually broad understanding of true knowledge.

Main works of the Mimamsa school of philosophy: Mimamsa-sutra, by Jaimini (probably 2nd century A.D.); Bhasya, by Sabara (c. 400); Brhati, by Prabhakara (c. 650); Commentary on the Rju-vimala, by Salikanatha (late 7th century); Naya-viveka, by Bhavanatha; Sloka-vartika, Tantra-vartika, and Tup-tika, by Kumarila Bhatta (c. 700); Nyaya-ratnakara and Sastra-dipika, by Parthasarathi Misra; Vidhi-viveka and Bhavana-viveka, by Mandana Misra (probably 8th century); Nyaya-mala-vistara, by Madhava (c. 1350); Artha-samgraha, by Laugaksi Bhaskara; Mana-meyodaya (16th century); Bhatta-dipika, by Khandadeva (c. 1650); Mimamsa-nyaya-prakasa, by Apadeva (c. 1650).

201

2. The Development of Philosophical Schools in Buddhism

Like Hinduism, and often in reaction to it, Buddhism developed a number of philosophical schools during the same period of time in which Hindu schools of philosophy crystallized in writing. These schools were in the first place a function of the great religious division within Buddhism itself, the division between Hinayana and Mahayana Buddhism. Hinayana Buddhism, it will be recalled, was more conservative, more individualistic, and less open to philosophical speculation on the whole. It was also that form of Buddhism which survived only in the southern parts of India, especially in Ceylon. Mahayana Buddhism was more communitarian, more accomodating to the ordinary layperson, and thus more open to foreign thought. Each form of Buddhism had many different philosophical schools. However, tradition came to accentuate four Buddhist schools of philosophy as especially significant, and it is these four that will be briefly discussed here: the Vaibhasika, the Sautrantika, the Madyamika, and the Yogacara. The first two are Hinayana schools, the second Mahayana schools. Thus it is especially the latter two which were of importance in the development of philosophical thought in Tibet, China, and Japan. Each school tended to develop on the basis of the preceeding school, the Vaibhasika being the earliest. And the development was clearly from the naively realistic (the Vaibhasika) to the more critical realistic (the Sautrantika) to the more extreme varieties of idealism (Madyamika and Yogacara). It is for this reason that the turn toward "the mental" in the Sautrantika is often taken as being of great significance for the overall development and flowering of later Buddhist philosophy.

a. The Vaibhasika School

The **Vaibhasika** school of Buddhism was the earliest philosophical school to develop. The school itself had an important center in the city of Kashmir. While the early history of the school is shrouded in obscurity, its earliest acknowledged spokesman was **Vasumitra** (2nd century), while its final flowering was the philosopher **Sanghabhadra** (4th century). After that time the school was largely a museum relic, having been devastated by the criticisms of the Sautrantika school and others.

The Vaibhasika school would seem to have been founded upon the general claim that "all things exist", or better, everything that really exists is perceived in some fashion. It is claimed that the mind has direct knowledge of objects in the world. The position is more complex than this statement might indicate, however. There are three important consequences that can be drawn from it: a) a theory of the substantiality of time; b) a theory of the substantiality of things; and c) a theory of the substantiality of mind.

202

(The notion of substance (<u>svabhava</u>) must be understood here not in the manner of Hindu thought—for which substance is usually understood as permanent substratum—but in a manner consistent with the Buddhist emphasis on change, namely, as that substratum logically required at the foundation of the experience of sense qualities. To avoid confusion here, some expositors actually speak as though the Vaibhasika school denied all substance whatever, when what is meant is that they denied substance as that term is understood in Hindu thought. However, there is a sense in which the bare notion of a logical substratum is affirmed by the Vaibhasika, and thus a legitimate sense in which one may use the term "substance" here. Another synonym for "substance" here might be "real" or "existent".)

First, if "all things exist", then the things of the past would seem to exist equally with the things of the present and the future. Or to be more precise: any part of time in its threefold structure is understood to be fully substantial or existent. An object can be past or present, or both at the same time, depending on the perspective of the knower; just as an individual can be a farmer, a tax-payer, and a citizen at the same time without contradiction. The divisions of time into past, present, and future is a consequence of ignorance, of taking the relative for the absolute. The things that do exist are beyond time, or rather one might say that time is something that "happens" to them. It is this doctrine of time that is perhaps the most distinctive of the Vaibhasika school, and which curiously demonstrates how close even a "realistic" school such as the Vaibhasika could be to the more "idealistic" versions of Buddhist philosophy, such as the Yogacara and the Madyamika.

The notion of perpetual change which underlies the Buddhist account of perception suggests that the world of objects is ultimately atomistic in structure. It is not certain that the early Vaibhasika embraced this view, though the doctrine was commonplace later on. In any event, the "objects" which they were analyzing were those which were the ultimate constituents of perceived objects. A distinction between these ultimate constituents and the larger objects of which they were composed was of signal importance to the Vaibhasika philosophy. For they distinguished sharply between empirical truth which is based on the objects of perception and absolute truth which concerns the nature of the ultimate constituents of reality.

Both the objects of perception and their ultimate constituents undergo change, but it is the change of the latter that is more fundamental. The Vaibhasikas analyzed change into four stages: production, momentary existence, decay, and annihilation. Now if the objects of perception did not endure for at least a

203

moment they could never be perceived at all. This would seem to suggest that the ultimate constituents were rather like substances, and the Vaibhasika school would seem to have believed that these substances were directly perceived and absolutely real.

Besides the substantiality of time and material things, the Vaibhasikas also argued for the substantiality of mind. Like objects which are perceived, the "mental" in a general sense includes both the characteristics of the mind, that is, its various states or qualities, and that which at each moment constitutes the substratum of these states or qualities. This substratum was that in which the impressions from the momentarily existing substances in the physical world were "stored": for without this supposition, it would be impossible to explain the knowledge of the continuity of time. This mental substance was understood to be unconscious in nature. Conscious perception, by contrast, was one of the mental events which was of momentary duration.

The Vaibhasika school is not noted for its internal consistency. Though the school's emphasis on the distinction between mind and matter was made in the context of the Buddhistic doctrine of constant change (unlike the dualism of the Hindu Sankhya school), the attempt to found this distinction on a theory of substance, and to apply this theory to the nature of time itself, led some to question whether the theory of substance was not too high a price to pay in order to defend the distinction between mind and matter. The issue was first posed in terms of the substantiality of matter, and only later in terms of the very notion of substantiality. The Vaibhasika may thus be said to have been the first (major) attempt to rationalize Buddhism, but an attempt which could not satisfy the more discriminating who recognized that Buddhism rests on the rejection of the belief in any kind of material substance, however momentary its existence.

Main works of the Vaibhasika school of philosophy: Jnanaprasthana sastra, by Katyayaniputtra; Dharmaskandha and Sangitiparyyaya, by Sariputtra; Dhatukaya, by Purna; Prajnaptisastra, by Maudgalyayana; Vijnanakaya, by Devaksema; Prakaranapada, by Vasumitra; Samayapradipa and Nyayanusara, by Sanghabhadra (possibly 5th century); Atthasalini and Visuddhimmagga, by Buddhaghosa (5th century); Abhidammavatara and Namarupaparicchecda, by Buddhadatta (5th century); Abhidharmadipa and Vibhasaprabhavrtti, possibly by Vimalamitra (possibly 6th century); Abhidhammatthasangaha, by Anuruddha (12th century).

b. The Sautrantika School

The Sautrantika was the second major school of philosophy to develop within Buddhism, and was largely responsible for the waning of the Vaibhasika philosophy and for the growth of more radical philosophies. Perhaps the greatest thinkers of the school were <u>Vasubandhu</u> (4th century) and his disciple <u>Yasomitra</u> (probably 4th century). Vasubandhu, however, was converted from Hinayana Buddhism to Mahayana by his brother, and subsequently became one of the great thinkers of the Yogacara school of Buddhist philosophy. This conversion is not only of biographical significance; it also well symbolizes the close connection between the Sautrantika position and later forms of idealism.

The Sautrantika school is known for its criticism of the Vaibhasika theory of direct knowledge of the object. To understand why the Sautrantika became an exponent of "indirect knowledge" only, one must understand their fundamental misgivings about the understanding of substance which dominated the earlier philosophy.

The Vaibhasika had understood change to involve four elements: production, momentary existence, decay, and annihilation. The second of these four implied that a thing did exist for at least a short time—long enough in any event to make it possible for the thing to make an impression upon the perceiver of the object. The substantiality of the thing, for the Vaibhasika, is a function of this notion of direct perception. The Sautrantika, however, rejected any notion of substantiality since the latter seemed to amount to introducing a theory of atman or self into metaphysics, that is, to introducing the notion of a permanent object into a system that requires the belief that all things are changing. Hence the Sautrantika theory began by denying two of the four elements of change—namely, the elements of momentary existence and decay. A thing is nothing more than production and annnihilation. There is no intermediate point of existence which can properly be called substance.

A great many consequences ensued with this rejection of substance. First, the Vaibhasika had explained causes and effects in terms of the nature of the substance; it would follow that the Sautrantika theory, rejecting the existence of substance, had to reject any understanding that linked cause and effect as closely as the Vaibhasika had. Indeed, the Sautrantika theory held that the effect was entirely nonidentical with the cause, that causes and effects were merely contiguous in time and place, and that there was nothing else connecting them. This theory has a certain resemblance to that of David Hume.

Another consequence with respect to the nature of time followed from this theory of causality. Since cause and effect are always temporally distinct, the relation between past and future is inherently involved in their relation. Significantly, the Vaibhasika had maintained that the past was as real as the future and the present. The Sautrantika theory denied that the past and future were as real as the present, and claimed to the contrary that the former were only known by inference from the latter.

This doctrine, then, added up to a claim that all things that exist are annihilated with their very production. This metaphysical atomism carried with it the radical claim that the "atoms" in question could not even have substance ascribed to them. This theory of substance-less atomism was of great importance in the subsequent development of Buddhist thought.

Perhaps the single most significant consequence of the Sautrantika denial of substance was the denial of direct perception of the object. If the object did not persist even long enough to be called a "substance", it did not exist long enough to make an impression on the perceiver. The impression that is made on the perceiver thus occurs at a point in time after the object has been annihilated. When I perceive an object, therefore, it is already quite "dead" and nonexistent. The object of knowledge is thus the representation or impression that object has made on me, and not the object itself. This is what is meant by the theory of indirect perception or knowledge, and it is the heart of the Sautrantika position.

The Sautrantika philosophy, like that of the Vaibhasika, was realistic in that it continued to distinguish between mind and matter. However, the Sautrantika greatly emphasized the role of the mind and knowledge, and especially of inference, in all knowledge of the external world. Thus this theory of indirect perception was the first dramatic step toward more idealistic philosophies which would build on the basis of the Sautrantika objections to the Vaibhasika philosophy.

Main works of the Sautrantika school of philosophy: Abhidharmakosa and Vyakhya, by Vasubandhu (4th century); Abhidharmakosa vyakhya, by Yasomitra (4th or 5th century); Nyayabindu, by Dharmakirtti (7th century); Commentary on the Nyayabindu, by Dharmottara (9th century).

c. The Madyamika School

The Madyamika school of philosophy was probably the first major philosophical school of Mahayana to develop. Its founder, and perhaps its most brilliant exponent, was Nagarjuna (2nd century). Other members of the school include Nagarjuna's disciple Aryadeva (late 2nd century), Buddhapalita (late 4th century), Bhavaviveka (early 5th century), Candrakirti (early 7th century), and Santideva (691-743).

The Madyamika position, as developed by Nagarjuna, is

206

devastatingly simple and even elegant. The various theses of the Vaibhasika school--that the past and the future are real, that cause and effect are identical in nature, and so forth--can be opposed by the Sautrantika theses--that the past and the future are not real, that causes and effect are nonidentical, and so forth. Each of these positions can be proved by argumentation, and then disproved by argumentation. The Madyamika school accepted all these possibilities as inevitable. Thus, if we argue that A exists, it can be argued that not-A exists; that both A and not-A exists; and that neither A nor not-A exists. Any thesis whatever can be subject to this kind of dialectical argumentation. If we substitute terms such as "mind" or "matter" or "substance" or "time" or "space" in this argument we generate a series of arguments which show that, for example, (a) substance exists; (b) substance does not exist; (c) it is true both that substance exists and that it does not exist; and (d) it is true that neither substance exists nor that substance does not exist. Each of these positions can be logically proven, and the Madyamika simply helped themselves to the arguments already available in the philosophical literature of the Hinayana schools to amplify the point. But what is the result of this curious position?

Logically, what followed was the utter emptiness (sunyata) of anything. That is to say, anything that can be spoken of, or thought of, has no reality whatever. Not only is the concept of something "empty", but any proposition generated about that concept is equally empty because it can be contradicted and its contradiction logically proven. If what appears can be spoken of, or thought of, then the apparent is logically incoherent and meaningless. When the Madyamika speak of the emptiness (sunyata) of appearances, they seem to mean something like the "meaninglessness" of things, where "meaninglessness" refers to the inability to provide positive conceptual content or propositional elaboration.

The Madyamika did not confine their dialectical invention to propositions about external reality or matter; they also insisted that "mind" and the mental, and propositions about them, were also empty and meaningless. As elaborated, the position has been called nihilistic, because it insists that contradiction can be found in all appearances and in all descriptions of appearance. But is "nihilistic" an adequate comment on this school? Did the Madyamika renounce the whole point of Buddhism, which is the attainment of Nirvana?

The Madyamika did not do anything of the kind; they only insisted that with the attainment of Nirvana, one reached a state beyond mind and matter, beyond subject and object, beyond appearance, and beyond concepts and propositions. This stage is one of unity with reality, a unity which simply cannot be thought or

207

spoken without involving oneself in contradiction. Thus, in the end, the Madyamika insisted on a distinction between the phenomenal realm and the realm of true reality. At this point, the idealistic nature of the Madyamika dialectic becomes apparent. And with this one of the most important philosophical differences between Hinayana and Mahayana also comes to light. For Mahayana Buddhism has always gravitated toward idealistic philosophical theories by comparison with Hinayana Buddhism which has always been more or less wedded to more realistic accounts.

This shift toward idealism is, however, clearly anticipated at certain stages in both Vaibhasika and Sautrantika philosophy. Thus, the Vaibhasika theory of time suggests that the substances of things are literally timeless, and thus that time is somehow "external" to things. One possibile interpretation of this, of course, is that time in itself has no divisions, and that such divisions are only relative to appearances. Again, the foundation of the Sautrantika position is that reality (the substances of things) is inferred from the appearances. Both positions often unwittingly draw a distinction between appearances and reality, without fully understanding the problem of the connection between the two. The Madyamika position argues that appearance and reality are related as the realm of language and thought is related to that which lies beyond both. The elaboration of this position is often compared with the philosophy of Kant and especially with a section of Kant's discussion of the ideas of pure reason which is called the "antinomies of pure reason". In that section, Kant sets out in parallel columns proofs for contradictory propositions such as "the world is infinite in time and space" and "the world is finite in time and space", in order to demonstrate in the end the necessity of drawing a distinction between the apparent and the ultimately real, and to insist that conceptual or propositional knowledge must be confined to the realm of appearances. While Kant was absolutely ignorant of Madyamika philosophy, it is interesting that elements of his position were anticipated some 16 centuries before, half-way around the world.

Main works of the Madyamika school of philosophy: Mulamadhaymakakarika and Vigrahavyavartani, by Nagarjuna (2nd century); Catuhsataka, by Aryadeva (late 2nd century); Karatalaratna, Tarkajvala, and Madhya-martha samgraha, by Bhavaviveka (early 5th century); Prasannapada and Madhyamakavatara, by Candrakirti (early 7th century); Siksa samuccaya and Bodhicaryavatara, by Santideva (691-743).

d. The Yogacara School

The Yogacara school of philosophy was founded by Asanga (4th century), who reputedly converted his brother Vasubandhu (4th century) from Sautrantika philosophy in particular, and Hinayana Buddhism more generally. Both wrote important works setting forth Yogacara philosphy. Other members of this school include the somewhat independent logician Dinnaga (late 5th century), Sthirmati (6th century), and Dharmapala (6th century).

The Yogacara school accepted the distinction between the apparent and the absolutely real which seemed to be at the foundation of Madyamika philosophy. However, they interpreted the foundation of the apparent to be "ideation": that which appears is in the nature of an idea. It follows that the absolutely real is mind, since ideas are always relative to mind. The transformation of mind into a world of appearances is in three stages.

The first transformation is the growth of certain "seeds" within the "store consciousness" of mind. The latter is a term used by the Vaibhasika to explain the unconscious storehouse where the various impressions from the external world are kept until remembered. The Yogacara school divested itself of any realistic account here, and simply relied on the notion that mind has within it a kind of unconscious storehouse with various potentialities in it, some of which are for the good, some of which are not. These seeds or germs have to do with the basic dispositions for action. Now the first transformation comes when these dispositions ripen or mature into mental activity generally.

The second transformation occurs when this mental activity comes to be regarded as a mind (manas) or self (atman), which is perceived falsely, and which is the subject of self-love and the like.

The third transformation occurs with the projection of the full range of material objects, first as perceptible qualities, then as having a material or substantial base beyond the mind. Consciousness of objects, then, comes not from external objects, but ultimately from the ignorance of the mind itself. Indeed, the existence of external objects is a consequence of ignorance, and not its cause, on this theory.

It is at this point that one can see how the Yogacara school tended away from the twofold division of the Madyamika into appearance and reality, and toward a threefold division based on reified object, reified subject, and pure consciousness or mind. While both object and subject were appearances, the Yogacara school felt it was important to emphasize that the object derived from the subject, and not the other way around, thus making the subject more fundamental than the object. Pure consciousness or mind in any event, existed beyond the categories of the object, as well as the categories of the subject, indeed beyond all concepts.

209

In order to proceed from the world of objects and subjects and their distinction from one another, back to the source of all consciousness, the Yogacara school relied on the technique of Yoga (Yogacara means "the practicing of Yoga"). This testifies well to the openness of the Mahayana school, and it was the inclusion of Yoga that helped to popularize Mahayana philosophy with the Chinese especially. The use of Yoga sharply distinguishes this school from the Madyamika who were unconcerned about such methods, and whose dialectical wizardry tended to make very sharp distinctions between the absolute and the relative. By contrast, the Yogacara school's emphasis on the subject as mediating the object and pure consciousness tended to soften some of the edges of the sharp distinction between appearance and reality.

Main works of the Yogacara school of philosophy: Abhidharmasamuccaya and Mahayanasangraha, by Asanga (4th century); Vijnaptimatrata-siddhi, by Vasubandhu (4th century); Madhyantavibhaga (sometimes ascribed to Maitreyanatha, [early 4th century]); Mahayanasutralankara (variously ascribed to Asanga and to Maitreyanatha); Alambanapariksa, by Dinnaga (late 5th century); Commentary on the Trinsika of the Vijnaptimatrata-siddhi, by Sthirmati (6th century).

3. Materialism in India

There is one last philosophical "school" which must be discussed, though its members and literature are not well known. That school is the Carvaka or materialist school, and it is a kind of a straw-man of both Hindu and Buddhist thought. That such a school ever existed is very doubtful, and indeed there is little extant literature that would seem to belong to it. In many respects, the "materialist philosophy" may have been a partial invention of the various religious intellectuals, an invention based on particular opinions voiced here and there which were critical of some of the more fundamental beliefs of Indian society. While the "systematic" nature of the Carvaka school is probably a product of the growth of other philosophical systems, the philosophical complaints voiced in the Carvaka philosophy probably go back long before the Christian era. There is some evidence of the existence of treatises critical of the Vedas in the centuries before the birth of Christ. The school itself was reputedly founded by a person named Carvaka, but his very existence has often been questioned.

As the "Carvaka" philosophy developed in the writings of its opponents, its main features seemed to be a strong emphasis upon perception as a source of knowledge, a rejection of most of the basic metaphysical beliefs of Hindu thought, and an adherence to a form of epicureanism.

The Carvaka school admitted only perception as a valid source of knowledge, claiming that inference and testimony were not valid. The claim was that only knowledge derived from sense perception is valid. If that is the case, then all knowledge was bound to particulars, and it would never be possible to arrive at universal laws or relations. Without the latter, inference is not possible. Further, the testimony of another person is either reducible to inference, which is not valid, or to perception. If the testimony of the other is reducible to perception, there is no problem. But if the testimony of the other is about things which are quite beyond perception, it is clear that such testimony must be disregarded as unreliable and untrue, since no inference to anything beyond perception has validity.

The Carvaka school did not deny that we could and did make inferences based on perception. Their point was simply that such inferences were only probably true, not certainly true, and only true if they concerned perception and did not extend beyond it. But in any event, no inference could ever be known with certainty.

The positive metaphysics of the Carvaka school is a function of its exclusive commitment to perception as a source of knowledge. The only things that can be known to exist are those things that are perceived or can be perceived. Now these are all material. The Carvaka school held that there were four elements out of which all material things were made: earth, air, fire, and water. What is of greater interest, however, is the "negative" metaphysics of the Carvaka. The school rejected the notion that either souls or gods existed. Thus the existence of a reified consciousness in the form of a soul is ruled out as beyond perception. Perception establishes that there is consciousness in various physical bodies, but that this consciousness is an emergent quality of the order of these bodies, and not an independent entity capable of survival after death. In a similar fashion, the Carvaka philosophy holds that the order of the world is immanent within it, and that no recourse to a transcendent deity is necessary in order to explain why the world is as it is. The physical world obeys its own laws founded upon the nature of the objects that compose it; thus there is no need to posit a creator-God.

Given the rejection of both the soul and God, it would seem to follow that the goal of life for the Carvaka school was simply the elimination of pains and the pursuit of pleasures in this life. The only release from pain, however, is that of death; in this life genuine happiness is not entirely possible, though it is possible to increase happiness considerably. The ethics of the Carvaka is essentially hedonistic.

The Carvaka philosophy, then, probably represents a melding

of a variety of views expressed over generations, all of which
were in one form or another critical of the dominant religious
values expressed in Hinduism, Buddhism, and Jainism. Whether any
single individual ever expressed all the views outlined above,
however, is very doubtful.

Main works of the Carvaka school of philosophy:
Tattvopaplavasimha (7th century); Sarvadarsanasamgraha (14th century).

E.   THE MEDIEVAL FLOWERING OF HINDUISM IN THE VEDANTA SCHOOL OF
     PHILOSOPHY

1.   Introduction

     The period from 500 to the influx of Westerners in modern
times was a time of growth for the various Hindu philosophical
systems. Perhaps the most important development was the flowering
of the Vedanta school, the sixth and last school. Its origins are
almost certainly more ancient, but it did not receive its classical exposition until the medieval period. The Vedanta school is
much more varied in its interpretation than some of the other
schools previously discussed. But it is the Vedanta school, and
especially the thought of Sankara, which more than any other has
become the paradigm case of Hindu thought for Westerners and
foreigners generally. While this has tended to obscure the diversity of Hindu thought, such judgment could not have been made
except by way of acknowledging the genius of Sankara. In any
event, it was Sankara, among others, who launched a strong attack
on Buddhism, and succeeded in virtually stifling its intellectual
development in India. Buddhism survived in India for a time, but
by the later medieval period (14th century) it was of no significance.

     Only three members of the Vedanta school will be discussed
here: Sankara, Ramanuja, and Mahdva.

2.   Sankara (788-820)

     Sankara's philosophy is one of the paradigm cases of pan-
theism in human history. His thought has been compared with that
of Meister Eckhhart and Spinoza in the West. He worked out the
Vedanta philosophy on the basis of those hints of pantheism in the
Vedas that had not been fully explored by other thinkers. As we
have seen, the Nyaya-Vaisesika philosophy is realistic and pluralistic, the Sankhya-Yoga philosophy is realistic and dualistic,
while the Mimamsa philosophy is again realistic and pluralistic.
By contrast we may say that Sankara's Vedanta philosophy is idealistic and monistic, rejecting both dualism and pluralism. It is

212

of some interest that his thought perhaps most resembles that of Mahayana Buddhism, especiallly Yogacara idealism. But unlike the latter, Sankara recognizes the authority of the Vedas, and of course differs from the Buddhists on many secondary and even primary issues—so much so, that he was one of the most effective opponents of Buddhist thought. Yet Sankara's Vedanta undoubtedly moved in directions that the Buddhists were moving, and did so on the basis of Vedic authority. This no doubt insured him a place in Indian thought.

Sankara openly brought to a head the potential conflict in the Vedas between polytheism, monotheism, and pantheism. His solution to this potential conflict is of considerable interest. Essentially he argued that these three religious and philosophical positions were stages on the road to the recognition of absolute truth. Polytheism and monotheism are both ways of regarding God from the viewpoint of the natural or physical world. In polytheism, the gods are not much more than personifications of natural powers; whereas in monotheism, God is separated decisively from any kind of plurality, but is still understood in relation to the plurality of things in the material world. In this last respect God is termed "Isvara" and his capacity for creating is regarded as part of his very essence. From both standpoints—polytheism and monotheism—the world is regarded as real, and God or the gods are regarded as real. And this is in fact the nub of the problem. God is certainly real, but is the world real as well? Sankara insists that the world is not real, and in that insistence comes to a different understanding of the relation of God and the world than is found in either polytheism or monotheism.

To be real is to be that which pervades through changes, which, by contrast, are called the apparent. One way in which the question of the reality of the world can be examined is by looking at the relation between the realm of apparent changes and that which is their cause. Now every effect is absolutely inseparable from its cause; without the cause, the effect would not come to be at all. Further, what transpires in the relation between cause (clay, for example) and effect (the pot made of clay) is simply the transformation of a substance from one thing to another. In this change, the effect is not something new at all. Indeed, the effect exists in the cause. This theory must be carefully distinguished between the Sankhya theory of the effect, while holds that the effect, even though potentially in the cause, is in fact really distinct from the cause. Sankara denies just this. He insists that the effect has nothing whatever within it which was not in the cause in the first place. If the effect was novel in some respect, that which is novel would have no cause—and that is absurd. Sankrara concluded that the effect is identical with the cause.

213

If the effect is identical with the cause, then all change is only apparent, not real. Sankara did not deny the fact that change is perceived, only that change is objectively real. What is objectively real is the substance of all change.

But one may argue that this only brings us to the reality of a plurality of substances, not to any kind of monism. Sankara agrees, and presses his question again: do not these apparent substances change? Is there not something which is the cause of their change, of the change in all substances? Wouldn't that "something" be that which is permanent in all so-called substantival changes—namely pure existence, or what is called Brahman, the ontological foundation of the world? Sankara asserts just this, but his argument spells out another step in the process: that step which mediates Brahman and the apparent world—namely Maya. It is his theory of Maya that is one of the more distinctive elements in his theory.

Maya—related to the English "magic"—is the power within Brahman of bringing about the great illusion which is called "the world". More specifically, Sankara identifies Maya with prakrti (the principle of nature or material substance in the dualistic Sankhya system). Unlike the Sankya theory of prakrti, Sankara insists that this principle is not ultimate or uncaused, but rather founded in the power of God. Maya's relation to God is like the relation of the power of shining in a diamond to the diamond itself. That the world is maya, an appearance, does not imply that God deceives us willfully in any way. Rather, it is simply that we can be deceived by mistaking the apparent for the real. And obviously God, who is perfect, is not deceived by Maya. Maya then only appears for those who are ignorant of the substantial reality of all things. It has no being other than this.

Does this theory of Maya imply a subjective idealism like that of the Yogacara? In one sense, it does, insofar as Maya does seem to be relative to at least divine consciousness in the end. But Sankara's theory of Maya does not entail the reduction of the external world to a series of ideas in our own minds—which is what he understands the Yogacara theory to involve. Quite the contrary: Maya, the external world, is not simply a function of our ideas, but a power in God himself. This power in God is a function of God's free will, which therefore has a beginning and can have an end.

If one recognizes with Sankara that there is one underlying substantial existence present throughout what we call the world—namely Brahman—and that what appears to be changing is a realm—namely Maya—which is a power rooted in God's free will, what then is the relation of the human soul to either of these? How does

Sankara conceive liberation?

Sankara's fundamental conviction was that Atman (the soul) is Brahman (God). God and humanity are one and the same, identical, and all suffering and misery can only come about by failing to recognize or know just this truth. Generally the soul appears not as Brahman, but as a particular entity, as the source of activity or knowledge or ritual/moral activity. In all these respects, the soul is being understood either covertly or overtly in its relation to the body, just as in monotheism God as the cause of the world is brought into a relation with a physical world which is taken as real. The belief in an ego or an "I" as a center of activity and knowledge is thus the effect of the belief in a body. The soul by nature is non-centered: perhaps the best indicataion of what this is like is the state of the soul in dreamless sleep. It is in this latter condition that the soul is experienced as unlimited consciousness and as absolutely joyful. It should be clear that the notion that there is just one soul for each body is also a consequence of ignorance, ultimately of Maya, and that in fact there is only one soul which in its very nature is pure consciousness and absolutely one.

Sankara was insistent that liberation could be achieved in this life, and that its achievement did not imply that the individual might cease to take part in life. To the contrary: the achievement of liberation meant for the first time the ability to take part in life with absolute detachment. This was especially necessary so that others would be led to the same recognition of truth. Thus Sankara's mysticism was not conceived in an exclusively other-worldly fashion, or as a cover for what we today would call social or political irresponsibility.

Main work: Brahma-sutra-bhasya.

3. Ramanuja (1017-1137)

The philosophy of Ramanuja, who has the distinction of being the longest-lived philosopher in history (120 years!), appears to be a careful modification of Sankara's, and is thus fundamentally a modification of the earlier Vedanta. If the latter is understood as an unqualified monism, Ramanuja's position is often called a qualified monism.

Ramanuja began by questioning Sankara's distinction between what was absolutely real and what was not so real, namely Maya. Now Maya is not mere nothingness; so it must be some kind of reality intermediate between Brahman and nothingness. But this is absurd. For either something is real or it isn't. From this Ramanuja drew the conclusion that the world is real—just as real as God. And it follows that God's creation of the world is not some kind of magic trick, but quite real.

One might think that Ramanuja was setting himself up for a return to monotheism, but this is not the case. Rather, Ramanuja attempted to restate the case for monism in terms that did not lead to the theory of Maya.

Ramanuja, like Sankara, referred to the world in general as prakrti and claimed that both it and the many finite souls that populate the world are present in God as God's parts. God is absolutely one but contains these many principles within him. Thus God's unity is a difference-in-unity, where the difference is entirely internal to God. The principles that compose God are on the one hand the unconscious (prakrti) and on the other hand the conscious (atman). These are but two of the infinite number of qualities that God possesses. All of God's parts are eternal with him. In this respect Ramanuja's understanding of praktri differs from Sankara's understanding of the same, since for Sankara prakrti was rooted in the free will of God. Ramanuja insists that the principle of the material world, prakrti, is eternal, having neither beginning nor end.

There is a curious resemblance between Ramanuja's theory and the Sankhya theory. Indeed, what Ramanuja appears to have done is to take the two principles of prakrti and purusa and to ground them within the one God. In this way, Ramanuja may have hoped to avoid what he considered to be the unfavorable consequences of Sankara's theory of Maya.

Obviously, Ramanuja's understanding of liberation differed considerably from Sankara's. Certainly, to the extent that each finite soul is found in God's nature, each soul may be said to be both the same as God, and different from God. For Ramanuja, this translates into a dual goal for the human soul: to recognize our inseparability from God (identity), and to overcome attachment to the body (similarity). The latter occurs through the performance of religious rituals and those tasks proper to one's caste. But the final method of detachment from the body occurs with meditation, prayer, and especially devotion. It is in this context that Ramanuja insists that making God an object of love and thus recognizing a similarity with God is more important than any kind of absolute mystical union with God. Indeed, the only element in Sankara's identity theory that Ramanuja sympathizes with is the bare element of inseparability between the soul and God. It would seem, then, that Ramanuja sought to establish traditional devotional theism on a panentheistic foundation.

Main work: Brahma-sutra bhasya.

216

4. Madhva (1197-1276)

The views of Madhva originated in a passionate attack on the Vedanta philosophy of Sankara which led him to a philosophy even more pluralistic than that of Ramanuja.

Madhva's fundamental insight rested on the notion of the particular, and of how one particular differed from another. It was typical of Hindu thought to conceive of the particular as characterized by one or several distinctive qualities, which were common to all the particular things of that class. Thus consciousness was a quality uniquely characteristic of, and common to, all souls, and so forth. But it was precisely the status of the "universal" quality pervading all the members of a class that drove thinkers like Sankara to posit identity beyond all differences, and thus to deny the reality of differences. Madhva's insight was that the particular was a combination of an infinite number of qualities which were uniquely combined in that particular entity, such that while two things may be alike or similar in virtue of this or that quality, they are always different in terms of many others. This uniqueness was not just a matter of qualities, however—it pertained to the very nature of the substance of the thing. A substance just is this particular collection of qualities. As a consequence it makes no sense to ask what the one thing is that pervades the many, as though that would be more real than the many. The many material substances of this world are each real, and real in their own individual way.

Madhva's metaphysical system, then, is founded upon the rejection of identity in favor of differences, specifically the difference that exists between God, the realm of souls, and the realm of material substances. Further, each soul was uniquely individual among all souls, just as each material substance was unique among all material substances. God is the creator of all the souls and substances, but not some kind of universal quality at the foundation of all of them.

One of the important differences between souls and substances is the changelessness of the former. Material substances are created from the chaotic prakrti by God; thus prakrti would seem to be the material cause of the world of substances, while God is an efficient cause (to use scholastic and western terminology). A more importance consequence of this view is the reduction of the notion of karma to both the creative activity of God and the particular qualities of a given individual. In short, Madhva's theory eliminated the necessity for a theory of karma independent of his understanding of God and the nature of individuality.

An interesting consequence of the doctrine of particulars is its application to the traditional question of liberation. Madhva drew the consequence that liberation from ignorance differs from one individual to another, and that some individuals are doomed to never find release. Indeed, Madhva is unique among Indian thinkers in positing a conception of hell after death.

It is not surprising that many have found Madhva's way of thinking to be similar to that of Christianity, and this has led some scholars to suggest some kind of contact. Such theories are doubtful, but there is a curious resemblance. Madhva's monotheistic pluralism has been influential clear up to modern times.

Main works: <u>Mahabharata-tatparya-nirnaya</u>; <u>Tattvoddyota</u>; <u>Visnu-tattva-nirnaya</u>; <u>Commentary</u> <u>on</u> <u>the</u> <u>Brahma-sutra</u>.

F. RECENT INDIAN PHILOSOPHY

1. Introduction

While India has always been influenced by contacts from the West throughout its history, it was not until the advent of British colonialism in recent centuries that this contact became increasingly virulent and violent. In the wake of British subjugation, Indian society underwent a great deal of soul-searching, which led in the end to a philosophical renaissance, as well as to social reform and political independence after World War II. It is not possible to detail all the developments in the last century or so, but some short outline of the major thinkers is in order.

Several features of contemporary Indian thought stand out. The first is that many subscribe to one version or another of the Vedanta school. Indeed some have argued that the Vedanta philosophy is the very heart of Hinduism and the epitome of the Indian religious spirit. Secondly, many Indian thinkers have been anxious to reinterpret the Vedanata philosophy, and Hindu philosophy more generally, in a way which would be more open to Western scientific thought. Thirdly, Indian thinkers have often been quite critical of all things Western—from Western government and wars, to some aspects of Western religion and Western culture generally. Thus, while Indian philosophy has sought for its own distinctive foundation in its philosophical past, it has been been both critical and accomodating in its relation with the West. These ambivalent tendencies will no doubt persist as India continues its modernization and Westernization.

2. Rabindranath Tagore (1861-1941)

Tagore, who received the Nobel Prize for literature in 1913, and who was knighted by the British government in 1915, was one of the most indefatigable writers of the early 20th century, and probably the single most representative figure of his generation in India. Tagore was not simply a philosopher; he was an accomplished poet, playright, painter, educational experimenter, and social reformer.

Tagore's fundamental philosophical conviction rested on a rejection of classic Sankya dualism, and on that element in Indian thought which demeaned the importance of the natural and physical world. He was convinced that the true spirit of Indian thought lay in its acceptance of one absolute truth which appears in many different perspectives. In one of his more famous passages, Tagore suggested that this view was of the unity of the "humanity of God" with the "divinity of man", of Indian religion with Western science. This suggested both an emphasis upon the many modes of knowledge of the divine, just as much as it suggested that the quest in life was for the unity of knowledge. While the former perspective implied pluralism, the latter implied a rejection of individualism. The result is a kind of affirmation of unity-in-plurality, and difference-in-unity.

Of great concern to Tagore was the question of Indian nationalism. Unlike others, he was quite critical of nationalism and individualism, both of which he regarded as Western aberrations, and thus inappropriate to the spiritual destiny of India. He emphasized the importance of personality, which is denied by both nationalism and individualism, and insisted that personality was closely linked with the notion of unity-in-plurality. But while he rejected nationalism, he did not champion British control either. Instead, he favored internal social and cultural reform, so that India, by coming to a better awareness of its own spiritual destiny, might be better capable of facing the problems of Western civilization. Tagore was instrumental in setting up a school for the realization of his aims as early as 1901.

Overall, then, it would seem that Tagore championed a synthetic unity of what he considered to be good about Western society (its concern for nature, its science), and what he thought was good about Indian religion (the vision of the impersonal Brahman at the foundation of all things). This vision was to be realized in primarily cultural and spiritual ways, rather than in any easy political solution. In the latter regard, he was not heeded.

Main works: Sadhana: The Realisation of Life (1913); Personality (1917); Nationalism (1917); Creative Unity (1922); The Religion of Man (1931); Man (1937).

3. Mohandas K. Ghandi (1869-1948)

Ghandi always denied that he was a philosopher, and there are

219

many who would take him at his word. It is true that he had no
formal education in philosophy, though it is also true that he was
a well trained lawyer and enormously well read. Ghandi's works
are eminently practical and never systematic. However, it is
possible to derive from these works a more or less consistent
philosophical framework, and indeed many who have admired his
political stances have done just that.

Ghandi's overall view would seem to be an interpretation,
sometimes rather novel, of the basic message of the Bhagavad-Gita.
His concern throughout life was with the pursuit of Truth (satya),
and in many ways it was Truth which was fundamental to his
thinking and his acting. Indeed, his position might be summed up
by saying that Truth (satya) is God or Reality (sat). This stands
in contrast to saying that God is Truth; for Ghandi's commitment
to God was only through Truth.

The ideal of each human person must be holding firm to the
truth (satyagraha), which suggests independence and self-
sufficiency. The latter concept of satyagraha is foundational for
Ghandi's political and economic views, which emhasized Indian
self-sufficiency and self-determination and strongly rejected
economic dependence on Western countries, and especially Western
industry and technology which negated the ideal of self-
determination. The ideal of satyagraha meant that each individual
should be economically self-sufficient, and this led Ghandi to
champion a life-style based on the making of one's own clothes,
and so forth. Yet the ideal of satyagraha is only one part of
Ghandi's philosophy.

Just as important as satyagraha is the notion of sarvodaya.
Whatever is done in firmness for the sake of Truth must be done
for the welfare of all (sarvodaya). It is in this respect that
action must be sacrificial and altruistic, indeed performed with
utter detachment. The realm of action is in general the realm of
karma, and the only release from it is through the way in which
the individual is oriented toward the Truth in all action. Thus
one is most detached from action when one does it for the sake of
love of all, and vice-versa. It is at this point that one can
begin to understand why Ghandi's perspective on action is intrinsically social and political.

There is one final aspect that is important, indeed central
to Ghandi's fame in the political world: the insistence on non-
violence (ahimsa). Non-violence is to be extended not just to
humans, but to all living things. Ghandi recognized the pragmatic
necessity of killing at times; and he acknowledged that at times
if the only choice is between being cowardly and acting violently
it is better to do the latter. But the higher course, the overall
commitment of one's life, should be toward non-violence. This led

Ghandi to reject wars and revolutions of all kinds, to insist on vegetarianism, and to preach a message of universal love not unlike (or uninfluenced by) the message of the New Testament.

Non-violence (ahimsa) cannot be understood apart from satyagraha, however. Non-violence is an end, and satyagraha is a means to that end. The point here is that non-violence does not entail passivity; Ghandi insisted that being non-violent meant that one stand firm in the truth as one did so, that one allow universal love to pervade one's refusal to practice violence. It is for this reason that Ghandi's political method can be right-fully called active non-violence, or non-violent resistance. Thus Ghandi turned a traditional Hindu ethical prescription (ahimsa) into a radical political method with curiously Christian over-tones.

Ghandi's views did not derive simply through meditation on the Bhagavad-Gita. He was deeply influenced by many Western sources, including Tolstoy and Thoreau. While he called himself a Hindu, he could be very critical of Hindu scriptures at times, and appreciative of the Islamic Koran and the Christian Bible. While he was a deeply religious man in his private life, he rejected the claim that there was any one religion that had the final word on the human situation. While he stood for the revitalization of Hinduism, he rejected some of the most typical Hindu beliefs, such as belief in the Untouchables and in the inferiority of women. It is not surprising, then, that he was assassinated, not by a foreigner for being "too Indian", but by an orthodox Hindu, for not being Indian enough.

Main works: An Autobiography (1929); In Search of the Supreme (1931); Satyagraha: Non-violent Resistance (1958); Discourses on the Gita (1960); Nonviolence in Peace and War (1962); Caste Must Go: The Sin of Untouchability (1964).

4. Sri Aurobindo (1872-1950)

Aurobindo was educated in the classics in England, for the explicit purpose of eliminating whatever was "Indian" in his upbringing. That education failed in one sense: Aurobindo re-turned to his mother country as a confirmed nationalist and even-tually became a revolutionary. He was finally imprisoned in 1908 for about a year. It was during his imprisonment that he had a powerful religious experience which changed the course of his life, though the authorities never ceased believing he was still dangerous. Aurobindo founded a religious commune at Pondicherry, where he remained for the rest of lis life.

Aurobindo's thinking was in many ways a realization that the whole purpose of nationalism, as he understood it originally, was

221

at odds with the soul of the nation he was fighting for--i.e., India. That India had a supra-national destiny in the world he never doubted. But it was only in his imprisonment that he came to question whether the emphasis on violent revolution and nationalism was at odds with this destiny. He never ceased to champion freedom from Britain; but his vision from 1909 onward was tempered by more religious concerns.

Aurobindo set out in his writings to combine a kind of qualified monism with some aspects of Western thought, especially evolutionism and the doctrine of the emergence of the Overman. Aurobindo, like many others of his generation, accepted the Vedanta tradition, but was sharply critical of the world-negating attitudes of Sankara. Aurobindo proposed a theory of evolution which was directly contrary in its implications to Sankara's theory of Brahman standing in transcendent aloofness beyond the illusory world. Thus Aurobindo argued that Brahman was immensely powerful, so powerful in fact as to be able to descend into matter, and little by little to cause matter to evolve to a higher plane. Now for matter to evolve, it is necessary to assume two things: (1) that Brahman is a necessary condition for the evolution; and (2) that matter has within it the potentialities of development with respect to new stages. In the latter sense, for example, inorganic matter must have within it the potentiality for life, if life is to evolve at all.

With the evolution of each new phase, there is an integral reorganization and restructuring of all lower forms of existence. Thus the emergence of life profoundly affects the realm of the inorganic; the emergence of animal life profoundly affects the realm of plant life, and so forth.

The end of evolution is the emergence of the Overman, the highest manifestation of Brahman. The Overman must not be understood in any narrow individualistic sense; for the illumination of each individual leads inevitably to the divinization of the human community. The means whereby this will be achieved is called "integral yoga", which is simply the way all lower forms of existence will be spiritualized in accord with the realization of Brahman in human life. Thus integral yoga is more than just a means of ascending upward and inward to God; it is even more a means by which God embraces all material existence in a downward and outward movement of universal love.

It is the destiny of India to promote this spiritual destiny of the human species, a destiny which is compromised by Western emphasis on technology and government. In one sense, then, Aurobindo never ceased being a nationalist; the only real change for him came with the realization that the destiny of India could not be realized by a reliance on Western violence and technology.

Main works: Essays on the Gita (1926-1944, 1950); The Renaissance in India (1946); The Riddle of the World (1946); The Life Divine (1947); The Synthesis of Yoga (1948); The Human Cycle (1949); The Ideal of Human Unity (1950); The Supramental Manifestation upon Earth (1952).

5. Sarvepalli Radhakrishnan (1888-1975)

Radhakrishnan has been prominent both in the academic world and in the Indian government. He is probably one of the most widely read Indian philosophers in the West. His philosophy is essentially concerned with the essence of religion, and devolves around a contemporary interpretation of Sankara's monistic Vedanta.

Radhakrishnan has argued that two aspects especially of Sankara's views have been repellent to Westerners and others: the emphasis on the impersonality of Brahman, and the corresponding rejection of a personal God, and the belief in the world as maya or illusion. Radhakrishnan has argued that in fact the impersonality of Brahman is only prominent when Brahman is understood non-relationally. But Brahman can be understood as related to the finite and temporal, however, and when this standpoint is taken Brahman is personal. The relation between the personal and the impersonal then is entirely a logical one within the nature of Brahman. Thus the religious worship of a personal God, and mystical vision of an absolute impersonal unity go hand-in-hand, and do not contradict one another.

Secondly, Radhakrishnan argues that Sankara's notion of Maya simply amounts to the logical and ontological claim that the world depends on Brahman. It does not entail the view that the world is totally unreal. Such a view is absurd, and Radhakrishnan argues at length that Sankara did not believe any such thing. In this way, Radhakrishnan hoped to champion a properly Hindu understanding of the universe which was not adverse or hostile to the Western concern for scientific understanding.

Radhakrishnan has argued against any fully naturalistic view of the world, and in this regard he has shown that he can be quite critical of the West. Perhaps the most inadequate aspect of naturalism , he suggests, is its inability to take into account the obvious spiritual intuition and nature of the human person, not to mention the clear presence of order and design in the world. To defend himself, Radhakrishnan has argued at length for the inclusion of intuition, in addition to perception and inference, as a source of knowledge. Intuition includes both religious, scientific, aesthetic, and ethical insights—none of which can be explained by any narrow naturalistic account of the world.

223

Radhakrishnan's understanding of intuition is at the heart of his interpretation of religion. The very essence of religion is founded upon intuition, and all religions have the same essence or intuition at their heart. The task then is to realize in the fullness of real life the religious vision; to do this is to transcend the narrow boundaries of denominations and religious organizations.

Radhakrishnan's vision of religion is founded upon his interpretation of Vedanta, which he claims is the highest religion of all, at least in its spiritual essence. All other religions are at heart the same, because they all point in the same direction. Radhakrishnan wrote extensively about other religions, but his interpretations of them have been sharply questioned.

Main works: The Ethics of the Vedanta and Its Metaphysical Presuppositions (1908); The Reign of Religion in Contemporary Philosophy (1920); The Religion We Need (1928); Kalki--or the Future of Civilisation (1929); Eastern Religions and Western Thought (1939); Education, Politics and War (1944); The Heart of Hindusthan (1945); Freedom and Culture (1946); Religion and Society (1948); East and West in Religion (1949).

CHAPTER 10

A BRIEF HISTORY OF CHINESE PHILOSOPHY

A. INTRODUCTION

Philosophy seems to have emerged with relative suddenness in ancient China in the final centuries of the Chou dynasty, which lasted from 1122-256 B.C. The rule of the Chou dynasty had been generally marked by a return to humanistic ethical ideals, by contrast with the much more strong-armed tactics of the previous Shang dynasty. Chinese philosophy, as it emerged in the declining centuries of the Chou dynasty, was marked by a concern for ethical conduct, and especially for the kind of conduct befitting a gentleman. Yet the late centuries of the Chou dynasty were not peaceful especially, and there was a great deal of internal turmoil and economic and social upheaval. Perhaps it was the turmoil of the period that provided the more immediate impetus to the flowering of philosophy.

Although there were some six classical schools of philosophy in ancient China, they did not all continue to be of importance in later ages. Two especially stood out and persisted: Confucianism and Taoism. In the period from the end of the Chou dynasty to the end of the T'ang dynasty (10th century A.D.), there was a great deal of philosophical consolidation among these two schools. And perhaps most important of all was the rise and decline of Buddhism, which exercized an indelible influence on China, but which had ceased being of philosophical relevance by the 10th century. What followed in the centuries after this was a remarkable growth of various kinds of Neo-Confucianism—that is, a Confucianism that had absorbed elements from Taoism and Buddhism and other sources. This gave Confucianism an incredibly important hold on the intellectual life of China until the end of the Manchu dynasty in 1911. The years 1911-1948 were years of transitional chaos, culminating in the communist revolution led by Mao Tse-tung. Yet even under communism, certain traces of the Chinese past—namely, Confucianism and even Taoism—survived in new forms.

The history of Chinese philosophy can, therefore, be divided conveniently into four periods: (1) the ancient schools; (2) the consolidation of Confucianism, Taoism, and Buddhism in the first millenium A.D.; (3) the emergence of the great Neo-Confucian systems from about 960 to 1800; and (4) modern Chinese thought.

Before embarking on this history, however, it is important to say something here about the various "Classics" of Chinese culture and civilization, since these texts were of extraordinary

225

importance for the subsequent development of Chinese thought. There are either five or six "Classics", depending on whether one counts a work on Music which is no longer extant. The Five Classics that have survived include: The Book of Changes or I Ching, as it is popularly known; The Book of History or Shu Ching; The Book of Odes or Shih Ching; The Book of Rites or Li Chi; and The Spring and Autumn Annals or Ch'un-ch'iu. All of these works were thought to have been written at least in part by Confucius, but that ascription is very doubtful for the most part. Indeed, just when these texts were written is not very clear. They had assumed their final form as we know them now in the first century B.C., when they came to constitute the essential texts on the basis of which all Confucian thought and education developed. A few comments about these texts are in order at this point.

The Book of Changes or I Ching will be discussed below in reference to the Yin-Yang school. The book is in general founded upon methods of divination, which were undoubtedly very ancient, and which were practiced for religious and political reasons. In time the book came to have great metaphysical significance, as will be seen.

The Book of History is a collection of documents pertaining to the various rulers of China, from the earliest legendary dynasties to the early Chou dynasty. Some of the material dates from a much later period and is not necessarily an accurate reflection of historical events, while some of it, especially that relating to the Chou dynasty, is relatively reliable in its information. The tradition has it that Confucius edited these texts. Similarly, it is believed that Confucius compiled The Spring and Autumn Annals, which is a history of the state of Lu from the late 8th century B.C. to the early 5th century B.C. The Book of Odes, also ascribed to Confucius' editorial activity, is a collection of nearly 300 poems or songs dating from various periods of ancient Chinese history.

Perhaps the most important of the Classics for the purposes of philosophy is The Book of Rites. This is in effect a collection of texts dealing with religious rites, compiled presumably by Confucius. Some of the texts are very obscure and particular; others are general and philosophical. It is the latter which are of interest here. One section of The Book of Rites came to be known as The Great Learning. It suggests that knowledge or investigation into the nature of things is the foundation of all things human. This is because wide and deep knowledge brings with it sincerity of will and rectification of the mind, which in turn leads to a cultivation of personal life as it is lived both in the family and in the state. And when the latter has taken place, there is the possibility of world peace. Obviously this makes knowledge very important, important not for its own sake, but for the sake of its ethical, social, and political consequences. This would become a recurrent theme in later Confucianism. Another text in The Book of Rites suggests a significant concern of Confucius' philosophy, namely the so-called doctrine of the mean (chung-yung). The Mean describes the "Man of Virtue", the one who who follows Tao (the Way) in all things, and thus achieves virtue (te). But what is human nature? The latter is described as center (chung) before the emotions, and harmony (yung) after the emotions (hence the doctrine of chung-yung). This realization of centeredness and harmony with the world is called sincerity (ch'eng). Sincerity is founded upon education and results in enlightenment. It is important to recognize here that the realization of virtue is closely tied in with various social ideals and realities—that following Tao means very much being in harmony with things in the world. This interpretation of Tao is almost certainly part of the general Confucian critique of Taoism which advocated a much more unworldly understanding of following Tao. This point should be clearer in the subsequent discussions of Confucianism and Taoism.

B. THE SIX SCHOOLS OF ANCIENT CHINESE PHILOSOPHY

1. Introduction

According to one very classical account, the six philosophical schools of ancient China were closely associated with certain divisions of the intelligentsia and reflected the interests of those divisions. The six schools were:

1. The Ju School, composed primarily of those who taught the Classics and the various ceremonies and music required for religious and political purposes. It is out of this school or group of intellectuals that Confucianism arose.

2. The Taoist school, composed primarily of hermits who had become disillusioned with society and politics.

3. The Moist school, found among the educated soldiers who had as their responsibility the teaching of the art of war to new recruits. The school received its name from Mo Tzu (Tzu = Master, Mo Tzu = Master Mo).

4. The School of Names, consisting of professional debaters and rhetoricians.

5. The Yin-Yang school, whose members were practitioners of the occult arts, magic, divination, astrology, and numerology.

227

6. The Legalist school, composed of intellectuals who served as advisors to the various Chinese rulers.

Ancient Chinese thought, even before the emergence of a written philosophical tradition, was founded on the notion of the Virtue (te) of the King. This virtue was seen in the performance of various religious rituals and duties which were understood in terms of following the mandate (ming) of Heaven (T'ien). Following the way (tao) of Heaven was the way in which one acquired virtue (te). If this occurred, then success in the harvest and in military duties was inevitable. The latter was founded on a deap-seated belief in the unity of Humanity and Nature. In some quarters there was a belief in a personal God-Ruler (Ti), but generally many intellectuals, especially the Confucianists, held that the impersonal principle of Heaven (T'ien) was a higher principle than any god. Thus the earliest components of the Chinese world-view consisted of a belief in an impersonal ultimate principle, coupled with a belief in the close relation between Humanity and Nature. The nub of this view was to be found in what is called moral virtue or ethical action. Chinese thought has always been eminently humanistic because of this emphasis on ethics.

Though religion and the state (in the person of the emperor) were very closely related in ancient China, religious life was generally unmarked by anything like "orthodoxy" and hence never exercized any restraining influence on the development of intellectual life. For this reason, Chinese philosophy has always had, from the very beginning, a persistent streak of humanism, secularity, and "this-worldliness". This must be qualified, of course, but it is important to note the extraordinary contrast that Chinese philosophy makes with Indian philosophy. It is not surprising to find Chinese philosophers who sound very much like other secular or humanistic voices in the West, and that may account, at least in part, for the traditional Western fascination for all things Chinese.

2. Confucianism

Probably the earliest philosophy in China, and certainly the most long-lasting and prestigious, was that of Confucius (551-479 B.C.). Confucius' philosophy is propelled by a strongly humanistic and ethical orientation, coupled with a tacit agnosticism about metaphysical questions. Thus on religious questions and on the issue of human nature, Confucius is reported to have been silent, or said nothing, or preached agnosticism. The record is not entirely clear, nor is the evidence all on one side. But it seems clear that Confucius generally was concerned with matters other than "the nature of things." Certainly he refers to the Mandate of Heaven (Tien-ming) as the moral foundation of human

228

existence, but it would appear that he also thought of Heaven (Tien) as impersonal in nature. The same is true of his discussion of Tao and the realization of te or virtue: the emphasis is all on the realization of virtue, not on the notion of Tao as such.

Confucius emphasized three ideals with respect to human virtue: Wisdom, Humanity (jen), and Righteousness (yi). Knowledge or Wisdom pertains to what is central or foundational in human existence; but Confucius interpreted such knowledge only in relation to the ethical ideals of Humanity (jen) and Righteousness (yi). Humanity (jen) has two aspects. The first, conscientiousness (chung), is positive; the second, altruism (shu), is negative and refers to the idea that one should not do to others what one would not want to have done to oneself (a kind of negative version of the Golden Rule). Righteousness is perhaps the real heart of humanity (jen) for Confucius, who says that righteousness is the very substance of things. Indeed, what the "Man of Virtue" possesses over inferior men (and Confucius was clearly speaking of men, not women) is precisely righteousness; by contrast, the inferior are concerned with the desire for profit. It is in this way that the Confucian gentleman is perhaps most clearly marked off from those who must work or trade for a living.

This rather conservative evaluation of the social superiority of the educated gentleman becomes apparent in a doctrine which is closely related to the call for righteousness in human conduct: namely, the question of the rectification of names. If one wants to know how to act, and specifically what it means to act righteously, the answer can be found in the very names that are used in designating the various social positions and offices of individuals. Thus, for Confucius, the superior individual is one who respects parents for what they are, brothers for what they are, women for what they are (and Confucianists consistently held to the belief in the inferiority of women), kings for what they are, and so forth. The matter can be put in a more positive light: if, to take a contemporary example, education has declined, it may be because teachers do not understand any more what it is to be a teacher, and students do not understand what it is to be a student. Thus the doctrine of the rectification of names simply means that the social situation is to be rectified by everyone becoming what their relevant names describe by nature. The rectification of names was an attempt to restore social order and harmony by insisting on the crucial significance of language itself. It is in this interpretation of righteousness in terms of the rectification of names that the political and social preoccupations of Confucianism can be clearly seen.

Confucius' social ideal was harmony built on restraint from

doing harm to others, and on the full development of one's nature. There is both a negative and a positive side to this ideal, and one can see this very clearly in his political philosophy. Thus the good ruler, as an instance of the "Man of Virtue", is marked both by virtue in the positive sense, and by inaction in the negative sense. Inaction is understood here as not doing anything unnatural. Later Confucianists would contrast this understanding of inaction with the Taoist ideal of inaction which had a much more radical tinge to it. In any event, Confucius emphasized virtue as the foundation of the political order in opposition to those who favored principles of violence or force. Confucius argued that those who use violence or force will never bring about peace because they disturb the fundamental harmony of things. It is interesting to note that while Confucius emphasized some very conservative social principles (the rectification of names in particular), he also drew some conclusions which may not always have been welcome among the ruling class: for example, the notion that extremes of poverty and wealth tended to promote violence and therefore a lack of harmony and balance. The state is thus founded upon an equal distribution of wealth, on harmony and on peace. The ruler of such a state is one who is primarily concerned with the realization of nature and thus of virtue, and with refraining from anything contrary to nature. "Nature" here clearly refers to the twin ideals of Humanity (jen) and Wisdom. Confucius' ideal may have been conservative, but its high ethical tone made it attractive to many different factions within Chinese society. But it certainly met with serious challenges in the ancient period, as will be seen.

Main works: The Analects (sayings of Confucius arranged by his pupils).

Confucius' philosophy underwent two important interpretations, the one idealist, the other realist. Representative of the first was Mencius, of the second Hsun Tzu.

Mencius (371-289 B.C.) represents the more idealistic, and, some might say, "mystical" interpretation of Confucian philosophy. Mencius seems to have begun with the question: why have people become so bad or evil? The answer to that question is implied in the question itself, insofar as it is presumed that people have become bad. This suggests that by nature humans are good, and that it is society or socialization which makes people evil. In the ancient period, Mencius was distinctive in maintaining this notion of natural human goodness. But the significance of this notion of an innate goodness was that it allowed Mencius to reconstruct Confucianism on what he considered to be a firmer foundation.

Perhaps the most unique turn in Mencius' thought is his recognition that realizing one's good nature means achieving unity with some kind of transcendent power or spirit. Mencius is notably vague about the nature of this reality, but it is clear that the experience of an innate human goodness is closely related to it. In any event, Mencius characterizes this transcendent power in one passage as a kind of moral destiny. This is not quite an extreme form of fatalism, but he was accused of holding a form of that theory.

Human moral nature is innate, and Mencius proposes what he calls the Four Beginnings of Human Nature, that is, four developments of human goodness: humanity (jen), righteousness (yi), propriety, and wisdom. His most important contribution here seems to be a kind of systematization of Confucian ethics. Perhaps a more important contribution, however, lies in his discussion of the realization of these Four Beginnings in love. Mencius very much emphasized love as the final goal of ethical life. By love he insisted that he meant love of all, no matter whom, a conception which was clearly universalist and ruled out any kind of egoism. But Mencius adds an important proviso and qualification to this notion of universalist love, a proviso which is very much in tune with the Confucian doctrine of the rectification of names. Specifically, Mencius argues that universal love cannot be extended to each and every person in exactly the same way. Universal love is not mathematically egalitarian. To the contrary, love must always respect the nature of the other, especially the social role or position that individual has. Thus love varies between parent and child, as compared with husband and wife, and so forth. A universal love which respects differences rather than wishes them away is the kind of love that Mencius urges.

Mencius' political philosophy is an amalgam of populist and elitist sentiments. On the one hand, he sharply distinguishes between those who labor and those who think, and asserts that the latter should rule the former in the ideal state. In this regard his proposals have been compared with the general thrust of Plato's Republic. Yet despite this conservative preoccupation, Mencius became known historically for his populist sentiments. Like Confucius he insisted that the ruler should govern through virtue. He strongly condemned those who employ force, and those who used double standards in their dealings with citizens. Further, the people should guide the ruler in all important political decisions. Mencius clearly suggests that the ruler should ignore the advice of his ministers and constantly seek what the people want. If the king does not do this, and if the king pursues actions that are evil, Mencius affirms the right of the people to overthrow the ruler. Clearly, Mencius' political philosophy is on the whole more critical of governmental leadership than Confucius' philosophy was.

Main works: The Book of Mencius (arranged by pupils of Mencius).

Although Mencius came to be regarded as the foremost interpreter of Confucius, his fame was eclipsed temporarily by another follower of Confucius who could not have been more different in his mentality and concerns: Hsün Tzu (fl. 298-238 B.C.). Hsün Tzu represents the "realistic" interpretation of Confucius. His influence on the highly authoritarian Ch'in dynasty (221-206 B.C.) was quite significant, and his influence on Chinese thought generally flourished for hundreds of years, until the advent of Neo-Confucianism which held Mencius in much greater esteem.

Hsün Tzu began with the same question that Mencius did: how have people come to be so evil? Hsün Tzu argued that they had become evil because they were born that way—that is, that humans by nature were evil. A clear sign of this can be found in the feelings of conflict and strife that pervade human emotions from the beginning of life. But this notion of the innate evil of human nature did not lead Hsün Tzu to any kind of fatalism: to the contrary, he developed the humanistic philosophy of Confucianism as a kind of antidote to human nature itself. Specifically, Hsün Tzu argued that while human nature was evil, the actions of humans need not be. Through knowledge, and especially through education, it was possible to become righteous, to set up good laws in the state, and to practice propriety. Because education is so important, Hsün Tzu made clear that the proper concern of all knowledge is the human—not the transcendent or Heaven (T'ien). Heaven was impersonal, and nothing could be gained by studying it. All knowledge of any use was knowledge of human nature, human behavior, and human wisdom.

If Mencius stressed universal love in his account, Hsün Tzu stressed knowledge or wisdom. Indeed, Hsün Tzu became one of the most important of the ancient Chinese logicians. Everything in human affairs was dependent on knowing nature or investigating things. But to investigate nature meant that one investigated names or language, since knowledge of language or human thought was presupposed for any other kind of understanding. Hsün Tzu argued that names (in language) had both logical and social causes. Logically, every name has its origin in something experienced through the senses or through the mind. Similar things have similar names, dissimilar things have dissimilar names. But names also have social causes. The names of things—that is, language generally—were first appointed by the ancient sage-kings of China, and thus all language is conventional and customary. Hsün Tzu lays more stress on the conventional nature of language, than on its supposed origin in sense perception, thus

232

confirming his emphasis on a humanistic as opposed to a naturalistic account of language.

Given this analysis of language, Hsün Tzu went on to offer
an analysis of the various kinds of error that are possible. His
point was that error, lack of knowledge, is at the root of human
evil, and only through an enlightened understanding of error
could humans do what was good. In any event, he argued that
there were two basic kinds of error: error that was purely linguistic or came about simply because of insufficient knowledge of
grammar, and error that stemmed from a lack of understanding how
language applied to reality. With regard to the latter, there
were two further possible kinds of error: one could attribute
some purely imaginary quality to some really existent thing; or
one could attribute some really existent quality to some purely
imaginary thing.

In all of this concern for language, one can see how an
ethical doctrine such as the rectification of names might lead to
a concern for understanding the nature and function of the names
that were used. It is for this reason that Hsün Tzu's thought
represents one of the high points of ancient Chinese logic.

Main works: Hsün Tzu (some chapters may have been written by
his students).

3. Taoism

The origin of the religion of Taoism is wrapped in obscurity. The primary document of both religious and philosophical relevance is the long, mystical, and enigmatic poem
traditionally called the Lao Tzu. It was supposedly written by
an individual also named Lao Tzu (Master Lao). Just who this
individual was, and when he lived, and whether he ever wrote the
book ascribed to him is a matter of intense controversy to this
day. About the only way one can summarize the matter is to say
that the individual lived, and the book was written, both sometime between the 6th and 3rd centuries B.C. Some would have Lao
Tzu as an older contemporary of Confucius; some would have him
living centuries later. The evidence is exceptionally unclear.
What is clear, however, is that this mystical and poetic work was
one of the most important in Chinese philosophy, and has come to
be known as a classic of World literature as well. It should
also be understood that Taoist philosophy is anti-Confucian at
almost every point, and cannot be sensibly interpreted otherwise.

Though the Lao Tzu is intensely mystical, often obscure, it
is very much concerned with traditional ethical questions, and
with political philosophy. But it is best to begin an account of
Taoist philosophy with the very notion of Tao.

233

The concept of Tao is not unique to Taoism--it is found in virtually all of the ancient Chinese thinkers. Taoism has come to be known by this term, however, because of its unusual emphasis on the transcendent reality of Tao, a term which literally means " the Way". The conceptualization of Tao in Taoism is somewhat like that of a transcendent God in some religions. Thus, Tao is said to be eternal and infinite, absolutely simple, unchangeable, and nondependent. But other characteristics ascribed to Tao are decidedly more "mystical" and impersonal in significance. Thus Tao is said to be vague and elusive, empty, bottomless. The non-existence of Tao is repeatedly asserted, and concomitantly it is said that Tao is without names, and thus cannot be spoken of. The closest parallel to this sort of thing is perhaps the notion of Nirvana in Madyamika Buddhism, or the radical negative theology of Plotinus.

Tao differs from the universe in that the universe can be said to exist, and can be named both as a whole and in its various parts. How the universe came to be from Tao is not made clear--there are several apparently conflicting accounts given. One passage seems to suggest that Tao and the universe are the same in origin, and that the difference between the two appears only when different names are given to the two. But this is not clear.

The ethics of Taoism consists in following the Way (Tao). But this standard ethical maxim, which can be found in many Chinese philosophical systems, is given an unusual twist in Taoism. To follow Tao for the Taoist sage is to become one thing so that one may be its very opposite. Thus if one wants to act, one should not act; if one wants to teach, one should be silent; if one wants to be the highest, one should be the lowest, and so forth. The point is that direct pursuit of a goal through the realization of desire will never accomplish that goal. One accomplishes things by inaction, by inward concentration, by appearing to be weak. One must realize within oneself the complete vacuity or nothingness that the Tao is by nature. With this mystical realization, one will become unified with the world and with nature, and thus impartial and universal. Love for the Taoist is universalist, but unlike that love preached by Mencius, it respects no differences because it is utterly impartial. The Taoist ethic is highly individual and notably unconcerned with social distinctions; it is in this sense that it is diametrically opposed to the general thrust of Confucianism. Further, Taoism holds that only through unity with the transcendent reality of Tao will the ethical ideal be realized. Although Mencius was moving in that direction, most Confucianist philosophy remained adamantly opposed to an other-worldly or mystical concern; indeed the Taoist mystics were part of the social problem from the

234

Confucian point of view. And the Confucians were victims of ignorance of the fundamental nature of things, at least according to the Taoists.

Somewhat surprisingly for a document reputed for its mysticism, a significant part of the Lao Tzu is concerned with political philosophy. The latter centers on two topics: the good and wise ruler on the one hand, and good government on the other hand. The good ruler, for the Taoist, is one who is unified with the Tao, and thus marked by a profound lack of selfishness, by an undifferentiated love for the people, and by a profound reserve and caution. If the sage has no desires, he seeks to keep the people without desires. Thus he makes sure that the people have enough food to eat; he discourages the pursuit of knowledge (surely a jab at the Confucianist emphasis on education); and he weakens their ambition (Confucian intellectuals were known at times for their ambition at court). The sage-ruler achieves his ends through inaction. The less that is done out of desire, the more the order of the state will appear.

The best government from the Taoist viewpoint, then, is one which is ruled by a sage (not by a Confucian!). This government succeeds by avoiding social strife, and it does the latter by minimizing every chance of raising the level of desire. Thus the good government does not single out some people for honor and praise, since that will create resentment and strife; the good government does not create rare treasures which citizens will want to possess for themselves. The Taoist philosophy strongly rejects the use of violence and force, condemns all wars, all capital punishment, any strong army, indeed any weapons. The ideal government is quite literally that which does nothing, and which thus allows all to live in peace and tranquility. There is a strong note of protest in all this against government as such; and while the Lao Tzu continued to acknowledge the need for a good and wise ruler, it understood ruling largely in terms of inaction. Confucian political philosophy also emphasized inaction, but its conception of inaction generally meant doing what the full development of human nature required—that is, it was an essentially positive conception of inaction. By contrast, the Taoist notion was decidedly and radically negative in its understanding of inaction. For if all action is based on desire, and if all desire is contrary to the Tao which is quiet and self-contained, then it follows that the highest ethical standpoint will be one of non-action and non-desire. So, although both Confucianist and Taoist philosophy capitalize on the concept of inaction, they differ radically in their interpretations of that concept.

Perhaps the point can be made more clearly by contrasting the Confucian emphasis on the rectification of names, with the

235

Taoist notion of the Tao as name-less. For the Confucian, the attainment of virtue meant the recognition of the social structure embedded in language itself. The project of the rectification of names was an attempt to take language and the social distinctions founded upon it as having fundamental significance. By contrast, the Taoist sage who identified with the nameless absolute recognized the relativity of all names, and thus of all language. The Taoist was not radically egalitarian; but certainly the Taoist denied that names had ultimate significance. If the Taoist sage became "empty", that was as much as saying that no name was applicable to the sage. In the end, both the Confucian and the Taoist followed nature: but for the former "nature" had a clear social and hierarchical meaning, whereas for the latter, its meaning transcended all language.

The first identifiable Taoist philosopher other than Lao Tzu is Chuang Tzu (fl. 399-295 B.C.), who was very likely a contemporary of Mencius. Chuang Tzu did not add very much to Taoism, but did draw out some of its implications in interesting ways.

Chuang Tzu's understanding of Tao is that of a unity immanent in the multiplicity of things. His metaphysics plays a great deal on the difference between multiplicity and unity. He suggests a kind of cosmology or cosmogony, based loosely on the Lao Tzu, whereby all things originate with Tao (which is non-being). From Tao comes The One which is named Being. From The One comes the duality of Yin and Yang. From this duality come the multiplicity of things that exist. Things either have life or physical form (li), or they have spirit or nature. By following nature, humans return to that out of which all things were produced, i.e., the Tao. Chuang Tzu is at pains to emphasize the necessary character of this process. This leads him first of all to deny the existence of a personal deity—a point which he has in common with many Chinese philosophers. Secondly, the process of the emergence of things seems to be eternal, with neither beginning nor end. Time is divided into cycles, each cycle being characterized by the emergence of the complex and multiple from the simple. Chuang Tzu even suggests a kind of primitive account of evolution, holding that from germs came plants, from plants insects, from insects horses, and from horses—humans! (Suggesting that humans "evolved" from horses may seem odd, but the Chinese had a great love and respect for horses [as may be witnessed in their ceramic art especially]. Perhaps the Darwinian theory was doomed in the popular mind from the outset, given the Western contempt for monkeys and apes.)

Chuang Tzu's more important philosophical contribution came with his meditation on the nature of knowledge. He distinguished between great and small knowledge on the one hand, and between waking and sleeping knowledge on the other. The distinction between great and small knowledge is based on the difference between knowing the whole, and knowing only the parts or fragments of the whole of reality. The sage possesses great knowledge, the inferior individual only small knowledge. But how does one come to possess great knowledge? Essentially, one must come to see that opposites are not distinct, but are bound together by unity. Small knowledge insists on recognizing in opposites some kind of ultimate difference. The difference between great and small knowledge can also be understood in terms of waking and sleeping knowledge. Chuang Tzu understood that waking knowledge is about the absolute distinction between this thing and that thing. By contrast, sleeping knowledge or dream knowledge is knowledge in which this thing and that are understood as existing together in unity. The knowledge of the sage is based on the recognition that the experience of things in this life is like that in a dream where all things are blended together into a unity. The inferior individual does not recognize the dream-like character of this life, and so assumes that one thing is really distinct from another.

There is an important corollary for Chuang Tzu in this distinction between "wholistic" knowledge and fragmentary knowledge. Both reason or logic and speech or language are oriented toward the expression of fragmentary knowledge. Knowledge of the unity of things, that is, knowledge of Tao, is beyond reason and language.

It is through the possession of great knowledge that an individual becomes a sage. For great knowledge means seeing the unity in opposites. Now those who see this unity in opposites recognize that life and death, for example, are not ultimately real in themselves, but are bound together in the unity of Tao. For this reason, the sage is capable of standing beyond both life and death, which become a matter of indifference.

The sage who has become one with Tao is both active and tranquil, according to Chuang Tzu, who here modifies to some extent the Lao Tzu's emphasis on inaction. As tranquil, the individual is a sage; but as active, the individual is a king. Thus king and sage are opposites bound together in unity. It is at this point that Chuang Tzu's emphasis on the dialectical relation of opposites in unity brings him to express the ideal of the sage in terms slightly different from that of the Lao Tzu.

Chuang Tzu's emphasis on the dreamlike nature of life and on the unity within multiplicity tended to cast an idealistic interpretation on Taoism. This orientation would help make Taoism relevant to the various forms of Mahayana Buddhism that emigrated to China about the time of Christ.

237

Main works: <u>Chuang Tzu</u> (parts by Chuang Tzu, most written by pupils).

4. Moism

This ancient school of Chinese philosophy was named after its most prominent member, <u>Mo Tzu</u> (fl. 479-381). Mo Tzu was a member of the warrior class, and Moism as a philosophy was associated with this class and its perspective on reality. There has been some speculation, however, that Moism may reflect the interests of the lower, rather than the upper, classes of China. However, that must remain speculative.

Mo Tzu was a prominent and well-known opponent of Confucianism. Whereas the latter emphasized humanity (<u>jen</u>), the former emphasized righteousness and love. Both of these were understood in ways quite opposed to that of Confucianism, however. Righteousness was understood as obedience to the Will of God or Heaven, and thus understood not so much in terms of human nature, but in terms of a transcendent spirit of some kind. Secondly, love was understood as universal and without distinctions of any kind. This was clearly opposed to the philosophy of Mencius and of Confucius. Concomitant with this emphasis on universal love without distinctions was a strong condemnation of war. Ironically, much of Mo Tzu's philosophy was concerned with the details of military preparedness. This is to be expected for those who were professional warriors; what is unusual is the strong emphasis on love and condemnation of war.

If being righteous was a matter of obedience to the Will of Heaven, the emperor's righteousness stemmed from his being elected by Heaven itself. That there is an emperor is a function both of divine ordination, and of the nature of society, which seems to be one of moral anarchy. Thus the function of political rule for Mo Tzu was to create moral order.

There was present in Mo Tzu's philosophy a strong tendency toward a form of humanism at variance with the Confucian version. The Moist humanism was founded upon the rejection of fatalism. As he understood the concept, Mo Tzu seems to have thought that both Confucianists and Taoists were fatalistic. Fatalism—the belief that all things happen because of the mandate of Heaven— had actually corrupted society. But how is this rejection of fatalism connected with the emphasis on obedience to the will of God or Heaven? Was Mo Tzu contradicting himself? It would seem not. Indeed, his point may have been that righteousness presupposes a certain freedom, a freedom which is rooted in Heaven itself. For Mo Tzu clearly indicates his belief in a loving God and various spirits that inhabit the universe. If so, the doctrine of righteous obedience may be founded not so much on human nature, as on the nature of the higher spirits in the universe.

That freedom is what is involved here becomes especially clear when one encounters in Mo Tzu the unusual and perhaps unexpected condemnation of music and funeral ceremonies. This condemnation, which is an attack on the Confucianists who championed proper performance of religious ritual, was founded on an overt appeal to utilitarianism. Mo Tzu is amazingly frank about the basis for determining what is good for the individual or society. In essence, that which is virtuous is so because it gives pleasure, while that which is evil is always the cause of pain and harm. If universal love is championed, then, it is because it is that which gives the most pleasure and happiness to all. Thus there is the strange fact that Confucianists, who were mostly agnostic about God and spirits, defended religious ritual because human destiny hung in the balance, while Moists, who believed in God and the spirits, attacked such ritual as fatalistic. Confucianism, like the Mimamsa philosophy of Hinduism, emphasized ritual at the expense of agnosticism, while Moism emphasized the evaluation of ritual by frankly external norms, ultimately founded upon obedience to God.

The thought of Mo Tzu thus shows that beneath its apparent contradictions there is a kind of internal unity based on a hedonistic utilitarianism and a denial that religious ritual has any value. What is interesting is that this philosophy defended both God and an egalitarian pleasure principle against the Confucianist espousal of an impersonal heaven and the cultivation of virtue among an elite group of intellectuals.

Moism had a brief moment of glory in ancient China, but it did not survive the Confucianist attack on it. Interest in Moism, as in so many of the ancient Chinese doctrines, has been revived in modern times, in part because of the peculiarly modern ring to Western ears of the Moist doctrine.

Main works: Mo Tzu.

5. The School of Names

The School of Names consisted of a group of debaters or rhetoricians whose interests apparently turned to serious logical questions centering on the relation between names or language and reality. As such, it was unique in the history of Chinese philosophy, having virtually no influence on subsequent developments.

There are two thinkers of some note associated with this group. The first is Hui Shih (380-c.305 B.C.), who was most likely a friend of Chuang Tzu. It is difficult to unravel

239

exactly what Hui Shih believed, since almost all of his recorded sayings consist of riddles and paradoxes. One fairly convincing interpretation of these paradoxes is that Hui Shih was arguing in favor of the relativity of space and time--that is, that space and time were unreal and marked by genuine contradictions. There is some indication that his fundamental view may have centered on the absolute unity of all things--a view not unlike that of Chuang Tzu. Indeed, it has been proposed that the relation between the Hui Shih and Chuang Tzu is not unlike that between Zeno and Parmenides in ancient Greek thought. Certainly some of Hui Shih's paradoxes are remarkably similar to those of Zeno.

Main works: Most information on Hui Shih's philosophy can be found in several chapters of the Chuang Tzu.

A second logician was Kung-sun Lung Tzu (380 B.C.-?). The significance of his theory is even less clear than that of Hui Shih, in part because of a very abstract argument, coupled with a hopelessly corrupted text. It would seem that Kung-sun Lung's starting point was the Confucian project of the rectification of names, and that his intellectual energy was poured into the endeavor to understand the logical relation between names and things. One interpretation of his theory is that there is a difference between each name and every other name, and that each name is permanent and universal in its denotation. Or, to put it in other words, a name like "white" denotes what in the West is called the idea or concept or universal of "whiteness"--and not any particular or concrete reality. As so interpreted, Kung-sun Lung's theory would seem to be similar to Plato's theory of forms. However, this interpretation is only tentative and provisional, if for no other reason than that Kung-sun Lung's writing is so obscure. In any event, it does seem that while Hui Shih emphasized the relativity of space and time, Kung-sun Lung emphasized the non-relativity or absoluteness of names or concepts, in relation to real things.

Main works: Kung-sun Lung Tzu.

6. The Yin Yang School

This "school" consisted largely of a text of extraordinary importance for Chinese thought generally--the I Ching or Book of Changes--and one philosopher named Tsou Yen.

The I Ching, or the basis of it, goes back to ancient practices of divination. The theory of divination is that there is an inherent connection between humanity on the one hand, and Heaven and Earth on the other. By understanding the structure of the universe, one can gain insight into those human actions that are either best related to, or harmonized with, that of the

240

universe. Originally, there were two sets of principles of great importance: the Yin and Yang principle, and the Five Elements. Yang perhaps originally meant sunshine, while yin meant the absence of such. They were regarded as cosmic principles, yang being associated with masculinity, activity, heat, brightness, and odd numbers, and yin being associated with femininity, passivity, cold, darkness, and even numbers. Yang is represented by an unbroken line, yin by a broken line. Yin and Yang are dynamic principles, and like the union of the male and the female produce all the various things that make up the universe. Each thing in the universe is thus some amalgam or rational proportion of yin and yang.

All of this was symbolized in the 64 hexagrams of the I Ching. A hexagram is simply a six-line figure. The six lines are written one on top of the other. Each line is either unbroken (the Yang principle) or broken (the Yin principle). The theory of the I Ching is that each hexagram was formed by the "mating" of two trigrams (figures with just three lines in them), of which there were 8. These eight trigrams, from which all 64 hexagrams could be formed, were:

1. Ch'ien (Heaven)   ☰

2. K'un (Earth)   ☷

3. Chen (thunder)   ☳

4. Sun (wood, wind)   ☴

5. K'an (water)   ☵

6. Li (fire, sun)   ☲

7. Ken (mountain)   ☶

8. Tui (marsh)   ☱

Just as a given hexagram can be regarded as the "marriage" of two trigrams, so each trigram can be regarded as the intermingling of the two kinds of lines (broken or unbroken), symbolizing the two principles of yin and yang. The point of all this is that the universe as a whole has rational principles; that those rational principles, and the changes that occur in the world in accordance with them, are comprehensible in terms of a dynamic interaction of two fundamental principles; and that all things in the world are founded upon some kind of numeric proportion. While these principles are not unlike those found in Pythagoreanism and are thus not unallied with a scientific

241

spirit, Chinese science never developed in the way Western science did.

Besides the principles of Yin and Yang, there was also a tradition of the Five elements. These elements were water, fire, wood, metal, and soil. To each of these elements there corresponded five human phenomena: appearance, speech, vision, hearing, and thought. This kind of schema was broadened so that time itself could be divided into five's.

It is in connection with the latter that the philosopher Tsou Yen (305-240 B.C.) proposed a theory of history based on the notion of the Five Elements. Though nothing of his writings has survived, it appears that he proceeded to a theory of history by an extraordinary gathering of inductive data about the world in the present, and proceeded to work backwards through time. On the basis of this monumental gathering of data, he proposed a cyclical theory of history, based on the succession of yin and yang principles, the latter succession being determined by the "rotation" or relative importance of each of the Five Elements-- water, fire, wood, metal, and earth--in a given period of time. Obviously, by knowing which particular cycle of yin or yang one was in, and under which predominant element, one might better know how to live virtuously. It seems likely that Tsou Yen's ethics were Confucian; it is known that he was better accepted for the latter, than for this rather speculative philosophy of history.

7. The Legalist School

The last of the six ancient schools of philosophy was in fact the last to take shape before the onset of the Han dynasty around 200 B.C. While some of the ideas of this "legalist" philosophy probably date back to the period of Confucius, the most prominent member of this school, and one who was associated with the Ch'in dynasty's brief experiment in government (221-206 B.C.), was Han Fei Tzu (?-233 B.C.). His philosophy is original--startling so, at times--and combines various elements from Confucianism and Taoism. But his thinking is generally original and independent.

Like Hsün Tzu, who was his teacher for a time, Han Fei Tzu seems to have held to the belief in the inherent evil of human nature. But from this premise of an evil human nature, Han Fei Tzu derived very different consequences than did Hsün Tzu. The latter emphasized education and humanity as a remedy for this evil. But Han Fei Tzu denounced the whole Confucian program of education and virtue as unworkable and irrelevant. From his point of view, the evil of human nature can only be corrected through political solutions.

242

Han Fei Tzu realized that, if one wants the majority of human beings to do the good and avoid evil, no solution dependent upon individual initiative is practicable. What is required is a way of forcing everyone to be good. This can be done in two ways: by rewarding the good, and by punishing the evil. Reward and punishment are a function of laws. Hence, the most important way in which human evil can be eliminated is through strong laws. As a consequence, Han Fei Tzu was ruthlessly critical of the notion of love as the Confucians practiced it: law is for everyone, and should apply equally. In this regard, he sounds like a Moist.

Did Han Fei Tzu think of the ruler of government as a kind of modern dictator? In one sense he did; but in fact his rhetoric is curiously Taoistic. The good ruler rules by means of inaction, he insists. Inaction means that the ruler takes no deliberate action. This can only happen, however, if the ruler practices statecraft and uses laws. Statecraft involves the wise appointment of subordinate ministers. These ministers are also to be subjected to the laws, so that their deeds correspond to their "names" (that is, that they actually do what their position requires them to do). This is, of course, a version of the Confucian rectification of names. But, as has been pointed out, names are rectified here not on the basis of personal virtue but on the basis of law itself.

In the end, the ruler takes no action only because his ministers do; and they are controlled through the laws. One can see in all this a kind of rationalization of the "inaction" ideal, an attempt perhaps to show how order can emerge from what appears to be a negative ideal. Thus the curious marriage of a politics of power with a rhetoric of impotence.

Significantly, Han Fei Tzu did add in an interesting way to Taoistic metaphysics. He proposes that each thing that is produced by Tao has its own principle (li). Indeed, he says that Tao is realized only when principle (li) is definite. This is because Tao in itself is nondeterminate and without principle. This emphasis on li as mediating between concrete things and Tao is perhaps the only element in Han Fei Tzu's thought that did have some subsequent influence. His political thought seems to have fallen into permanent disrepute with the fall of the Ch'in dictatorship.

Main works: Han Fei Tzu.

C.   CONFUCIANISM,   NEO-TAOISM,   AND   THE INFLUX OF BUDDHISM (200
B.C.-960 A.D.)

1.   Introduction

After the notorious incident of the Burning of the Confucian
Books in 213 B.C. and the fall of the infamous Ch'in dynasty in
206 B.C., there was a strong return to more traditional government and eventually to a state-sponsored Confucianism in the Han
dynasty (206 B.C.-220 A.D.).   This period of time was at first
dominated by the rise of Confucianism, but then declined with the
emergence of Neo-Taoism in the 2rd century A.D.   But perhaps the
most important event philosophically was the importation of
Buddhism, which began in the middle of the Han dynasty, grew
steadily during the period of Inner Turmoil (220-589) and the Sui
Dynasty (589-618), and reached both its climax and decline in the
the T'ang dynasty (618-907).   After this long period (nearly
eight or nine hundred years) of influence from the outside, there
was a strong reaction against Buddhism, and after a period of
internal strife (907-960), the first of several more stable
dynasties arose under which the great neo-Confucian systems would
be produced.   What is important to realize is that the neo-
Confucianism of this later period relied upon the various advances in Confucian, Taoist, and Buddhist thought made in the Han
dynasty and afterward. Indeed, this later neo-Confucianism is in
many ways unthinkable without these earlier developments.

2.   The Development of Confucianism Before the Rise of Buddhism

In the centuries immediately after the fall of the Ch'in
dynasty, Confucianism dominated the intellectual scene.   It was
during this time that the debate arose about the relative merits
of the interpretations of Mencius and Hsün Tzu.   For the most
part, it was Hsün Tzu's interpretation that was favored.   But
perhaps the most interesting development was the tendency to
incorporate elements of the **Book** of **Changes** into Confucianism.
The I Ching itself did not reach its present day form until the
3rd century A.D., but the interest in it by the other philosophical schools was significant.

Three Confucian philosophers seem to sum up the development
of this school during much of the Han dynasty.   The first, **Tung**
Chung-shu (179-104 B.C.), helped to make Confucianism a state
philosophy (which occurred in 136 B.C.), and was known for his
efforts in synthesizing the Yin-Yang school with Confucianism.
Thus he argued that the Universe as a whole is made up of a
trinity of Heaven, Earth, and Man. Heaven and Earth are fundamental, while Man is a microcosm of these two principles.   Now
Heaven and Earth are formed by the principles of Yin and Yang,
and so Man, as the microcosm of Heaven and Earth, is also formed

by the same principles. Changes in the relative balance of the one principle with respect to the other demands a natural adjustment on the part of Man to those changes.

It is important to note here that Tung Chung-shu emphasizes not so much the complementarity of yin and yang, as the tendency for one to dominate over the other. In this regard, yang is inherently superior to yin, as the male to the female, and so on. When Tung Chung-shu went on to apply this notion of the yin and yang to various social relationships, the conclusion was to emphasize the asymmetric nature of those relations in a way that was quite consistent with the Confucian project of the rectification of names.

Tung Chung-shu also formulated a theory of the three kinds or types of historical ages. There is, first, the "Black Age", symbolizing the black void which exists before anything acts. Second, there is the "White Age", symbolizing the initial growth and formation of all things in the world. Third, there is the "Red Age", symbolizing the full activity and realization of all things. These three ages are related to Tung's threefold cosmological schema: The One or Origin, from which all things come; Heaven and Earth as the initial growth and principle of all things; and the full development of Man and the multitude of things. The sage is understood as the one who is able to trace Man back to the Origin of all things. This is clearly a different understanding of the "sage" than can be found in Confucius, insofar as it emphasizes the cosmological over the ethical.

Tung Chung-shu also demonstrates some independence from Confucius, as well as an admiration for Hsün Tzu, in his discussion of humanity and wisdom, and in his theory of human nature. He strongly emphasizes the equal importance of Humanity (jen) and Wisdom, and the dependence of the one on the other. This emphasis is typical of the influence of Hsün Tzu. But just as strong is Tung Chung-shu's emphasis on an evil human nature. Interestingly, Tung Chung-shu believed that it was not merely wisdom and learning that were needed to correct this situation-- it was a state-enforced education that was needed. Thus, there is here a hint of the kind of political realism typical of Han Fei Tzu (also influenced, it will be remembered, by Hsün Tzu), a realism which led to the adoption of Confucianism as the state philosophy in 136 B.C.

Thus, while Tung Chung-shu is noted for his amalgamation of the Yin-Yang school's cosmology with the traditional Confucian emphasis on ethics, that project was clearly subordinated to, and suffused throughout by, an emphasis on authoritarianism that grew out of the political realism of the age--a realism which was fostered by Hsün Tzu's interpretation of Confucius. Though Hsün Tzu would eventually lose favor among Confucianists, it was precisely Tung Chung-shu's achievement in the political and educational realms which helped to insure the long-term survival and triumph of Confucianism in China.

Main work: Ch'un-ch'iu fan-lu (Luxuriant Gems of the "Spring and Autumn Annals").

A second Confucianist of the Han Dynasty, although of lesser importance, was Yang Hsiung (53 B.C.-18 A.D.). His thought is not terribly profound, his eclectic spirit typical of the age. Yang Hsiung is noted for two developments in Confucian thought. The first is the suggestion, and it is not more than that, that human nature is both good and evil. That is, there are good elements in human nature and evil elements in it, and what one becomes in life is a matter of which elements one cultivates. One can see here a tendency toward synthesizing Mencius and Hsun Tzu. But the theory is not well explained or defended.

A second tendency in Yang Hsiung is toward the use of Taoist ideas. Specifically, Yang Hsiung speaks of an ultimate principle which he calls T'ai-hsüan, which literally means "the Supremely Profound Mystery". T'ai-hsüan is understood as utterly vacuous and formless, akin to nothingness, and it is said to be the origin of all things. This Supremely Profound Mystery gives rise to the world of myriad things, and specifically makes possible the fulfillment of human destiny. In this regard, the Confucian ethic is understood as the means whereby the Supremely Profound Mystery comes to pervade human life. In all this there can be seen an attempt to merge Taoist concepts with Confucianism. Yang Hsiung remains strongly Confucian, however.

Main works: Fa-yen (Model Sayings); T'ai-hsüan ching (Classic of the Supremely Profound Mystery).

The third thinker to be considered is Wang Ch'ung (27-100 A.D.), whose classification as a Confucianist may be somewhat questionable. For Wang Ch'ung represents a thoroughly independent spirit, sometimes quite Confucianist in orientation, and sometimes quite Taoist, though in surprising ways. However, it is probably best to see Wang Ch'ung as representative of a Confucianist reaction against certain elements within the Confucian tradition itself.

Wang Ch'ung's cosmology is borrowed from the Taoists. But he turns the fundamental principles of Taoism to a somewhat different purpose. Thus Tao is traditionally said to produce all things spontaneously. But that means that what is in the world occurs without conscious purpose and toward no external end. The

246

world just is because it has been produced by Tao: that is all that can be said. On this foundation, Wang Ch'ung draws the conclusion that any religious or philosophical tendency toward belief in the purposefulness of what goes on in the world, any tendency toward superstition or divination, and so forth, is based on a false assumption. Humans are distinct from Heaven and Earth and do not determine the activity of the latter. Religious ceremonies and rites have no effect on the world; for the activity of the world is purely spontaneous and founded on Tao.

Wang Ch'ung does not stop with this. He goes on to insist that humans are not immortal. One must remember here that the popular Chinese religion always centered on veneration of the immortal ancestors. Thus Wang Ch'ung was attacking religious life at its heart in his denial of immortality. He is quite explicit. He insists that human life is closely tied to the life of the body, and that human consciousness is dependent on sense-perception. He points out the effects of sickness on consciousness, which suggests that consciousness is essentially related to the health of the body. Reports about the existence of ghosts are obviously fraudulent, since ghosts have a way of having bodies and wearing clothes even after they are dead. Clearly, the life of ghosts is peculiarly similar to life as it occurs elsewhere—it depends on bodily life and not otherwise.

In all of this, it is not implausible to see Wang Ch'ung as developing the naturalistic and skeptical elements inherent in the Confucian tradition. But what is of interest is that much of this seems to be based on his acceptance of Taoist metaphysics.

Wang Ch'ung was a Confucianist, however, and that can be more clearly understood when examining his rather original comments on human nature. Three theories had been proposed in the history of Confucianism—those of Mencius, Hsün Tzu, and Yang Hsiung. Mencius had argued that all were good by nature, Hsün Tzu that all were evil, and Yang Hsiung that all were both good and evil by nature. Wang Ch'ung resolved to synthesize these three positions into one that was more coherent. He argued that some people were born good, others were born evil. He then suggested that each of the three Confucian masters had been correct in one sense, and incorrect in another. The implication of this view is that education and learning will be far more essential for some than for others.

The overall emphasis in Wang Ch'ung's thought was toward naturalism. He was probably at odds with the general tendency of most Confucianists of his age, however, in that the latter favored a highly religious interpretation of Confucianism, and some were even suggesting that Confucius was a kind of divine being. Wang Ch'ung's naturalism was a form of protest against

247

this tendency.   Yet his defense of naturalism and skepticism was
founded upon the most pre-eminent religious philosophy of China--
namely Taoism.   Ironically, he furthered the tendency toward combining the two philosophies, even as he fought against some
implications of this tendency.

Main work: Lun-heng (Balanced Inquiries).

3. The Development of Neo-Taoism

Though much of the Han Dynasty was dominated by Confucianism, there was a tendency toward synthesizing elements from
other traditions, especially insofar as those elements provided a
firm metaphysical and cosmological base for the development of
Confucianism.   Ironically, this meant that in time Taoist philosophy would come back into play, precisely insofar as it offered
either a new way of interpreting Confucianism, or insofar as it
offered a genuine alternative to Confucianism.   Until the end of
the Han dynasty, Taoism was largely a secondary philosophical
movement; but in the third century A.D., and with the fall of the
Han dynasty, a reaction against Confucianism set in, and there
developed a strong, if brief, movement toward Neo-Taoist philosophy.

The earliest philosopher in the Han Dynasty was Huai-nan Tzu
(?-122 B.C.).   He was not an original thinker, but he was important for two reasons: first, he showed a tendency toward rationalism in the cosmological scheme he elaborated, which would be
important for later developments; and secondly, he was a renowned
Taoist scholar at a time when there were few.

Main work: Huai-nan Tzu.

A second development can be found in a work entitled Lieh
Tzu.   This work is a product of the late Han Dynasty, and undoubtedly produced by Taoists of the time, who for various
reasons were not happy with the social situation of the 3rd
century A.D.   The work's nature is rather complex and confusing.
It is nominally a work by Lieh Tzu who supposedly lived in the
5th century B.C.   It contains a separate chapter, nominally by
Yang Chu, who lived in the 4th century B.C., which is quite
different in its character from the rest of the Lieh Tzu.   But
the work of the whole, while incorporating elements of these two
ancient philosophers, is clearly the work of another age.   The
philosophy expressed in the Lieh Tzu is a kind of Taoist skepticism; that of the Yang Chu Chapter is a form of hedonism. Both
are quite unorthodox within the Taoist tradition.

The skepticism expressed in the Lieh Tzu is rather profound.
It is claimed that the human mind cannot know anything about the

beginning and end of the universe, about the nature of the many things in the world, or about the nature of Heaven and Earth. This kind of skepticism is almost certainly related to the naturalism of Wang Ch'ung. However, it is well to remember that skepticism certainly may be an outcome of Taoist metaphysics, and one can perhaps see that in the ancient logician Hui Shih whose friend was Chuang Tzu. In any event, the skepticism of the <u>Lieh Tzu</u> is also combined with an unusual interpretation of the spontaneity of Tao: if Tao produces all things without effort, then the sage who is utterly vacuous because one with Tao produces all things without effort. This is stated in a way which suggests a fatalistic resignation about life, however. It is not clear that this philosophy of effortlessness is quite orthodox.

Even less orthodox perhaps is the open hedonism expressed in the Yang Chu Chapter of the <u>Lieh Tzu</u>. Here skepticism about the next life and the Taoist ideal of indifference with respect to life and death leads to an open embrace of the pleasures of this life. There is certainly implicit in all this an attack on the Confucian ethics, but this hedonistic strain is most unusual.

The most significant development of Taoism, however, came during the period of turmoil (220-589), during which the political situation was hopelessly corrupt and intellectual circles turned increasingly toward more religious views for solace and intellectual creativity. It is interesting that this period saw the rise not only of Taoism, but also of Buddhism.

Among the Taoists of this period, three especially stand out. The first is <u>Ho Yen</u> (?-249) who strongly emphasized Tao as the nameless and formless, beyond all knowledge and language. Ho Yen shows no originality, but his writings are marked by a kind of freshness and intellectual vigor.

Main works: <u>Tao lun</u> (<u>Treatise</u> on <u>Tao</u>); <u>Wu-ming lun</u> (<u>Treatise</u> on <u>the</u> <u>Nameless</u>).

The second Taoist of this period, and one who served as a government official for a time, is <u>Wang Pi</u> (226-249). He shows a tendency to combine elements of Confucianism within an overall Taoist perspective. But like Ho Yen, he strongly emphasizes the transcendent nature of Tao, its essential non-being. Indeed he says that non-being is the function (<u>yung</u>) of things, while being (which derives from non-being in Taoism) is the substance (<u>t'i</u>) of things. This distinction between function and substance will be of considerable importance to later neo-Confucianism, and it is first found in Wang Pi. Further, Wang Pi develops a distinction between the principle of things and the activities of things, and suggests that the former can be understood through the latter. This too would be important for later developments.

249

Wang Pi's ethics relies on Confucian terminology, but his conception of virtue seems to be rooted in Taoist metaphysics. Thus he insists that the sage-ruler will assist things in the development of their nature, and help them become what they are. By contrast, he will not institute new forms or establish new names in order to restrain things. The suggestion seems to be that the rectification of names can be justified if it is understood in terms of the spontaneous development of nature. But the emphasis in Wang Pi seems to be on a positive activity, and this may be because of his Confucian sympathies.

Main works: Chou-i lueh-li (Simple Exemplifications of the Principles of the "Book of Changes"); Commentary on the "Book of Changes"; Commentary on the "Lao Tzu".

The third Neo-Taoist of this period is Kuo Hsiang (?-312). Kuo Hsiang's approach was largely through a reinterpretation of the Chuang Tzu, rather than the Lao Tzu. Of some interest is his emphasis on the term Tzu-jan or Nature, as opposed to the notion of Tao. The implications of this are only partly verbal. For Kuo Hsiang emphasizes an entirely naturalistic and even this-worldly account of things. Each thing is said to have Nature as its norm or principle. Indeed, Kuo Hsiang goes so far as to say that Nature is in each thing, and therefore does not produce it. If one asks: where and how are things produced, does being come to be, the answer can only be that each thing spontaneously produces itself--which is simply another way of saying that nothing is caused by anything else.

If Nature is an ultimate principle with respect to things, does that imply that there is nothing beyond the multitude of things or being? Kuo Hsiang suggests that that is not the case. For Tao is non-being. Tao produces nothing, causes nothing to be at all. But Tao, not Nature, is ultimate as a principle. This is a curious way of putting matters; for here Tao seems to be totally other than being, such that there is a kind of ultimate dualism between being and non-being. But the result of this ultimate non-causal dualism is that the principle which explains why things are and why they change must be found within the things themselves. All things are transformed in accordance with their own nature. One need not look further.

Kuo Hsiang draws from this the conclusion that there is no Creator God. Tao does not create; and the world is not created. Hence there is no need for a Creator God.

With this underlying metaphysics, Kuo Hsiang proposes as the ideal of the sage that of following nature. To follow nature is to be in accord with the self-transformation of all things

250

according to the principle of Nature within them. Spontaneity becomes the ethical ideal, and with this a strong rejection of any effort whatever. Coupled with this is a sense of fatalism—a sense which is quite lacking in Wang Pi, whose Confucianism may have prevented him from lapsing into that quandry.

Main work: Commentary on the Chuang Tzu.

4. The Rise and Fall of Buddhism in China

Buddhism first entered China about the time of the birth of Christ. Translations from Sanskrit or Pali into Chinese did not begin until the second century. There rapidly arose a number of philosophical schools, the traditional number being seven. The doctrines of each of these schools is not very clear, though it does seem that they were dominated by Neo-Taoism—so much so, that some have found these early "Buddhist" schools more Chinese than Indian. Indeed, the rise of Neo-Taoism was undoubtedly influential on later Buddhists, whose philosophy was often expressed in terms and issues that were remarkably similar to those of Taoism.

The height of Buddhist philosophy in China occurred between the 5th and 7th centuries. By the mid-9th century Buddhism had become quite powerful, and reaction had set in. In 845 the Taoist emperor Wu-tsung initiated a forceful persecution of the Buddhists. The result of this was the virtual disappearance of the philosophical schools. Popular Buddhism survived in China after this, however, but it is of no concern here. Buddhism did undergo a revival in 19th century China, but it was not marked by any new philosophical development.

The discussion of Chinese Buddhist philosophy will first center on the major Chinese representatives of the Indian schools, especially the Madyamika and Yogacara schools which flourished in China. Then two distinctive philosophical schools original to China will be discussed, namely the T'ien-t'ai school and the Hua-Yen school. Finally, some of the tenets of the popular sect called Ch'an will be discussed.

The Madyamika school of philosophy was represented in China by three important thinkers: Seng-Chao, Tao-Sheng, and Chi-Tsang. Seng-Chao (384-414) represents the first genuinely significant Chinese Buddhist thinker. He was well read in Taoism, and helped translate various Indian works into Chinese.

Seng-Chao's philosophy centered on the issue of what was ultimately real. Change, which involves rest and motion, appears to be real. But to believe that change is real is to be one of the common people, without insight into the nature of things. For rest and motion have no meaning except in relation to one another,

251

and this implies that ultimately they are the same, since two things which are not radically different must ultimately be the same. Using a similarly reductive logic, Seng-Chao argues that what is past is truly past and cannot endure into the present; the present is what it is only in the present; and the future remains wholly other. It follows that temporal change, indeed time itself understood as the passage of time, is wholly an illusion and thus unreal.

The sage is the one who recognizes that beyond all the differences between things there is absolute unity. This absolute unity of all things is the Supreme Vacuity which is the source of all existence, and is beyond all names and words. If all things are one then the Absolute and the universe are identical. This identification of reality and appearance is a typical twist in the Chinese interpretation of Buddhism.

Main works: Chao lun (Seng-chao's Treatises).

A contemporary of Seng-Chao was Tao-Sheng (?-434). Tao-Sheng argued that if the sage achieves unity with original non-being, that experience is such that it is not susceptible of degrees or additions. Thus either one has such an experience, in which case it is absolute, or one does not. This represents the beginning of a long discussion in Chinese Buddhism about whether enlightenment is gradual or sudden. Tao-sheng's significance lies in his defense of the latter alternative.

Tao-Sheng also insists on the absolute identity of reality and appearance. Thus nirvana is not about some other world beyond this one: enlightenment means recognizing that this world and the real world are one and the same.

Perhaps the most radical theory Tao-Sheng proposed, however, was that each individual possesses a Buddha nature. This, of course, follows from the identification of the real world with the apparent world, for all things truly are Buddha on that account. It follows that not only may Buddhists achieve liberation, but so also may non-Buddhists. This conclusion did not set well with all Buddhist monks, needless to say.

Main works: Pien Tsung lun (Discussion of Essentials), by Hsieh Ling-yun (d. 433).

The third philosopher, and probably the most important expositor of Madyamika doctrines, is Chi-Tsang (549-623). Chi-Tsang's defense of the two levels of truth is fundamental for his method. According to this, there are two levels of truth, that which is possessed by the ordinary people, and that which is possessed by sages and saints. Chi-Tsang proposes a three-step dialectical process to clarify the relation between these two levels.

In the first stage, worldly truth——that things are——is sharply contrasted with absolute truth——that things are not. In the second stage, worldly truth insists that both being and non-being are ultimate principles, while absolute truth insists that neither being nor non-being are ultimate. In the third stage, worldly truth affirms both the duality of being and non-being and the non-duality of them, while absolute truth affirms neither duality nor non-duality. Absolute truth is thus the middle path, avoiding either the affirmation of both being and non-being, or the affirmation of both duality and non-duality.

Chi-Tsang employs this dialectical method in his writings to some advantage, though for many Chinese thinkers it was exceedingly scholastic. In any event, most of his doctrines are typical of the Madyamika school, and these will not be repeated here.

Main works: Erh-ti Chang (Treatise on the Two Levels of Truth); San-lun hsüan-i (Profound Meaning of the Three Treatises).

The Yogacara school of Buddhist philosophy was most prominently represented in Hsüan-Tsang (596-664), certainly one of the most famous and brilliant of the Chinese Buddhists. Hsüan-Tsang's teaching centers on the three transformations of consciousness. This theory, which is a restatement of the theory advanced by Indian thinkers of the Yogacara school, holds first that only consciousness is ultimately real. The first transformation of consciousness is that of the storehouse consciousness, which is a kind of repository for all the possible effects of good and evil deeds; it is consciousness understood as a potential moral self involved in a world of action. The second transformation of consciousness is that of deliberation, whereby consciousness becomes a centered self, capable of delusion, pride, and egoism. The third transformation of consciousness is that of the discrimination of the spheres of objects. This involves the projection of an external world through the five senses and the picturing of that world as a whole in the sixth or sense-center consciousness (not unlike the scholastic notion of sensus communis or common sense).

Two important consequences can be drawn from this understanding of the "projective" nature of consciousness. The first is that every notion of the self is an illusion; for the idea of a self arises only when consciousness is encrusted with either overt or covert notions of phenomenal reality. In short, every notion of a self is a by-product of the transformations of consciousness. Secondly, every notion of a thing (dharma) is an illusion, for all things are projections of consciousness in the third

253

transformation.

Consciousness is the only reality whatever. Things or dharmas are neither absolutely real nor absolutely unreal. They are obviously not absolutely real; but they are not absolutely unreal either, since their reality simply is pure consciousness or pure suchness or thusness. If consciousness is not empty, then the dharmas cannot be absolutely empty.

Main work: Ch'eng wei-shih lun (Treatise on the Establishment of the Doctrine of Consciousness-Only).

The Chinese did not merely import the already existent Indian Buddhist schools to their soil. In time, new schools arose which were distinctively Chinese. The first of these to be considered is the T'ien-T'ai School (T'ien-T'ai being the name of the mountain on which the reputed founder of the school meditated), and the most famous philosopher associated with this school was Hui-Ssu (514-577). Hui-Ssu argued that there were three levels of truth. The first is the Truth of Emptiness: this consists in the recognition of Pure Mind, that realm in which there is no differentiation of one thing from another. Because there is no differentiation it is a realm of non-being. The second level is the Truth of Time: this consists in the recognition of the phenomenal realm made up of differentiated things (dharmas). The third level is the Truth of the Mean: this is the realization that the first two levels are identical, or rather, that Pure Mind is the reality of the phenomenal realm of dharmas. The formula that is used to express this is that Pure Mind is substance, dharmas function.

One of the consequences of this view is that each phenomenal thing is only apparently different from all others; in fact, there is no proper nature to any given phenomenal thing. All things are one; the vision of an instant is necessarily the vision of the whole of time.

One can see from this that Hui-Ssu's philosophy embraces elements of both Madyamika and Yogacara, without being reducible to either. What is interesting in this is the identification of pure Mind with phenomenal reality. This certainly emphasizes the natural world once again, a trait distinctive of Chinese thought and untypical of Indian Buddhism.

Main work: Ta-Ch'eng chih-kuan fa-men (The Method of Concentration and Insight).

A second distinctively Chinese Buddhist philosophical school was the Hua-Yen (= Flowery Splendor, the name of the scriptures the school especially emphasized). The most important philosopher of this school was Fa-Tsang (643-712). In many respects

Fa-Tsang's philosophy depends much on a synthesis of the other schools. He recognizes the distinctive contributions of the Hinayana and Mahayana schools (the Indian contribution, if you will) as consisting in knowledge of the causal dependence of the phenomenal realm and knowledge of the emptiness of the phenomenal realm. He also recognizes the contribution of the T'ien-T'ai school in the knowledge that the phenomenal realm exists as an illusion of Pure Mind. What Fa-Tsang contributes to all this is a recognition that reality is not static and unchanging, but dynamic and self-transforming. Each phenomenal thing in itself has no substance--in this respect it is empty. But when combined with other things, that is, as seen in relation to other things, each thing is in accord with principle. This means simply that all things are together and pervade one another precisely because of principle, and principle means the absence of substance and the omnipresence of function. Everything is in everything else, all of time is in each instant, precisely insofar as reality is appearance, that is, Pure Mind simply is the world of phenomenal things. It is in this fashion that spontaneity is to be understood: for spontaneity simply is the manifestation of all things in each thing and vice-versa.

Fa-Tsang's philosophy is very close to a kind of organicist metaphysics, and it is of some note that he, among others, had an influence on the development of Neo-Confucian metaphysical systems.

The third and last of the more distinctively Chinese schools of Buddhism is the Ch'an school (known in the West by its Japanese name Zen). Ch'an Buddhism is more of a popular sect than anything else, though some of its writings are of intellectual interest, to say the least. Unlike the other philosophers, those of the Ch'an school were not systematic for the most part.

Ch'an Buddhism was founded by Hung-Jen (601-674). It broke into two different branches, the one in northern China founded by Shen-Hsin (605-706), the one in southern China founded by Hui-Neng (638-713). The Northern school emphasized enlightenment (the achievment of Nirvana) as a gradual process of concentration, while the Southern school emphasized sudden enlightenment. The tendency to insist that all of time is grasped in a single instant has been noticed before, and this belief is not unrelated to the notion of sudden enlightenment. Various methods of bringing about sudden enlightenment were developed. The most famous is perhaps the koan, which was a story, riddle, or question and answer, which did not make sense. These stories were often bizarre and shocking, and their intention was to provoke the individual into recognizing that ultimate reality was beyond that which could be discussed logically or rationally. Also employed as methods were shouting and especially beating. All of these rather bizarre

255

developments were distinctively Chinese, and were loosely founded on the various philosophical developments of other schools that have been previously discussed.

D. THE TRIUMPH OF NEO-CONFUCIANISM (960-1800)

1. The Late 8th/Early 9th Century Confucian Revival

The reaction against Buddhism in the political realm was anticipated by an intellectual reaction, specifically in the form of a revival of Confucianism, which had been quite dormant for hundreds of years. The two philosophers associated with this revival were not particularly good thinkers, but they were of immeasurable importance for the re-establishment of Confucianism as a living intellectual tradition.

The first of these two philosophers was Han Yǔ (768-824). Han Yǔ proposed the theory of the three grades of human nature-- the superior, the inferior, and the average--based probably on the theory of Wang Ch'ung whom Han Yǔ admired. But his chief contribution was probably his stinging attack on Taoism and Buddhism. This attack centered first of all on the claim that to follow Tao did not culminate in the practice of virtues such as humanity (jen) and righteousness; and that it was possible to be a sage without recognizing the proper relationships that formed the basis for the family and the state. In short, Taoists and Buddhists praised and practiced a way of life which bore no virtue as its fruit, and which discarded all the relationships which made society what it was. The conclusion was inevitable: Taoists and Buddhists had made people into barbarians!

Main works: Yǔan-hsing (An Inquiry on Human Nature); Yǔan-tao (An Inquiry on Tao).

The second philosopher associated with this early Confucian revival was Li Ao (late 8th century-c. 844). Li Ao also spoke of the dark ages brought on by the popularity of Taoism and Buddhism, and he urged a return to the Confucian classics. Yet for all his emphasis on the Confucian classics, Li Ao's own contribution was to reinterpret the doctrine of the goodness of human nature in terms that were quite Taoist. Li Ao distinguishes between a good human nature and the evil feelings that come to exist in time. Now, what could possibly put an end to evil feelings? It is clear that using feelings to combat feelings will only make things worse. It follows that only through the cultivation of the originally quiet and inactive mind will human nature be recovered. In this respect, Li Ao was more concerned about the recovery of a tranquil mind than he was about the cultivation of the classic Confucian virtues.

256

Main works: Fu-hsing shu (The Recovery of Nature).

2. Confucianism in the Sung Dynasty (960-1279)

The Sung Dynasty, while politically unstable, represents one of the greatest periods of Chinese philosophy. Within a period of a century and a half, Confucianism had not only been provided with a firm metaphysical foundation, but had also undergone systematization into two distinctly different schools, first demarcated by the remarkable brothers Ch'eng Hao and Ch'eng I. The period ended with the systematic philosophy of Chu Hsi, who many reckon as one of the greatest Chinese philosophers of all time. Given this flowering of thought, it is not surprising that Confucianism dominated the history of philosophy until virtually the 20th century.

Perhaps the first great Neo-Confucianist philosopher was Chou Tun-i (1017-1073). His contribution was significant on a number of different intellectual fronts. First of all, Chou Tun-i made a point of returning to the Book of Changes as a source for Confucian cosmology and metaphysics. In part, this was an attempt to avoid using either Taoist concepts or terminology. In fact, Chou Tun-i was often inclined toward Taoist concepts, despite his desire to avoid the terminology.

Chou Tun-i suggests that there is a "Non-Ultimate" called Non-Being and along with it the "Great Ultimate" (T'ai-chi). The notion of Non-Being is derived nominally from the Book of Changes, but is also central to Taoism. There is considerable disagreement among the commentators as to how this notion of Non-Being is to be interpreted. Some argue that Non-Being is the Ultimate before any other distinction comes to be made; others argue that Non-Being is other than the Great Ultimate, and that Chou Tun-i's metaphysics is fundamentally dualist. The text does not suggest a clear answer to this question. In any case, the Great Ultimate through its movement generates Yang or the principle of activity; and when activity has come to its end, there is tranquility and thus the principle of Yin. From these two principles of Yin and Yang there comes first of all Heaven (the realization of Yang) and Earth (the realization of Yin), and then the 5 Agents (water, fire, wood, metal and earth). These 5 Agents or material forces (ch'i) constitute the basis for the order of the universe. They are also the foundation for the order of human nature which is fivefold: humanity, righteousness, propriety, wisdom, and faithfulness. When these five moral principles interact with the world there emerges the realm of moral activity, of good and evil.

Chou Tun-i explicitly draws from this metaphysical theory the conclusion that reality can be understood as the relationship

257

between the one and the many. The many, he says, are ultimately one (since everything is founded upon the Great Ultimate), and the one is differentiated in the many. Each thing has its own proper reality or state of being and its own proper function. This suggests both an organicist conception of reality, and one which is balanced in its evaluation of the various factors.

Chou Tun-i attempted to work out the notion that there is a distinction between principle, nature and destiny. He does not always use these terms, which would become commonplace among later Neo-Confucianists, but their sense seems implied in the discussion at times. Principle refers to Yin and Yang, and the five agents. Nature refers to the Mean, and that includes primarily sincerity (ch'eng) and thought (in human beings). Destiny (for humans) refers to the distinction between substance and function (or substance and its manifestations, such that destiny is understood as the realization of substance).

The five virtues present in human nature are rooted in sincerity (ch'eng), and it is Chou Tun-i's fame to have regarded it as genuinely fundamental. Essentially sincerity is tranquil and inactive. But if one considers sincerity not as substance but as function, then it is clear that it realizes itself in cautious activity. Similarly thinking is tranquil by nature—so much so that it is accurately described as "having no mind" (a Taoist ideal)—but in its activity it pervades all things. It is clear that although Chou Tun-i relies on Taoist concepts, he seeks everywhere to avoid the consequences of Taoism. He does this by systematically distinguishing between principle, nature and destiny, and between substance and function. While principle, nature, and substance are understood at times in Taoist terms, destiny and function suggest that following Tao is to realize virtue in a Confucianist way; thus destiny and function clearly modify any Taoist interpretation of principle, nature and substance. This is, of course, the kind of solution that would become foundational for Neo-Confucianism.

Chou Tun-i was also concerned about social and political philosophy, and wrote a great deal about the woes of his own "modern" age. He decried the immorality of contemporary music and literature, and insisted on the importance of good education and sagely rule from above. In all this he remained true to his Confucian origins.

Main works: T'ai-chi-t'u shuo (An Explanation of the Diagram of the Great Ultimate); T'ung-shu (Penetrating the "Book of Changes").

The tendency toward providing a metaphysical base for Confucianism probably reached its apogee in the thought of Shao Yung

(1011-1077), whose cosmological philosophy was in many ways at odds with the traditionally humanistic concerns of Confucianism. Shao Yung was led in this direction by his preoccupation with the I Ching. He began by recognizing that all things come from the Great Ultimate through inaction. (In this respect he shows clearly a certain Taoist influence, especially by comparison with Chou Tun-i who stated that the Great Ultimate produced all things through movement.) In any event, the Great Ultimate is the One, and from the One arises the two forms of activity (the principle of Heaven) and movement (the principle of Earth). From the two forms come the four emblems of things. Thus, from activity comes the dual principle of Yang and Yin; and from tranquillity comes the dual principle of Weakness and Strength. From each of these four come two further manifestations, depending on whether the principle is manifested in a major or minor way. Thus there are eight cosmic and earthly substances generated (sun, stars, moon, zodiacal spaces, water, earth, fire, and stone).

There are a number of important features in this account, though its details are rather arbitrary and mechanically derived. Perhaps the most important point lies in the understanding of principle in Shao Yung's account. Principle is inherent in each thing, and to account for any given thing is to invoke a series of hierarchical principles. Secondly, principle is closely related to number, which is said to derive from principle. Shao Yung even says that Heaven and Earth are numbers in nature. The whole account given above depends on the generation of eight categories of things from four "emblems", from two forms, from one ultimate. It is not surprising that Shao Yung's schema has been compared with the Pythagorean tendencies of some pre-modern Western meta-physicians.

Shao Yung also proposed an elaborate theory of time based on his interpretation of the hexagrams from the I Ching. According to this theory, all of time is cyclical, and each cycle is re-peated infinitely. Now time, and its progress, is fundamentally numerical, and proceeds according to principle. Each cycle con-sists of 12 epochs (corresponding to the 12 months of the year), each epoch consists of 30 revolutions (corresponding to the days in a month), each revolution consists of 12 generations (corres-ponding to the 12 divisions of the day), and each generation consists of 30 years (= 1 human generation). If one does the requisite arithmetic, the cycle turns out to be exactly 129,600 years in length. Shao Yung went on to carefully describe the changes that each cycle underwent from its inception to its end. All of this was based on his intepretation of cosmic processes. The theory of time-cycles may well have been indirectly influenced by Buddhist ideas on the subject, but it was more immediately inspired by the I Ching.

259

Shao Yung emphasized the importance of the distinction between principle, nature, and destiny. Principle and nature were complementary concepts. Destiny he understood as abiding or being rooted in principle and nature. This linking of destiny with nature and principle was of some importance for future thought.

Shao Yung also discussed the nature of the universe in terms of the interaction of material force and spirit. Each principle is said to be one in its nature; but while material force is spatial, spirit transcends space, and can change and transform through material force. While this sounds dualistic, it is not, if one recalls the schema outlined above. It is interesting to see how this duality of material force and spirit is worked out in the thought of the next important neo-Confucian, Chang Tsai.

Main works: Huang-chi ching-shih shu (Supreme Principles Governing the World).

A third philosopher of the early Sung dynasty is Chang Tsai (1020-1077), who in his early years studied both Taoism and Buddhism, but then later returned to Confucianism. However, his system, which is nominally balanced between metaphysical and ethical concerns, is marked by some original ideas.

In metaphysics, Chang Tsai was noted for his simplification of previous cosmological schemas. He urged that the Great Ultimate was nothing other than material force (ch'i)--perhaps the first time in Chinese thought that this principle was made fundamental. In itself material force (ch'i) has principle (li) within it. The Great Ultimate is thus subject to a twofold movement: the one toward integration, which is the source or origin of the myriad of things, each with their physical form; the other toward disintegration, which is the tendency back toward the Great Vacuity. In the first case, material force can be called the Great Harmony; in the second case the Great Vacuity. Now spirit is nothing other than the Great Vacuity, which is in turn the name for the Great Ultimate is its disintegrative movement. Because spirit is identified with material force, Chang Tsai's philosophy has been called materialistic. It is, however, a rather dynamic kind of materialism, since ch'i suggests not some kind of unchanging, rigid form, but a positive activity, involving either contraction or expansion (integration or disintegration).

It is in terms of this schema that Chang Tsai interprets various other cosmological terms in common use. Thus the Great Ultimate is Tao (which, since it has both a positive and a negative, both an integrative and disintegrative, aspect, is distinct from the Taoist notion, which is only negative). Yin and Yang are not distinct forces but simply the names of the two tendencies of ch'i. Further, material force is substance as the Great Vacuity,

260

function as the Great Harmony.

Chang Tsai's theory of human nature and ethics was also of great importance. Human nature is subject to the dual principles of integration and disintegration, and thus one speaks of the unity of nature and destiny. Nature represents integration, destiny represents the disintegration of ch'i. Specifically, there is a distinction between the principle of nature and human desires. Human desires represent the possibility for the emergence of evil, but are not understood as evil in themselves. What is important therefore is the cultivation of knowledge as a means of eliminating evil desires. But knowledge, it is claimed, is rooted in sincerity (ch'eng), a term which also connotes genuine existence. Thus sincerity, because it is the key for the development of knowledge, is also the foundation of the moral life and thus of the formation of proper desires.

Of great interest is Chang Tsai's re-interpretation of jen (humanity). Indeed his understanding of this central Confucian virtue became standard for subsequent Neo-Confucianism. In virtue of the unity of all things, which is founded on the principle of ch'i, and which is identified with spirit, one may legitimately speak of the unity of spirit between the individual and all others, as well as the individual and the universe. Jen is that love which one should have not only toward all others, but toward everything in the universe. Clearly, this love presumes distinctions; but it is founded upon the identical reality that lies at the base of all things whatever. This is the first time that a truly universalist conception of jen or humanity was successfully defended in Confucianism, and it is significant that it was only made possible by a monistic metaphysical schema.

Main works: Cheng-meng (Correcting Youthful Ignorance); Hsi-ming (Western Inscription).

Two of Chang Tsai's nephews were the brothers Ch'eng Hao and Ch'eng I. While both had studied Buddhism, Taoism, and the thought of Chang Tsai, they each set out on independent paths. In so doing, they became the traditional founders of the two wings of Neo-Confucianism—Ch'eng Hao the founder of the idealistic wing, and Ch'eng I the founder of the so-called rationalistic wing. In fact, they shared a great deal in common, as will be seen.

Ch'eng Hao (1032-1085), as well as his brother, insisted on the centrality of principle in his metaphysical account of the universe. All things have the principle of Heaven or Nature (T'ien-li) which is specific to each individual thing, and thus the many things are essentially one, and that one principle pervades the universe. Principle is the origin of all things, of the equality and inequality of things, and thus at the heart of all

261

changes.   As Ch'eng Hao uses the term, T'ien-li virtually has the meaning of "natural law" as that term is used in Western philosophy.

One of the most important tasks of the sage, according to Ch'eng Hao, is to investigate things.   Now the investigation of things means simply to investigate the principles of things, and those principles are ultimately one, as has been seen. Ch'eng Hao also declares that investigating principles is the same thing as developing one's nature to the full and fulfilling one's destiny. Thus principle, nature, and destiny are virtually identified.

One of the most distinctive contributions of the two brothers was their understanding of jen or humanity.   Ch'eng Hao declares that jen is the principle of the unity of all things, that is, it is humanity by which all things in the universe are related in an organic unity.   For this reason, it is wrong to think that Nature and the Self are two distinct realities: in view of the unity of principle there is an unquestionable unity present throughout reality, such that it does not make sense to distinguish between the internal and the external with respect to the self.

As the unifying principle of all things, jen has as its substance sincerity (ch'eng), while seriousness (ching) is its function.   Sincerity is understood simply as the unity of the three virtues of wisdom, humanity (jen), and courage.   In this way, Ch'eng Hao continued the trend of defending the importance of sincerity, even though it seems clear that jen was of greater ethical and metaphysical significance.

Ch'eng Hao's philosophical system is as monistic as Chang Tsai's, but unlike the latter it rejects the notion that material force underlies all of reality.   The factor which most closely corresponds to ch'i in Ch'eng Hao's system is the principle of Nature (T'ien-li), and jen seems to be synonymous with this. Nevertheless, there are passages where Ch'eng Hao seems to identify material force with spirit, or at least to assert that they are the same.   However, it is principle which is stressed, not material force.   Thus Ch'eng Hao's philosophy preserves a strong humanistic cast to it, while rejecting a materialistic foundation.

Main works: I-shu (Surviving Works); Wai-shu (Additional Works); Ming-tao wen-chi (Collection of Literary Works); Ts'ui-yen (Pure Words).   All of these are from Erh-Ch'eng ch'uan-shu (The Complete Works of the Two Ch'engs).

Ch'eng I (1033-1107) also subscribed to a fundamental monism, but his emphasis tends at times toward dualism.   This dualistic tendency is clearest when he explains physical form as itself due to the formlessness of Tao, from which all things originate, and

262

as resulting in material force and the principles of Yin and Yang. Material force, Yin, and Yang are those factors which have to do with the explanation of the outcome of things in their activity, while Tao has to do with the explanation of the being of things in their substance. However, despite this account, Ch'eng I makes clear that all things--even material force, Yin, and Yang--are one with the Tao. It is apparent that the difference with his brother Ch'eng Hao is more a matter of emphasis than doctrine.

It may be this awareness of his own dualistic tendencies that led Ch'eng I to strongly condemn Buddhism for its dualistic rejection of this world. In this regard, Ch'eng I shows that his philosophy is thoroughly worldly. His point was not merely abstract; like all Confucianists, he found Buddhism guilty of moral irresponsibility, precisely insofar as it neglected important worldly virtues.

Ch'eng I's theory of human nature was of great importance for later Neo-Confucianism. Jen was fundamental because it was the unity which provided a moral and metaphysical ground for seriousness and the extension of knowledge. What is especially emphasized in all this is the extension of knowledge through the investigation of things. Like his brother, Ch'eng I emphasizes not the investigation of concrete things so much, as the investigation of the principles of all things, especially since this principle is ultimately one. What is important here is that our native goodness can only develop on the basis of the investigation of the principle of things. Thus knowledge is crucial in Ch'eng I's understanding of human destiny. In this respect, he follows Mencius' emphasis on the goodness of human nature (as most Neo-Confucians did), but stressed the importance of knowledge. What is evil in human affairs occurs as the result both of ignorance, or the lack of knowledge, and material force. Ch'i, Ch'eng I thought, could impede the development of knowledge in some people, and thus it was not just lack of knowledge that explained why some people were evil. Again, one senses a certain dualism in his account.

To sum up: the major difference in metaphysics between the two brothers seems to stem from Ch'eng I's distinction between principle and material force; while the major difference in their ethics stems from Ch'eng I's emphasis on knowledge as opposed to Ch'eng Hao's emphasis on jen. Yet as has been seen there are many similarities in their thinking, and many common premises.

Main works: I-shu (Surviving Works); Wai-shu (Additional Works); I-ch'uan wen-chi (Commentary on the "Book of Changes"); Ching-shuo (Explanations of the Classics); Ts'ui-yen (Pure Words). All of these are from Erh-Ch'eng ch'uan-shu (The Complete Works of the Two Ch'engs).

After the profusion of thinkers in the 11th century, one might expect a kind of lull in philosophical development, but this did not happen. Indeed the 12th century saw two philosophers of great importance: Lu Hsiang-shan, who continued the idealistic tradition of Ch'eng Hao; and Chu Hsi, who continued the rationalistic tradition of Ch'eng I, and who many reckon as the finest Neo-Confucian philosopher in Chinese history. Of the two, Chu Hsi was certainly more important historically, and it was his version of Confucianism that dominated Chinese thought for many centuries.

Lu Hsiang-shan (1139-1193) was probably uninfluenced by Ch'eng Hao, but his thinking is in many ways similar to the latter's. He was acquainted with Chu Hsi, and the two were ardent philosophical opponents.

Lu Hsiang-shan's metaphysics was simple and straight-forward. He identified mind, principle, and humanity (jen) as being the same. One might say that the principle of all things simply is mind, and humanity (jen) is another term for this principle. Mind is said to be infinite and the same for all. Yet principle, insofar as it is mind, is in each of the myriad things of the universe. Mind is the same thing as the natural universe, which is constituted by space and time.

Mind, as the Great Ultimate, cannot be called non-being. Chu Hsi had defended just this interpretation of the Great Ultimate, and Lu Hsiang-shan roundly condemns it as Taoistic and as absurd. The Great Ultimate has always existed, he says, and thus non-being is an utterly incorrect ascription. The Great Ultimate can be called Tao; but Tao in man is not non-being, but simply humanity (jen) and righteousness. And Lu Hsiang-shan's interpretation of these virtues clearly suggests that there are unequal social roles in society which must be respected on the basis of humanity and righteousness.

Lu Hsiang-shan's condemnation of Taoism and Buddhism is very strong. The Taoist conception of non-being, he claims, simply eliminates all social differences and creates social havoc. And he interprets the difference between the Confucian and the Buddhist as the difference between the man of righteousness and the man who seeks profit. Thus one can see the strongly moral cast of Lu Hsiang-shan's thought, a moral cast which is continued from Ch'eng Hao and which would reappear in later Neo-Confucians.

Main works: Hsiang-shan ch'uan-chi (Complete Works of Lu Hsiang-shan).

Chu Hsi (1130-1200) falls into the rationalistic tradition begun by Ch'eng I. His contribution was substantial; for he not only synthesized Confucianism in a fully coherent way, he also systematized the educational system of Confucianism for later generations. He established a kind of "orthodox" line of Confucianists, which left out thinkers such as Hsun Tzu and Shao Yung, and which made Mencius and the Ch'eng brothers among the more important. He oriented Confucianism somewhat away from the speculations of the I Ching and back toward the Analects of Confucius. Yet at the same time, he did not neglect some of the more traditional metaphysical questions.

Chu Hsi's philosophy is, like Ch'eng I's, moderately dualistic, resting on a distinction between principle (li) and material force (ch'i). Yet in many respects, Chu Hsi's final vision emphasizes the way in which this duality is constitutive of each and every being, such that every being is inherently related to every other being. Concretely, one might say that Chu Hsi begins with an organic universe, and proceeds to invoke a duality of factors to explain that universe.

The Great Ultimate is explicitly identified with Principle (li), or Tao. Principle has two basic characteristics: it is utterly undifferentiated in itself and it is the highest good. Each thing possesses this Great Ultimate in its entirety, that is, principle is wholly in each thing. As such each thing may be said to have a nature and to be complete in its actuality. However, a given being is not merely constituted by principle. Rather, with the presence of principle in the actualization of nature, there comes to be material force. Logically, material force (ch'i) is posterior to the physical nature, while principle is anterior to it. Material force is the principle of the incompleteness of the being. Thus each being in its actualized nature is in a sense complete by virtue of the presence of principle in it, and incomplete by virtue of the material force. Another way of saying this is that principle is what is permanent in each thing, while material force is what is impermanent or changeable in each thing. This is how Chu Hsi can say that principle is eternal, while material force is temporal. Despite this, there is an insistence that these two factors always belong to one another: principle cannot be realized with out material force, and material force is empty without principle.

To understand the implication of this theory, one must explore further the relation between principle and mind, a relation which adds another dimension to Chu Hsi's metaphysics. Principle simply is Mind; indeed he says that Mind is the reservoir of all principle. Now inherent to mind is both life and consciousness. It then follows that if everything has principle in it, everything has mind, consciousness, and life. It is important to note, however, that there are clearly degrees of consciousness and life in things: they are obviously not equally alive or conscious. The reason for this inequality can be found in the fact that material force obscures and keeps hidden the principle in different beings in different ways. Thus the degrees of life and consciousness in things is a function of material force, not principle itself.

It should also be clear that principle as such is not actual, but potential. Actual consciousness and actual mind is thus quite distinct from principle which is mind in its undifferentiated potentiality. To put it another way: actual consciousness pre-supposes both principle and a physical nature and thus material force.

It is this distinction between principle and actualized being that allows Chu Hsi to identify destiny with principle in its inner meaning, but to insist that destiny has to be actualized in and through physical nature. Thus correct destiny is destiny insofar as it is principle; modified destiny is its actualization.

Chu Hsi does provide a cosmology somewhat distinct from his metaphysics, though relying on the concepts he has elaborated. He suggests that at the beginning of the universe there was material force in a state of constant turmoil--that turmoil being the movement of activity (Yang) and tranquility (Yin). (Chu Hsi insisted that the principles of Yin and Yang, as well as the Five Agents, were both subsequent to the existence of physical nature, and not prior.) Through a process of contraction the earth came to be at the center of the universe, while the heavenly bodies were essentially material force in a state of relative expansion. It is this ethereality of the heavenly realm which allows it to move; and it is the compactness of the earth that makes it motion-less.

Given his emphasis on material force as inherent to any actual being, one might ask just what Chu Hsi thought of the existence of ancestor spirits and other such beings. It has been noted before that Confucianists generally were agnostic about such matters. Chu Hsi's philosophy is clearly inimical toward the existence of such things as ghosts. However, his expressed opinion is more cautious. He urges people to attend to what is important in life first of all, and only then consider questions such as the existence of ghosts. In short, the existence of purely spiritual beings is a matter which should not interfere with the ethical life.

Chu Hsi's metaphysics is founded upon the one concern which he thought sharply separated Confucians from Taoists and Buddhists: and that was the concern for concrete actuality. Per-haps no other Chinese philosopher has been more preoccupied with the explanation of concrete things than Chu Hsi. In this regard he was defending what was genuinely unique to Chinese thought.

266

Chu Hsi's theory of human nature derives from his metaphysics. He distinguishes between human nature on the one hand, and feelings and desires on the other, the two being related as substance and function. There is indication of some change in Chu Hsi's understanding of mind as actualized in the human person. In some passages (the earlier ones, it seems), Chu Hsi identified mind with both nature and feelings. In time, however, he came to change his opinion, and identified mind with nature. The implication of this was to ally mind with that which is originally good. Principle, which is the highest good, is nature in its actualization. Thus mind, as actualized, and as identical with nature, is inherently good. In all this, Mencius is clearly Chu Hsi's source of inspiration.

Chu Hsi was critical of those Buddhists who attempted to reduce actual consciousnesses to objects of some pure mind, that is who insisted that pure undifferentiated mind is not principle but fully actual subjectivity. Although Chu Hsi identifies mind with principle, he recognizes that mind is potential, not actual, insofar as it is principle. What is actual, what truly exists, is an actualized consciousness. Chu Hsi was clearly aware, then, that there is an ineradicable subjectivity found in actualized consciousness, and his metaphysics is founded on the recognition of that subjectivity.

The distinction between mind and feelings is a distinction between a state of equilibrium and a state of harmony. The development of feelings does not cause the mind to change as such. Nor is the development of feelings in and of itself evil. Some feelings are good. In the same way, some desires are good. Evil is only possible presuming that there is a good nature, which does not change, and that there are good feelings and good desires. Evil, in short, is consequent upon goodness and could not exist without it. All of this suggests that evil is metaphysically rooted in material force, not principle. Indeed, Chu Hsi has already argued that material force is that factor which can obscure and hide principle. Chu Hsi relies on material force to explain the origin of evil. Yet while evil is inevitable as a possibility, humans are able to avoid it. Chu Hsi is not a fatalist about evil. For if evil has its source in material force and its effects, it does not follow that evil cannot be avoided.

How is evil to be avoided? There are essentially two means to this end, and they are closely related. The first consists in nourishing human nature in its ethical dimension, and the second consists in preserving mind through the investigation of things. Of the two, Chu Hsi was perhaps more remembered for his emphasis on the investigation of things, and generally on the importance of knowledge. But in fact he had much to say about the importance of _jen_ and humanity.

Fundamental to the pursuit of good is the cultivation of seriousness, which Chu Hsi understands as the mind's self-mastery or self-control. Without this self-mastery, there is no way that feelings and desires (function) can be brought into proper relation with nature (substance), no way in which the external can be unified with the internal. Yet while seriousness is the root of all cultivation, there is more required. The whole of the ethical life is fundamentally a responding to things in the world, and that response requires both activity and tranquility, both concern for the principle of nature and concern for feelings.

Ethically, Chu Hsi insisted on the centrality of _jen_ for human beings. He defended the traditional four virtues--humanity, righteousness, propriety, and wisdom. But of these four, humanity or _jen_ was central and unifying. Some had identified _jen_ with human nature, that is, with consciousness; while others had identified _jen_ with the feeling of love. Chu Hsi argues that in a sense both theories are correct. However, _jen_ is essentially consciousness insofar as it is substance, and it is love insofar as it is function. It is best to understand _jen_ as the unity of substance and function, of consciousness and love, rather than to identify it simply with either one.

But for all the emphasis on the importance of _jen_, Chu Hsi did suggest that _jen_ is itself founded upon impartiality in human nature. And this would seem to make _jen_ derivative, perhaps ultimately from seriousness to which impartiality would seem to be related.

If _jen_ is not quite fundamental in human nature, it is universal. Every being, insofar as it has nature or principle, has _jen_; thus Chu Hsi preserves the Neo-Confucian emphasis on a cosmic understanding of _jen_.

Of great importance to Chu Hsi is the investigation of things, and it is on this subject that he expounded at length. He insists that everything in the world should be investigated; he constantly shows an enthusiasm about learning, no doubt because of its central importance in his ethical theory. But he did not restrict his conception of knowledge to the metaphysical principles of things: he also he insisted that there was much to learn about ethical principles and that these must be learned for the sake of the moral life itself.

It was in regard to the latter that Chu Hsi elaborated his theory of the relation between knowledge and action. While he insisted that each requires the other, he tended to emphasize knowledge and tended to emphasize the relative distinction between knowledge and action. Knowledge prior to action was important if one was to root out selfishness; however, even when this occurs, it is also important to recognize the knowledge that one gains after one has acted. For knowledge of ethical principles always increases after action. This, of course, presents a dilemma: doesn't this increased posterior knowledge call into question the adequacy of the moral decision as it was originally made? Chu Hsi answers that one must only be satisfied that one acted originally with knowledge founded upon seriousness; it does not make sense to hold that one should have absolute knowledge in advance of a decision. In this way, Chu Hsi emphasized the dynamic nature of ethical life, as opposed to unchanging principles. It is not, of course, that there were no unchanging principles; but the clarity of knowledge was mitigated by material force in varying degrees. Hence moral knowledge was not given in any absolute fashion, even though it was entirely present in human nature. It is in this regard that one can see why knowledge was so important in his ethical theory.

Main works: Chu Tzu wen-chi (Collection of Literary Works by Chu Hsi); Chu Tzu ch'uan-shu (Complete Works of Chu Hsi); Chu Tzu yu-lu (Classified Conversations of Chu Hsi).

3. Confucian Philosophy in the Ming Dynasty (1368-1644)

There is only one prominent philosopher of the Ming Dynasty, and he was Wang Yang-ming (1472-1529). Wang Yang-ming's philosophy was born of a reaction against the intellectualism of Chu Hsi and the civil servants trained under the Confucian educational philosophy. Thus Wang Yang-ming stands in a tradition with Lu Hsiang-shan and Ch'eng Hao. But there are some distinctively different elements in Wang's thought.

Wang Yang-ming took aim at two revered doctrines of the Neo-Confucians: the doctrine of the investigation of things, and the doctrine of the distinction between knowledge and action. Both were of cardinal important to Chu Hsi, and both were at the heart of the disease which affected society in the time of Wang Yang-ming, at least by his own thinking. In two separate events, Wang Yang-ming underwent a kind of "religious conversion", though it was only late in his life before he wrote much of his thinking down.

Wang's philosophy assumed that mind and principle were the same. If that were the case it followed that nothing whatever was outside mind. Indeed, it must be true that all things and events occur inside the mind, not outside it. In this regard, one source of intellectual (and moral) error is the belief that there are objects outside the mind, and further that there is a distinction between this object and that object. The doctrine of the investigation of things, as formulated by Chu Hsi, would have the individual believe that each thing has its own principle, that the principles of things are external to the human mind, and that there are a myriad of things each of which is distinct from the other. This mentality, Wang insists, is that of the small man who pursues learning as though the latter were simply a matter of fulfilling idle curiosity.

By contrast, the great man, according to Wang Yang-ming, is one who regards all things as one, that is, as principle and as mind. Even more significantly is the realization that mind and principle are good by nature. Now if this is understood, then it is possible to give a new meaning to the investigation of the principles of things. For this can only mean the investigation of the goodness in things; and since all things are mind, the proper object of mind is the goodness inherent in mind.

Evil exists only to the extent that mind recognizes the distinction between good and evil. Before that distinction, mind is fundamentally indifferent. Because of this assertion, Wang Yang-ming was sometimes accused of being a Buddhist. But that ignores the logic of his position. His point is quite clearly that the mind is inherently good, even if the use of that term only comes into play when evil is to be distinguished from mind.

The sage who recognizes the inherent goodness of mind, and the fact that nothing is outside the mind, has as his goal the forming of one body with all things. To love the people is thus to fulfill the heavenly mandate to form one body with all things. Now this is not to erase proper distinctions in love: for while love must be universal, it has a proper form with respect to the king, to the father, and so forth. Thus Wang distances himself from Moism, even if at the expense of internal theoretical consistency.

But perhaps the most radical aspect of Wang's doctrine is the identification of knowledge and action. He accused Chu Hsi of fostering this distinction between the two, a distinction which Wang argues is in the service of a selfish individual. Equally abhorrent is the belief that knowledge must precede action. Wang insists that since all things are in mind, such that nothing is outside it, it follows that action is not different from knowledge. Thus to know the good is to extend it to all beings. One cannot distinguish knowledge from ethical behavior.

Clearly Wang's concern was that the sage had come to pursue knowledge as though it had nothing to do with "loving the people". But the latter is the whole point of wisdom. In this way, Wang Yang-ming proposed one of the most dynamic and intensely ethical theories in Chinese philosophy.

Major work: <u>Wang</u> <u>Wen-ch'eng</u> <u>Kung</u> <u>ch'uan-shu</u> (<u>Complete</u> <u>Works</u> <u>of</u> <u>Wang</u> <u>Yang-ming</u>).

4. Confucian Philosophy in the Ch'ing Dynasty (1644-1912)

Philosophy in the Ch'ing Dynasty reacted strongly against the highly speculative and idealistic theories advanced in the Sung and Ming periods. The reaction was against both Chu Hsi and Wang Yang-ming, or better, against their emphasis on the abstract and especially on the notion of principle (<u>li</u>). To some extent this reaction may have been indirectly stimulated by the introduction of Jesuit education, not so much with regard to religious, as with scientific matters. Thus this philosophy may owe something indirectly to increasing contact with the West. But despite that, the emphasis throughout is on re-establishing Confucianism on its original grounds. A movement of return to the classic texts, and away from medieval speculation, was especially prominent. Three thinkers--Wang Fu-chih, Yen Yüan, and Tai Chen--each illustrate some of the typical concerns of this period of Chinese thought.

<u>Wang</u> <u>Fu-chih</u> (1619-1692) was one of the most interesting, though least influential of his generation. He took aim at the whole tradition of Neo-Confucianism, and specifically at the importance that had been accorded principle (<u>li</u>). Wang argued for the centrality of the concrete thing, reducing principle to the material force of the concrete thing, specifically to the order of one thing with respect to another. In short, principle was an aspect of material force. Wang was thus a materialist in the tradition of Chang Tsai. But Wang Fu-chih also argued that principle was greatest where material force was greatest. Now material force developed, was produced and reproduced, in accordance with the principles of Yin and Yang. Since Yang is the principle of activity, it is with Yang that the greatest material force accumulates and that principle reaches its greatest extent and influence. To follow Tao is simply to realize principle; but this means having much material force. The notion that Tao is some kind of non-being or that principle is some kind of mind is so much nonsense. Material force exists, and mind is just one aspect of material force.

With this "overthrowing" of the supremacy of principle, it is not surprising to find that Wang Fu-chih also did away with the notion of the supremacy of human nature or mind over desires. He argues that knowledge of substance comes about only through knowledge of function, and clearly not the other way around. Function is the only way in which it is possible to know what a thing is. Since desires are function in relation to mind which is substance, it follows that desires, far from being those factors which <u>hide</u> substance, actually <u>reveal</u> what mind is. Thus Wang strongly

271

emphasized the importance of desires in a way that most Confucians had never done.

Given his strong emphasis on the concrete thing, and on the constant change of things due to the constant change of material force, it is not surprising to find Wang arguing in favor of change toward the better. He accepts a kind of view not unlike that found in the Western enlightenment--a view, namely, that looks forward to future development, and downplays the way things were done in the past. This was an extraordinarily dynamic and "progressive" philosophy for the Chinese. It is not surprising that it was of little influence until the 20th century.

Main works: Ch'uan-shan i-shu (Surviving Works of Wang Fu-chih).

Yen Yüan (1635-1704) represents a second reaction against Neo-Confucianism. Like Wang Fu-chih, Yen Yüan identified principle and material force, and thus stands in the materialist tradition. But what is interesting about Yen Yüan is his championing of a return to the fundamentals of Confucianism--to the Analects and to the works of Mencius. The reasons for this become clear when Yen Yüan attempts to spell out his own ethical views. By accepting the reduction of principle to material force, Yen Yüan realized that it was quite impossible to argue that material force was the source of evil. Indeed, he took many of the earlier Neo-Confucianists to task for having identified principle and material force, and then insisting that the former is good while the latter is evil. It follows for Yen Yüan that material force can only be good, and thus that evil does not derive from material force. But what does it derive from? Yen Yüan was able to answer this question by returning to the simpler social ethics of the ancients. For the view of Confucius and Mencius had been that evil was a function of the bad influence of others, that is, that the explanation of evil could only be social, not metaphysical. The attempt to ascribe evil to material force, of which Chu Hsi, for example, was most especially guilty, was probably due to the influence of Buddhism on almost all Sung and Ming philosophers. Thus Yen Yüan advocates a simpler ethical view based presumably on the classical Confucian sources.

Even more striking is Yen Yüan's strong rejection of the notion that knowledge is rooted in substance. He claims that knowledge's substance lies in things themselves, and that it follows that all learning must be through acquaintance with the things themselves. Thus, for example, to know what music is is to play a musical instrument, sing, dance, and so forth. One cannot know what music is simply by thinking about its components conceptually. This theory is radically experiential and inductive in tone, and again is strikingly at odds with much of the speculative

272

nature of classical Chinese philosophy.

Main works: Ts'un-hsing pien (Preservation of Human Nature); Ssu-shu cheng-wu (Corrections of Wrong Interpretations of the Four Books).

Tai Chen (1723-1777) is commonly reckoned as the most brilliant Chinese philosopher of the 18th century. His fame was secured in part because of his immense learning and his application of the inductive method to various studies, including mathematics, textual analysis, and variety of other disciplines. For all his brilliance, however, his thinking often repeats what other Ch'ing Dynasty thinkers had already said. Thus he accepts the basic emphasis on the examination of particular things that was promoted by Yen Yuan. While he strongly emphasized the importance of principle, his understanding of it is very much at odds with that of the Sung philosophers such as Chu Hsi. For him principle (li) is simply a natural feeling for the differences between things, and for their order. In this sense, principles are simply feelings that are correct or good. There are other kinds of feeelings, but the important point here is the reduction of principles to feelings.

Tai Chen strongly condemns those who make of principle some kind of "thing" or "reality" beyond things themmselves: the tendency to do this among the Sung Neo-Confucians was due to their preoccupation with Buddhism. Tai Chen insists that neither Confucius nor Mencius made principle into some kind of supernatural metaphysical reality.

One of the consequences of this way of thinking is to regard desires as not only good, but inevitable and necessary. Indeed, Tai Chen asserts that one cannot be fully human without desires. But in the spirit of Mencius one should have few desires rather than many, since this makes for greater fulfillment in life. Further, there is a question of what kind of desires one will have. Principle is correct desire, desire that corresponds to the mean and avoids extremes.

Main works: Meng Tzu tzu-i shu-cheng (Commentary on the Meanings of Terms in the "Book of Mencius").

E. CONTEMPORARY CHINESE THOUGHT

1. Introduction

Just as the Westernization of India brought forth a number of intellectual efforts to defend the core or essence of Indian philosophy, so also the Westernization of China provoked a number

273

of responses which centered both on revitalizing the philosophical tradition and on bringing that tradition into close alignment with typically Western concerns. Unlike Indian philosophy which was strongly tinged with mysticism, classical Chinese thought was imbued with a strong sense of the "worldly"--both in its metaphysics and in its ethics--and this made a rapprochement with Western philosophy both plausible and viable. Yet in all the exchange of ideas, the Chinese, as much as the Indians, have insisted on continuity with their own past. This even appears with the emergence of Communist China and the "Marxism" of Mao Tse-tung, which is heavily tinged with specifically Chinese concerns.

2. K'ang Yu-wei (1858-1927)

K'ang Yu-wei began as a reformer in the late Ch'ing Dynasty, and ended up as a great defender of the Emperor after the institution of the Republic. It was his fate to have lived in a period of transition, and specifically in the transition from China's ancient form of government to the modern form. His philosophy is a curious amalgam of concerns and shows a deep-seated interest in establishing Confucianism as the philosophy of the new China. In this effort he did not succeed.

K'ang was part of a generation of Confucian scholars who reacted strongly against the anti-Sung philosophers of the early Ch'ing dynasty. K'ang realized that what was needed was a Confucian philosophy for the new age, a philosophy based not just on a return to Confucian classics, but on a recognition that Confucius was a great religious teacher, and Confucianism itself a dynamic religion. K'ang strongly sympathized with the dynamic and ethical elements of Lu Hsiang-shan and Wang Yang-ming. He openly acknowledged Buddhist influence, and drew from this some radical conclusions--radical, at least, for a Confucian.

K'ang emphasized the concept of jen as central to his beliefs. Jen was not just a matter of universal love, the bond uniting all things--it was identified with the universe itself, which K'ang held was fundamentally a form of electricity. Jen is nothing but the unity of electricity (the universal ether) and consciousness. This theory is reminiscent of previous forms of dynamic materialism in Chinese thought, but the emphasis on electricity is quite new and inspired by Western science.

The dynamic nature of the universe is such that it advances through periods of growing progress. There is first a period of Relative Disorder; second, a period of Rising Peace; and third, a period of Lasting Peace. This theory is evolutionary in spirit, and is probably inspired by Tung Chung-shu's theory of historical cycles. But K'ang's theory is not about the repetition of cycles of time--it is clearly in the tradition of Western evolutionary schemas, such as that of Auguste Comte. In any case, K'ang's theory was meant to explain his own reform activities in the late 19th century. For he understood his own age to be at the end of the second period, with the inauguration of the third period within sight. His predictions were perhaps quite correct—except that peace has not been a notable characteristic of the 20th century!

Kang's theory about the new age was proposed in a book which was only published posthumously. In it he explicitly draws on the Buddhist desire to relieve suffering in the world. The heart of jen or humanity is precisely the inability to bear the sight of the suffering of anything whatever. The new age will seek to eliminate all the sources of suffering. Now the fundamental cause of suffering is the very existence of distinction among things. This sentiment is radically opposed to the whole thrust of Confucianism, and K'ang did not hesitate to draw some very radical conclusions. He proposed the elimination of distinctions among nations, classes, races, physical configurements (including that which divides male and female), families, occupations, and even the various animal species. To abolish suffering is simply to recognize the equality of all. K'ang hoped for the establishment of a Utopia on earth.

K'ang's philosophy can thus be seen as an attempt to blend the monistic but ethically dynamic philosophy of Buddhism and the idealistic wing of Neo-Confucianism, with some Western ideas. This synthesis culminated in a wholesale rejection of classical Confucianism's emphasis on social distinctions. Thus while K'ang's philosophy is thoroughly modern, much of it can be found in older sources.

Main works: Lun-yu chu (Commentary on the "Analects"); Chung-yung chu (Commentary on the "Doctrine of the Mean"); Kung Tzu kai-chi k'ao (An Investigation on Confucius' Institutional Reforms); Meng Tzu wei (Subtle Meanings of the "Book of Mencius"); Commentary on the "Book of Rites"; Ta-t'ung shu (Book of Great Unity) (1935).

3. Chang Tung-sun (1886-1962)

Perhaps the most Western of all the Chinese philosophers to be considered here is Chang Tung-sun, who was for a long time the leader of the State Socialist Party in China, but who in the late 1940's converted to Marxism. Chang's fundamental philosophy can be found in a series of books that he published after World War II. Overall these show some change from his pre-World War II thought, though not a great deal. He was himself much influenced by John Dewey and Bertrand Russell, both of whom had lectured in China. But in the end Chang's own thinking drove him to a kind of sociologism.

Chang argued that it was the social situation that conditioned or influenced how individuals, including philosophers, thought about things. A social situation certainly included class relations, but Chang was often preoccupied with the influence of things such as institutions, values, and so forth. The situatedness of all thought does not imply the elimination of the individual's uniqueness, or the absolute reduciblity of all thought to the situation. Rather there is a kind of dialectical interplay between the individual and the situation, and reality as it is known is constructed both by the mind and by the natural growth of things.

Epistemologically, Chang argued for a version of Kantianism, which emphasized the difference between subject and object, between appearance and reality. Yet he insisted that any simple bifurcation along these lines would not do: the order of the world is a function not merely of the mind, but of the world itself. This view he called epistemological pluralism, the view that reality is neither a function of the object or the subject alone.

Chang's political views were of some importance. Originally his sympathies were with democratic socialism. He felt that what was most important in the short run for China was the elimination of poverty through massive industrialization and Westernization. He insisted that this could only mean the growth of distinct social and economic classes in China, but felt that for the time being this was a small price to pay for the overwhelming good that would be done. He advocated moderate government, democratic in nature and concerned for the welfare of the least advantaged. He was sharply critical of Marxism, which he thought was irrelevant to China's immediate needs, because it tended to concentrate on class conflict at a time when China's economic structure was still feudalistic.

But Chang's own emphasis on the sociology of knowledge led him to sympathize with the Marxists, and after the Communist Revolution in 1949 he joined the government for a short time, before retiring from public life.

Although Chang's ideas seem to flow entirely from Western sources, he was well read in the Chinese classics, and there is speculation that his fundamental theory of epistemological pluralism may have been influenced by Neo-Confucianism. But clearly he chose to keep these more traditional elements in the background of his theory.

Main works: Jen-shih lun (Epistemology) (1934); Ssu-hsiang yü she-hui (Thought and Society) (1946); Chih-shih yü wen-hua

276

(Knowledge and Culture) (1947); Li-hsing yu min-chu (Reason and Democracy) (1946); Min-chu chu-i yu she-hui chu-i (Democracy and Socialism) (1948).

4. Fung Yu-lan (1895-)

Like Radakrishnan who was both an original philosopher and one of the great historians of Indian philosophy, Fung Yu-lan is one of the great synthesizers of Chinese philosophy and one of its great historians as well. It is important to say something about each, since it is his historical writings which may contain a clue to his fate under Communism.

Fung Yu-lan's greatest philosophical work was The New Rational Philosophy published in 1939. In this and in a number of subsequent works, Fung Yu-lan developed an original philosophy based substantially on concepts found in Chu Hsi and others of the medieval rationalist school.

The foundation of Fung Yu-lan's theory was a sharp distinction between reality which was concrete, and conceptualization which was abstract. The conceptualization of what is or what exists is elaborated through four fundamental beliefs or concepts that describe the nature of reality. Thus, the first two concepts are those of principle (li) and material force (ch'i), which are correlative concepts needed for explaining what constitutes a given being. Each thing must have both some kind of specific principle in its nature, and must be actualized with material force. Fung Yu-lan is quite explicit in identifying principle (li) with the Platonic understanding of form, and material force with matter. Thus principle is both eternal and intrinsically intelligible; the totality of all principles is called the Great Ultimate (to be distinguished from the Great Whole, which is the principle of the unity of all things). Fung Yu-lan rejects any hint of a supernatural world which is the repository of such principle, however. Rather, both li and ch'i are analytical components of concrete reality and nothing more.

The third and fourth concepts are those of Tao and the Great Whole (to be distinguished from the Great Ultimate). Tao is simply the principle of constant change, of self production and transformation. This understanding of Tao is typical of the medieval Sung philosophers more than of Taoism as such. The fourth concept is that of the Great Whole. This is simply the idea of the unity of all things, of the interrelatedness of all things. As such, the Great Whole is a principle which functions as the goal of human life. In regard to this latter, Fung has proposed an ethical theory based on the fourfold development of the human spirit which begins in ignorance, moves on to utility as the highest principle, and penultimately to service of society, and finally culminates in becoming a part of the Great Whole. This ethical theory is quite traditional in some respects, and it is likely that Fung has modified it in later years under the impact of Communism and the Cultural Revolution.

The question of Fung's philosophy under Communism is not clear, and there has been much discussion about it. Some things should be clear, however, from Fung's own comments and from his outstanding work in the history of Chinese philosophy. First of all, Fung had always emphasized a materialist approach to history. His account of Chinese philosophy gives due recognition to the social class backgroud of the various philosophies. This was true long before his relation with Marxism became an important issue. Secondly, his overt comments after the revolution strongly suggest that while he has not changed his philosophy, he now realizes two things that he did not before: first, that his previous philosophical work, which was premised on the distinction between the concrete and the abstract, had entirely overemphasized the abstract to the detriment of an analysis of society in the concrete; and secondly, that his abstract conceptual schema was still too beholden to the mind-set of medieval feudalism. While both of these "discoveries" were no doubt prompted by his Communist surroundings, it should be clear that the first point is well taken on many grounds, and that Fung's history certainly indicated sympathies for a Marxist view of things. The renuntiation of his previous philosophy as "too elitist" may or may not have been voluntary. However, his early work still stands as perhaps the most important statement of Chinese philosophy in this century.

Main works: History of Chinese Philosophy (1930); Hsin li-hsüeh (The New Rational Philosophy) (1939); Hsin shih-lun (China's Road to Freedom) (1939); Hsin shih-hsün (A New Treatise on the Way of Life) (1940); Hsin yüan-jen (A New Treatise on the Nature of Man) (1943); Hsin yüan-tao (The Spirit of Chinese Philosophy) (1944); Hsin chih-yen (A New Treatise on the Methodology of Metaphysics) (1946).

5. Hsiung Shih-li (1885-1968)

The second greatest Chinese philosopher of this century, and perhaps Fung Yu-lan's only serious rival, is Hsiung Shih-li. Hsiung's philosophy also relies on elements in Neo-Confucianism, but more on the idealistic philosophies of Ch'eng Hao, Lu Hsiang-shan, and Wang Yang-ming, than on Chu Hsi. His original interest was in Buddhism, especially in the Yogacara school of Consciousness, but eventually he turned back to Confucianism, especially to the I Ching. Hsiung Shih-li was also aware of a number of contemporary currents in Western philosophy, and while he makes few references to them it is likely that some of them—especially Bergson—influenced his own thinking at least to some extent.

278

Hsiung begins with the assertion of an Original Substance which consitututes all things. All things that exist come into being and perish again in the constant production and transformation of things that are characteristic of the Original Substance. There are two fundamentally diverse tendencies of the Original Substance, and neither of them can be reduced to the other. The first tendency is toward external integration and physical form, that is toward "closing"; the second is toward internal self-awareness and consciousness, that is, toward "opening". Clearly, consciousness is not quite fundamental in the way that perpetual transformation of the Original Substance is. Yet consciousness does represent one of the most fundamental tendencies of Original Substance.

Hsiung's explanation of principle (li) and material force (ch'i) is of considerable originality and interest. He argues that principle (li) refers generally to both substance and function insofar as it captures the whole of what is involved in the transformation of Original Substance. By contrast, material force (ch'i) refers primarily to function, not to substance, and emphasizes the dynamic outcome of transformation. In effect, Hsiung identifies material force with principle, but claims that principle is a broader concept than material force.

Consciousness, insofar as it is rooted in Original Substance as one tendency of the latter, is one, whole, and undifferentiated. Consciousness is said to be plural insofar as Original Substance is transformed and changed. Hsiung again suggests that terminology be clear. Thus he points out that mind and will refer to substance properly speaking, while consciousness refers to function. Will refers to substance insofar as the latter develops in a certain or definite direction. Specifically the direction of will (and of mind) in its transformation is toward "opening", that is, toward resistance to materiality and more generally toward mastery of the material. Thus consciousness means, for all practical purposes, coming to have self-mastery or mastery over the material aspects of things.

Hsiung's original monism is perhaps compromised by this development of consciousness struggling to overcome matter; for since both of these are simply aspects of Original Substance, it would seem that Original Substance is in conflict with itself. This is not a fatal objection, but some have argued that Hsiung's commitment to Buddhism here runs up against his sympathies for the cosmology of the I Ching.

Main works: Hsin wei-shih lun (New Doctrine of Consciousness-Only) (1944); Yüan-ju (An Inquiry on Confucianism) (1956).

6. Mao Tse-tung (1893-1976)

Like Stalin, Mao cannot be credited for being a great philosophical thinker. His "wisdom", such as it was, grew initially out of his revolutionary experience, and was used in time for mass political education. Mao's "philosophy" thus belongs not to the history of philosophy so much, as to the history of political struggles in the 20th century.

Yet despite this, there are certain elements in Mao's expressed writing, which not only help to explain his political goals, but show how and why Marxism has been transformed in China. The heart of that transformation may lie in the pragmatization of Marxist dialectics. Mao himself was always a good pragmatist, even suggesting at one time that Marxism, far from being a religious dogma, was simply a general guide to activity. Perhaps the most important statement about the nature of Marxism was Mao's doctrine of the Sinification of Marxism. Mao argued that Marxism itself urged this sort of thing insofar as the cardinal doctrine of Marxism was the grounding of theory in practice, of knowledge in action. Mao was critical of Marx for ignoring this theory of the unity of knowledge and action, and of the Soviets for doing the same thing.

But how are theory and practice related? What kind of epistemology is correctly grounded in practice? Mao suggested that there were essentially two kinds of philosophical outlooks, the metaphysical or static outlook, and the dialectical or dynamic outlook. The metaphysical kind of philosophy argues that reality is static or unchanging, and constituted by individual entities, each of which exists harmoniously with all the others in a certain kind of order or hierarchy. This view is clearly rooted in feudalism; it is in fact the ideology of feudalism, and it is this ideology and social system that Mao recognized needed to be destroyed if the development of China was to occur. (It should be remembered that the same process occurred in the West, with much social and political upheaval, but more slowly and gradually than in either the Soviet Union or China.) The dialectical or dynamic philosophy is one which recognizes that reality is constant change, and all change is conflict between opposites, that is to say, contradiction. This philosophy is rooted in actual revolutionary practice.

If contradiction is a permanent feature of reality and of society, it follows that even in a classless society (and China's political establishment considers itself to be classless) there will be class conflict and contradiction. Hence the arrival of a classless society is not the same thing as the arrival of a period of peace and harmony.

It was this notion of contradiction that led Mao to postulate a theory of permanent revolution. While Marx and the Russians urged that only one revolution was needed to bring about the new order, the Chinese under Mao argued that the new order was nothing but perpetual revolution and perpetual change. And this was deduced from the dialectical nature of social reality.

Mao's insistence of the unity of knowledge and action (with strong emphasis on the latter as fundamental) and his emphasis on perpetual revolution led to some radical consequences, most notably the so-called "Cultural Revolution". Differences developed between the left-wing idealists following Mao and so-called Confucian Marxists. The latter emphasized the establishment of peace and order based on industrial development and the growth of minimal class differences; they were periodically persecuted and murdered, but some of their faction were among Mao's closest associates (notably Chou En-Lai). And since Mao's death, the Confucianists (the term is used of a form of Marxist, not a follower of Confucius) have been in power. Mao's theory of perpetual revolution emphasized agricultural communes, and the downplaying of industry, as well as an emphasis on absolute egalitarianism at all costs. Thus the "Cultural Revolution" of the 1960's succeeded in closing down the universities, and sending intellectuals off to the farms for forced labor (thinking rooted in action was translated into hard work with no thinking). The emphasis in the Cultural Revolution was on the elimination of the intellectuals as a class distinct from the people. The result was the elimination of all thought, whether scientific, artistic, or philosophical. The end of the Cultural Revolution has meant the beginning of intellectual life once again, but it has also meant the growth of class differences in China.

A point which is important to make about Mao's influence, and especially something like The Little Red Book, is that much of the political propaganda, while Marxist in inspiration, sounds not unlike certain extreme forms of traditional Chinese wisdom. Undoubtedly Mao's Sinification of Marxism is a development from within Marxism itself; yet it is also, it seems, in accord with some of the traditional emphases in the history of Chinese philosophy. This is not to reduce Maoism, say, to the idealistic voluntarism of Wang Yang-ming. But it is to point out certain similarities with previous Chinese thought, which tend to get overlooked by those Westerners who fail to recognize that Marxism in practice is a family of theories, each developed in different cultural, economic, and political conditions, and each influenced by those conditions, as much and often more than by the writings of Karl Marx. Maoism may be Marxism, but it is Chinese Marxism.

Main works: On Correcting Mistaken Ideas in the Party (1929); On Practice (1937); On Contradiction (1937); Against Liberalism

(1938); The Chinese Revolution and the Chinese Communist Party (1939); On New Democracy (1940); Talks at the Yenan Forum on Art and Literature (1942); On People's Democratic Dictatorship (1949); On the Correct Handling of Contradictions Among the People (1957); Where Do Correct Ideas Come From? (1963).

CHAPTER 11

AFTERWORD

There are but a few questions to be considered at the end of this work. First, are there some general features which characterize the development of Western, Indian, and Chinese philosophy? Second, has this development been one of intellectual progress or not? And finally, given the account in the preceeding pages, what if anything may be said about the future developments of philosophy?

1. The development of philosophy in the three major civilizations discussed in this work may be characterized as having had a Grand Beginning, a subsequent tendency toward Scholasticism, and in every case has entered its "Modern" Period. This simple scheme will be used to clarify some aspects of the history of philosophy.

Western philosophy, Indian philosophy, and Chinese philosophy began in rather different circumstances. Perhaps the most interesting variable is their respective relations with the dominant religions of the civilizations in question. Western philosophy began in Greece some five or six centuries before the appearance of the religion—Christianity—which was to dominate Western civilization. Indian philosophy grew rather naturally out of its own religious traditions, both Vedic and non-Vedic. Chinese philosophy originated in the religious concerns surrounding the conduct of the ancient king, and of those classes attached to the king. These different origins betray or suggest a very different flavor for each tradition of philosophy.

Western philosophy has been traditionally independent of Christianity. Christianity has accomodated itself to this philosophical tradition on many occasions, and in many different ways; but philosophy in the West originated among the "pagans", not among the Jews or Christians. The result has been a rocky intellectual marriage, marked by periods of genuine unity between the two disciplines, as well as by periods of sharp separation and conflict. For every Thomas Aquinas, there is a David Hume. Western Philosophy is now very much indebted both to its Greek and Roman origins, as well as to its Christian upbringing; but it is for the most part today relatively independent of all these influences.

By contrast, Indian philosophy was the <u>direct result</u> of Indian religion, and was never fully independent of that religious tradition. The irony of this is that Indian philosophy, carried on by intellectuals whose education was quite beyond that of most of their co-religionists, was often rather far removed from the ordinary beliefs of the religious masses. It is doubtful, for example, whether the Mimamsa school of Hindu philosophy was ever genuinely popular; and there is no doubt that the atheism perhaps characteristic of this school at times in its history was quite out of step with the average Hindu. Yet the Mimamsa school is thoroughly dependent on the Vedas for its inspiration, and could not be understood as in any sense "secular" or independent of Hinduism.

Chinese philosophy originated not so much from particular religious texts, but from a general belief that human conduct was intimately and causally related to events in the universe. This belief was of great importance with regard to the king or emperor, and came to be of importance to intellectuals as they began to generalize from this fundamental belief. But the religious practices of the ordinary Chinese peasant or villager centered not around this, but around the veneration of ancestors. Chinese philosophy was religious in that it was deeply concerned with ethical conduct, and deeply concerned with theories of the universe, especially since these two seemed to be related in some fashion. But Chinese philosophy was sometimes relatively irreligious insofar as it challenged popular religion, and especially the belief in the value of religious ritual and the belief in ancestor spirits. Thus again, it can be seen how a philosophical tradition may be deeply religious and hostile to some aspects of religion at one and the same time. Perhaps one may sum up the difference between Indian and Chinese philosophy by saying that the former is sometimes hostile to religion under a veneer of religiosity, while the latter is deeply religious under an occasional veneer of skepticism.

The beginnings of all three philosophical traditions occurred in geographical areas remote from one another, at roughly the same period of time in human history—i.e., in the first millenium B.C. There were apparently no causal connections between the three Beginnings; and the circumstances vis-a-vis the religion of the host civilization were different in each case. But beginnings are followed inevitably by periods of intellectual synthesis and codification, constituting what might be called a tendency toward "scholasticism", where this is understood as either a genuine "school" with a collective tradition, or an intellectual movement whose exponents have no personal connection with one another. This tendency toward scholasticism occurred in all three civilizations, though in differing degrees. Western philosophy began this process with Plato and Aristotle, both of whom set up the first European "universities" for the propagation of their own philosophy. And the tendency was resurrected in the medieval period with the foundation of the great Universities and the growing dissonance among Dominicans, Franciscans, and others. Scholasticism was also an important element of Hindu and Buddhist

284

philosophy, with all the important philosophical movements within these religions being in effect "schools", or ongoing traditions in interpretation of religious texts. Philosophy was seen simply as the working out of a certain intellectual perspective, drawing on particular religious texts as a source of inspiration. A position was defined, and other positions objected against, with a certain inevitable intellectual narrowness as a result. The same tendency is noticeable in Chinese philosophy in the medieval period, where virtually all positions were incorporated into just two wings--the idealistic and the rationalistic--of Neo-Confucianism. While this unusual development helped to broaden Confucianism initially, the long-term result was an intellectual stasis whose overthrow seemed inevitable with the fall of the Manchu dynasty in the early 20th century.

Scholasticism is an inherent trait in the development of philosophy, and probably quite unavoidable. Its primary virtue is the preservation of traditions of learning and bodies of knowledge. Its primary vice is a tendency toward belief in self-sufficiency and completeness.

It was inevitable that philosophy would generate reactions against this tendency toward organization of knowledge for its own sake. Protests against "tradition" in philosophy are rampant in philosophy itself, and have prevented it from suffering an early death.

One form this protest has taken in all three civilizations is the emphasis on "modernity". Modernity is a Western phenomenon, partly intellectual, partly technological. Western modernity began with Cartesianism philosophy and Galilean science in the 17th century and has continued unabated until the present day. Some of its philosophical concerns have been the centrality of the human subject, scientific reasoning, history, and language, to name but a few of the major issues. Of all these phenomena, the one that has been most prominent for those outside Western culture is scientific reasoning, and that is because long before Western culture and languages are understood in foreign civilizations, there is contact with Western technology.

Modernity in Indian and Chinese philosophy has in the first place meant a concern with Western technology and the epistemology intrinsic to it. To this end, many Indian and Chinese philosophers have been interested in accomodating themselves to certain aspects of modern science, because it appears that, for better or worse, Western technology has been and will continue to be of great importance for all on the planet.

But the relative enthusiasm for Western scientific epistemology in the East has not generated an equal enthusiasm for other aspects of Western philosophy. This is because of the often strong conviction or suspicion that Western civilization is hostile to the interests of those outside its geographical borders. Western economic and political imperialism has generated a strong reaction against "Westernization" among Indian and Chinese thinkers. Modernism in this sense has usually meant an explication of anti-imperialist philosophy. Ironically, the one philosophy that has been most available in this regard is itself a Western product—namely, Marxism, whose political success has been almost entirely outside the Western world. But Marxism is no more a perennial philosophy than anything else; Marxism transported to China is no longer "pure" Marxism. Thus even Western "exports" in this intellectual domain are utilized in ways that are sometimes quite alien to the intentions of those Westerners who formulated the relevant theories.

At the heart of Western modernity is what one might call in a very broad sense philosophical anthropology. At the heart of Indian and Chinese modernity is the appreciation of scientific rationality and the commitment to anti-imperialism. This accounts for the rather different flavor of the word "modernity" insofar as it is used to describe these various philosophical traditions.

2. Any lengthy submersion in the history of philosophy inevitably generates questions about its apparent progress or lack of such. Does the history of philosophy, especially in the international context presented in this book, suggest that there is some progress toward an ultimate or final goal? This question was never seriously raised until the 18th century in the West, when grave doubts about the adequacy of previous philosophical thought had arisen. The thinkers of the Enlightenment set out to provide an intellectual framework that would indeed give philosophy some direction, some sense of accomplishment, after centuries of what appeared to be semantical asides. The Dark Ages would at last be subject to Enlightenment.

However, this and every attempt to create "progress" in philosophy has failed, however, and almost always for the same reason. To create such progress, it is necessary to formulate a philosophical view that would be so self-evident in its starting-point and its conclusion, as to preclude the possibility of further substantial development, as well as to relegate all previous thought to the dust-bin. But starting-points in philosophy are endlessly open, as open as human experience; and, just as yesterday's trash, viewed from a new perspective, is today's art-work, so yesterday's "outmoded way of thinking", when reconsidered in the light of novel experience, has a way of turning out to be tomorrow's "guide to the future".

286

Philosophy is progressive in the sense that the possibilities of new thought are never over with, because human experience is always expanding and reconstituting itself in new ways. What is constantly happening is not only an enrichment of the mind with new experiences and new questions, but a deeper exploration of language and thought, of conceptual expressiveness and conceptual precision. The progress of philosophy is inseparable from the progress of the human species. But it is quite impossible to see with finality just what direction such changes will continue to take, or whether and how they will terminate altogether in some final "system". Indeed, whether philosophy has a direction in this last sense at all is very much a debatable matter.

3. If one cannot say whether philosophy is progressing toward some ultimate goal, it is quite possible to say something about the kinds of starting points that philosophers will increasingly take up. These are scarcely hinted at in this book, because the newest of the new are not old enough to have yet a history. The following perspectives are put forward with an undeniable recklessness:

(1) The history of philosophy has been largely made by unmarried males living in the northern hemisphere. It seems obvious that, precluding a world-wide disaster of some kind, this characteristic of previous philosophizing will change. There is no doubt that there is a greater sensitivity among male philosophers toward the question of women and non-privileged groups. There is also, since the advent of higher education for women, the beginning of philosophical traditions of women (not just feminists). And there is the experience of those in the southern hemisphere in the planet, in third world countries, whose contributions to the intellectual culture of the world seem assured in time. The course of philosophical thought is bound to change as the economic and political dominance of America, Great Britain, and Europe begins to decline with respect to other civilizations and cultures. This is not to suggest that the philosophical traditions of the West can be consigned to the dust-bin; but it does mean that the philosophers of the future are likely not to make the same assumptions about this philosophical history as others have to date.

(2) The preoccupation with human nature, considered biologically, socially, psychologically, or religiously, is bound to exercise a controlling influence on all other thought. The human has not always been the center of thought in the history of philosophy; but whatever the past has been like in this regard, there is not much doubt about the relevance of this preoccupation for the immediate future of thought. The human constitutes the center of all centers for philosophical thought, not because of any simple minded narcissism (as some TV evangelists would have

it), but because of the need to reflect on the enormous growth of power not only over the forces of nature, but over the human race itself. The growth of technological and political power has thrust philosophical psychology and anthropology into the limelight with a vengeance. Questions about metaphysics may continue to be of interest, but they are bound not to excite interest as they once did, unless they are viewed in connection with human self-reflection and interests.

(3) Correlative to this is the incontrovertible centrality of ethics and of "value-theory" to philosophy in the future. This has been thrust to the fore not only by the increasingly unusual violations of traditional ethical norms, but by the questionable relevance of such norms in the face of technological change and the ability of humans to control their fate in ways that were previously inconceivable. The manufacture of new life forms, even of human lives, and the concomitant ability to destroy all life, human or otherwise, is bound to raise—is already raising—shattering questions about human nature and experience, about the ethical and political purposes of social organizations, and of the rights of individuals to control what is happening to them. Intense debates rage today about not only the "begining" and "end" of human life, but of the value of human life, of animal life, of the life of the environment. These debates are not "traditional"; many of them have been triggered by practical and technological developments that are new to human history. But if these debates are only in their infancy, they are by no means of passing interest only, a kind of temporary distraction from the "universal" questions that traditional academic philosophers might prefer to discuss. For many of these questions have been posed by the requirements of human and planetary survival. The urgency of these questions is not likely to go away soon, and the need for thoughtful action with regard to them, and thus the need indirectly for a philosophical account, is similarly fixed.

In short, it may well be the case that philosophy in the future will be concerned, as it always has been, with ontology, epistemology, ethics, and the like. But its perspective on these issues is bound to be rather radically different from anything in the past, both in terms of whose perspective is at issue, and in terms of the guiding intellectual and ethical concerns of that perspective. While some may find these considerations unsettling, others may find consolation from the openness of the future. The task of philosophy in an age of anxiety is to face the present, without either fleeing to the past or the future. It is between the past and the future that the human mind can first come to know the difference between the static and the fluid. And with this realization one has finally caught up with the Beginnings of Philosophy.

ABOUT THE AUTHOR

Eugene F. Bales attended Conception Seminary College from 1964-69, graduating with a B.A. in Philosophy in May, 1968. From 1969-1973, he pursued graduate studies at the University of Missouri-Columbia, where he earned his M.A. and Ph.D. degrees in Philosophy. He taught at the University of Missouri, Stephens College, the Missouri School of Religion, and the University of North Dakota at Grand Forks. From 1975-76, he had the distinction of being the only Ph.D. in Philosophy employed as a full-time secretary in the Department of Veterinary Pathology at the University of Missouri. Since 1976 he has been a member of the Philosophy Department at Conception Seminary College. In 1980, the author was privileged to be accepted for a NEH summer session in Philosophical Anthropology, under the leadership of Dr. Calvin Schrag.

The author's wife, Deborah Bailey, is Assistant Professor of Special Education for the Associated Colleges of Central Kansas. A husband who is a philosopher and a wife who specializes in behavioral and emotional disorders have much whereby to understand one another, and their relation has been a very happy one. They have three cats, if "having" cats is free of logical contradiction.